Feminist Economics

Feminist Economics

Interrogating the Masculinity of Rational
Economic Man

Gillian J. Hewitson

Edward Elgar
Cheltenham, UK • Northhampton, MA, USA

© Gillian J. Hewitson 1999

Published by
Edward Elgar Publishing Limited
Glensanda House
Montpellier Parade
Cheltenham
Glos GL50 1UA
UK

Edward Elgar Publishing, Inc.
136 West Street
Suite 202
Northampton
Massachusetts 01060
USA

A catalogue record for this book
is available from the British Library

Library of Congress Cataloguing in Publication Data

Hewitson, Gillian J., 1961–
    Feminist economics : interrogating the masculinity of rational
    economic man / Gillian J. Hewitson
    Includes bibliographical references (p.)
    1. Feminist economics. 2. Neoclassical school of economics.
    3. Economic man. 4. Poststructuralism. I. Title.
    HQ1381.H48   1999
    330'.082—dc21   98–38336
                                                                      CIP

ISBN 1 85898 946 9

Printed and bound in Great Britain by
Biddles Ltd, Guildford and King's Lynn

Contents

Preface

This book is based upon my PhD thesis, completed in 1997 at La Trobe University in Melbourne, Australia. I am deeply grateful to my supervisors John King in the School of Business and Professor Marilyn Lake in the Women's Studies programme and the School of History for their support and mentorship, their invaluable guidance and their many concrete suggestions, all of which contributed significantly to the quality of the PhD thesis. I would like also to extend my thanks to Philipa Rothfield who supervised me during 1995, and whose advice I found extremely helpful. Other people to whom I am particularly grateful for their support of my endeavours include my mother, Hilda Hewitson, my twin sister, Sally Hewitson, and my brother Tom Hewitson, as well as Jo Moore, Dennis Moore, Fran Hattam and Sisira Jayasuriya. I would especially like to acknowledge and thank my close friends and fellow PhD candidates Margaret Barkley and Allison Craven. My greatest debt is to Gregory Moore, whose love, friendship and support were critical in bringing this project to fruition.

PART ONE

Feminist Economics/Feminist Poststructuralism

1. Introduction

Current critical thought holds that knowledge is not discovered but socially produced, and that it is therefore never neutral reflecting instead ambient power relations. Thus traditional conceptions and taxonomies are viewed less and less as mere images of the order of things being instead subjected to a 'deconstructionist' critique that seeks to uncover the underlying assumptions and thereby establish the possibility of alternative thinking (Schick, 1990: 349).

1.1. Introduction

The subject of this book is neoclassical economics as a sexually-specific knowledge. It is an interdisciplinary work in which I draw on feminist theory from a range of disciplines to develop a critique of neoclassical economics and the claims of its practitioners that this framework is universally applicable and sexually indifferent, and a theoretical position from which to undertake alternative, feminist, readings of neoclassical economics. These readings illustrate the ways in which neoclassical economics constructs particular meanings of sexual difference, and hence illuminate the limitations of neoclassical economics for women and enable productive interventions into its discourse. Such a work is situated within the newly emerging field of feminist economics, or, more specifically, within the even more recently-developed field of 'feminist poststructuralist economics'. These fields are marginal within the discipline of economics, in part because feminism has taken a long time to obtain a foothold within the economics discipline, particularly compared to its advances in disciplines such as philosophy, law and legal studies, history, cultural studies, film theory and sociology. Further, many feminist economists reject poststructuralist and related feminist insights, preferring to maintain, implicitly or explicitly, the epistemological commitments which neoclassical economics itself requires. In short, then, the feminist poststructuralist approach is a nascent programme within a fledgling subfield of economics, and this book should be interpreted as an exploration of the way in which one particular version of feminist poststructuralism may be employed to analyse the masculinity of neoclassical economics and generate insights into the means by which neoclassical economics produces

3

the 'economic condition' of women and men.

The central figure in neoclassical economics is the universal individual, commonly known as 'rational economic man'. My aims in this book are to employ a feminist poststructuralist approach to reveal the masculinity of this allegedly unsexed figure, and to point to some of the real effects of his masculinity. Rational economic man engages with the world in order to maximize his utility or profit subject to the constraints he faces. In a world of two sexes the alleged universality of rational economic man implies that he or she is characterized by a pure (disembodied) consciousness within which his utility-producing desires are articulated. Neoclassical economists further assume that 'rational economic man' is a referent who preexists the discourse about him. Indeed, the essential epistemological assumption of neoclassical economics is that it is able to describe the real world (in the positivist tradition) or to predict what will happen in the real world (in the Friedman tradition). That is, economists have what is known as a referential view of language in which language is regarded as a transparent medium by which knowledge of real economic objects is communicated. Neoclassical economists therefore claim simply to label a set of preexisting characteristics relevant to 'economic behaviour', which itself is seen as inherent within preexisting individuals or 'human nature'. Thus the economic individual is claimed to be the exogenous foundation of neoclassical economic theory. It is my intention to show that, contrary to these claims, neoclassical economics is a discourse which does not describe an independent 'real world', but rather contributes to the production of the real. It will further be argued that meaning is constructed in ways beyond the control or the intent of an individual author. I aim to show that 'rational economic man' is not an abstract, unsexed consciousness, but a textual production of a male subject position which has real effects in women's and men's lives, despite any particular economist's commitment to the gender-neutrality of the discipline. In this introductory chapter, I outline the emergence of feminist economics and discuss in general terms its relationship with feminist theory (section 1.2); delineate the central argument of the book (section 1.3); address some key criticisms of my approach and indicate in broad terms the significance of the book (section 1.4); and outline the way in which the argument of the book proceeds in the chapters to follow (section 1.5).

1.2. The Emergence of Feminist Economics

Both feminist and non-feminist economic literature on women grew dramatically during the 1970s, a fact which may be attributed to the extension of rigorous microeconomic foundations to the behaviour of families, [1] the increased visibility of women in the labour market, [2] and feminist interest in, and pressure on, the discipline following the social revolutions of the 1960s. [3] Since this time, historians of economic thought have demonstrated that there is an extensive history of feminist contributions to the economics discipline as well as considerable debate about the role of women in the economy (see, for example, Thomson 1973; Pujol 1992; Folbre 1993a; Groenewegen 1994a). However, the use of 'feminist economics' as a label for a recognized field of research within economics is a very recent phenomenon. The recent emergence of feminist economics as a formal field of intellectual endeavour has yet to be rigorously delineated. Nor has there been a systematic survey of all the strands of research activity which may be classified as feminist economics. [4]

Indications of the recent development of the field are given by a number of institutional facts. The first association of feminist economists, the International Association for Feminist Economics (IAFFE), was not founded until 1991; the first of IAFFE's annual conferences on feminist economics was held in Washington in 1992; the first international conference on feminist economics, entitled 'Out of the Margin: Feminist Perspectives on Economic Theory', was held in Amsterdam in 1993; the first anthologies of feminist economics were published in 1993 and 1995 (Ferber and Nelson 1993a; Humphries 1995a; Kuiper and Sap 1995a); and the first journal devoted to feminist economics, entitled *Feminist Economics*, was launched by founding editor Diana Strassmann on behalf of IAFFE in 1995. Evidence of the recent rise of feminist economics can also be found in the literature. It was only in the early to mid-1980s that scholars directly addressing deficiencies within neoclassical economics began self-consciously to refer to themselves as feminist economists, with an independent research programme or conceptual framework, although non-economists and radical economists had begun this process earlier. Early papers linking the terms 'women' and 'economics' include those of Barbara Bergmann in 1973 ('The Economics of Women's Liberation'), and Joan McFarland in 1976 ('Economics and Women: A Critique of the Scope of Traditional Analysis and Research'). It was in 1977 that the terms 'feminism' and 'economics' were first linked when the Marxist feminist Ann Markusen published her paper entitled 'Feminist Notes on Introductory Economics', and wrote of the development of a feminist political economy and the importance of teaching 'women's economics'. Other papers making this connection include the paper by Anne Phillips and Barbara Taylor entitled 'Sex and Skill: Notes Towards a Feminist Economics', in which they argued, against conventional Marxists, that capital is not indifferent to sex and that definitions of skills are 'saturated with sexual bias' ([1980] 1986: 55); [5] Lisa Leghorn's and Katherine Parker's book, *Women's Worth: Sexual Economics and the World of Women* (1981), which they viewed as a contribution to 'women-centered economics' (ibid: xi); [6] Barbara Bergmann's ([1983] 1990; 1984a) paper entitled 'Feminism and Economics', in which she used the term 'feminist economists', and briefly reviewed the criticisms of labour economics and the new home economics made by such economists (who may be of either sex); and Martha MacDonald's (1984) paper, 'Economics and Feminism: The Dismal Science?', in which she surveyed the way in which women are studied within the economics discipline, writing that she was 'intrigued by the possibility that feminism and economics can be combined within the discipline and not just left to the sociologists', but concluding that 'We are a long way from a feminist economics' (1984: 170). In Australia, the term 'feminist economists' was used at a conference on women and employment in 1984 (Ministry of Employment and Training 1984: 199). Despite the relatively recent development of the terms 'feminist economics' and 'feminist economist', in this book I use these terms to refer to research prior to the early 1980s which was critical of the treatment of gender by neoclassical economists.

From these early references it is apparent that feminist economics can be preliminarily defined as an independent research programme (rather than, for example, merely an arm of neoclassical labour economics), which has as its primary goal the advancement of understandings of the disadvantaged economic conditions of women. This aim is revealed by most recent definitions of the field, definitions which identify the content and/or the methodology of neoclassical economics as androcentric or masculine, and feminist economists as those who wish to eliminate this androcentrism. For example, Myra Strober defines feminist economics as 'a rethinking of the discipline of economics for the purpose of improving women's economic condition' (1995: 1), and Edith Kuiper and Jolande Sap contend that 'Feminist economists believe that uncovering the gender biases in economics is a necessary prelude to constructing an economics which can encompass the perspectives and embody the realities of both women and men' (1995b: 4; see also Seiz 1995a: 111; Hyman 1994a: 53; Day 1995: 139–40; Woolley 1993: 497). Feminist economists have adopted a number of feminist theoretical frameworks and approaches, so that different orientations toward orthodox economics can be discerned within the writings which fall under the umbrella of feminist economics.

Even though feminist economics is pluralistic rather than univocal, a theme which unifies many of the different works is the common use of the sex/gender distinction. The development of the sex/gender distinction as an analytical tool was crucial in enabling feminist developments in most of the disciplines. It has already been mentioned that social movements which arose in the 1960s and 1970s have played a major role in facilitating the emergence of feminist economics. Indeed, it can be argued that many forms of women's economic disadvantage became visible only once the sex/gender distinction had been made explicit, and hence that early feminist economics relied heavily upon its theorization within radical, socialist and liberal feminist theory. Specifically, so long as the dominant understanding of the social roles of men and women was that they were biologically determined, and hence fixed, it was difficult for women to argue credibly that these social roles were inappropriate or unfair. It became possible for women to make this argument by appealing to the body of knowledge which theorizes gender as expressed in 'sex roles' as socially constructed and hence malleable. Thus, although the words feminism or women and economics or political economy were not linked before 1977, feminist work drawing on the sex/gender distinction began earlier. Carolyn Shaw Bell, for example, in her paper entitled 'Economics, Sex, and Gender' (1974a), drew on this distinction to argue that economic analyses consistently assume and reinforce societal assignations of roles to individuals on the basis of sex, and specifically the primacy of the homemaker role for women. Economists, she contended, study women as mothers and housekeepers, and take for granted the detrimental influence which their socialization into this role has on women's labour market choices and economic outcomes (1974a: 630). The sex/gender distinction was, then, critically important within feminist theorizing in this era, and continues to play an important role in feminist economics (see Ferber and Nelson 1993b; Nelson 1995b; Chapter 4 below).

The distinction drawn between 'sex' and 'gender' is based upon a distinction between the role of the biological and the social in the formation of identity and social relations. As noted, the development of 'sex' and 'gender' as distinct analytical categories was critical to the development of feminist theory in the 1960s and 1970s (see the feminist classic *Sexual Politics* by Kate Millett [1969] 1977; for discussions of the sex/gender distinction, see Gatens 1983; Eisenstein 1984; Edwards 1989; Threadgold 1990), and these categories remain of particular relevance to a discussion of feminist economics. In the context of the sex/gender distinction, the category of 'sex' refers to 'natural', anatomical differences between the bodies of men and women. As Michèle Barrett has pointed out, the sex/gender distinction isolates the biological from the social 'by presupposing that a pre-social "state of nature" exists and that we have categories of thought that are uncontaminated by the social which would thus allow us to apprehend this state' (1988: xxviii). Thus, within this framework, sexed bodies are natural, ahistorical and presocial referents, the meanings of which are assumed to be transparently available to socially-situated individuals. This is seen, for example, in the common pronouncement that 'biology is destiny', in which feminine and masculine characteristics are assumed to be predetermined by biological sex. This argument is known as the 'natural complement' theory of sexual difference, and it continues to be employed by those, such as sociobiologists, who assert that what is understood by some to be an oppressive system for women is really just the cultural expression of a natural truth. [7] As explained by the feminist philosopher Ann Ferguson (1977: 47):

> According to the Natural Complement theory, there are traits, capacities, and interests which inhere in men and women simply because of their biological differences, and which thus define what is normal 'masculine' and normal 'feminine' behavior . . . Thus it is natural that men are the breadwinners and play the active role in the production of commodities in society . . . Since women bear children, it is natural that they have a maternal, nurturing instinct which enables them to be supportive of the needs of children.

Discrimination against women, in this view, is non-existent: women's preferences for, or at least their presence in, work of low value follows from their biologically-determined dispositions, and neither employers nor society as a whole can be held responsible for the labour market outcomes which result. The argument here is that women are biologically disposed to remain in the private sphere of home and family, but, when forced by economic circumstances to take up paid work, they prefer part-time work or work which requires a minimum of commitment. Hence the well-known claim that women have a low attachment to the labour force. Further, discrimination is considered a dangerous concept by those who argue that social roles are biologically determined, as women may well be encouraged by anti-discrimination laws to move outside their natural terrain of home and family; that is, women may attempt to live in opposition to their biologically-mandated role as the helpmate and complement of men. Barbara Sullivan has noted this reaction in her examination of the discussion surrounding the introduction of the Australian Sex Discrimination Bill: 'For supporters of the biological discourse the Sex Discrimination Bill was attempting to eliminate innate differences and encourage an unnatural "sameness" between the sexes' (1990: 178).

The category of 'gender' in the sex/gender framework of analysis is regarded as a social rather than a biological category. 'Gender' refers to a complex of social and familial assignations of sex roles to individuals. It is 'the culturally and socially shaped cluster of expectations, attributes, and behaviors assigned to that category of human being by the society into which the child was born' (Eisenstein 1984: 7; see also Millett [1969] 1977; Caddick 1986). Gendered individuals therefore can exist only within the social as opposed to the natural realm, because their identity relies on a process of socialization. The concept of gender was taken up by feminists from Robert Stoller (1968), whose work on transsexuality and transvestitism caused him to argue that biological sex or 'anatomical facts' and social gender are separable and arbitrarily connected (Eisenstein 1984: 7; see also Oakley 1972: ch. 6; Gatens 1983). The social acquisition of a gendered, rather than a sexed, identity subsequently became a widely-adopted tenet of early second-wave feminisms. The following passage was written in this period and exemplifies this attitude: 'I follow the convention of distinguishing between sex (female and male) and gender (feminine and masculine). Sex is biological, whereas gender is psychosocial. Thus, for example, a person who is biologically female may be – in terms of psychological characteristics or social roles – feminine or masculine, or both' (Trebilcot 1977: 70).

Those feminists who have adopted this account of the social production of gendered identity are sometimes known as 'social constructionists' (Grosz 1994a: 17; Barrett 1988: xxiv) or 'feminist constructionists' (Ferber and Nelson 1993b: 9). However, in this book those feminists who draw, implicitly or explicitly, on the distinction between the biological and the social in their accounts of the production of identity, and who argue that the masculinity of economics is a function of the current social construction of the masculine gender, will be denoted as 'gender feminists'. The source of this term is Moira Gatens, who also describes feminists seeking equality on the basis of the sex/gender distinction as 'feminists of equality' (Gatens 1983: 144). This label is by no means a derogatory one, for its political purchase is such that it 'probably provides the best basis for a dialogue between feminist theory and economics' (Ferber and Nelson 1993b: 9). In fact, feminist economists have been particularly enthusiastic in adopting the argument that gender is a social construction which is the basis of discrimination and other negative economic outcomes for women.

Gender feminists combined the concept of a socially-acquired gender identity with the ideal of equality to construct a political program for change. By definition, the concept of equality requires that there are differences between the categories under examination, as well as something which is the same across these categories. In this context, gender feminists argue that the biological differences between men and women are self-evident but irrelevant, and that the 'something' shared by men and women is their pre-given consciousness, their humanity, which is the essence of personhood or self. The essence of personhood is therefore deemed to be unsexed, and a process of socialization is said to inscribe gendered identities upon these unsexed consciousnesses. As Gatens explains, in gender feminism's account of subjectivity, or selfhood, 'the mind, of either sex, is a neutral, passive entity, a blank slate, on which is inscribed various social "lessons". The body, on [this] account, is the passive mediator of these inscriptions' (1983: 144). The expulsion of the body from the essence of personhood in this account can be situated within a long philosophical tradition which has privileged the mind over the body as constitutive of identity: Descartes's axiom 'I think therefore I am' is the quintessential statement of this privileging.

The gender feminist program of change therefore entails achieving social and economic equality by eliminating gender as it is currently constituted. This is to be achieved by forcing society to undergo a 'degendering' process in which the system of gender ideology would be transformed by a combination of reeducation and legislative acts. The gendered characteristics, traits, behaviours and tasks would be eliminated, and the gendered individual would be succeeded by an androgyn (see Elshtain 1987). As Gatens wrote: 'The result of [gender theorists'] analyses is the simplistic solution to female oppression: a programme of re-education, the unlearning of patriarchy's arbitrary and oppressive codes and the re-learning of politically correct and equitable behaviours and traits, leading to the whole person: the androgyn' (1983: 144). The 'androgyn' is an individual who 'would combine some of each of the characteristic traits, skills, and interests that we now associate with the stereotypes of masculinity and femininity' (Ferguson 1977: 45–6). [8] An androgyn, then, is a person who has no gender, in-so-far as gender implies masculinity and femininity. The solution to women's oppression is to eliminate differentiated sex as the substructure of gender, since the individual is to have no sex-specific gender characteristics.

The effects of degendering will be felt in both the public and the private spheres. The public/private distinction is a problematic though useful classificatory device which demarcates the boundaries between the spheres of paid and unpaid work, or between the domains of the market and the family (see Pateman 1987). Gender feminists believe that the distinction between these two spheres has been premised upon the 'patriarchal' distinction between men and women which derives from the 'natural complement' view of identity. Further, they argue that the public/private dichotomy both abets the construction of gendered identities and disciplines those who attempt to transgress them. Specifically, the public realm of paid work is portrayed as a masculine pursuit, while the private realm of unpaid work and the related activities of the family are portrayed as feminine responsibilities. Representatives from each realm act as role models in the socialization process, and the resulting artificially-created physical space and qualities of the spheres enable individuals to be easily identified and penalized for attempting to take on roles which are deemed unsuitable for their gender (see Chodorow 1978; Millett [1969] 1977). It is therefore apparent that the gender feminists' degendering programme necessarily must take place in both these spheres, and ultimately eliminate them as separate conceptual entities.

It should be noted that, although gender is conceptually distinct from sex, feminist economists have conflated the terms on the basis of the predominant understanding that biological women are feminine while biological men are masculine. Francine Blau's (1987) entry on 'Gender' in *The New Palgrave: A Dictionary of Economics*, which exemplifies the empiricist feminist view of the role of gender in economics (discussed in Chapter 2 below), begins with the following explanation: 'The term gender has traditionally referred, as has sex, to the biological differences between men and women. More recently a movement has arisen both in social science writings and in public discourse to expand this definition to encompass also the distinctions which society has erected on this biological base, and further to use the word gender in preference to sex to refer to this broader definition' (ibid.: 492). Gender is therefore equated with sex, since the social construction of gender is built upon the biological base of sex. It is not, then, feminine persons, who may well be men within the logic of the sex/gender distinction, against whom employers discriminate, but women. The ubiquity of this collapsing of gender into sex is indicated by the use of the term 'gender' to elicit information as to the conventional category of biological sex. In this context, Gatens has asked 'Should a feminine man tick F [for femininity], a masculine woman, M [for masculinity]?' (1989: 33).

I have argued in this section that the sex/gender distinction, and consequently the gender feminist approach, is very important within feminist economics, and that many of the arguments and aims of feminist economists rely heavily on the ability of feminism to eliminate socially-constructed differences between men and women and, hence, socially-constructed differences in economic outcomes between the sexes. The advantage of the approach, as articulated by Ferber and Nelson (1993b: 9), is that economists are likely to be much more open to arguments based upon it, in part because the alternatives, as outlined by Ferber and Nelson, are so unconvincing and foreign to economists' ways of thinking. This advantage should not be underestimated, given the cultural hegemony of economic theorizing. However, it is also important not to underestimate the disadvantage of the gender feminist approach, which may well, paradoxically, be the source of its advantage. This disadvantage is that feminist economists who adhere to a degendering program, whether in terms of the content or methodology of economics, remain within the terms of neoclassical economics itself, and hence fail to challenge its underlying reliance upon the exclusion of the feminine. The task of substantiating this argument is left to the following chapters. For now, I turn to an introduction to the feminist poststructuralist approach used in this book.

1.3. Elements of the Theoretical Framework of the Book

The aim of this book is to reject the abstract individualism of neoclassical economics, where this abstract individualism rests on a supposed sexual indifference. Sexual indifference is essential for the abstract individualism of neoclassical economics because the universally-applicable portrait of the individual constructed within neoclassical economics is necessarily a portrait of a disembodied, and hence unsexed, individual. Feminist scholars have frequently noted the implicit masculinity of such 'universal' theories or knowledges of humanity, and there has been more than one response to this perception of 'masculine bias'. Of relevance to this book is the distinction that has been made between two approaches to the relationship between women and knowledge. The first approach is to introduce women or the feminine as objects of knowledge within the relevant discipline. That is, the framework of the knowledge is adopted, but its content is expanded or adjusted in order to make the knowledge a more complete representation of the real world. This is sometimes known as the 'add women and stir' strategy, as if, in Judith Allen's words, women 'had somehow slipped out' (1986: 181). If this were the approach to be taken here, the rejection of abstract individualism would lead to a call for neoclassical economics to particularize its assumptions and categories with respect to sex (or gender), and to enlarge its domain of inquiry to include questions of specific interest to women, on the basis that 'women are abstract individuals too'. A second approach to the relationship between women and knowledge, used in this book, is to take the theory underpinning the discipline as the object of investigation. Whereas the first approach is to maintain, and supplement, the framework of the discipline in question, the second approach involves an exposure of the arbitrary and partial nature of the framework and the delineation of the ways in which that framework's 'truth-claims' shape social relations. [9] Thus my project is not one of adding women or the feminine to an already-existing paradigm, but rather one of taking that paradigm as the object of a specifically feminist analysis. Those feminists taking the second approach often, but not necessarily, use a poststructuralist position. [10] This is the approach used in this book. Thus my examination of the masculinity of neoclassical economics is based on recent feminist theory influenced by poststructuralist thought, and in this section I delineate aspects of this poststructuralist and feminist thought.

One of the most important aspects of the poststructuralist position, and feminisms which draw upon it, is its rejection of the referential or empiricist view of language. In this view, language, made up of words or signs, is a transparent medium of communication, a set of symbols which refer to or represent things in the world, by which meaning is transferred between individuals. In this referential view of language, the sign is 'put in the place of the thing itself, . . . "thing" here standing equally for meaning or referent. The sign represents the present in its absence. It takes the place of the present' (Derrida 1982a: 9). The poststructuralist challenges this empiricist model of language as a tool of communication, in which a word or symbol captures the essence of a thing or referent, representing it in its absence. Instead, language is posited as a set of relationships or a structure within which meaning itself is produced. This view of language derives from the structuralist model of language, most closely associated with Ferdinand de Saussure, in which words are not representational symbols, but signs which are made up of two parts, a signifier and a signified. The signifier is a written or spoken mark, and the signified is the concept evoked by this mark. For example, in the empiricist view, the word 'tree' is a symbol which represents the referent 'tree', whereas in the view of language as a structure, the sign 'tree' encompasses both a signifier and a signified, where the signifier is the written or spoken word 'tree', and the signified is the concept evoked by this mark. However, in distinction from the referential view of language, the concept 'tree' only has meaning through the differentiation of its sign from all other signs within the language system. Thus meaning is constructed through difference, rather than through naming that which preexists the language system. [11] Note that to argue that meaning is created through difference rather than through naming, that is, to assume the arbitrariness of both the signified and the signifier, is not to say that the 'real world' does not exist as is sometimes suggested, but rather to seek insight into the construction within language of that 'real world'. The meaning of a referent – its conceptual existence, and hence its 'reality' – relies upon language: 'Whether we take the signifier or the signified, language has neither ideas nor sounds that existed before the linguistic system, but only conceptual and phonic differences that have issued from the system' (Saussure [1916] 1974: 120). [12] Saussure used the game of chess to illustrate his conclusions about the language system (ibid.: 88–9, 110). Within a game of chess, the meaning of a piece is constituted by its difference from other pieces. Outside the system of rules which characterize the game, any chess piece is simply a piece of wood or plastic. But the material existence of the chess piece outside of the game is not extinguished by its lack of meaning. A significant implication of the structuralist view of language, then, is that individual language-users do not preexist the language system and do not create the meanings that are available within this system. This means that no individual language-user has transparent access to 'reality'; rather, the language system precedes the individual language-user, so that the 'reality' perceived by that user, including his or her own unified and sexually-specific selfhood, is itself produced within the language system.

Those who view language as a structure therefore take a radically different view from empiricists. Many structuralists have nevertheless often inadvertently assumed a centre to this structure, an assumption known as logocentrism. This centre is the origin of meaning, where the origin may be anything from the senses or intellect of man to the word of God. Of interest in the present context is the centring of the speaker/author in Saussure's structuralist linguistics. The centring occurs because speech is privileged over writing through the idea that writing is a representation of speech, rather than a structure which creates meaning through difference just as does spoken language. [13] This privileging of speech implies that the source of meaning is the language-user, since if writing simply represents speech then it contains the intended meaning of the author, which, with greater or lesser effort, can ultimately be divined from the written work. In Jonathan Culler's words, this privileging of speech over writing 'involves the belief that sounds are simply a representation of meanings which are present in the consciousness of the speaker . . . And the written word is an even more derivative and imperfect form: it is the representation of a sound sequence which is itself a representation of the thought' (1976: 109). This retention of the centre to the structure is an implicit endorsement of the empiricist claim that the meaning of speech, or of a piece of writing or text, is controlled by the speaker or author of that text. Within the structuralist analysis of language, then, there is a contradiction, and it was this contradiction which was the point of departure for the poststructuralism which is now closely associated with the name of Jacques Derrida. [14] The poststructuralist critique of structuralism showed that there can be no centre or 'transcendental signifier' which fixes meaning, or from which meaning emanates. Instead meaning is always deferred, through the differentiation of the signs within the language structure, much like the endless deferral involved in the use of a dictionary. In other words, every signified is also a signifier, so that, as Saussure himself argued, within the language system there are only differences without positive terms ([1916] 1974: 120). To say that meaning is always deferred is to say that meaning is never fully self-present or complete in and of itself (it can never be fixed), just as one is always directed to a new word in the dictionary. This in turn implies that a term will have multiple meanings, each a function of the particular context in which it appears.

Logocentrism, or the singularity of meaning, therefore relies on the self-presence of meaning, a self-presence or identity which is constructed within the binary pairing of presence and absence. An understanding of binary oppositions and the role they play in the production of knowledge is crucial to understanding the poststructuralist claim that language itself produces or constitutes the 'real world' as knowable. Binary oppositions obey three laws: the law of identity, which means that if a thing is A, it is A; the law of non-contradiction, which means that if a thing is A it cannot also be not-A; and the law of the excluded middle, which means that A and not-A contain all the possibilities of a given situation (Gross 1986a: 26–8; Jay 1991: 92–3; Lechte 1994: 106). Within this binary structure the A term gains positive value and self-presence through appearing to define what it is not, or its other, the not-A term. The not-A term is thereby cast as lacking self-presence or positive qualities of its own, a negatively-defined, unbounded space made up of everything which A is not. The A term is therefore privileged at the expense of the not-A term. [15] However, despite its claims to self-presence, the A term requires the existence of the other for its own identity. This interdependence between the terms cannot be acknowledged if a logocentric view is to be retained, for acknowledging the interdependence of the terms is sufficient to disrupt the self-presence of the A term, and hence the referential view of language. Examples of binary oppositions which operate to structure knowledges are mind/body, subject/object, culture/nature, reason/emotion and self/other. As mentioned above, a binary opposition of vital importance to logocentric knowledges is that between presence and non-presence (or absence), since it is this binary opposition which constitutes Western notions of scientific objectivity, truth and being, and hence underpins knowledges which claim to describe the real world and constitute truth. The poststructuralist view of language undermines these binary pairings, since meaning is created through difference within the sign or language system. This means that there is always an absence within presence (one is always directed to another word in the dictionary), so that no term can be self-present, present in and of itself, including the 'I' of language or the subject (Derrida 1981: 17–29, 1982a: 11; Grosz 1989: 26–37).

Within this context, the term 'subject' is not simply a synonym for 'individual'. The term 'individual' 'carries with it a sense of one who is unified, whole, the source of conscious action' (Marshall 1992: 81). If language is referential, the individual is the centre or the source of meaning. The term 'subject', on the other hand, does not imply, within poststructuralist theory, autonomous individuals who construct knowledge. The subject is produced or actualized within language, and it is language itself which creates the belief that one is fully self-present and hence the source of meaning. Although the subject is constituted within, and therefore decentred by, language, particular words can have different meanings within different contexts, and hence subjectivity is not fixed or determined in a 'once-and-for-all' production. These different contexts may be understood as discourses. In poststructuralist writing, the term 'discourse' refers to a set of meanings which constitute a system and the range of institutions and social practices which articulate and support those meanings. In the words of Joan Scott, 'A discourse is not a language or a text but a historically, socially, and institutionally specific structure of statements, terms, categories and beliefs' (1988a: 35). [16] Different discourses therefore form different systems (Macdonell 1986: 12). For example, the discourse of neoclassical economics refers not simply to conversations between economists but also to institutions such as policy-making bodies, universities and economic journals, and social practices such as media representations of economic matters, the privileging of economics graduates in the employment practices of various government departments, the structuring of policy around the concept of efficiency, and the marginalization of certain kinds of interdisciplinary research within economics departments. The discourse of economics, however, is not the only discourse to which an economist is subject. An economist is also positioned in relation to other discourses which exist at a particular historical juncture, such as those pertaining to the family, law, biology and feminism (see Weedon 1987: ch. 2). These discourses in relation to which subjects are positioned are not independent of each other, and meanings produced within them interact in a range of ways. For example, the discourse of neoclassical economics interacts with dominant legal and political discourses to construct a mutually-supportive set of understandings of the inhabitant of the public sphere (discussed in Chapters 5 and 7 below).

It is also important to note that this decentring of the subject does not eliminate agency, as is sometimes supposed by those who would oppose determinism to agency within a binary relation. Discursively-constituted subjectivity does not imply determinism: subjects are situated in a range of contradictory positions within the set of existing discourses, and may actively resist some of these positions. For example, patients can resist a medical discourse of interventionist birth by demanding 'natural' birth (Pringle 1995: 209–10), sex-workers can resist a feminist discourse constructing them as passive victims of men by asserting that they themselves exploit men for pecuniary gain (Sullivan 1995), 'wives' can resist the discourse of the nuclear family by taking up the 'head of household' position on census forms, and economists can resist the discourse of neoclassical economics by drawing on feminist theory to deny the universal applicability of its theoretical framework. These different subject positions are therefore the source of agency: 'agency is created through situations and statuses conferred on [subjects]' (Scott 1992: 34; see also Davies 1991; Hekman 1991; Butler 1992: 12–14). So the use of the term 'subject' may be taken to mean a move away from the liberal conception of the individual to the poststructuralist view of a potentially-resistant subject-within-language, rather than to a deterministic view of the individual.

The decentring of the subject is also not simply a decentring of consciousness, which would involve the Cartesian privileging of the mind over the body (Rothfield 1990: 136; see also Rothfield 1995 who discusses the privileging of brain over body within biomedical discourses). The mind/body split is itself the product of humanist discourses. Liberal philosophy and neoclassical economics, for example, both privilege mind over body and hence enable the experience of the body as a possession and as subordinate to the mind. Within these discourses, the mind/body binary opposition is allied with that of culture/nature. 'Body' is relegated to nature; it is outside the social, and can be known and represented within culture through the language of biological, medical and other sciences which take the body as their object of knowledge. The body, within this binary structuring, is excluded from the process of the production of scientific knowledge, which relies upon the construct of 'pure mind', or mind unadulterated by body. Within poststructuralism, on the other hand, it is argued that discourses produce embodied subject positions, and that the body is enacted as a lived, experienced and experiencing body within discourse. Discourses operate to differentiate bodies through categories such as race, class and sex, and those with different bodies do not necessarily occupy the same subject positions in the same way. For example, the subject position of 'citizen' is made available through the discourse of politics, but Australian women may experience this subject position rather differently from Australian men. This is because 'citizen' has historically been linked with, indeed, constructed as, the ability to defend the country in war, and, until recently, men have been the only group actually or potentially able to do so. [17] Furthermore, the meanings produced when men and women both take up a particular subject position may be different because their bodies are already signified in particular ways. For example, even if a woman asserts that she is a citizen in precisely the same way as a man, her already signified female body may be read by others as incapable of the aggression and discipline required to defend the nation state, and hence unable to be a citizen in the same way as a man. Such readings of the female body have real effects; in this case, the armed forces exemption from Australian sex discrimination legislation allows women to be excluded from combat duty. In this account, then, the sexed body is not a preexisting referent, to which discourses simply refer, but a cultural product, or a 'text' which is both 'written' by discourses and which produces particular meanings in particular contexts. The sexed body is 'naturally social', and is always a situated, acculterated body (Grosz 1987: 7). Thus bodies do not have essential or natural meanings to which we have an unmediated access, as required by the arguments of sociobiologists, for example, nor can they ever be neutral. In short, sexed bodies are central to the experience of subjectivity, an experience which is made available within, and structured by, language or discourses.

These poststructuralist understandings may be employed for feminist ends, and those who do so are called 'feminist poststructuralists'. Feminist poststructuralists draw upon Derrida's view of language as a centreless structure within which discourses are elaborated, and in which sexed subjectivities are produced: 'If meaning and value are produced rather than simply given, then sexual identity, like any other identity, is a relational construct, enmeshed in language and its peculiar economy' (Kirby 1991a: 5). Indeed, sexed bodies will always be produced as meaningful, although these significations are historically variable and discourse-dependent, and cannot fix the meaning of sexual difference. Moreover, within logocentric knowledges, or those knowledges which are premised upon language as a reflection of the real world, sexed bodies are signified within a hierarchical structure. Specifically, feminist poststructuralists argue that the binary opposition of man/not-man is critically important in the construction of the meaning of 'woman', knowledge, truth and being, and is integrally connected to a range of other oppositions crucial to the production of knowledge in Western culture, such as the mind/body, reason/emotion, culture/nature, objectivity/subjectivity, universal/particular and presence/absence oppositions. The privileged term in each of these oppositions is that associated with 'man'. That is, 'woman' is constructed as the 'other' of 'man' into which is cast all that the term 'man' cannot tolerate within itself: body, emotion, subjectivity, nature, particularity and absence. Thus 'woman' is cast as the material foundation of the endeavours of 'man' in the realms of the social, political and economic, as well as within knowledge production. Phallocentrism is the term used to signify this construction of 'woman' as the other of 'man'. Specifically, phallocentrism is the discursive construction of the world in binary terms in which the binary opposition of man/not-man restricts 'woman' to representation only in relation to 'man', as its not-A term, its inferior or its complement (Threadgold 1990: 1; Gross 1986c: 134). [18] In Grosz's (1989: xx) words:

There are three forms phallocentrism generally takes: whenever women are represented as the opposites or negatives of men; whenever they are represented in terms the same as or similar to men; and whenever they are represented as men's complements. In all three cases, women are seen as variations or versions of masculinity.

Thus, within phallocentric knowledges, only one of the two sexes exists as a positive, or self-present, term. This means that the elaboration of a single truth requires not only the absence of absence, but also the absence of 'woman' or the 'feminine'. Feminist poststructuralists therefore argue that logocentrism, or the claim that there is a single truth, is premised upon a 'one-sex' model of sexual difference in which 'woman' is represented (and constructed) as not-man within the man/not-man binary opposition. They seek to identify the ways in which this one-sex model operates to exclude 'woman' from allegedly universally-applicable theoretical systems, as well as those which explicitly deal with the question of sexual difference, and to find ways in which the two sexes can be represented as autonomously different, rather than different only in terms of the presence or absence of masculinity (Gross 1986c: 135–6, 1986b). Thus the implication of phallocentrism as opposed to simply logocentrism is that the self-presence of terms and subjects relies not simply on a centre, but on a male centre. [19]

It is apparent that 'experience' loses its authority as the source of truth within the feminist poststructuralist framework. The subject's experience is not in some transparent relation with reality, but is only available from within discourse: 'It is not individuals who have experience, but subjects who are constituted through experience' (Scott 1992: 25–6). From this perspective, then, feminist theories which draw on some notion of an authentic 'female experience' to ground their critique of patriarchy are neglecting the way that women's experience, as well as their resistance to patriarchal representations of woman or the feminine, is produced and available only within discourse. Moreover, to install 'experience' as the privileged foundation of feminism is to attempt to reverse the terms within the phallocentric binary oppositions, while leaving the binary structure itself in place. This strategy is in danger of simply reinforcing the phallocentric alignment of sexual difference with that set of oppositions. A related point, and an important sub-theme in this book, is that men's experience, in particular the benefits that accrue to them as men, cannot be theorized as the originating or ultimate driving force of 'patriarchy'. In other words, it is problematic to assume that men have particular interests and needs which preexist the language system and particular discourses, and that men have been able to ensure the satisfaction of those interests and needs through the conscious establishment of a patriarchal system. However, this is not to argue that men (or masculinity) do not have sexually-specific interests, but rather that these interests preexist individual men and are intimately related to the production of masculine identities in contemporary, phallocentric, cultures. Some feminist economists place great importance on the dominance of men and masculine modes of viewing the world within the economics discipline, but there is a fine line between arguing that economics in one way or another serves the interests of men, as they are currently understood, and implicitly accepting the idea that men preexisted economics and created it to meet their (preexisting) needs. Accepting this idea is to essentialize men and masculine interests, reifying the very construction of sexual difference which is problematic. In the words of Maria Black and Rosalind Coward, 'language is reduced to being an instrument of expression, simply reflecting the "interests" of given social groups, i.e. men and women. [It is to say that language] constructs the positions of men and women, but men pre-exist language and use it to perpetuate their interests' (1990: 112; see also Threadgold 1988).

Another important sub-theme of the book is the inadequacy of the sex/gender distinction, which, as mentioned in the previous section, is an important unifying structure for many works within the developing school of feminist economics. The sex/gender distinction derives from the dichotomous construction of sexual difference as either fully biological, anatomical, or natural, or as fully social. It therefore relies on a binary structure opposing culture, or the social, to nature or biology, and constructs the essence of personhood (and sexual difference) as either anatomically predetermined, a function of the body understood as pure biology, or as a function of consciousness or the mind. This dichotomy has allowed feminists to argue that gender roles are social products which are arbitrary with respect to their bodily designations. They have thereby been able to offer an alternative to the conservative position that social roles are inherent within the biology of the sexes, which in turn has enabled them to argue that there is no natural basis to justify women's exclusion from any activities and positions from which men are not also excluded. Many feminist economists have also drawn upon the sex/gender distinction to argue that 'rational economic man' is of masculine gender and, for this reason, needs to be transformed into a human through the addition of feminine traits. They therefore theorize entirely on the plane of gendered consciousness and fail to take issue with this individual's (theoretical) disembodiment, or the issue of sexual difference as an embodied difference, the meaning of which is constituted within discourses.

Indeed, those feminists working within the sex/gender distinction seem to fear considerations of the body on the grounds that they invoke, in agreement with sociobiologists and others, the anatomically-defined body of conservative theory (Allen and Grosz 1987). This generates the curious paradox that 'the very thing that sexual difference cannot afford to be about, in feminist theory, is the difference between men's and women's bodies' (Ferrell 1991a: 173). Clearly, however, the fear of a return to a conservative position, which would have us believe that the body dictates the social in ways which are not amenable to social amelioration, is a function of the dichotomous structure within which these feminists are working. If the body is theorized as a social product, the experience and meaning of which is produced within discourses (not only of the body but also those discourses which efface the body, such as neoclassical economics), then the dichotomous construction of the social and natural, and the mind and the body, breaks down. At this point, it is possible to examine the critical importance of the construction of women's bodies variously as chaotic, emotional, uncontrollable, irrational, maternal, and more generally a product of nature and therefore the 'constitutive outside' of the social (and the economic). In short, then, the use by feminist economists of the sex/gender distinction leads them to adopt, along with neoclassical economists, the assertion of an underlying essence of personhood, and hence to accept the logic of a universally-applicable knowledge, in which exchange relations are theorized as relations between self-present, autonomous, and conceptually-disembodied individuals. The fantasy of abstract individualism is reinforced, and the implications of the female body (or a two-sex model) for neoclassical economics are once more erased.

In summary, then, in this book I use a feminist poststructuralist account of sexed subjectivity to challenge the claims of neoclassical economics to describe the real world and to be universally applicable or sexually indifferent. The subject of neoclassical economics, 'rational economic man', is an individual which neoclassical economics claims either simply to describe and render intelligible through mathematical formulations of his environment and his activities, or to use as the basis for predictions of his behaviour. This individual is characterized by an essence which preexists his entry into economic activity, an essence of the mind which allows economics to claim universal scientific status. Specifically, the mind-based essence of humanness allows neoclassical economics to avoid the question of sexual difference. A feminist poststructuralist approach to economics, on the other hand, puts the question of sexual difference at the heart of the analysis. Thus my central aim in the book is to examine the ways in which neoclassical economics produces sexual difference as meaningful within a one-sex model. Once discourse is seen as productive, rather than merely descriptive, neoclassical economics can be understood as constituting specific texts which are productive in particular ways. Specifically, I examine the embodied, and hence sexed, subject positions produced within the discourse of neoclassical economics. This is not to argue that men and women preexist neoclassical economics and simply become represented, in their absence, within its texts. I argue instead that particular meanings of 'femininity' and 'masculinity' and of female and male bodies are produced within neoclassical economics, and that 'femininity' operates as the not-A term not only for masculinity, but also for neoclassical economics as a whole, with real, and deleterious, effects in women's lives. In other words, neoclassical economics produces femininity as that which must be excluded for it to operate. 'Femininity', then, is the 'other' of neoclassical economics.

1.4. The Importance of a Poststructuralist Approach

Poststructuralism has been very influential in feminist theory, and has been taken up in a variety of ways within a range of disciplines, including law and legal studies, literary criticism, sociology, history, philosophy, and film and cultural theory. Although there is by no means a consensus on the usefulness to feminism of poststructuralist insights, the resistance to accepting such insights seems particularly prominent within feminist economics. [20] In this section I seek to explain and counteract this resistance by addressing several related criticisms of feminist poststructuralist work: that poststructuralism is relativistic and nihilistic; that it has nothing to do with the concrete realities of oppressed persons' lives (an interpretation of Derrida's famous dictum that 'there is nothing outside the text'), and that it is (therefore) unable to form the foundation for a political position (or a feminist politics); that it is jargonistic, impenetrable and obscure; and that poststructuralism is a patriarchal subterfuge which feminists would do well to dismiss without further ado. Although these criticisms may be well-founded in relation to some uses of poststructuralist theory, I respond to them only in relation to the feminist poststructuralist work upon which I draw in this book. These criticisms are outlined and answered in the following paragraphs.

Feminisms which draw upon poststructuralism are often accused of relativism and nihilism. Relativism posits the existence of a multitude of truths, as opposed to a single truth. Since critics argue that none of these multiple truths can be claimed to be any more true or of any greater value than the others, the criticism of relativism is closely related to the charge of nihilism. [21] Within Western or scientific knowledges, relativism is understood through the binary opposition of absolutism/relativism. In this binary structure, absolutism – a single truth, or the existence of criteria which establish truth – is the privileged A term. The criticisms of relativism and nihilism are, therefore, 'parasitic on the assumption of the necessity for a foundation of knowledge' (Hekman 1990a: 153; see also Harding [1986] 1987: 294–5). Within this structure, the analysis of this book, which reflects the assumption that economic texts always produce meanings beyond the control of the author (and this book is no exception), can hardly be redeemed, since the rejection of the idea of a single absolute truth seems to imply a sanctioning of relativism. However, poststructuralists do not share this definition of relativism with their critics. In Terry Eagleton's words, 'To say that there are no absolute grounds for the use of such words as truth, certainty, reality and so on is not to say that these words lack meaning or are ineffectual' (1983: 144). In rejecting absolutism, then, poststructuralists are not simply espousing the relativism which modernists reject. Rather, they are rejecting the Western or Enlightenment epistemology which defines knowledge as either absolute or relative (ibid.: 152). However, this rejection does not confer an ability to work outside the binary opposition of absolutism/relativism. Rather, it entails a deconstruction of this framework, or a subversion of the framework from within. [22] To undertake a deconstruction allows the question of the political implications – the real effects – of posing a particular truth to be examined. As Mia Campioni and Elizabeth Gross have argued: 'There is nothing relative about politics or power unless for those who presume themselves to be outside of it in some universal position of knowledge' (1983: 123). The politics of absolutist positions are masked and effaced, but, none-the-less, operate in particular ways and produce particular outcomes or 'truth effects'. Perhaps what poststructuralists find most interesting about the absolutism/relativism dichotomy is the source of its supporters' desire for, and investment in, absolutes. As Judith Butler asks, what does the theoretical move which establishes foundations authorize, and what is excluded or foreclosed? (1992: 7).

Since feminist poststructuralist analyses deconstruct the binary opposition of absolutism and relativism, they seek to offer neither an alternative single truth, nor one of a range of equally valid truths, as feminists such as Susan Bordo (1990) and Susan Strickland (1994) have suggested. Rather, such analyses offer insights into the commitments and foundations of 'truth' and their 'truth effects', while acknowledging the irony that any analysis establishes foundations. Thus feminist poststructuralists cannot be called 'anti-foundationalists', since this would imply the very Archimedean point which is the object of their critique. Neither can feminist poststructuralists be accused of a lack of interest in meaning, or of being apolitical. Rather, they are vitally concerned with particular meanings, how these meanings come to be effected, and the consequences of these meanings, particularly in relation to women and 'woman'. Feminist poststructuralists are therefore necessarily political, and hence not relativist, since they are interested in the consequences of particular meanings. In the words of Hilary Lawson, 'From a non-realist perspective what matters are the consequences of . . . stories about truth' (1989b: 4).

The criticisms of relativism and nihilism are closely linked to a particular interpretation of Derrida's dictum, 'There is nothing outside of the text' (1974: 158), an interpretation which is captured by the phrases: 'if you stub your toe you'll know what reality is', or 'if you are a poor black woman you'll know what reality is'. In Niall Lucy's words, 'Somehow the statement "there is no outside the text" has been taken to mean that there is no truth, no reality, no history, no actual flesh-and-blood people in the world, no rocks and trees, disease, sex, poverty, or physical violence' (1995: 1). In other words, 'there is nothing outside of the text' is taken to mean that poststructuralism relies on a disjunction between reality and representation, between theory and practice, and/or between academic theorizing and 'grassroots' activism: 'All there is . . . is a form of fiction *in extremis*: nothing can be said to *be* except in so far as it has been made up, constructed, put together from language, discourse, signs' (ibid.; see also Eagleton 1983: 143–5; Cheah 1991: 117–20). In this construction, feminist poststructuralists are seen as operating only within the realm of representation or theory, rather than in the realm of reality or practice. [23] This interpretation follows directly from the referential view of language which enables a completely literal interpretation based on a distinction between reality and mere appearance. To argue that rape is a discursive event, to take an example which Mary Hawkesworth has argued is one of 'the realities which circumscribe women's lives' (1989: 349), is not to deny that rape occurs, but to challenge claims that, for example, rape is due to men's testosterone and a 'natural' need for sex, as the judge-economist Richard Posner (1992: 106) has argued. That is, the constructions of women as rapable and men as rapists are themselves politicized, leading to very different strategies for women from that of rape prevention. [24] Thus, the phrase 'there is nothing outside of the text' may be read to mean that knowledge of 'reality' can only be apprehended and experienced through text or language (Barrett 1992: 209). To say that there is nothing outside the text is to acknowledge the power and materiality of language and its truth effects.

Critics of poststructuralism also accuse feminist poststructuralists of failing to offer a political project for feminism. Christine Di Stefano, for example, has argued that 'the postmodernist project, if seriously adopted by feminists, would make any semblance of a feminist politics impossible' (1990: 76; see also Hartmann *et al.* 1996). This argument relies on the notion that without an ontologically-grounded subject there can be no politics, let alone a feminist politics. The notion of 'politics' which underlies this criticism is one of representational or identity politics: women can only demand social change – the satisfaction of their interests or the extension of rights – on the basis of their shared identity as women. The concern of some feminists is that, without this well-defined category, this fixed identity of 'woman', there can be no politics. Poststructuralist feminists, on the other hand, argue that the installation of the subject 'woman' as a self-present category upon which a feminist politics might rest results in the foreclosure of analyses of the political construction and regulation of this category (Butler and Scott 1992b: xiv). That is, to premise a feminist politics upon 'woman' as a stable, foundational, subject is to deny the political nature of that premise, that is, to exclude from the political sphere the very construction of subjectivity. This does not mean that the term 'woman' loses its ability to signify, since, in Butler's words, 'To refuse to assume . . . a notion of the subject from the start is not the same as negating or dispensing with such a notion altogether; on the contrary, it is to ask after the process of its construction and the political meaning and consequentiality of taking the subject as a requirement or presupposition of theory' (Butler 1992: 4, 1994b; see also Derrida 1984: 125; Cornell 1991: ch. 2; Kirby 1991b). Feminist poststructuralism can be argued, then, to enlarge the sphere of the political rather than to diminish it, since foundational concepts, such as the subject, reality, nature, truth, being and sexual difference are brought within the sphere of the political and historicized, rather than being excluded from examination through a process of naturalization or the creation of a 'constitutive outside' which is denied a productive role in establishing the meaning of the inside (the political, the social, the economic). Ironically, then, it is the referential view of language which can generate political conservatism through its naturalization of foundational concepts. Nevertheless, it should not be forgotten that feminists have achieved substantial gains for women in the political and economic spheres precisely on the basis of posing 'women' as a self-present and unifying category. These gains, however, have come at a cost, because in being achieved they naturalize a particular essence of woman. A feminist poststructuralist politics also requires coalitions or alliances, but these are formed not on the basis of a supposed essence, but on the basis of localized, particularized struggles.

A further criticism commonly made of poststructuralist and feminist poststructuralist writing is that it is 'jargonistic', impenetrable and even deliberately difficult and obscure. [25] The first point to make is that 'jargon' or specialized language develops within all disciplines and within new areas of research. To argue that poststructuralism is unusually 'jargonistic' is to forget that, as Terry Threadgold has noted: 'What were once technical 'jargons', metalanguages, have made the transition from theory into the everyday world of the ordinary' (1990: 19). [26] However, given the widely-available array of dictionaries, glossaries and introductory texts of modern thought and thinkers, psychoanalysis and feminist theory, there is clearly more at stake here. [27] The prominent feminist economist Julie Nelson's comment is a slightly petulant indication of what it is that might be at stake: 'The deconstructionist literature seems to assume that all its readers have the time and inclination to become versed in its vocabulary and rules through extensive scholarly study of contemporary literary criticism; either that, or it assumes that theorizing best be left with the literary elite. I doubt the practicality of the first option and deplore the parochialism of the second' (1992a: 148). Vicki Kirby has discussed this response to feminist poststructuralism, pointing out that 'complex work of this kind is often criticized *because* it is complex' (1993: 26). But, she argues, to demand simplicity, clarity and transparency is to make those who have invested significant effort in understanding and putting to use this body of work 'responsible for rendering the difficulties of this new material immediately accessible to those who have not engaged [its] challenges, as if the difference between doing the work and not doing it were of no particular value'. The effect of this demand for clarity is to reduce the potential of this work to 'resist familiar frames of reference' (ibid.). In other words, a completely 'transparent' rendering of feminist poststructuralist writing empties that work of its political possibilities, because in its alleged transparency, or single, graspable meaning, it invokes as self-evident the very categories, assumptions and foundations which it is seeking to undermine. [28]

The 'jargon' criticism has also been closely related to the criticism that feminist poststructuralist work is not political. This follows from the belief that academic feminists have a duty to make their theorizing and writing accessible and relevant to *all* women, which requires the simplified and transparent rendering referred to above. If feminist poststructuralism is unlikely to be understood by waitresses, migrant 'women, the 'woman next door', and other non-academic women, then it must be elitist 'mumbo-jumbo' with no possible relevance to those women or their lives. Elizabeth Grosz's response to the charge that her work is not feminist because it not accessible to everyone is to argue that: 'There is an immense amount of intellectual arrogance which presumes that factory workers, for example, should be reading philosophy . . . It is elitist to assume that every theory should be of universal relevance' (1994a: 22–3). She contends that 'if one says something of relevance to everyone then one says nothing of particular relevance to anyone. Politics is occurring at many different levels, in many different places and with many different kinds of tactics'. She argues that the view that political action is the domain only of 'real workers' is a remnant of a Marxist notion of politics, but that academics are also workers who are able to contest politics in their own workplaces, and who should not presume that they can dictate the strategies of others who are differently situated (ibid.: 23). Furthermore, such a criticism presumes that feminist theorizing and research in the academy is irrelevant to those outside academia, as if challenging dominant modes of representation had no effects, or as if there was a clear distinction between 'pure' and 'practical' knowledge (on this distinction, see also Norris 1987: 157–61). This assumption is not borne out by the history of feminist interventions into policy and modes of organization in both the public and private spheres, often premised upon the sex/gender distinction which itself brought about new representations of the meaning of 'woman'.

The concept of closure is also relevant to the discussion of the 'jargon' criticism. 'Closure' refers to the fixation of meaning or the closing off of possibilities beyond a single interpretation. Closure therefore refers to logocentrism, within which the fixation of meaning allows the reader to acknowledge the author as the centre and to master the meaning which that author has intended. Structural linguistics, as well as the referential view of language, offers such a sense of a centre through its implicit identification of the signifier as that which represents the signified. This identification enables the meaning of a text to be conclusively comprehended. For poststructuralists, on the other hand, closure can never be effected, since each signifier is a signified for another signifier: poststructuralists operate with the notion that a text can never be mastered since there is no transcendental signifier. Thus poststructuralists such as Lacan and Derrida enact their critiques of the self-knowing *cogito* with their writings. [29] Their writings are so difficult precisely because there is no closure, no satisfying sense that 'I understand what was meant (and therefore I, too, can be the source of meaning)'. As Derrida has remarked: 'Play [the play of meaning] is the disruption of presence' (1978: 292). In other words, the slippage that occurs within texts, or the inability of the reader finally to master or contain the author's intended meaning, is disruptive of the self-presence of the reader. [30]

Finally, some feminists have accused those feminists who use poststructuralism of falling for a patriarchal trick. Nancy Hartsock, for example, argues that it seems highly suspicious that, just as women and other marginalized and silenced groups are claiming the right to name themselves and act as subjects rather than the objects of history, the concept of the 'subject' is brought into question (quoted in Hazel 1994: 92–3). Again, this criticism is intimately related to the idea that poststructuralism denies the possibility of feminist political struggle and social change through its problematization of the notion of a preexisting referent or constituency which feminism is thought to represent, and of concepts such as truth, reason, justice and progress. But, as Valerie Hazel has pointed out, 'to assume that it is possible for women to gain access to unified subjecthood understands subjecthood to be a category amenable to such an accession [which] is precisely the dilemma that feminism poses for the Enlightenment subject: just how is it going to be possible for women to gain access to a category whose very identity requires their exclusion?' (1994: 94–5). And even if women were able to claim the subjectivity of the Enlightenment subject, many feminists have argued that this is not desirable in any case, since to become subjects on the basis of sameness requires that (sexual) difference be effaced (ibid.: 95).

The project of this book should certainly be seen as political in the sense of wanting to generate positive change for women. However, although destabilizing readings of neoclassical economics such as that offered by this book have political implications and may be used to intervene in economic discourse, it seems unlikely that these effects will be felt within the economics profession for some time, as Randy Albelda's (1995) survey of 400 US-based members of the American Economic Association shows. Some of the more salient results of this survey are as follows: the surveyed economists believed that feminism had made virtually no impact on the methodology of economics or on economic theory; [31] less than one-fifth believed that more space in economics journals should be devoted to 'Feminist Perspectives on Economic Analysis' (ibid.: 263); and nearly 70 per cent either strongly disagreed with, somewhat disagreed with, or had no opinion on the statement that 'Mainstream economics would be enriched if it incorporated more feminist analysis' (ibid.: 267). As I show in Chapters 2 and 3 below, feminist economics is still in its infancy. Feminist economists can perhaps take heart, however, from the successful installation of feminist perspectives in the teaching of other disciplines. [32]

1.5. Outline of the Book

The major object of this book is to employ feminist poststructuralist insights to investigate neoclassical economics as a productive discourse within which 'rational economic man' is produced. The book is divided into two parts. The first part consists of this and the following three chapters, and may collectively be interpreted as a critical survey of the existing feminist economics literature. In Chapter 2 I examine feminist economic writings which adopt the 'add women and stir' strategy; that is, that work in which women as economic agents are incorporated into the existing neoclassical framework (this is the first approach to the women and knowledge mentioned in section 1.2 above). The authors of these works also adhere to an empiricist philosophy. They maintain a commitment to the singularity of truth and believe that the addition of women to the content of neoclassical economics will produce a more realistic economics. They are therefore on common ground with those neoclassical economists who believe that the economic individual is a preexisting referent. In Chapter 3 I continue the critical review of the feminist economics literature by focusing on feminist works which take the theoretical underpinnings and the methodological precepts of neoclassical economics as the object of investigation (the second approach to women and knowledge mentioned in section 1.2 above). The authors of these works believe that the existing theoretical framework and methodology suffer from an androcentric bias, and hence must be adjusted or overthrown. In Chapter 4 I argue that the sex/gender distinction is of central importance to the feminist economics projects delineated in Chapters 2 and 3, and provide a critique of this distinction and those feminist economic works which draw upon it. I develop the feminist poststructuralist framework delineated above in order to overcome the limitations of the sex/gender distinction, and interpret the feminist economics projects from this perspective. In particular I draw upon a body of theory which has been named by an English writer 'New Australian Feminism' (Barrett 1988: xxix). 'New Australian Feminism' is a poststructuralist feminism of difference with a focus on the production of sexed bodies.

Part One of the book, then, is a 'building block' exercise in which I situate the book in terms of current scholarship on economics, feminist economics and feminist theory, and develop those aspects of feminist poststructuralist theory employed in the analyses that comprise Part Two of the book. The devotion of four chapters to these tasks is necessary because of the fledgling nature of the field of feminist economics. As noted above, feminist economics has only recently gained the various institutional forms necessary for its establishment as a legitimate field of endeavour; namely, an association, a journal devoted to its articulation, a presence within economics conferences and its own conference program. Consequently, the small but growing literature in this area has yet to be surveyed in any detail, and the main directions and boundaries of this field have not been clearly delineated. The feminist economics literature has also not been comprehensively situated in relation to feminist theory, and in particular, in relation to the discussions on the question of women and knowledge within recent feminist scholarship. This is a task of vital importance because, as I demonstrate, different approaches have different implicit commitments, and these commitments, and associated advantages and limitations, must be explicitly analysed. Such an analysis is especially warranted in the case of feminist poststructuralism, which has received relatively scant attention from economists and is little understood by many practitioners of feminist economics.

The second part of the book encompasses the final four chapters, and entails a consideration of neoclassical economics as a productive discourse, and, specifically, an examination of the masculinity of 'rational economic man'. I address the incompatibility of the female body and neoclassical economics, the production of masculinity and the one-sex model within neoclassical economics, and more broadly the problematic inclusion of woman or the feminine within neoclassical economic theorizing. In Chapter 5 I explore the figure of Robinson Crusoe, which is used as a teaching device in neoclassical economics, looking at both the Daniel Defoe ([1719] 1945) novel and economic textbook representations. I use this analysis to reverse and displace the one-sex model upon which neoclassical economics relies. The next two chapters develop a case study of the surrogate motherhood exchange. In Chapter 6 I develop a formal neoclassical model of this exchange. In Chapter 7 I undertake a feminist poststructuralist reading of this model and argue that it requires, and produces, a one-sex model. Chapter 8 concludes the book, and comprises a brief outline of the ways in which my analysis has contributed to the literature.

Part Two of the book, then, is an application of the feminist poststructuralist approach developed in Part One. Such an application is of central importance because feminist poststructuralism has yet to be extensively adopted within feminist economics, and my analyses may be taken as examples of the way in which the insights of feminist poststructuralism may be usefully employed to shed light on the discourse of economics and the economic position of women. Feminist poststructuralism has also been adopted by feminists working within a range of other disciplines, and hence a detailed application of this approach is long overdue in economics. Unlike other feminist frameworks, such an approach focuses on the productivity of discourses, and hence reveals the limitations imposed by language and institutions on the ways in which woman can be theorized. The limitations imposed by the discourse of neoclassical economics are the focus of the feminist poststructuralist analysis of Robinson Crusoe and surrogate motherhood.

Notes

1. See Gary Becker (1973, 1974a, 1974b) and section 2.3 below. Becker was awarded the Nobel Prize for Economics in 1992, in part for his theorizing of the family as an economic institution.
2. Cynthia Lloyd, Emily Andrews and Curtis Gilroy pointed out in their introduction to an anthology of papers on women in the labour market that: 'Many of the most recent methodological breakthroughs in the analysis of labor market problems have been prompted by the challenge of unraveling the true facts about women's relative economic contributions and economic rewards . . . the external economies to the field of labor in general generated by research on women have been substantial and have encouraged many with no particular

ideological commitment to women's issues to move into this challenging research area' (1979: xiv). An example of such research rewards is given by Martha MacDonald, who points out that since women's labour market participation tends to vary more than men's, empirical examination of the income and substitution effects of a wage change requires data on women (1984: 156).

3. Susan Himmelweit has recently argued that: 'One of the earliest moves in the late 1960s in what has now come to be called feminist economics, was the attempt to incorporate women's domestic labor into the domain of economics, to analyze it as a form of work comparable with, though underprivileged in relation to, paid work' (1995: 1). The 'domestic labour debate' began in the late 1960s and continued throughout the 1970s, involving some Marxist or socialist economists, some of whom are now known as feminist economists (Nancy Folbre and Heidi Hartmann, for example), but largely undertaken by feminist sociologists and other feminist theorists interested in the relationship between Marxism and patriarchy. Specifically, the debate examined the relationship between class and patriarchal relations, and sought to clarify the status and value of domestic work within the capitalist system as understood by Marx. Although the debate certainly falls under the umbrella term 'feminist economics', it is a debate that is largely internal to Marxism, and led to the development of Marxist and socialist feminisms as distinct forms of feminism (see Jaggar 1983). This debate is briefly discussed in section 3.2 below.

4. The likely reason for this failure is the recent, and even nascent, nature of the field. For partial, article-length surveys, see Ferber and Nelson (1993b), Hyman (1994a, 1994b), Grapard (1995b), Nelson (1995b) and Humphries (1995b), as well as Chapters 2 and 3 below.

5. Phillips was a politics lecturer and Taylor a feminist historian, indicating (as contended in note 3 above) the multidisciplinary nature of feminist interest in issues arising from the problem of fitting women and their work into conventional Marxist categories.

6. The non-economists Leghorn and Parker were motivated to write the book by their active participation in the women's movement of the 1970s.

7. As Philipa Rothfield has pointed out, sociobiology was a contemporary of the women's liberation movement (1991b: 110), and others have argued for a causal relationship between the two. For example, Ann Oakley remarked that it is no coincidence that each time feminism erodes the 'system of gender-differentiation', arguments that sex differences are innate are reenlisted (1972: 189). Elizabeth Fee argues more explicitly that sociobiology was part of a conservative ideological movement within science which was mobilized in response to feminism (1986: 43).

8. See also Nancy Chodorow (1978), who draws on object relations theory as well as on Stoller's work on the distinction between sex and gender to argue that equal parenting will break down the link between women and the feminine qualities associated with mothering, and that between men and the masculine qualities associated with their distance from parenting (ibid.: 211–19). Chodorow's work has been particularly influential in feminist economics (see Chapter 3 below).

9. These two approaches have been drawn from Moira Gatens's (1986) discussion of the relationship between feminism and philosophy. She there makes the point that feminists often begin with the first approach, but find themselves having to take up the second. Alternatively, feminists who begin with the first approach may continue to believe that they are simply extending or altering the *content* of the knowledge, or, as Gatens writes, 'adding to and tidying-up' philosophies or other knowledges, but they have also modified the *framework* of that knowledge, often in ways not always readily visible to them (1986: 22). This is particularly relevant to my discussion of feminist economics in Chapters 2 and 3 below (see also Grosz 1988a).

10. The terms 'postmodernism' and 'poststructuralism' are terms which have been used interchangeably to refer to the philosophical projects outlined in this section (see Huyssen 1990: 258–67; Milner 1991: 110–16; Appleby *et al.* 1996: 385–92). However, these terms

can also connote quite different concerns. Postmodernism is often associated with the fields of architecture, literature, photography, film, painting, video, dance and music (Hutcheon 1989: 1), while poststructuralism is associated with knowledge production, subjectivity and philosophy. In this use of the terms, 'Postmodernism is to art what poststructuralism is to philosophy and social theory' (Ryan 1988: 559). In other works, poststructuralist theory is treated as a subset of postmodern theory, and postmodern theorists are viewed as extending poststructuralist insights in the realm of philosophy to new areas within social theory (see, for example, Best and Kellner 1991: ch. 1). The term 'postmodernity', on the other hand, is also used to indicate both the general terrain of aesthetics and of knowledge production (see, for example, Seidman 1994; Grosz 1986: 10). In this book, as in Australian writings in general, the term 'poststructuralism' will be used to denote theoretical writings which take as given the productivity of language and which are concerned with questions of subjectivity, truth and knowledge, keeping in mind that, in the United States, the term 'postmodernism' also covers this terrain. Note, however, that exceptions to this geographic divide exist. For example, Vicki Kirby (1994), an Australian author working in the United States, has written within an Australian text that 'As an intellectual phenomenon, postmodernism is a critique of Reason that examines the status of what constitutes knowledge and the "knowing subject" ' (1994: 120), while the American feminists Judith Butler and Joan Scott write that ' "post-structuralism" indicates a field of critical practices that . . . interrogate the formative and exclusionary power of dis-course in the construction of sexual difference' (1992b: xiii).

11. Saussure's *Course in General Linguistics* ([1916] 1974) inaugurated this view of language. Note that, despite the implications of his work, Saussure himself falls into the trap of using language as nomenclature: 'the signified "ox" has its signifier *b-ö-f* on one side of the border but *o-k-s* (*Ochs*) on the other' (ibid: 68). Sturrock (1986: 16) argues that Saussure's apparent confusion is a result of the construction of his *Course in General Linguistics*, which was an amalgam of students' lecture notes produced after his death. Jacques Derrida, however, notes that (for poststructuralists) the importance of the *Course* is as a text, rather than as a set of authorial intentions (1974: 329n38).

12. If the meaning of referents were not arbitrary, as Saussure implied in the just-quoted sentence, language would be a simple naming system. Sturrock has argued that the nomenclature position retains plausibility only if language consists entirely of verbs and nouns. The nomenclature position cannot be sustained when other categories of sign, or the complex logical relations which signs enter into when used, are considered (1986: 17). For an introduction to the structuralist view of language, see Culler (1974, 1976, 1983), Norris (1987), Selden and Widdowson (1993), Lechte (1994: 14–53), Lucy (1995) and Nöth (1995). The view of language employed by poststructuralists derives from Saussure's structuralist linguistics (see below).

13. Saussure's privileging of speech over writing, and his implicit retention of the author as the source of meaning, is revealed in the title of Chapter VI of his *Course in General Linguistics*: 'Graphic Representation of Language'. In this chapter he states that: 'Language and writing are two distinct systems of signs; the second exists for the sole purpose of representing the first' ([1916] 1974: 23; see also Culler 1983: 97–102).

14. See Derrida (1974: ch. 2, 1981: 'Semiology and Grammatology: Interview with Julia Kristeva') for his analysis of Saussure's privileging of self-present speech over writing. See also Derrida (1978, 1982a, 1982b, 1991). Derrida's work is notorious for its difficulty. Useful introductions to his work include Spivak (1974), Culler (1976, 1983), Johnson (1981), Young (1981), Norris (1982, 1987), Eagleton (1983: ch. 4), Gross (1986a), Sarup (1993: ch. 2), Selden and Widdowson (1993), Troup (1993) and Lechte (1994: 105–10).

15. Nancy Jay gives the example of men/not-men, where the not-men term refers to women and children, non-white persons, and perhaps others. Here the term 'men' has positive value, while 'women and children' have only the negative commonality that they are not men, or that they are infantile in relation to men (1991: 98). See Lloyd (1984) for the history of the

binary construction of reason as masculine.

16. Scott attributes this definition of discourse to Michel Foucault, and it is in this sense, rather than in the linguistic sense, that the term is used in this book. For discussions of this distinction, see Nöth (1995) and McHoul and Grace (1993: ch. 2). Note also that discourse in the Foucauldian sense cannot be equated with 'ideology', since discourse is productive of embodied subjectivity and reality rather than offering an interpretation of a separate, given reality (see Foucault 1972, 1980a, 1980b, 1981a; Campioni and Gross 1983; McHoul and Grace 1993: ch. 1).

17. See Huston (1985), Lloyd (1986) and Lake (1992a) for discussions of the connections between the masculinity of war, the masculinity of citizenship and the construction of motherhood.

18. Derrida coined the term 'phallogocentrism', a conflation of phallocentrism and logocentrism, to indicate Jacques Lacan's elevation of the phallus to the status of transcendental signifier or a mark of presence (Smith 1992; see also Cornell 1991: ch. 2; Kamuf 1991b). In this book I use the term 'phallocentrism' to signal that the feminist poststructuralist position developed here relies more heavily upon Derrida and feminist theorists of the body than on Lacan and psychoanalytic theory. However, as Rosemary Pringle suggests when she writes that phallocentrism is 'phallogocentrism for the purists', the two theoretical systems are closely aligned in their focus on 'sexuality, fantasy, representation and the constitution of the sexed body' (1995: 199).

19. Elizabeth Grosz (1989: 34) argues that Derrida himself raises the question of whether sexual difference precedes or follows ontological difference, and hence recognizes that sexual difference may underlie logocentrism. Drucilla Cornell declares more strongly that Derrida 'explicitly argues that fundamental philosophical questions cannot be separated from the thinking of sexual difference' (1991: 98). Peggy Kamuf (1991b) concurs, noting that in typical fashion Derrida shows that what appears to be marginal – that is, sexual difference – is actually central to philosophical thought. Supporting this view is Derrida's response, in an interview in 1973, to a question about the relationship between logocentrism and phallocentrism: 'It is one and the same system: the erection of a paternal logos . . . and of the phallus as "privileged signifier" ' (quoted in and translated by Culler 1983: 172). On phallocentrism, see Irigaray (1985), Cixous and Clément (1986), Gross (1986a, 1986e) and Grosz (1989, 1990a, 1990c); and for feminist poststructuralism more generally, see Barrett (1988, 1992), Weed (1989), Hekman (1990a), Rothfield (1990), Threadgold (1990), Ferrell (1991a), Kirby (1991a, 1991b, 1993, 1994), Butler (1992), Butler and Scott (1992a, 1992b), Dallery (1994) and Elam (1994).

20. See, for example, Nelson (1992a, 1996a), Folbre (1993b), Ferber and Nelson (1993b) and Seiz (1993).

21. Eagleton agrees that some Anglo-American poststructuralists embrace this supposed nihilism and hence view themselves as unconstrained by the requirement to take a position on important issues. This follows from their failure to acknowledge the productivity or real effects of language, leading to the churning out of closed (empty) critical texts in an 'endless power game' which is a 'mirror-image of orthodox academic competition' (1983: 147). However, feminist poststructuralists, who self-consciously take a political stance in their challenges to the various investments made in the concepts of, for example, 'woman', 'man' and 'sexual difference', cannot be accused of supporting the existence of a series of equally valid truths (see, for example, the papers contained in Butler and Scott 1992a).

22. The term 'deconstruction' has a particular meaning within poststructuralist writing. Briefly, the term does not simply refer to a 'pulling apart' or destruction of binary oppositions and textual structures. Rather, it involves a close and strategic reading of a text and the demonstration that the argument of the text is a political position rather than a self-evident or self-present 'truth' through the strategy of revealing its reliance upon a binary opposition, and simultaneously the presence of the not-A term within the A term within that binary structure. I discuss deconstruction in Chapter 4 below.

23. As Butler and Scott note, this charge is often accompanied by the contradictory claim that, within poststructuralist writing, reality is completely determined by discourse (1992b: xvii). See, for example, Alcoff (1989: 306–8).

24. See the brilliant discussion by Marcus (1992) for a poststructuralist reading of rape and a rebuff to Hawkesworth's argument that rape is 'real' (fixed, determinate and transparent to understanding), rather than a 'fiction', which, Hawkesworth suggests, is the inevitable conclusion of 'postmodern thought' (1989: 349). For other poststructuralist discussions of rape, see Smart (1990), Cheah (1991) and Butler (1992: 17–19).

25. See, for example, Christian (1988), Stefano (1990) and Brodribb (1992). Note that economics is itself notorious for its jargon.

26. Note, however, that although there is a metalinguistic function, since language can be used to discuss language, there is no metalanguage, 'only more language piled upon language' (Culler 1981: xi).

27. See, for example, Grosz (1990b), Best and Kellner (1991), Milner (1991), Wright (1992), Lechte (1994), Humm (1995), Nöth (1995) and Appleby *et al.* (1996).

28. The difficulty for poststructuralist writers is that while necessarily remaining within logocentrism, and hence constantly invoking logocentric assumptions, they are also seeking to undermine logocentrism and its effects. As Derrida has argued: 'We have no language – no syntax and no lexicon – which is foreign to this history we can pronounce not a single destructive proposition which has not already had to slip into the form, the logic, and the implicit postulations of precisely what it seeks to contest' (1978: 280–1; see also Irigaray 1989). There is, then, no question of a meta-language created by poststructuralism, but rather a re-working of language from within language itself.

29. Mitchell has called attention to the 'preposterous difficulty of Lacan's style', pointing out that: 'Humanism believes that man is at the centre of his own history and of himself; he is a subject more or less in control of his own actions, exercising choice . . . The matter and manner of all Lacan's work challenges this notion of the human subject: there is none such' (1982: 4; the relevance of Lacan's work to the project of this book is delineated in Chapter 4 below). Similarly, as previously noted, Derrida's work is notoriously difficult, or, as Kamuf remarks, 'disconcerting and deliberately so' (1991a: ix). She warns readers of her anthology accordingly: 'Be advised that the most familiar may well begin to appear strangely different. As Derrida writes in one of the extracts from *Of Grammatology* . . . his final intention is "to make enigmatic what one thinks one understands by the words 'proximity', 'immediacy', 'presence' ", that is, the very words with which we designate what is closest to us' (ibid.). She further notes that readers trained in the importance of clarity of style may find Derrida's work obscure. However, 'Derrida never cultivates this "obscurity" for its own sake; on the contrary, the apparent density of his writing has its correlative in a relentless demand for clarity of another order, which may be called, in a seeming paradox, a clarity about the obscurity, opacity, and fundamental difference of language. Standard notions of clarity or "correct" style, when viewed from this perspective, must be seen as, themselves, obscurantist since they encourage a belief in the transparency of words to thoughts, and thus a "knowledge" constructed on this illusion. Deconstructing this knowledge will necessarily be a matter of some difficulty' (ibid: xi–xii). Nevertheless, as Culler (1983: 17–18) argues, 'Critical debate should stimulate, not stupefy', and hence clarity, although not simplicity (and here I agree with Kirby 1993, whose arguments were previously delineated), on the part of the expositors of theorists such as Lacan and Derrida, or at least those within the introductory genre, is something of an obligation.

30. The logical response that Derrida, for example, establishes an authorial intention even when enacting the disruption of presence, was dealt with in the famous debate between Derrida and John Searle (see Lucy 1995: ch. 2). This debate consisted of a paper by Derrida (1982b), a critique of this paper by Searle, a rejoinder from Derrida, a book review by Searle in which he 'lambasted' Derrida, and Derrida's response to Searle's review (see Lucy 1995: 23). Derrida's initial paper was a critique of J.L. Austin's speech act theory. In

Searle's 'Reply' to this paper, he argued that Derrida had misunderstood Austin. Derrida replied that Searle had misunderstood his (Derrida's) meaning. In Niall's words, 'Each accuses the other of being wrong. But it is only Derrida whose theory is supposed to make this into a self-contradiction' (ibid.: 34). In other words, Derrida was making the point that, in Searle's misreading of Derrida's critique, Searle had confirmed precisely what he was arguing against. To quote Niall, 'according to Derrida, Searle is wrong, and so Derrida has tried to put him right, but that is no guarantee that Searle won't still be wrong or go being wrong forever. And of course this logic can be reapplied even if the proper names are inverted: according to Searle . . . and so on. Understanding is therefore contextual: otherwise it would be a universal principle of every semiotic exchange, and there would be no need of pedagogy. And it is contextual *because* the possibility of misunderstanding is always at work, in play, in general' (ibid.: 37; see also Norris 1987: ch. 7, 1990).

31. Only 1 per cent of the surveyed economists believed that feminism had made a 'substantial, positive impact' on the methodology of neoclassical economics, and less than 10 per cent believed that feminism had made a 'substantial, positive impact' on most of the other specific fields examined. The exceptions were 'Labour Market Analysis' (12.3 per cent) and 'Household Behavior and Family Economics' (11.1 per cent) (Albelda 1995: 260).

32. For an introduction to the debates about the radical potential of feminism in the academy, see Stanton and Stewart (1995a, 1995b).

2. Women and Knowledge I: Adding Women to Neoclassical Economics

2.1. Introduction

In Chapter 1 it was pointed out that there have been two broad and overlapping historical stages in the feminist analysis of the relationship between women and knowledge. The first stage is associated with the feminist writers of the late 1960s and early 1970s and is characterized by the aim of incorporating women into the existing disciplines, both as research practitioners and as objects of study. In this stage the incumbent disciplinary frameworks are largely taken as given, and the domain of inquiry is expanded to include women in order to make these knowledges a more complete representation of the real world. In other words, the goal is to enlarge the content rather than challenge the disciplinary paradigms, and it has therefore been referred to as the 'add women and stir' strategy. The second stage began at different times within different disciplines, but it had commenced in most by the early 1980s. Feminists began to conclude that the existing disciplinary frameworks were simply unable adequately to incorporate women or the feminine, and such frameworks themselves became the objects of a specifically feminist analysis. In other words, the goal was to alter (or to challenge) the character rather than the content of the frameworks. Early feminist writing, then, elaborated women's unfair treatment by the practitioners of various disciplines, including discriminatory behaviour which acted as a barrier to women entering the relevant professions and the dismissal of women as important objects of study within the disciplinary knowledge, while later feminist writing has sought to develop specifically feminist perspectives on the disciplines and the place of women and/or the feminine within those disciplinary knowledges (see Pateman and Gross 1986). Note, however, that the research projects undertaken by scholars within each feminist project can, perhaps fruitfully, continue to develop alongside one another.

This overlapping two-stage development of feminist scholarship has been discussed in relation to most fields of study. Moira Gatens, for example, has detailed these two approaches in the context of philosophy. Feminist philosophers who assume that philosophy as a discipline and method of inquiry is neutral with regard to sex expand the content of philosophy as if philosophy and feminism were complementary projects, where feminism undertakes the role of transforming philosophy from a male-dominated enterprise into a human enterprise: 'feminist theory adds to, or completes, traditional or existing philosophy, by filling in the "gaps" in political, moral and social theory' (1986: 16). The second approach has involved taking feminist theory or a feminist perspective as the starting point and philosophy itself as the object of study, 'demonstrating not only *what* is excluded from a particular philosophy but also *why* it is crucial, for the very existence of that philosophy, to exclude it' (ibid.: 24–5).

Another case in point is the discipline of history. Feminist analysis began with what Marilyn Lake, following Gerda Lerner, has labelled 'contribution history' and other feminists have referred to as 'her-story', in which women's 'roles' in history were delineated (1986: 116; see also Lake 1988: 1; Scott 1988b: ch. 1). Lake argues that the rescue of the forgotten women of history within women's history follows an 'assimilationist' model, practitioners of which fail to challenge explicitly the ruling categories of historical analysis. In labour history, for example, 'Women have been incorporated and rendered similar to the male subjects of labour history' (1992b: 1). Feminist history, in contradistinction to 'women's history', 'added gender as a problematic relationship', and interrogated the disciplinary paradigm of history itself (Lake 1988: 1; see also Allen 1986).

Suzanna Walters has also documented two distinct approaches within feminist cultural theory. Early research focused on content analysis, or the documentation of sexist representations in the mass media: 'early feminist researchers worked largely within the dominant framework of a quantitative, content-based methodology . . . In this sense, early feminist research can be seen as a classic case of the "woman question" being applied to a pre-existing framework of analysis' (1995: 37). Criticism of this early approach led to the emergence of a second approach – there was a shift from 'images of women' to 'woman as image', in which feminist work moved from the question of sexist images to questions of the production of cultural images and the ways in which those images become meaningful (ibid.: 38–49). However, reflecting the experience in other disciplines, this shift from sexist content to meaning production was 'by no means a simple and chronological one' (ibid.: 39).[1]

Even though feminist economics as a self-conscious feminist endeavour is a relatively new field of research, the two broad stages of feminist analysis can be demarcated within the feminist literature on economics. Indeed, the development of feminist economics has mirrored the development of feminist analysis in other disciplines. In this chapter I survey the writings of those feminists who have been guided by the first strategy of expanding the content of neoclassical economics to include women, and in the next chapter I overview the writings of those feminists who have been guided by the second strategy of interrogating the nature of neoclassical economics from a specifically feminist perspective. In section 2.2 I delineate feminist writings which document and explain the male domination of the profession of academic economist. In section 2.3 I delineate the historical development of neoclassical theory which has positioned women as economic actors in the same way as men. In section 2.4 I discuss the criticisms of feminist economists who fit within the category of 'feminist empiricism' (Harding 1986). These feminists argue, on both theoretical and empirical grounds, that the neoclassical modelling of women is inadequate. These criticisms lead to the development of new work, which builds on the perceived 'oversights' of male economists in their analyses of women's work within the neoclassical framework, rather than not to a rejection of that framework. Section 2.5 concludes the chapter.

2.2. The Absence of Women from the Economics Discipline

One of the earliest feminist critiques of Western knowledge production pointed to the exclusion of women from the social environments and institutions in which knowledge is produced (Poovey 1995: 136). The research underpinning this critique has been labelled 'equity studies' by Sandra Harding (1986: 21), and entails drawing attention to those discriminatory practices which cause very low numbers of women to attempt to enter particular professions, rather than necessarily highlighting any biases within the knowledge itself.[2] An equity study therefore involves the documentation of the quantity and forms of this discrimination against women. Feminist economists, too, have documented the absence or under-representation of women from academic positions within economics departments, from journal publications specializing in economic matters, from the histories of economic thought, and from economics textbook examples. They attribute these absences either to women choosing not to be part of a workplace which is tacitly hostile to their attributes and skills, or to women actively being excluded from the workplace through discriminatory practices inherent in the disciplinary employment selection procedures, the journal refereeing process and the allocation of research funds. Within the context of equal opportunity legislation, most would agree that such discriminatory practices should cease. The policy response to the absence of women within the profession, then, is to eliminate sexist practices and encourage more women to enter the discipline.

An assumption, implicit or explicit, which underlies this documentation of the absence of women within a discipline is that the male domination of a discipline generates bias in the content of that discipline's knowledge. This link between male domination of a discipline and knowledge may be made by arguing that women, but not men, look at issues and problems relevant to women. As Evelyn Fox Keller has remarked of feminists in science, 'Scholars began to ask how that under-representation has skewed choices of problems, and then, how inadvertent bias has crept into the design of experiments and the interpretation of data' (1985: 177). Thus the context of discovery may be biased because of male domination, and furthermore, male domination may also affect the context of justification, since, as Janet Seiz has argued in her discussion of gender and economics, 'the lack of diversity in the scientific community produces a commonality of interests and of limitations of vision; androcentric and enthnocentric [*sic*] theories are not rooted out, and better explanations are not advanced, because those who might challenge the prevailing arguments lack numbers and influence' (1992: 277). Thus, 'In the sciences, as in other fields, the male near-monopoly on knowledge production means that the discipline's notions of the good and the true (as well as the interesting) are notions that *men* find appealing' (ibid: 275–6). There are at least two reasons, then, to examine the extent of male domination in economics: to satisfy equity considerations, and to establish grounds for a critique of the content of the discipline (see Seiz 1992: 275–7).

One of the most frequent observations made by feminist economists in this context is the absence or under-representation of women within the ranks of economists (see Bell 1973a, 1974a, 1974b; Reagan 1975a, 1975b; Strober 1975; Ferber and Teiman 1981: 126–8; Blau 1987; Seiz 1992: 285–6; Ferber and Nelson 1993b: 2–4; Albelda 1995). This observation is certainly justified. For example, in 1992, 0.67 per cent of professors and associate professors, 9 per cent of senior lecturers and 25 per cent of lecturers in the economics departments of New Zealand universities were women (Hyman 1994a: 70–1). In the same year, 9.9 per cent of the staff of the 17 economics departments in Australian universities were women, and nine of these departments had two or fewer women (Thornton 1994: 3; see also Rosewarne and Meagher 1994). In the United States, women made up 16 per cent of the faculty at undergraduate institutions in 1988–9, and 9 per cent of the faculty at universities with graduate programs (Ferber and Nelson 1993b: 2–3). These proportions are low, but a further disturbing element is that women are concentrated in the lower level academic positions, with, for example, women making up only 3 per cent of full professors in universities in the United States (ibid.; and see Jones and Lovejoy 1980). Economics also has a very low proportion of women graduating with the degree of PhD compared to other disciplines such as psychology, anthropology and political science (Nelson 1996a: 26). Women's minority status in the profession of economist is also reflected in the granting of academic awards. No woman has achieved the Nobel Prize in Economics (commencing in 1967), women have never been awarded the Francis A. Walker or the John Bates Clark medal, and only one of forty distinguished fellowships awarded in the United States between 1965 and 1989 was given to a woman (Ferber and Nelson 1993b: 2).

A further problem for women in economics is the finding of a statistically significant difference in the number of citations to other authors of the same sex in the journal articles of economists (Ferber 1986, 1988; see also Paludi and Bauer 1983; Paludi and Strayer 1985). Relatedly, Marianne Ferber and Michelle Teiman (1980) have shown, using a small sample, that double blind reviewing raises the acceptance rate of papers by women. This issue continues to be of interest to feminist economists, with Rebecca Blank carrying out a more comprehensive study in 1991 which revealed no statistically significant correlation between gender and acceptance rates (Blank 1991). However, women may well publish less than men, or publish under more difficult circumstances, since, as Klamer (1991: 134) argues, they tend to be burdened with a disproportionate amount of committee work and student support.

Feminist economists have also noted the tendency for those women who have entered the academy to undertake research within 'feminine' fields such as labour economics. In 1971 the American Economic Association established the Committee on the Status of Women in the Economics Profession, and a roster of women economists was established (American Economic Association 1972).[3] Myra Strober and Barbara Reagan (1976) used these data, as well as the 1974 American Economic Association Directory of Members, to examine the relationship between economists' specializations and their sex, finding evidence that women disproportionately enter female-intensive specializations such as labour and population economics. They suggested: 'It may be that influences bearing on choice of dissertation research or allocation of postdoctorate research programs to women and/or to specific fields of specialization involve the most subtle forms of occupational segregation and sexism – differential encouragement on the part of male mentors' (ibid.: 317). Strober and Reagan also alluded to the possibility that female-intensive specializations may have a lower level of reward than other fields (ibid.: 316). Laurie Bassi's experience reinforces this possibility. She argues that research on 'women's issues' is a derogatory term within the economics profession, and a female academic economist must 'narrow her field of study to that which is acceptable in a male-dominated discipline', or she will not get tenure (1990: 44).

Some feminist economists have also suggested that the intellectual contributions of women and feminists to economics have been invisible, motivating the work of recovering the careers of important women within the history of economic thought (see, for example, Madden 1972; Thomson 1973; Pujol 1992; Hammond 1993; Groenewegen 1994b, 1994d; O'Donnell 1994; Alexander 1995; Dimand 1996; Hill 1996). Furthermore, feminist economists have contended that debates amongst (both male and female) economists about women and their roles in the economy have been ignored in the discipline's histories of thought. Michèle Pujol (1992), for example, has elucidated the late nineteenth and early twentieth century debates about women's role in the labour market; Nancy Folbre (1993a) and Frances Hutchinson (1995) have outlined the feminist contributions of nineteenth and early twentieth century socialist thinkers; and William Dugger (1994) has discussed the feminism of Thorstein Veblen (see also Folbre 1992; Cooper 1993; Nyland 1993a, 1993b; Nyland and Ramia 1994; Groenewegen 1994c; White 1994).

There is also a relatively large literature on how women have come to be excluded from the economics profession. Some economists have argued that women's own choices, rather than such external constraints as direct discrimination and barriers to women's employment, explain why there have been so few female economists (Johnson and Stafford 1974). Feminist economists argue that even if no direct discrimination has taken place, indirect discrimination affects women's career choices and their success in those careers. Indirect discrimination can take a number of forms. Reagan (1975b) cites male attitudes regarding female colleagues as a barrier to women's full career development, although Ferber (1988), writing twelve years later, is optimistic that as the number of women in the discipline grows, it will become more difficult for women's contributions (and hence women themselves) to be ignored. The neglect or stereotyping of women in textbooks is also an important form of indirect discrimination, since the invisibility of women as role models for students might discourage females from continuing with their economic studies. Susan Feiner and Barbara Morgan (1987) evaluated both quantitatively and qualitatively the coverage of race and gender issues in introductory economics textbooks over the period 1974–87 by counting the number of pages on which references to such issues appeared, and by assessing the coverage using the criteria set out in the guide to sexist and racist biases in research compiled by the American Sociological Association. They concluded that economic theory is gender- and race-blind, that there is a tendency to define the economic problems or experiences of white men as the norm, and that minorities and women are most frequently portrayed in stereotypical ways, with their experiences being treated as anomalous or deviant (ibid.: 387). Feiner and Roberts (1990) concur with these results, arguing that the distinction between positive and normative economics and the focus on equilibrium both contribute to the failure of texts to deal adequately with such topics as income inequalities, discrimination and inequality of opportunity (see also Bartlett and Feiner 1992).

A related issue is the failure of economists to incorporate into their teaching women as economic agents in their own right. Ferber (1984), Barbara Bergmann (1987b) and Strober (1987) urge the profession to include teaching about women's roles in the economy in their courses, and Jean Shackleford (1992) advocates the use of feminist pedagogical methods by academic economists. One of the first courses on women in the economy, entitled 'The Role of Women in Modern Economic Life', was taught by Cynthia Lloyd at Barnard College in 1972 (Lloyd 1975c). To encourage others to initiate courses on women and economics, members of the Pedagogy Committee of the International Association of Feminist Economists have been working on the *Feminist Economics Curriculum Project* which has seen the release of collected curriculum materials to interested parties since 1993 (Quade 1994; see also Bergmann 1990). Many of the courses listed in this document seek to elucidate women's roles within the economy. As pointed out by Lake (1988) in relation to history, one problem with this approach is that the masculinist categories of the discipline remain unquestioned.

Other classroom issues include the effects of a 'classroom climate' which is unfriendly to women (Ferber 1984; Sandler [1988] 1994; Ferber and Nelson 1993b: 3), and the denial to women PhD students of the encouragement given to men by their departments (Strober 1975; see also Berg and Ferber 1983; Shelburn and Lewellyn 1995). An additional indirect form of discrimination arises from the method by which economics is taught. Ferber, Bonnie Birnbaum and Carole Green (1983) critically review the evidence that there are sex-linked differences in learning economics which advantage men, concluding that the test instruments, such as standardized multiple choice questions, favour men. The authors claim that this is because of men's 'well-known . . . relative advantage in spatial and numerical skill' (1983: 29). Women, on the other hand, have a relative advantage in verbal skills, and hence would be expected to perform better than men in essays (ibid.). Hence different test instruments yield different conclusions with regard to men's as opposed to women's aptitude for economics (see also Lumsden and Scott 1987; Heath 1989; Hirschfeld, Moore and Brown 1995). Moreover, Katrina Alford argues that in secondary education girls' subject preferences are more 'socially oriented and humanitarian' than those of boys, who prefer technical, mechanical and manipulative educational activities. In general, then, girls prefer 'subjects which contextualise knowledge and skills in a broader fabric of understanding', and boys prefer 'abstract, "disembedded" studies' (1993: 14). Hence, as 'economics becomes more abstract, technical and severed from applied and contextual analysis, it is more likely to bias the selection process even more towards males' (ibid.: 15). We should not be surprised, she argues, that 'females tend to lose interest as economics has become more abstract and "disembedded" from its social and historical context' (Alford 1996: 24; see also Krueger *et al.* 1991). Sue Richardson also argues along these lines, suggesting that 'women tend to have a strong sense of the importance of the social and the collective and the non-material' and hence are not interested (along with 'sensitive, socially-concerned men') in disciplines which expunge 'feminine skills and motivations' such as creativity, communication, social concern and intuition in favour of 'applied maths' (1996: 19–20). Thus, an 'excessive' use of mathematics in economics has been argued to 'masculinize' the discipline, making it less likely that women will be attracted to it. Strober's (1975) research supported this conclusion, showing that a low level of training in mathematics was an important factor in women's decision not to enter the economics profession (as well as in their decision of field of specialization). However, mathematics has a higher percentage of women completing PhDs than does economics (Nelson 1996a: 26), pointing to a more complex relation between masculinity and economics than that suggested by Alford, Richardson and Strober.

As is apparent from this brief overview, there is a rich and lengthy literature in which the absence of women within economics as a profession, particularly in the United States, has been documented, criticized and explained. The majority of the early literature implied or stated that discriminatory barriers were responsible for women's virtual absence from the professional ranks of economists; hence the solution was to demand equal opportunity and the elimination of discriminatory behaviour and institutions. Bergmann and Irma Adelman, for example, argue that 'Given a fair shake, there is no doubt in our minds that women can make it to full equality with men in the job market. The problem, as we see it, is one of how to implement the transition to "sex-blind" hiring practices, in the presence of prevalent conscious and subconscious discrimination and role casting' (1973: 513). The Committee on the Status of Women in the Economics Profession was established expressly for this purpose (American Economic Association 1972).

However, the project of establishing equal opportunities for men and women is not as straightforward as some feminist economists appear to have assumed. Margaret Thornton, in her discussion of the operation of the Australian affirmative action legislation within the academy, makes a number of relevant points. She argues that affirmative action is based on the liberal myth that merit is gender-neutral: 'while merit continues to be used as though it were self-defining, the construction of excellence is shaped by the subjective and institutional perceptions of decision-makers. Furthermore, merit is used as a means of allocating scarce resources and of rationalising the *status quo* so that individual Anglo-Celtic, heterosexual, able-bodied, middle class men continue to be the beneficiaries of a disproportionate percentage of societal goods in the form of well-paid and prestigious jobs. Nevertheless, it is one of the most deeply-cherished myths of liberal society that the "best" person emerges triumphant in the competition for jobs and that a fair and just allocation has been made' (1989: 117). Thornton also points to the implicit white male norm and consequent association of affirmative action policies with a supposed inferiority of those who do not match that norm. She links this with the idea of 'homosocial reproduction' or the idea that 'senior men see youthful images of themselves as the ideal candidates within the recruitment process' (ibid.: 122). In order to establish themselves within the academy and other forums, women may well be forced to conform to this norm, as noted by Bassi (1990). Yet it must be emphasized that few contemporary feminist economists limit their explanation of the androcentrism of neoclassical economics to the under-representation of women economists. Indeed, the task of adding women to the profession of economist can be seen as the least confronting of the tasks demanded by feminist economists critical of the discipline of economics. A more challenging critique is to challenge the absence or inadequate incorporation of women as objects of research within the intellectual endeavours of the discipline. It is to this topic that I now turn.

2.3.   The Inclusion of Women as Objects of Knowledge: the 'Chicago School of Feminist Economics'

In this section I discuss the work of those feminist economists who have either documented the way in which women have been excluded as objects of investigation within neoclassical economics or endeavoured to correct this state of affairs by actually incorporating women as objects of study within the neoclassical framework. The absence or invisibility of women is a problem which characterizes many disciplinary frameworks. It 'involves women being completely ignored or neglected because the subject of such theories are [*sic*] explicitly male or male-dominated institutions and activities. Women are excluded by default; they become invisible by being disregarded' (Thiele 1986: 31). Those scholars who have sought to overcome this problem by incorporating women within neoclassical economics usually implicitly adhere to the principles of feminist empiricism, and hence I shall refer to such writers as feminist empiricists. 'Feminist empiricist' is the term employed within the feminist literature to describe the work of those feminists in the sciences who believe that androcentrism in its various forms can be eliminated through the more rigorous deployment of the scientific method (Harding 1986: 24–6, 1989: 191–4, 1993a: 51). The scientific method entails the use of scientific procedures to attain value-neutral or objective conclusions unbiased by the social interests of the observer. In the sense of the subject of this section, then, feminist empiricists are those who implicitly or explicitly attribute the absence of women from the theoretical relationships of neoclassical economics to 'bad science' in both the context of discovery and the context of justification. Social bias arises within the discovery process because questions, data and hypotheses relating to women are seen as unworthy of attention or as outside the scope of the discipline, while social bias arises in the justificatory process because the scientist fails to see that the resulting 'universal theories' do not have applicability to women.[4] Thus the solution to the absence of women is not so much to challenge the core assumptions which underpin the neoclassical framework, but to deploy the scientific method correctly in order to make neoclassical theories more representative of the real world. In other words, the solution is to correct 'bad science' by, as Helen Longino put it, 'taking the sex out of science' (1989: 205) In this section I examine the most important research areas in which women have been incorporated as objects of research; specifically, the definition of economics as a discipline, the household, human capital accumulation, discrimination and the national accounting framework.

Women as objects of study have been excluded from the formally defined domain of economics for a large part of the history of the discipline. As Beverly Thiele has noted, the exclusion of women in this way 'is not a simple case of lapsed memory; these theorists don't just forget to talk about women; rather, women are structurally excluded from the realm of discourse or, for the sake of theoretical preoccupations and coherency, they are deliberately dropped' (1986: 32). This omission arose in the nineteenth century when economics was defined explicitly to exclude the home, housework, reproduction and childrearing (and hence activities primarily associated with women) as sites of economic activity. Specifically, political economy was defined as the study of any activity relating to the production or distribution of wealth, where wealth was defined to exclude the realm in which the majority of women's activities took place. Nassau Senior's *An Outline of the Science of Political Economy* ([1836] 1965) was pivotal in establishing these boundaries for the science of political economy. Senior defined political economy as that science which 'treats of the Nature, the Production, and the Distribution of Wealth' (ibid.: 1), and wealth was defined to include all those things which are transferable, limited in supply, and either directly or indirectly productive of pleasure or preventative of pain (ibid.: 6). Under this definition, then, the study of female labour market activity is included within the scope of political economy, while the study of female activity within the home is excluded, since the former and not the latter result in transferable objects for an explicit exchange price.

Senior makes this clear in the following passage where he is responding to a critic:

> Colonel Torrens supposes a solitary family, or a nation in which each person should consume only his own productions, or one in which there should be a community of goods, and urges, as a *reductio ad absurdum*, that in these cases, though there might be an abundance of commodities, as there would be no exchanges, there would, in our sense of the term, be no wealth. The answer is, that, for the purposes of Political Economy, there would be no wealth; for, in fact, in such a state of things, supposing it possible, the Science of Political Economy would have no application. In such a state of society, Agriculture, Mechanics, or any other of the Arts which are subservient to the production of the commodities which are, with us, the subject of exchange, might be studied, but the Science of Political Economy would not exist (ibid.: 25).[5]

This exclusion of the private sphere from political economy was not formally redressed until 1935, when Lionel Robbins successfully redefined political economy as 'the science which studies human behaviour as a relationship between ends and scarce means which have alternative uses' ([1935] 1948:

16). Under this definition, no exclusions of non-market exchanges are possible, since any activity can be interpreted as falling within the domain of economics. Gary Becker made this clear in 1976 with his claim that the assumptions that individuals maximize utility, that market equilibria exist, and that preferences are stable through time, are all that is needed to be able fruitfully to analyse any human or non-human behaviour (1976b: 14). Thus, at least from a definitional point of view, it now appears impossible to exclude women or their activities from economic research. Indeed, post-war neoclassical economists (particularly Chicago economists) have developed theories in which consideration of the two sexes is essential.

The formal incorporation of the female labour supply decision within the neoclassical framework began with Jacob Mincer's classic paper ([1962] 1993). Mincer explains the development of women as a focus of labour economists like himself as the result of a 'puzzling contradiction' which emerged in the 1950s (1993: ix–x). Using cross-sectional data, economists had identified an inverse relationship between the participation rate of married women and the wage earnings of married men. Using time-series data, however, economists identified a positive relationship between the participation rate of married women and family real income. Mincer resolved this puzzle by arguing that the wages of both married men and women were important in determining married women's labour supply. Normally, economists had assumed that time not spent at work was spent in "leisure". Married women, on the other hand, chose between hours of paid work, leisure, and work in the home. The demand for hours of work at home 'is a demand for a productive service derived from the demand by the family for home goods and services' (Mincer [1962] 1993: 5). An increase in the wages which married women could earn would cause them to substitute market goods and services for home goods and services and leisure, since such an increase raises the implicit cost of both leisure and home-produced goods and services. Empirically, this substitution effect had outweighed the income effect of the wage increase. In Mincer's words: 'Other things equal (including family income), an increase in the market wage rate for some family member makes both the consumption of leisure and the production of home services by that individual more costly to the family, and will as a matter of rational family decision encourage greater market labor input by him (her)' ([1962] 1993: 5; see also Amsden 1980b: 14–15; Mincer 1993). Mincer's pioneering work encouraged other neoclassical economists to study the labour supply decisions of females (particularly wives) and women's education and training, and 'family' variables such as marriage, husband's earnings and children have been an important theoretical and empirical aspect of these works (see the classic works of Cain 1966; Mincer and Polachek [1974] 1993; Schultz 1973, 1974a, 1974b; for overviews of economic analyses of women's labour market participation decision, see Kahne and Kohen 1975; Lloyd 1975b; Humphries 1995b).

The decisions and activities related to the entire private sphere (including the labour supply decision) were formally incorporated within the neoclassical framework with the development of 'new home economics', a research programme closely associated with the name of Gary Becker. This field of research formalizes the role of women in the home, and was nascent within Becker's 'A Theory of the Allocation of Time' (1965). In this paper, Becker extended the neoclassical paradigm to add time to the resource constraint faced by the household, permitting, as noted by Lloyd, 'an integration of labour market economics and home economics through a unified theory of economic decision making', which significantly raised the respectability of the household as an object of economic analysis (1975b: 8).[6] Becker's focus in this initial paper was not the sexual division of labour within households *per se*, but his analysis had important implications for the way economists understood this division of labour. For example, as briefly noted by Becker, multi-person households allocate the time of different members, with the allocation of the time of any member being greatly influenced by the opportunities open to other members. If a member should become relatively more efficient at market activities, other members would reallocate their activities toward consumption in order to allow that person to spend more time at market activities (1965: 512).

The new home economics developed when the theory of the allocation of time was combined with human capital theory (for human capital theory, see Schultz 1960; Becker 1964, 1975). In the new home economics, non-market exchanges, such as the decision to marry, are theorized as the utility-maximizing choices of individuals, and decisions such as that to have children are theorized as the utility-maximizing choices of the family. It is in this second category that the sexual division of labour is placed. The family seeks to maximize the utility of its altruistic head by producing market and home-produced goods and services.[7] Because women usually have a comparative advantage in housework, they will specialize in housework while men specialize in market work. The early work on the economics of marriage, fertility and the family was further developed during the 1970s (Gronau 1973; Becker 1973, 1974a, 1974b, 1974c; Becker and Lewis 1973; Mincer and Polachek [1974] 1993, 1974; Schultz 1973, 1974a, 1974b; Becker, Landes and Michael 1977; Bahr 1980), Becker's *A Treatise on the Family* appeared in 1981 (Becker 1981a, 2nd edn 1991), and this has been followed by, for example, Fuchs (1988, 1989) and Cigno (1991).

Theoretical relationships addressing the question of the earnings of women relative to men were formally incorporated within the neoclassical framework with the development of new home economics and human capital theory. It is well known that the average earnings of women are less than those of men. In a classic 1974 paper Mincer and Polachek used the neoclassical framework to demonstrate that female workers devote less time to investing in human capital, such as education and on-the-job training, and hence earn lower wages ([1974] 1993). They argued that the decision to invest in human capital is costly in terms of forgone earnings, and therefore individuals take into account the period of time over which the benefits of such investments will be reaped. Women, it is assumed, expect to have discontinuous labour market participation, and will rationally choose lower levels of investment in education than men, who expect continuous labour market participation. Furthermore, it is rational for women to choose jobs with little on-the-job training (another form of human capital investment), and hence the model offers an explanation of occupational segregation by sex in terms of individual optimization. In short, women are less productive than men, due in large part to their chosen role in the family, and hence earn lower wages (see also Polachek 1975, 1979, 1981; for appraisals of this work, see Amsden 1980b: 16ff; Mincer 1993). If labour markets value the human capital of men and women equally, then women's lower earnings can be attributed in full to their individual optimizing decisions. This model leaves little role for discrimination in the determination of women's wages. However, empirical work consistently showed that the difference between male and female earnings could not be fully explained by human capital and other supply-side variables. It appeared, then, that sex discrimination was a salient reality in the operation of labour markets, and an issue demanding theoretical attention.[8]

Theoretical relationships addressing the question of the earnings of women relative to men were further incorporated within the neoclassical framework with the development of the neoclassical theory of discrimination. Although research on discrimination had begun in earnest during the 1960s, it was focused on racial discrimination. Becker's foundational model was based on the idea that either employers, employees or customers have a preference for associating with whites (men) rather than non-whites (women), and hence have a 'distaste' for non-whites (women) and a 'taste' for discrimination.[9] Such individuals require some form of compensation in order to overcome this distaste. Discriminating employers pay non-whites (women) lower wages than they pay whites (men). Discriminatory workers demand a wage premium if they must work with non-whites (women). Discriminatory customers require lower prices if they are to come into contact with non-white (women) workers, and hence such workers must be paid a lower wage. These wage and price differentials, however, cannot persist in a competitive system. Discriminating employers will be driven out of the market, since non-discriminating employers are able to employ the non-white (women) workers at the lower wage. Similarly, wage premiums which arise to compensate discriminatory workers will be eliminated, since firms will segment their workforces geographically instead of paying a wage premium. Finally, customer preferences will also lead to a segmented workforce, with both kinds of workers earning the same wage. Nevertheless, despite these predictions it became clear that discriminatory behaviour, and the associated wage differential, was not being eliminated by market forces even in the long run (Arrow 1972; Mueser 1987).

Neoclassical economists developed the literature in a number of ways in response to this empirical finding. One development was the argument that employers who begin with a white (male) workforce, which refuses to mix with blacks (women), will not find it profitable to replace them with outsiders because of the transactions costs associated with such change (Arrow 1972b). In Kenneth Arrow's words, 'in a situation in which costs arise in the process of change, history matters a good deal' (ibid.: 95). Another development was the theory of statistical discrimination, in which it was argued that, if employers believe that women are, on average, less productive than men (or have higher average turnover rates), and if it is costly to acquire information about relative productivities, then it is rational for them to discriminate against women (Phelps 1972; see also Arrow 1972b: 96; Thurow 1975). Still another argument was that variables which could explain the wage differential without resort to discrimination were missing or had been mismeasured. Becker, for example, claims that 'since child care and housework are more effort intensive than leisure and other household activities, married women spend less effort on each hour of market work than married men. Hence, married women have lower hourly earnings than married men with the same market human capital' ([1985] 1995: 153; see Taubman 1991 for a challenge to the 'unmeasured variable' theory, and Yachetta 1995: 133–4 for a critique of Taubman). Furthermore, some economists believe that since marriage provides women with access to male income, women do not bear the full brunt of sex discrimination. Black people, on the other hand, have no such access to white income, and hence they do bear the full brunt of racial discrimination. Racial discrimination is therefore a more significant problem, and should be the focus of attention, at least when tradeoffs are required (Lazear 1991: 12–15; see Yachetta 1995: 133 for an appraisal of this argument).

Although housework had been viewed since the 1960s as an activity with economic relevance, the next step of valuing that unpaid work and including it in the national accounts which economists consult to determine an economy's changing levels of production has been slow to be realized. In fact, one of the most frequently-cited claims of the exclusion of women as objects of research is the omission of unpaid work in the home, around three-quarters of which is undertaken by women (Bittman 1991), from the national accounts or the conventional measurement of the value of the productive work of an economy (see, for example, Benería 1981; Waring 1988; Goldschmidt-Clermont 1983, 1990; Ciancanelli and Berch 1987). Desley Deacon (1985), Katrina Alford (1986), Nancy Folbre and Marjorie Abel (1989) and Folbre (1991) have documented the historical processes which led to the exclusion of housework from the national accounts in Australia and the United States respectively. Others have discussed the economic effects of this omission. These effects are significant: the value of national output is seriously underestimated when the value of goods and services produced in the household is excluded; accurate comparisons between economies with differences in the relative size of the household and market sectors cannot be made; measures of income distribution are distorted when the value of household production varies between households; the tax system is distorted when taxes are levied on market income alone; homemakers are disadvantaged in divorce cases by the failure to value their work; reliable estimates of home production are needed for injury cases and life insurance; and the efficiency of an economy cannot be determined, since the full costs and benefits of production are unknown, and therefore rational decision-making about the allocation of resources is not possible (Ferber and Birnbaum 1980a: 387–8; Cohen 1982: 150–1; see also Ferber and Teiman 1981: 131–2; MacDonald 1984: 164–7; Goldschmidt-Clermont 1990: 281–5; Benería 1992).

There were three main arguments against the inclusion of housework in the national accounts. First, housework is not exchanged on the market. Even so, the national accounts include the imputed values of analytically identical non-market items, such as the value of housing services to home-owners and the food grown by farmers and eaten on the farm (Ciancanelli and Berch 1987: 248). The second argument against including housework in the national accounts is that it is too difficult to measure. These difficulties have clearly been overcome in the cases of other non-market items. In any case, there now exists a large literature which identifies and evaluates several methods by which housework might be valued (Kendrick 1979; Murphy 1978; Ferber and Birnbaum 1980a; Goldschmidt-Clermont 1982; Ferber and Green 1983; Ironmonger 1989a, 1989b; Australian Bureau of Statistics 1990; United Nations 1993), and there exist any number of estimates of the value of housework (Clark 1958; Gauger 1973; Hawrylyshun 1976; Eisner *et al.* 1982; Murphy 1982; Eisner 1988; Snooks 1994). The third argument against including housework in GDP is that, in the words of Paul Samuelson, 'So long as the number of women working at home does not change much in relative importance, the ups and downs of GNP will be about the same whether or not we count in this or similar items such as home-grown vegetables and other do-it-yourself activities' (1976: 199, quoted in Cohen 1982: 150).[10] But as Marjorie Cohen remarks, it cannot be known whether the relative importance of household work changes if its value is not being measured (1982: 150). Indeed, empirical examinations reveal that the value of home production relative to GNP has fallen during the twentieth century and that it varies significantly across the economic cycle (Jefferson 1995, 1997), and several Western governments, including Australia, Canada and the United States, are now formalizing supplementary accounts which include valuations of home production (United Nations 1993).

In this section I have considered a number of research areas within the discipline of economics from which women have traditionally been excluded as objects of study. However, I have also demonstrated that the definition of the scope of economics, which includes all behaviour undertaken within a framework of choice, no longer excludes women or their activities, and that women have been explicitly incorporated within the several areas of economic analysis which have previously been the subject of this criticism. Indeed, it is interesting to note that it was a number of well-known, white, male, Chicago-based economists who have been responsible for enlarging the domain of economic research to incorporate areas of traditional interest to women, including the family, married women's labour supply and labour market discrimination. A vast literature has also grown up exploring alternative methods of estimating women's work in the home. Thus the problem of the absolute exclusion of women and problems of interest to women from the content of economics is a problem of the past rather than the present. Yet, for all this, feminist economists and others have not been completely satisfied with the neoclassical account of women as economic actors, on the grounds that the neoclassical framework is founded on a number of faulty assumptions and misunderstood empirical relationships. The arguments of these feminist economists are the subject of the next section.

2.4. Feminist Empiricists and the Modelling of Women Within Neoclassical Economics

In this section I examine the work of those feminist economists who object to the way in which women have been incorporated into the existing neoclassical framework on the grounds that it has generated conclusions which are biased against women, and who seek to adjust and supplement the theoretical relationships of this framework in order to eliminate these distorted inferences. Like the scholars considered in the previous section, these feminist economists may be called feminist empiricists, since they wish to adjust the neoclassical models through the use of the scientific method. However, unlike the scholars considered in the previous section, these feminist economists believe that the 'bad science' arises not from the absence of women from the neoclassical framework as objects of research, but from the expansion of this framework to include women in a way which fails to capture the realities of women's lives. Rebecca Blank has characterized such feminist economists as believing that 'much of the problem of economics lies not with the model itself but with its interpretation and use' (1993: 134), and Blau and Ferber remark that such analyses produce a picture of 'a more complex reality' (1992: 35). They criticize, for example, the kind of research which takes male patterns of mobility and other labour market behaviour as the norm, the study of institutions associated with these patterns, the invoking of nature as the ultimate determinant of the sexual division of labour, and the failure to integrate societal discrimination into analyses of the earnings gap (see Blau and Ferber 1992: 1; Cohen 1982: 156; Humphries 1982). As Cohen remarks: 'Women simply have not had access to the market under the same conditions as men, yet this fact is not recognized by economic analysis . . . There is a real danger when neoclassical ideals are used by economists who appear to be sympathetic to women and who seem to want to truly understand the economic condition of women. Ultimately, they merely reinforce the androcentric view of female behaviour' (1982: 156–7).

The depiction of women within new home economics has perhaps raised the greatest concern amongst feminist economists. In the new home economics, the family is assumed to seek the maximization of its utility, where utility is derived from market and home-produced goods. The sexual division of labour is based upon comparative advantage in the production of these two types of goods. Under increasing returns to scale, complete specialization occurs: women have a comparative advantage in home-produced goods and allocate all their time to their production, while men have a comparative advantage in market goods, and it is efficient for them to specialize in the production of these goods. Under more general conditions, it is efficient for the family to allocate men to the market and women to both the market and home production. In either scenario, the sexual division of labour is the result of rational economic calculations. However, these calculations are premised upon the initial distribution of endowments, and hence on comparative advantage. In order to explain why it is women who have a comparative advantage in home-produced goods, new home economists either simply assume this distribution of endowments and provide no explicit explanation, or they cite 'natural' differences between men and women. Becker, for example, begins his analysis with two identical individuals, but to explain why it is that women tend to specialize in the home rather than the market, he argues that they have a 'heavy biological commitment to the production and feeding of children [and] are also biologically committed to the care of children in other, more subtle ways' (1991: 37).

Feminist economists have taken issue with this explanation of the sexual division of labour. Their arguments can be divided into three categories, and each will be discussed in turn. The first criticism is logical in nature. Isabel Sawhill ([1977] 1980), in a widely-cited paper, pointed out that the sexual division of labour was simply assumed within a self-perpetuating circle of explanations. Specifically, the sexual division of labour was taken as an exogenously-given explanatory variable in order to explain the wage differential between men and women, but the wage differential between men and women was taken as an exogenously-given explanatory variable when economists attempt to explain the sexual division of labour. In Sawhill's words, 'we have come full circle. We have seen that women earn less than men because of their special role within the family, but that their special role within the family – and indeed the desirability of marriage and children – are [*sic*] importantly related to the economic status of women' (ibid.: 133).

A second criticism is that neoclassical economists have ignored a number of costs associated with the traditional sexual division of labour. For example, if men have a comparative advantage in some household tasks, it is inefficient for the woman to carry out all of those tasks; if market and home work yield (diminishing marginal) utility in addition to income and home-produced goods, both parties can increase their utility by undertaking both activities rather than one; if leisure is subject to diminishing marginal utility, complete specialization is likely to yield an inefficient distribution of leisure; women over-invest in the human capital required for childrearing, which lowers their productive value in all activities once children no longer require care, or when the marriage dissolves due to death or divorce; men's over-investment in market work leaves them without necessary survival skills once the marriage breaks down; and specialization reduces welfare when tasks are more efficiently performed together, or if people prefer to undertake them with others (Ferber and Birnbaum 1977; Sawhill [1977] 1980; Bergmann 1981; Ferber and Teiman 1981: 128ff; Blau and Ferber 1992: ch. 3). Thus, in the words of Bergmann, 'Gary Becker's economium to the advantages of the division of labor among spouses addresses some of the issues, but its perspective seems to be that of a male member of a "traditional" family' (1981: 81).

Given these costs of the sexual division of labour, the question arises as to why this division of labour persists. This brings us to the third criticism of the new home economics, which is its biological reductionism, especially the recourse to sociobiology, a literature which Becker explicitly recommends to his readers. Feminist economists have pointed out that, under the assumptions of the new home economics, women's choice to work in the home or in lowly paid employment appears to be the result of voluntary and rational decision-making on the basis of certain biological imperatives (Cohen 1982: 153; see also Jennings 1993: 126). Thus the socialization of women into a particular role within the economy is ignored and the benefits which accrue to men from the sexual division of labour are hidden (see Bergmann 1989). Feminist economists have also pointed out that, while natural biological difference may explain the sexual division of labour in earlier societies, it is now an historical relic which can be accounted for by the socialization of women. In the words of Lloyd, 'Marriage as an institution has evolved from and been reinforced by the original economic advantages of a sexual division of labor . . . However, as child-care responsibilities have declined with declines in fertility and other forms of household production have become less time consuming with technological change, the economic underpinnings of marriage have been eroded. The gains from specialization depend on the level of technology and the size of the group involved in exchange, and in today's market an exclusive group of two is too small to reap such gains' (1975b: 7; see also Bergmann 1981; Blau and Ferber 1992: ch. 2). Feminist economists have also argued that two key assumptions, required to inflate what may be insignificant differences in the productivity of household partners into 'an irreversible widening of relative comparative advantages' (Gardiner 1993: 6), are simply not empirically substantiated. These two assumptions are that the skills and expertise developed within the household are not transferable to the market, which reflects, according to Jean Gardiner, the 'social devaluation of skills acquired through domestic or voluntary labour' (ibid.: 5), and that there are increasing returns to specific human capital (ibid.: 6). Finally, feminist economists have contended that biological difference is not required as the basis for the sexual division of labour, which then implies that such specializations are social as opposed to natural and can be changed. To support this argument, feminist economists have delineated a number of economic benefits from marriage which economists ignore by focusing on the allegedly natural basis for marriage and the sexual division of labour. Examples include economies of scale – a meal for two takes less than half the preparation time of two meals for one – and externalities – holidays with a partner are more fun than holidays alone (see Lloyd 1975b: 1–7; Ferber and Birnbaum 1977; Madden 1979: 166; England 1982: 359; Humphries 1982; MacDonald 1984: 164; Boserup 1987: 824–5; Ciancanelli and Berch 1987: 246; McCrate 1988).

There have been two theoretical developments within the neoclassical paradigm which allow conflict and distributional issues within the household to be examined. The first is the application of non-cooperative game theory to the family (Manser and Brown 1979, 1980; McElroy and Horney 1981; Lundberg and Pollak 1993). The household is modelled as consisting of two interdependent individuals maximizing the joint gain from the marriage, with the non-marital economic position operating as the threat point, or the situation to which each individual will retire if a solution is not reached. Thus household decisions become a function of relative economic bargaining power (Folbre 1986: 250). One key disadvantage of the specialization of labour within the family is the depreciation of women's labour market skills. In the event of divorce, this loss puts the woman in a far worse financial position than the man, who has participated continuously in the labour market (Ferber and Teiman 1981: 131). In the static analyses of Becker (1981a, 1991) and others, such a cost of specialization could not be incorporated. In the game-theoretic model of the family, however, this depreciation is reflected in the ever-diminishing value of the woman's threat point, and hence her ever-diminishing ability to extract concessions from her husband. Specialization is a less likely outcome in such models (Ott 1995: 85–8). England and Barbara Kilbourne (1990) add the insight that the skills which women develop within marriage are more 'relationship-specific' than those developed by men. This difference supplies a reason for the oft-cited but rarely explained assumption that, even though marriage is theorized as an exchange, market earnings are more valuable in terms of power than is housework. Economists have also begun to analyse the family as the site of non-cooperative bargaining in which outcomes may be theorized as a

maximizing behaviour on the part of women, who choose to enter occupations requiring low levels of human capital investments because of their expectation of discontinuous labour force participation. Effectively, then, in the view of the neoclassical economist, it is women who determine their employment fate (Cohen 1982: 155; see also Blau and Jusenius 1976).[12] Feminist economists, by contrast, claim that occupational segregation is a result of direct as well as indirect discrimination and is a major determinant of wage relativities. In the 1970s a number of feminist economists drew on the work of Henry Sanborn (1964), who showed that the more detailed the occupational breakdown used in empirical work on earnings determination, the more of the earnings differential between men and women could be explained. They developed explanations of occupational segregation which used some kind of 'gate-keeping' function on the part of consumers, employees or employers, often pointing to the role of men's interest in maintaining the sexual division of labour. Bergmann, for example, who formalized the 'crowding hypothesis' in relation to race (Bergmann 1971), and then in relation to sex ([1974] 1995), suggested that women are systematically excluded from certain occupations by men, generating an artificially-expanded supply of labour and low wages in those occupations into which they are 'crowded'.[13] Bergmann implicitly expanded the role of the sexual division of labour on the demand side of the labour market by arguing that 'attitudes concerning which occupations are "proper" for women and blacks are part of the social system and are learned, and most employers have learned pretty much the same thing' ([1974] 1995: 313). Furthermore, as Francine Blau Weisskoff points out, even if employers were indifferent to the sex of their employees, they may be 'coerced' into sex segregation by the costs imposed by 'the resistance to women coworkers and customers to women in certain "non-feminine" occupational categories' (1972: 164; see also Strober 1972; Zellner 1972, 1975; Malkiel and Malkiel 1973; Sawhill 1973; Madden 1975; Stevenson 1975). In short, then, a small amount of direct discrimination can create a large cumulative effect, and it is essential to examine both direct and indirect discrimination in explanations of earnings determinations (Ferber and Lowry [1976] 1995: 438; Blau 1984, 1987: 492; Blau and Ferber 1992: 140).

Feminist economists have also criticized neoclassical economists for undertaking empirical studies which underestimate the degree to which discrimination and occupational segregation determine gender wage relativities. Bergmann (1989), for example, has taken issue with those empirical studies in which the importance of the sex discrimination variable is marginalized through the laboured delineation of less threatening independent variables, such as length of male job tenure relative to female job tenure. In the case of some economists' search for explanatory variables which will reduce measured sex discrimination to zero, she points out that no economist has yet suggested that there are missing data on men: 'Data demonstrating men's greater tendency to alcohol abuse, drug abuse, smoking, bad driving, resort to violence, criminal records, bankruptcies, back problems, history of heart attacks, are entirely missing from [empirical] studies.' Including such data, she notes, would increase measured sex discrimination (ibid.: 45). She cites empirical evidence that men and women have the same quit rates when they earn the same salary to counter economists' claim that men's longer average tenure explains their higher wages. She also argues that on-the-job training, usually cited as a worker's choice variable, is actually decided by the employer rather than the employee. She cites empirical work which shows the extent to which firms segregate workers by job title and pay workers accordingly. Thus jobs are 'earmarked' for a particular sex, with the segregation and associated differential earnings perpetuating such earmarking (ibid.: 49). Indeed, when firms recruit both men and women to the same job title, they usually work separately, as in the case of 'apartment house manager'. Bergmann remarks of this example: 'the firm's 149 different managers worked in 149 different buildings, a classic case of the exception that proves the rule' (ibid.: 46).

A further point is that whether or not women in general choose low-paying employment, there is no explanation of the fact that when women are in exactly the same fine occupational grouping as men, doing the same tasks and adjusted for experience, they are paid less than men. In response to Becker's assertion that women have less energy than men, Bergmann points out that slicing and cutting machine operators of whatever sex must operate the machine with care or face serious consequences, and yet women earn only 63 per cent of the wages of men in this particular occupation. Recent empirical work supports Bergmann's claim. Sheila Rimmer (1991) draws upon Australian data to argue that the desegregation of occupational employment would be likely to result in reductions in women's earnings. She finds that most of the differences in earnings between the sexes is due to differences within the same occupation, pointing to the need, not for affirmative action or desegregation, but for policies which eliminate discriminatory pay practices (ibid.: 215). Bergmann argues too that the presence of children does not explain women's lower earnings: 'If the wages of all women with children were raised to the level of wages earned by women with no children, 94 percent of the male–female gap would remain' (ibid.: 48). Other feminists have noted the inadequacies, at an empirical level, of the models used to explain earnings differentials. Blau and Jusenius note that human capital explanations of occupational segregation can only explain why women are in low-skill occupations, and cannot explain why women tend to be concentrated in a small number of occupations within each skill category (1976: 187). Janice Madden (1979) argued in a commentary on Solomon Polachek (1979) that it is impossible to determine which of occupational outcomes and labour force attachment is cause and which is effect, and that methods for disentangling the relationship need to be developed.

Feminist empiricists have also undertaken their own empirical work to refute mainstream theories about women and the labour market. Paula England (1982, 1984), for example, responded to Polachek (1979) by dismissing human capital theory as a complete explanation of occupational segregation. Polachek (1979) argued that women who plan intermittent employment prefer occupations with lower penalties for such behaviour. England's empirical analysis shows that, on the contrary, women in predominantly female occupations are no more penalized by lower earnings for intermittent labour market participation than are women in two-sex occupations, and that a woman's time out of the labour force is not systematically related to her occupation (1982: 360). She concludes, in a reiteration of the complaints cited above, that 'Bearing in mind that supply- and demand-side explanations are not mutually exclusive, social scientists need to investigate the complementary relationships between sex role socialization and market discrimination' (ibid.: 369). Feminist economists, then, have not been content with the incorporation of women into neoclassical analyses.

This section has shown that there is a tradition of feminist empiricism in which theorists seek to overcome the inadequate incorporation of women within the subject-matter of neoclassical economics. Since economists already treat women extensively, in large part 'adding women' has meant the development of new implications arising from the existing theoretical framework, and empirical observations showing that the theoretical models do not adequately account for reality. Although these feminist empiricists did not question the core assumptions of neoclassical economics, in seeking alternative explanations in areas given scant attention by their male colleagues, they are, as Barbara Reagan and Martha Blaxall put it, challenging the implicit or explicit assertions of female deficiency in relation to labour markets (1976: 2). Thus feminist empiricists attack the 'bad science' which has produced theoretical implications which are disadvantageous to women. However, not all feminist economists have been content with this solution. Many challenge the core assumptions of neoclassical economics from a specifically feminist perspective. This is the subject of the next chapter.

2.5. Conclusion

In this chapter I traced the way in which feminist economists have attempted to incorporate women within the existing neoclassical framework. This was done in three steps. First, I delineated the various measures of male dominance of the discipline and the arguments put forward as to how this has occurred and is maintained. Second, I outlined the ways in which women as objects of research have been incorporated into the neoclassical framework. Third, I identified a number of criticisms of, and theoretical and empirical developments from, this early integration of women into the framework of neoclassical economics. In each case, the 'add women and stir' strategy is evident. In other words, the feminist economists discussed in this chapter argue that the problem with neoclassical economics is either the physical absence of women from its institutions – its economics departments, classrooms and textbooks – or the absence of women within its theoretical framework. To overcome these deficiencies, both the institutions and the theoretical framework must be supplemented with the addition of women. The framework of neoclassical economics itself remains unchallenged. In the case of the 'Chicago school of feminist economics', it is actively developed to incorporate women. In the case of the feminist critics of the Chicago school, the framework is adjusted but not rejected or even questioned as to its adequacy. Much of this work was undertaken in the 1970s and 1980s, but it continues to be an important, but certainly not the only, feminist approach to economics.

In addition to incorporating women within existing institutional and theoretical frameworks, the feminist economists considered in this chapter follow an empiricist methodology. They believe that the absence of women from the existing theoretical frameworks, or the way in which women were modelled within the existing theoretical frameworks, was at variance with reality and therefore the product of 'bad science'. They are therefore feminist empiricists (Harding 1986: 24). This position has been vehemently advocated by Solomon Polachek, who believes that the empiricist methodology is the common theme binding the different strands of feminist economics together. Polachek is one of the few economists to have directly addressed the criticisms of feminist economics, and is a member of the 'Chicago school of feminist economists' discussed in section 2.3 above. He argues that the 'main point of feminist economics is that economics infrequently deals with women's issues, and when it does, it does so incorrectly because inherent "male" biases are deeply ingrained in economic practitioners, at this time mostly men' (1995: 61). He suggests that feminist economics is different from other criticisms of economics in that 'it takes a woman's perspective and concentrates predominantly on issues dealing with gender' (ibid.: 64). Such work, Polachek points out, is consistent with the scientific method: the 'more moderate' of the critics of orthodox theory seek 'to modify some standard economics assumptions so that economics can be more attuned to women, and hence become more realistic, accurate and bias free' (ibid.: 62–3). Polachek therefore sees the feminist economics project as a continuation of the scientific enterprise, in which science progresses by finding fault with the status quo and finding new problems to explain (ibid.; see also Blank 1993; Solow 1993; Vaughn 1994).

The feminist empiricist strategy of adding women to the existing framework, with some minor modifications, seems to pose no threat to neoclassical economists, since it appears not to challenge the neoclassical framework in any significant way. The fundamental assumptions, concepts and relationships of neoclassical economics remain largely intact. As Polachek claims, his own work and that of any number of mainstream economists such as Jacob Mincer and Gary Becker, all of whom examine 'gender issues', *is* feminist economics under this definition (ibid.: 62–4). In the chapter I have focused on the women economists who criticized aspects of ways in which women have been incorporated into neoclassical economics. However, there were and are numerous men also working to improve the explanatory power of neoclassical economics when women are examined. Thus the question arises as to the exact contribution of the women economists discussed. Specifically, have they added anything that can be called unique to a feminist approach? The simple answer is that they have not – they do not even have to maintain that they are feminists in order to undertake this work. This kind of feminism is what Carole Pateman has named 'domesticated feminism': it 'seems neither to be theoretically innovative nor to be raising questions that have not already been asked, albeit in different contexts' (1986: 5).

However, as Sandra Harding (1986, 1989) has argued, the work of feminist empiricists can undermine their own implicit or explicit claims to be simply correcting 'bad science', and hence be more challenging to the actual framework of neoclassical economics than they initially seem. This is because, in seeking to ensure the more rigorous application of the scientific method, feminist empiricists bring to light the importance of the context of discovery, or the social environment of the researcher. This occurs in several ways. First, feminist empiricists point to the importance of women scientists in bringing about the required theoretical changes. Lloyd, for example, argued that the Women's Liberation Movement 'has manifested itself within the economics profession in terms of a sudden increase in interest, particularly among young female economists, in research pertaining to all aspects of women's economic role [and] spurred an interest in undergraduate and graduate courses focusing on women's often-neglected role in all fields within the humanities and the social sciences' (1975c: ix). Second, feminist empiricists have shown the importance of the origins of scientific hypotheses by pointing to the significance of the context of discovery – the selection of phenomena to be investigated, and the definition of what is problematic about these phenomena – in creating bias in scientific results. Bergmann (1981), for example, made clear the importance of men's role as husbands in traditional families in producing theories which were blind to important aspects of women's experience. Lastly, feminist empiricists have shown the failure of the scientific method to detect and eliminate biases. In this sense, these feminist economists are implicitly positing a feminist, or at least a female, standpoint. Thus, in introducing or expanding the role of women as objects of research within the neoclassical framework, feminist empiricists fall into Gatens's (1986) 'add women and stir' category of the relationship between women and theory. However, with their implicit critique of, in particular, male economists, they are also laying the foundations for others who seek to adopt a specifically feminist position in relation to neoclassical economics, and who explicitly challenge both the core assumptions of the framework and its methodology.

However, this is not to argue that the feminist empiricist project of incorporating women into the disciplinary knowledge need necessarily end. Indeed, this project continues to be an important one, since such work more easily finds a legitimate place within the discipline's self-definition. In economics, in particular, such work feeds into new theoretical developments and into policy-making with the potential, within the context of the dominant neoclassical framework, to improve women's economic condition. However, there are limitations to the changes which such 'feminist empiricism' can generate, precisely because it works within and reproduces the established disciplinary framework. It is to those feminist economists who challenge that disciplinary framework that I turn in the following chapter.

Notes

1. See also Roberts (1981) for feminist approaches to literature, Shapiro (1981) for

anthropology, Wajcman (1981) for sociology, Whyld (1983) for education, Pateman (1986) for political theory, Longino and Hammonds (1990) for science, Naffine (1990: ch. 1) for law, Marecek (1995) for psychology and Spender (1981) for an anthology of feminist appraisals of their disciplines.

2. Aldrich (1978), for example, delineates the absence of women from science, and Mandelbaum (1978) undertakes the same task for medicine.

3. One of the major aims of this Committee has been to document and to increase the number of women within the profession of academic economist (see Bell 1973a, 1974b; Chapman 1975; Reagan 1975a, 1976, 1977, 1978; Friedlaender 1979, 1980; Bailey 1981, 1982, 1983; Bergmann 1984b, 1985; Sawhill 1986, 1987; Gordon 1988, 1989, 1990, 1991; Hoffman 1992, 1993; Blank 1994, 1995, 1996).

4. The context of discovery refers to the process of identifying and defining problems, the collection of data used in hypothesis construction, and the hypotheses themselves. The context of justification, on the other hand, refers to the process of justifying the hypothesis constructed in the discovery process through the repeated testing of that hypothesis against empirical evidence. The context of discovery has been considered irrelevant since the justificatory procedures of the scientific method will eliminate all 'impure' knowledge. However, the context of discovery becomes relevant when it gives rise to 'factually' incorrect or partial hypotheses which are not eliminated when the hypotheses are tested against the facts. Furthermore, the context of discovery may also limit the extent to which hypotheses of relevance to women are constructed. Therefore, feminist empiricists are seeking to correct 'bad science' as it arises in both the context of discovery and justification (see Harding 1986: ch. 4, 1989).

5. I would like to thank Gregory Moore for bringing these passages to my attention.

6. Earlier works on the economics of the household include Gilman ([1898] 1966) and Reid (1934), but these works lacked the prestige accorded by the discipline to the rigorous underpinnings of analyses such as Becker (1965).

7. Samuelson (1956) had earlier delineated a consensus model of the family, where family members maximized a 'social welfare function' which combined the utility functions of the family members subject to a combined budget constraint. The family therefore acted as a single individual in this model. Becker's model of the family was a development of Samuelson's model in that it explained the basis of the consensus between family members without requiring the combination of their utility functions.

8. There is an enormous empirical literature in which earnings discrimination against women and the sex segregation of occupations in Western nations is examined. For an introduction to this literature, see Kahne and Kohen (1975), Gunderson (1989) and Blau and Ferber (1992).

9. Neither the first nor the second edition of Becker's *The Economics of Discrimination* (1957, 1971) discuss sex discrimination in detail, although Becker (1957: 3) maintained that his analysis of race discrimination could equally well be applied to sex discrimination. Not all economists agree with Becker. The race discrimination model assumes the existence of two separate 'nations', one 'white' and one 'black', which trade with each other. A taste for discrimination implies the desire to remain physically distant from the black nation. Lester Thurow argues that physical-distance theories make no sense in the case of sex discrimination, since men want to live with women rather than achieve physical distance from them. It follows that the more income women earn, the higher are men's own consumption possibilities (1975: 162–3). However, as Barbara Bergmann has pointed out, there are other plausible, 'social distance', reasons for men's taste for sex discrimination. For example, men may not be keen to have their wives and mothers in jobs as good as their own. In addition, although it may not be rational for a man to discriminate against his own wife or girlfriend, he may discriminate against strangers' wives and girlfriends (1986: 96).

10. In an earlier edition of Samuelson's textbook, he remarked that 'A wife's housework services are not included simply because it is hard to find a market-price yardstick or any other to evaluate them', although, 'In all logic, [the value of the housekeeping services of a wife] should be included, and national income should be increased by one-fifth or more' (1955: 187). Estimates of the value of housework relative to national product are invariably greater than one-fifth, with the estimate for the United States in 1946 as high as 75 per cent (Ironmonger 1989b: 7).

11. Societal or pre-labour market discrimination, which 'denotes the multitude of social influences that cause women to make decisions that adversely influence their status in the labor market' (Blau and Ferber 1992: 140), should be distinguished from direct or labour-market discrimination. Direct discrimination occurs when employers, workers or customers treat two equally-qualified individuals differently (this was discussed in section 2.3 above). Note that indirect discrimination, which refers to the impact on women's human capital and occupational choices of the existence of labour-market discrimination against women, is a subset of societal discrimination.

12. That economists (especially women economists) were not content with the existing literature on occupational segregation, in terms of its development as well as its content, is shown by the organization, in 1975, of a conference entitled 'Women and the Workplace: The Implications of Occupational Segregation' by the American Economic Association Committee on the Status of Women in the Economics Profession. Papers from this conference were published as a special issue of the feminist journal *Signs* (Blaxall and Reagan 1976).

13. The 'crowding hypothesis' has been attributed to Francis Edgeworth, although Pujol suggests that it had been developed in the earlier writings of John Stuart Mill, Barbara Bodichon and Millicent Garrett Fawcett (see Pujol 1992: 94).

3. Women and Knowledge II: Theorizing Neoclassical Economics

3.1. Introduction

In Chapter 2 it was noted that feminist scholars in a range of disciplines have moved from a critique of their disciplines on the basis of their content (the 'add women and stir' strategy) to a critique of the disciplinary frameworks from a specifically feminist perspective. In this chapter I examine the work of feminist economists who have used the second of these two approaches to the relationship between women and knowledge and have therefore explicitly undertaken feminist critiques of neoclassical economics by identifying androcentric bias within its core assumptions and/or methodological procedures. These feminist economists hold beliefs analogous to those feminist philosophers identified by Gatens who claim that the problem is not 'what is said or what is not said about women, but rather, about what can and cannot be said about women within the terms of particular philosophical theories' (1986: 20). In other words, they believe that the central feminist problem in the field of economics is not that women are omitted from the disciplinary knowledge, but that the experience of women is distorted by that knowledge. The central feminist goal therefore shifts from merely expanding the content of the disciplinary knowledge in order to include women to radically altering (or even displacing) this disciplinary knowledge in order to eliminate its masculinist distortions. They believe that the discipline's self-description of its basic category, the individual, and the epistemological and methodological procedures used to produce theory based on this individual, cannot capture the realities of women's lives, while an approach guided by a specifically feminist perspective will do far better in this respect. Indeed, with few exceptions (see section 3.5 below), such scholars do not doubt that there are procedural criteria which feminists may draw upon to attain greater truth or realism, and, in this sense, they are similar to the scholars discussed in Chapter 2.

There are four main sections to the chapter. In section 3.2 I discuss the

criticisms of feminist economists who argue that a simple expansion of the
content of neoclassical economics, without an examination of its categories
of analysis, is inadequate because those categories, and in particular, the
category of rational economic man, are based upon the assumption of the
equivalence of man and humanity. Feminist economists who suggest
generalizations or variations in the core assumptions fall into two groups:
those who continue to maintain an allegiance to the neoclassical framework
and continue to view themselves as simply developing or expanding
neoclassical economics, and those who advocate alternative theoretical
frameworks such as institutionalist or Marxist economics. In section 3.3 I
discuss the work of feminist economists who challenge the 'add women and
stir' strategy by drawing on feminist research concerned with scientific
method and epistemology. I especially focus on the work which draws on
feminist standpoint theory, since this theory has been particularly influential
amongst feminist economists, and because its leading exponent, Sandra
Harding, has herself made a contribution to feminist economics (see Harding
1993b, 1995). In section 3.4 I examine the 'gender-compass' analysis
developed by Julie Nelson, one of the most published feminist economists,
and one who has developed the feminism-and-science literature in relation to
economics in a unique way. In section 3.5 I delineate the contributions made
by those feminist economists who draw on the work of Deirdre McCloskey
and others to show that masculinity operates as an implicit rhetorical tool,
and that this accounts for the success of the traditional assumptions and
methodology of neoclassical economics. Section 3.6 concludes the chapter.
In this chapter, then, I review work which challenges orthodox economics on
the basis of its claim that it is able to describe a given reality and to generate
truth using traditional scientific practice.

3.2. The Feminist Critique of Core Assumptions of Neoclassical
Economics

The feminist economists considered in this section argue that the core
neoclassical assumptions are androcentric and give rise to doctrines which
distort the realities of women's (and indeed men's) lives. Although many of
these scholars may also doubt the gender neutrality of the empiricist criteria
by which these doctrines have officially been judged, the questioning of such
traditional epistemological and methodological principles is not the focus of
their research. Feminist economists who fall within this category, then, focus
their critique on the theoretical distortions arising from the neoclassical
assumptions and contend that such assumptions have been readily and

erroneously accepted by economists because they justify the existing social production of patriarchal gender relations. More specifically, it is argued that the neoclassical assumptions devalue the contributions typically made by, and the traits traditionally deemed appropriate for, women, and valorize the contributions usually made by, and the traits normally associated with, men. This depiction of the world renders invisible both the important role played by women in economic activity (especially in the private sphere) and the many advantages and sites of dominance bestowed on men. The feminist economists who take this approach therefore endeavour to identify and revalue female characteristics and contributions and to alter the neoclassical assumptions in order to integrate such characteristics and contributions. These adjustments may be either minor and easily incorporated within the neoclassical framework, or fundamental and requiring the replacement of neoclassical economics with an alternative framework, such as feminist institutionalism or feminist Marxism/socialism. In other words, feminist criticisms of neoclassical economics have entailed attacks on both the core and peripheral assumptions of the neoclassical paradigm (this is in conflict with what is implied in Polachek 1995; see section 2.5 above). It must also be emphasized that the aim of such feminist economists is not somehow to naturalize as women's work the vocations traditionally assigned to women, but to revalue them within those theoretical frameworks concerned with these issues so as to encourage both men and women to take up such roles in equal proportions (see especially England 1993: 39).

The majority of these feminist criticisms are directed towards those neoclassical assumptions which are directly or indirectly related to the individual. As mentioned in section 2.3 above, neoclassical economics is currently defined within the discipline as the analysis of the choice of scarce means to achieve given ends. The basic unit of analysis, the chooser, is the individual, and is known as 'rational economic man' or *Homo economicus*. Rational economic man can be described by a utility function and a set of constraints. The utility function specifies the pleasure or utility an individual derives from the consumption of combinations of all possible goods and services, and hence represents that individual's preferences. This function is maximized subject to the constraints of income, prices and time. Goods and services are scarce relative to the unlimited wants of the individual, and the assumption of utility maximization ensures that the individual is efficient in the use of means to satisfy those wants. This analysis also applies to firms, which behave in accordance with the profit-maximizing motive of the firm's owner/s. Once these axioms are in place the majority of the neoclassical doctrines may be derived by analysing the way in which individuals (whether consumers or firm managers) alter their choices (demands and supplies) in response to changes in the constraints they face. This depiction of rational economic man has long been criticized by non-feminist economists (for a comprehensive overview of these criticisms, see Hollis and Nell 1975; Hargreaves-Heap and Hollis 1987), but has only recently been the subject of a specifically feminist critique (the relationship between these non-feminist and feminist critics is discussed in section 3.6 below).

The assumptions underpinning this representation of the neoclassical economic agent have been deemed androcentric by some feminist economists on the grounds that such an agent is a selfish, radically separate individual divested of those traits and uninvolved in those activities traditionally associated with women. These traits and activities are consequently devalued and rendered very nearly invisible within the neoclassical framework, while roles and traits traditionally associated with men are extolled (England [1989] 1995: 43). Interestingly, this interpretation of rational economic man to some extent mirrors the feminist interpretation of the individual as understood within social contract theory and liberalism (see Pateman 1988; Phillips 1994: 200) and within sociology (see Hartsock 1983: ch. 2; England [1989] 1995). The agent is depicted as an autonomous male who enters contracts to produce a civilized society, even though he is in fact dependent upon the caring but invisible activities of women, who are confined to the devalued and uninteresting sphere of natural functions. Moreover, when this sphere of natural functions is theorized within economics, as in Becker's analysis of the form and functioning of families, the imposition of the model of what Paula England (1993) has called the 'separative' self imposes a structure to the theory which inevitably excludes important aspects of the reality it is attempting to grasp. The more specific feminist criticisms of the postulates which underlie the construction of rational economic man, as well as the loss associated with its imposition on areas from which it had traditionally been excluded, will now be discussed in turn.

Feminist economists have argued that the shift from a cardinal to an ordinal conception of utility had negative implications for women. In the early history of neoclassical economics, it was thought that utility could be objectively measured by a universal unit called the 'util'. If this cardinal ordering were possible, interpersonal utility comparisons could be made. However, economists had realized by the turn of the century that no such common measure existed, and therefore the utility function had to be derived on the basis of the ordering of preferences rather than a cardinal measure (see Black 1987). Utility comparisons between individuals are therefore impossible, even in principle, and economists cannot determine which of the two parties to an exchange gain more from that exchange. Non-feminist critics of the neoclassical school have long objected to this exclusion of interpersonal utility comparisons.[1] England, by contrast, provides a specifically feminist perspective on this question, contending that the impossibility of interpersonal utility comparisons is a gender-biased assumption which helps construct the concept of the separative self. The separative self model explains economists' reluctance to deal with issues of endowment, wealth or income distribution, and hence removes a theoretical basis for arguing that existing arrangements benefit the rich more than the poor, and, more generally, men more than women (1993: 43). England argues that a more reasonable assumption is that individuals can make interpersonal utility comparisons by assuming 'the sort of emotional connection that facilitates empathy [which would mean] being able to imagine how someone else feels in a given situation'. The question of a standard measure would then become a practical measurement problem analogous to calculating shadow prices, and issues of inequality between individuals and between groups (such as men and women) could then be discussed (ibid.: 42). A further criticism of the exclusion of interpersonal utility comparisons is that it leads directly to the exclusion of the distinction between needs and wants. Julie Nelson points out that, if human ethical responsibility is not to be abdicated, one should be able to argue that a Guatemalan orphan needs her daily bowl of soup more than the overfed North American needs a second piece of cake (1993c: 33; see also Jennings 1993). Nelson's argument appears to be that the collapsing of the distinction between needs and wants is indicative of the masculine denial of his bodily existence, and it therefore renders invisible large parts of human experience which have traditionally been associated with femininity, namely 'the concrete, particular, embodied, passionate, "feminine" reality of material life' (Nelson 1993c: 25). The solution is therefore to reject the distinction between femininity and masculinity constructed within the separative self model, and which underpins the distinction between needs and wants, in order to construct a more human discipline focused upon the issue of provisioning rather than choice (ibid.: 33).

Feminist economists have also challenged the wisdom of assuming that rational economic man's preferences are exogenous and stable. Economists typically take preferences, which constitute the ends to be satisfied, as given, leaving the question of their formation to sociobiologists and psychologists (see, for example, Becker 1976b: 13–14). Indeed, the assumption of fixed and exogenously-determined preferences is vital to the neoclassical framework, since, if preferences are variable, welfare conclusions are made problematic and empirical results cannot uniquely identify the causes of economic behaviour (ibid.: 12–3). As Becker censoriously argues, examples 'abound in the economic literature of changes in preferences conveniently introduced ad hoc to explain puzzling behavior'. Instead, Becker maintains that economists must identify variations in the means by which the given ends are satisfied, such as changes in real income or the relative cost of different choices (ibid.: 12). Members of the Institutionalist and Marxist schools have long criticized this neoclassical tactical device, arguing that environmentally-induced changes in preferences have a major bearing on economic outcomes and hence must be the subject of study (see, for example, Bowles and Gintis 1993). Feminist economists similarly argue that even if preferences are fixed, economists should be interested in the formation of gendered preferences. Randy Albelda, for example, points out that to explain gender inequality in economic status in terms of differences in preferences of men and women is to beg the question in which feminists are interested: 'Why are women's tastes and preferences different from men's?' (1995: 270; see also Matthaei 1996: 29). Elaine McCrate has drawn on Amartya Sen's ([1977] 1990) notion of metapreferences to construct a framework in which this question may be analysed. She argues that individuals have preferences over their own identities as well as goods and services, but that these preferences are both produced and constrained by institutions of socialization in a male-dominated society. Although the resulting identities and associated tastes are endogenous, they do not respond simply to changes in relative prices, since 'men and women rationally make large and long-term investments in sex-typed preferences or identities, developing very different capacities for tastes, and severely restricting the possibility that they may elect at some future point to invest in significantly different tastes' (McCrate 1988: 237). These costly long-term investments in gendered identity explain, among other things, the failure of men to contribute time to housework, despite women's rising labour market participation (ibid.). England also argues that the assumption of exogenous tastes leaves out too much of human experience (1993: 44). She contends that changing preferences are a major consequence of the operation of labour, marriage and other markets, since variations in tastes are likely to result from long-term associations between particular individuals within these markets. She further argues that, by ignoring the endogeneity of preferences, the economist 'obscures some of the processes through which gender inequality is perpetuated'. If, for example, women develop preferences for occupations in which women already dominate in response to labour market discrimination, then markets create gender-related preferences which perpetuate women's lower earnings (ibid.). Indirect discrimination therefore entails a change in preferences in addition to women simply responding to the higher costs of entering male-dominated occupations, and in this sense it can be interpreted as a challenge to one of the core assumptions of the neoclassical framework rather than a mere extension of that framework.

Another matter of concern to feminist economists is the neoclassical assumption that rational economic man's utility function is independent of all other utility functions in the public sphere. Specifically, economists have traditionally assumed that individuals within the public arena have preferences which are independent of others, and which relate wholly to their own consumption of goods and services.[2] Exceptions include the economics of voting behaviour, blood donation, and other charitable activities (see, for example, Stewart 1992). The assumption of independence has been the subject of criticism by non-feminists (see, for example, Sen [1977] 1990; Frank 1990), but feminist economists are unique in pointing to the implications of independence for gender. Stephanie Seguino, Thomas Stevens and Mark Lutz (1996), for example, confirm earlier experimental evidence that economics students are more self-interested than others (see Marwell and Ames 1981; Frank, Gilovich and Regan 1993), and show in addition that gender is an important, though not conclusive, determinant of such self-interest. England, on the other hand, argues that the assumption of independent utility functions conceals men's altruism as well as that of women. 'Assuming selfishness in markets is not merely a "male" model of self that may fit women less well; it also fails to account for men's altruism in market behavior, altruism that may work to the disadvantage of women . . . For example, when male employees collude in order to try to keep women out of "their" jobs, they are exhibiting within-sex altruism' (1993: 46). Discrimination arising from such selective altruism will not be eradicated by competitive market forces (ibid.: 47).[3]

The assumed dominance of altruism in the family has also been questioned by feminist economists. Utility functions are assumed to be interdependent in the home because of the existence of a benevolent dictator (the market worker) who ensures that everyone acts in the best interest of the family (Becker 1981a, 1981b, 1991). Thus the family maximizes the altruist's utility function subject to the family budget constraint. Each family member, whether or not they are self-interested, seeks to maximize the altruist's utility in order to maximize their own utility, and hence also behaves as an altruist towards all other family members. Becker describes the case of a self-interested wife in the following way: 'Since a selfish beneficiary wants to maximize family income [in order to maximize her own utility], she is led by the "invisible hand" of self-interest to act as if she is altruistic towards her benefactor. Put still differently, the scarce resource "love" is used economically because sufficient caring by an altruist induces even a selfish beneficiary to act as if she cares about her benefactor as much as she cares about herself' (1981b: 5). Although the altruistic benefactor is much more likely to be male than female within Becker's analysis, since comparative advantage dictates that men undertake market rather than home-related work, feminist economists criticize the general association of altruism with the family in the new home economics. Nancy Folbre and Heidi Hartmann (1988), for example, discuss the rhetorical force of the assumption that there is 'Altruism in the Family and Selfishness in the Market Place' (Becker 1981b), arguing that the history of these associations has generated unstated, and self-serving, assumptions that women are irrational and non-economic, choosing to support men's market activities through their unselfish adoption of the role of housewife. They argue that the dichotomy of self-interest in the market and altruism in the home is both unrealistic and hides the power which men derive from their access to market earnings (see also England 1993; McCrate 1987). The institutionalists Ann Jennings and William Waller concur with these arguments. They contend that, although the new home economics relocates the family within the realm of the economic, it maintains the associations between women and the family, and men and the economy, to the detriment of women who are seen first as mothers and second as workers (1990: 627–9). This allows economists to avoid considering the means by which the lives of women and men are culturally ordered (ibid.: 629–30; see also Waller and Jennings 1990; Waller 1994).[4] Cohen, on the other hand, argues that there is a fundamental difference between the family and the market place, pointing out that the family has not been made to conform to the historically specific motives which drive market behaviour. She therefore rejects the assumption that emotional needs can be compared with material needs and that the basis of decision-making in the family – human motivation – is the same as that within the marketplace (1982: 151–3).

   Still another insight offered by feminist economists is that the joint utility function, which is meant to represent the preferences of the family members, cannot be used to address the question of unequal bargaining power within households consisting of individuals with unique preferences. In the single utility function formulation of family preferences, the family is a "black box" in which the distribution of income within the household is invisible. The family members are thereby assumed to be indifferent between a range of utility-maximizing distributions of production and consumption activities within the family; there is assumed to be a 'harmony of interest among all family members in maximizing the well-being of the "head"' (McCrate 1987: 75; see also Sawhill [1977] 1980; Manser and Brown 1979, 1980; McElroy and Horney; Edwards 1985a; Folbre 1986; Folbre and Hartmann 1988; England 1993; Phipps and Burton 1995; Ott 1995). The 'black box' approach, then, hides not only the benefits of the sexual division of labour which accrue to men, but also the extent of disharmony within households, in the form of inequality and conflict, which has been documented by Folbre (1986). She notes that inequality within households can be reconciled to the assumption of a joint utility function by introducing a taste for altruism or voluntary sacrifice on the part of the wife (ibid.: 248–9). Phipps and Burton (1995) and Findlay and Wright (1996) show that different assumptions regarding the allocation within the household of its financial resources generate quite different policy implications, and Haddad and Kanbur (1990) show that this is particularly important in developing countries (see also Browning, Bourguignon, Chiappori and Lechene 1994; Lundberg and Pollak 1996). To some extent, these problems have been overcome by the use of game-theoretic models of the family (see section 2.4 above). However, the individual bargainer in these models is simply rational economic man in a dynamic setting, and hence many of the criticisms delineated above remain relevant (see Sen 1990; Mehta 1993; Seiz 1995b). Moreover, as Seiz points out, bargaining models are yet to produce additional insights over and above those of feminist economists and other dissident economists, and may even be viewed as simply coopting such ideas and expressing them in the language which orthodox economists find acceptable (1995b: 616), with the implication that the potential of such ideas to destabilize the orthodox framework is thereby reduced or even eliminated.

The way in which the separative self model forces women's domestic work into masculinist categories has also been the subject of analysis by feminist economists. A market-based (and hence masculine) definition of work emerges from research which values housework, and this limits the extent to which the traditional female activities of the private sphere, such as caring, can be included (see section 2.4). The recognition that some forms of women's activity are marginalized when forced into 'masculinist' categories first emerged during the 'domestic labour' debate. Some participants in this debate argued that domestic labour produces no commodity or surplus value, and hence is unproductive, while others argued that domestic labour is necessary for the reproduction of the worker and hence produces the commodity labour power and is productive as defined within Marxist categories (Lovell 1990b: 71–3).[5] The debate was generally considered to have reached an impasse once it was recognized that domestic labour fits within neither the 'productive' nor the 'unproductive' categories of Marxian political economy, and therefore lies outside the terms of Marxian economics (ibid.: 72; see also Gardiner 1993). Some feminist economists have argued that the 'household work' approach to understanding domestic work is just as problematic as the Marxist approach. Chris Beasley (1994, 1996) and Susan Himmelweit (1995), for example, both argue that domestic labour can only be conceived of in terms of exchange or the market in household work studies, and hence such studies exclude from the categories of analysis those aspects of domestic labour which are neither work nor non-work. Beasley maintains that the application of the market model to the private labour of women fails to capture 'the specificity of sex relations and sexual hierarchy, let alone the specificity of women's private labour', and sustains a male norm which directs all political change towards the ideal that 'women should be treated like men and become like them' (1994: 45–6, 50). Himmelweit recognizes that the conceptualization of unpaid labour as work has allowed housework to be viewed as purposive activity with an opportunity cost, caused the tag of 'dependent' to lose its force, and contributed to the reinterpretation of housework as both men's and women's work, but nevertheless believes that there has been a net loss from such a recognition (1995: 3–4). Specifically, she contends that the process of valuing domestic activities as 'work' marginalizes the personal, relational, self-fulfilling and caring aspects of these activities to the point where they are forced into the background, 'essential to but unrecognized by the economics of work and by a society that operates within it' (ibid.: 2). These caring-related tasks have no counterpart in the market, and they subsequently 'retain the characteristics of invisibility that used to characterize all unpaid work' (ibid.: 9–11; see also Folbre 1995).

The question arises as to whether these critics of the core assumptions of neoclassical economics view neoclassical economics as fundamentally compromised, needing to be overthrown and replaced, or whether they seek to retain the neoclassical framework. Most appear to desire the retention of a less rigid, axiomatic and androcentric version of the neoclassical framework. England, for example, suggests that the neoclassical model needs to be changed substantially, and that although relaxing the assumptions that construct the separative self will 'entail a loss of deductive certainty', the final outcome will 'illuminate rather than ignore gender inequality in the social and economic world' (1993: 49–50). Others have argued that the masculine bias of the neoclassical framework cannot be rectified by mere extensions and adjustments. Cohen, for example, argues that women were excluded from the original conception of the neoclassical model, and 'fitting them in the existing analysis now does not work' (1982: 157). Michèle Pujol also insists that neoclassical economics cannot escape its sexist past, contending that early neoclassical thought was characterized by five explicitly sexist assumptions which helped sustain the status quo of women's disadvantaged economic position, and that these assumptions have left an indelible imprint on modern economic theorising ([1984] 1995, 1992, 1995). The five assumptions are that all women are married and have children, or will do so; that all women are or ought to be dependent on a male relative; that women are or ought to be housewives; that women are unproductive in the workforce; and that women are irrational and cannot make economic decisions (1995: 18). Thus, although the neoclassical model may be extended to include the rational actions of women, Pujol suspects that the 'logic, rhetoric and symbolism' of neoclassical economics are inseparable from the five sexist assumptions, and hence that women as economic agents will remain invisible to neoclassical economists.[6] Given the '*his*tory [within neoclassical economics] of stifling feminist approaches', feminists should seek to 'transcend' the neoclassical framework rather than waiting for it to change (ibid.: 29–30).

Numerous scholars have drawn a conclusion similar to that of Cohen and Pujol, and consequently advocate alternative economic paradigms as more productive for the development of a feminist economics. Some have turned to institutional economics, contending that the incorporation of gender into both neoclassical and Marxist economics has thus far been *ad hoc* and unsuccessful. They believe that the focus on power and institutions within institutional economics will enable the inclusion of the distinction between sex and gender, where gender is viewed as a system of power which benefits men (Waller and Jennings: 613, 624; see also Jennings 1990; Waller 1994; Waller and Jennings 1991; Whalen and Whalen 1994). Others have turned to Marxist economics, contending that it is the only theoretical framework which can accommodate the concerns of feminist, as well as anti-racist, economists. This is because neoclassical but not Marxist economics judges feminist perspectives as biased; Marxist but not neoclassical economics can incorporate analyses of gender and race as social constructs; and Marxism but not neoclassical economics uses the 'indispensable' concept of class (Matthaei 1996: 28–32; see also McCrate 1987; Feiner and Roberts 1990; Humphries 1992; Matthaei 1992). Thus, according to these scholars, no amount of relaxation of the assumptions upon which rational economic man is based will enable the neoclassical framework to incorporate what they see as the essential categories of gender, race and class. However, by articulating the belief that existing unorthodox frameworks are more suitable for considering feminist issues, these feminist economists open themselves to the charge that feminist economics is no more than another (unoriginal) dimension of those existing frameworks which advocate programmes for reducing social injustice. The question of the precise extent to which feminist economists of this orientation are committed to the unreconstructed concepts and relationships of these unorthodox frameworks, which many feminists argue to be just as androcentric as the neoclassical concepts and relationships, will be considered in the concluding section of this chapter.

The feminist economists discussed in this section focus their critique on the rugged individualism of rational economic man: his inability to make interpersonal utility comparisons; the exogeneity and stability of his preferences; the independence of his utility function in the market sphere; and the interdependence of his utility function in the non-market sphere. The androcentricity of this model is due both to its origin in the existing system of gender relations, and to the bias in favour of men's interests which are produced by the assumptions which follow from it. Men have an interest in maintaining the status quo, and these assumptions direct attention away from the disadvantages which women face both in the family and in the labour market (England 1993: 37–8). Some feminist economists seek to modify this model of the separative self, and hence other core assumptions of neoclassical economics, while others are led to reject neoclassical economics altogether in favour of an alternative framework. However, whatever their solution to the problematic assumptions of neoclassical economics, these feminist economists remain empiricist: each advocates a more realistic economics, one which is more like the real world of women and therefore more able to accommodate what women are really like. In the next section, I turn to those feminist economists who take up these issues of realism and truth, basing their critiques of the methodology of neoclassical economics on feminist work in the philosophy of science.

3.3. Masculinity and Science: Feminist Standpoint Theory

In addition to questioning the central theoretical relationships of neoclassical economics, some feminist economists have challenged the methodology and epistemology which the neoclassical economists have traditionally employed to derive and appraise these relationships. A feminist philosophy of science known as feminist standpoint theory, associated with the names of Sandra Harding (1986, 1989, 1993a, 1995), Evelyn Fox Keller (1983, 1985), Hilary

Rose ([1983] 1987), Nancy Hartsock (1987) and Dorothy Smith (1987), is particularly prominent as a basis for such challenges. Feminist economists adhering to the standpoint approach question the empiricist or positivist philosophies upon which most neoclassical economists rely, arguing that it is impossible for neoclassical economists to establish a value-neutral, objective knowledge, since knowledge production is always influenced by social background and, in particular, by gender. They further argue that masculine and feminine researchers have different perspectives or standpoints by which to view 'reality' (and, indeed, on how best to appraise 'reality'), and that, since the masculine perspective has dominated scientific activity in the past, neoclassical economics itself reflects this masculine perspective. In this section I delineate feminist standpoint theory as it applies to scientific research in general and then survey the writings of those feminist economists who have adopted this approach.

Feminist standpoint theory dominates the field of feminist philosophy of science. Standpoint feminists drew on the revolutionary work undertaken by male philosophers of science, such as Thomas Kuhn and Paul Feyerabend, in the 1950s and 1960s, to establish that the scientific process was a social activity which was unable to provide a single value-neutral, empirical truth. In other words, they argued that all knowledge is socially situated, and therefore there is no Archimedean point, or 'view from nowhere' (see Keller [1982] 1989: 178; Grosz and Lepervanche 1988: 16–19). This was an essential preliminary step in the standpoint programme, since standpoint theorists realized that they could not claim that science was in some way gendered without first showing that the traditional scientific claim of objectivity and neutrality was erroneous. As Evelyn Fox Keller argued: 'As long as the course of scientific thought was judged to be exclusively determined by its own logical and empirical necessities, there could be no place for any signature, male or otherwise, in that system of knowledge' (1989a: 178; see also Longino 1989: 208). Feminist standpoint theorists therefore argue that social factors enter the scientific process in both the context of discovery and the context of justification, notions first discussed in section 2.3 above. Bias enters the discovery process in the selection of research agendas and problems to be studied, in the choice of theories to be considered as explanations, in the choice of facts considered relevant, and in the language used to describe the problems. Bias enters the justificatory process, since preconceptions formed in social contexts shape and order the 'facts' which are used to test hypotheses. Note that emphasis is placed on both steps of the scientific process and that the discovery step (traditionally deemed not to fall within the domain of the philosopher of science) is included within the analysis because bias at this stage cannot be eliminated by a justificatory step which is itself biased. Moreover, as Helen Longino argues, 'a theory of scientific inquiry that focuses solely on the logic of justification neglects the selection processes occurring in the context of discovery that limit what we get to know about' (1993b: 101; see also Seiz 1992: 289; Longino and Doell [1983] 1987; Harding 1995).

Feminist standpoint theorists further argue that the bias arising from these social influences is intrinsic to the scientific process and cannot be eliminated. They therefore reject the feminist empiricist position (delineated in section 2.3 above) in which masculine bias is attributed to 'bad science' and can be eliminated by a stricter adherence to scientific practice and a removal of the social influences which shape the identity of the knowledge producer. In Harding's words, 'scientific method provides no rules, procedures, or techniques for even identifying, let alone eliminating, social concerns that are shared by all (or virtually all) of the observers, nor does it encourage seeking out observers whose social beliefs vary in order to increase the effectiveness of scientific method' (1993a: 57; see also Harding 1989: 191ff, 196). In contrast to the empiricist philosophers, feminist standpoint theorists seek to use the identity of the scientist to produce more 'objective knowledge', where 'objectivity' ceases to connote the Archimedean standpoint, or 'view from nowhere', of traditional scientific practice. The identity of the knower is relevant because individuals of different gender, race and class are positioned differently within society, and these different positionings shape the different visions of reality upon which, ultimately, the more objective knowledge is based. As Sondra Farganis argues, 'individuals, men and women, are historically embodied, concrete persons whose perspective is a consequence of who they are; therefore in a society divided by gender, women will see and know differently from men' (1989: 208). It is further argued that science as traditionally practised has been dominated by a masculine standpoint. Indeed, there is a congruence between the scientific method and norms of masculinity, and non-science and norms of femininity. These connections have led not only to the historical exclusion of women from the processes of knowledge production – that is, women's access to universities and the practice of science was limited – but also to the absence of femininity from those processes. In Evelyn Fox Keller's words, the 'exclusion of values culturally relegated to the female domain has led to an effective "masculinization" of science – to an unwitting alliance between scientific values and the ideal of masculinity embraced by our particular culture' (1989b: 80).

The question arises as to the ways in which these different standpoints emerge, and the ways in which they shape conceptions of science. The feminist standpoint literature draws upon object relations theory to explain how feminine and masculine standpoints arise. Object relations theory, most closely associated with Nancy Chodorow (1978), offers an explanation of the process of individuation and the development of gender personality structures. Since infants spend the majority of their lives with their mother, who is female, the process of individuation operates differently in relation to boys and girls. Boys are a different sex from their mother, so the process of individuation involves conflict, which is resolved by a repudiation of femininity. Girls are the same sex as their mother, and their individuation is not as complete as that of boys; they do not need to experience a sharp break with their mother in order to gain a sense of selfhood. Hence girls grow up experiencing empathy and connectedness to others, while boys, who must repudiate their early identification with their mother, and hence femininity itself, experience themselves as much more separate from others. Thus girls (women) value connection, intimacy and merging, and do not clearly distinguish between subject and object. Boys (men), on the other hand, value autonomy, distance and separation, clearly differentiating between subject and object. As Chodorow remarks, 'men [have] a psychological investment in difference that women do not have' (1994: 47). This investment in difference is reflected in men's conception of the world, a conception which is premised upon these valued terms, and which is congruent with the scientific conception of objectivity (Worley 1995: 141–2). Note, however, that these personality structures are not inevitable: early childcare arrangements, in which the mother plays an important role, and the absence of a concrete male with whom male infants can identify, are key factors in establishing the masculine and feminine personality structures which in turn produce the historically dominant masculine conceptions of scientific knowledge (see Chodorow 1994; Keller [1978] 1983, 1985, 1989a, 1989b; Flax 1983; Scheman 1983; for critical views of object relations theory, see Fee 1986; Moi 1989; Young 1990: ch. 2).

The object relations theory of the origin of gendered standpoints may be complemented by a Marxist-inspired account of the sexual division of labour in capitalist societies. A representative scholar who adheres to this approach is Nancy Hartsock (1983: ch. 10), who argues that women undertake specific kinds of work within the private sphere, namely housework (their contribution to subsistence) and the care of men and children (their contribution to childrearing). Although there are similarities between the work of men and women, there are also a number of key differences which establish the particular standpoint of feminists within patriarchal capitalism.

These differences include women's longer working hours (the 'double day') and the importance of quality rather than quantity in their work, which means that women, and not men, are in constant contact with concrete material life (ibid.: 235–6). Hartsock recognizes that not all women contribute to both subsistence and childrearing, but she argues that since women are institutionally responsible for both, they are thereby forced to become the kinds of persons who can do both (ibid.: 234). This enables a particular standpoint or view of society which is denied to men, who, in undertaking instrumental work within the public sphere, lack the material basis of the feminist standpoint, and provide further role models to male infants in the form of an abstract masculinity (ibid.: 241; see also Smith 1974; Rose [1983] 1987, 1986; Harding 1989: 194–5; Keller 1989a).

Feminist theorists have argued that the masculine personality structure which evolves from the process of individuation in a patriarchal society has operated historically to produce science as a masculine endeavour. The masculine personality structure comes to be reflected in valued social activities, such as science, because of men's power and cultural hegemony: 'Men have the means to institutionalize their unconscious defences against repressed yet strongly experienced developmental conflicts' (Chodorow 1994: 47). The shaping of science by the masculine standpoint occurred with the very birth of science in the Cartesian era. As Londa Schiebinger put it, over the course of the eighteenth century and the development of capitalism, 'Skills such as reason and objectivity became required for participation in the public spheres of government, commerce, science and scholarship. At the same time, feeling and subjectivity became skills confined to the private sphere of hearth and home' (1987: 32; see also Merchant 1980; Keller 1985). In her discussion of Descartes, Susan Bordo uses object relations theory to argue that the historical development of science and the scientific method involved a cultural repudiation of the feminine as an enactment of the male child's experience of individuation, in which feelings about the mother's capricious comings and goings are converted from helplessness to autonomy through an aggressive pursuit of separation and control of boundaries (1987b: 451). Thus the masculine epistemological stance rigorously separates the inner and outer worlds, and values objectivity or separateness above all else. The outer world, Nature, is viewed as a perverse and uncontrollable female other, the taming or conquering of which was the project of empirical science and rationalism (ibid.: 454–5). The production of scientific knowledge is, then, reliant upon a series of hierarchical dualisms or binary oppositions which structure knowledge itself. Particularly important dualisms are subject/object (of knowledge), objectivity/subjectivity (in knowledge production), abstract/concrete, fact/value, reason/emotion and culture/nature. Since these dualisms arise within the male's Oedipal drama of individuation, they are culturally mapped onto masculinity and femininity (see, for example, Lloyd 1984; Keller 1985: ch. 4; Harding 1986: ch. 6; Bordo 1987b; Hartsock 1987: 241). It must be emphasized that the particular gender system which supports the construction of a scientific method characterized by objectivity, dispassion and reason is a social construction rather than a biological given (Bordo 1987a: 263; Keller 1985: 4).

Most feminist standpoint theorists reject what they regard as the nihilistic implication of these standpoint conclusions: the promotion of a 'female subjectivity' to replace 'male objectivity' and hence the condoning of a pure feminist relativism. They want to reconceptualize objectivity and indeed to redefine what is regarded as science so that it ceases to be distorted by masculine bias (see, for example, Keller 1989a: 178–9). Two widely-cited reconceptualizations have been proposed. The first calls for a different kind of scientific practice in which the researcher adopts the feminist standpoint in order to transcend the dichotomies, such as the subject/object distinction, which characterize traditional scientific practice (Keller 1989a, 1989b, 1985; Rose 1986). Hilary Rose, drawing on the materialist foundation for women's standpoint, argues that 'women's labour constitutes a material reality that structures a distinctive understanding of the social and natural worlds', and that a feminist epistemology derived from such labour will produce 'a truer knowledge' which 'transcends dichotomies, insists on the scientific validity of the subjective [and] on the need to unite cognitive and affective domains' (1986: 72). Another example of the first approach is the work of Keller, who draws on object relations theory to contend that science is an Oedipal project (1989a: 182–3). Masculine science entails the scientist (the subject) seeking to be radically separate from the object and to dominate the object. The feminine approach to science, on the other hand, entails the subject interacting or communicating with the object, becoming a part of the system in which the objects are located, and conversing with nature (ibid.: 184). This 'dynamic objectivity' is the 'pursuit of knowledge that makes use of subjective experience . . . in the interests of a more effective objectivity' (Keller 1985: 117). Keller illustrates this approach through the work of the Nobel Prize-winning geneticist Barbara McClintock, who made revolutionary breakthroughs in her field of research by refusing to be divorced from the organisms she was studying (1985: 184ff; 1983; see Grosz and Lepervanche 1988: 21ff for a commentary). The feminine approach, then, provides an alternative to the masculine approach which currently dominates science. However, science as such is not rejected outright. The aim of feminists is to reclaim science as a human rather than a masculine enterprise: 'it is a transformation of the very categories of male and female, and correspondingly, of mind and nature' (Keller 1985: 179; see also Keller 1989a: 179).

The second approach to the reconceptualization of the scientific project is best illustrated with the work of Harding (1986, 1989, 1993a). Harding's reformulation of objectivity takes the form of a rejection of 'weak objectivity', or the ineffectual attempt to produce value-neutral knowledge independent of the context of discovery, and a replacement of weak objectivity with 'strong objectivity'. Strong objectivity increases objectivity by identifying the cultural values and interests that differ between researchers and research communities. It rejects the 'debilitating relativist stance' which is usually seen as the only alternative to weak objectivity, and it actively seeks out socially marginalized locations, vantage points or standpoints, not to discover uncontestable facts but to maximize objectivity (1995: 7, 11). In fact, the existence of different cultural values actually encourages scientific progress by increasing the probability that previously hidden values will be uncovered (ibid.: 19–20). The feminist perspective plays an important role in this process. In Harding's words, the 'experience arising from the activities assigned to women, seen through feminist theory, provide a grounding for potentially more complete and less distorted knowledge claims than do men's experiences' (1989: 194). Thus, as Helen Longino points out, Harding's position implies that 'the ideal epistemic agent is not an unconditioned subject but the subject conditioned by the social experiences of oppression' (1993b: 106). In this way, the standards of objectivity are strengthened rather than weakened by the feminist standpoint (Harding 1995: 11; see also Harding 1993b).

The question of whether feminist standpoint theory advocates a women's or a feminist standpoint is yet to be explicitly addressed. The answer varies amongst theorists. Hartsock, for example, argues that a feminist standpoint is not available to women simply because they are women; rather, women must strive to achieve a feminist standpoint. It is because the standpoint is an achievement that Hartsock names it a feminist rather than a women's standpoint. Nevertheless, it remains the standpoint of women, based upon the material nature of their labour (1987: 232). Harding also contends that the feminist standpoint is an achievement, arguing that only 'through feminist inquiry and struggle can the perspective of women be transformed into a feminist standpoint – a morally and scientifically preferable site from which to observe, explain, and design social life' (1989: 196). However, she rejects the idea that only women can achieve a feminist standpoint, and argues that in any case the category of universal woman, from which the new, more objective science is to emanate, is inadequate since it more often than not reflects the social experience of white, heterosexual, bourgeois Western women.

Feminist economists have employed these theoretical insights from the feminist philosophy of science literature in their criticisms of the methodology of neoclassical economics. This literature is relevant to economics because, despite the fact that most economists 'should have heard the news that "positivism is dead" . . . they seem little inclined to alter their practice – and there is little agreement among methodologists as to just how economic practice should be affected' (Seiz 1992: 273). Of those feminist economists who have cited this literature (see, for example, the papers in Ferber and Nelson 1993a), Janet Seiz (1992) has most explicitly delineated its use to feminist economists. She rejects both the positivist faith of feminist empiricism and the alleged relativism of feminist postmodernism in favour of feminist standpoint theory. However, like Harding, she rejects those versions which rely upon the idea of 'male' and 'female' viewpoints, since this produces the problematic notion of a 'female' science. She therefore advocates a feminist standpoint theory which is premised upon feminist and non-feminist views (ibid.: 281–2). Seiz maintains that those scholars who adopt the feminist standpoint in economics will be able to work on a number of fronts. They can, for example, provide analyses of particular economic texts and research programmes in which they 'reveal the operation and weaken the authority of gender ideology in economic discourse' (ibid.: 290). Such studies would show precisely where and how androcentric bias enters economic research, why 'bad' arguments are retained over time, and why theories are ultimately accepted or rejected (ibid.: 289). Seiz believes that the work undertaken by Arjo Klamer and Deirdre (Donald) McCloskey on the 'rhetoric of economics' (see section 3.5 below) is ideally suited to this sort of research, and she herself draws on this approach to describe the way in which readers bring various unstated assumptions to their readings of economic texts (ibid.: 290–1).

Seiz believes that feminist standpoint theorists could also examine the way in which neoclassical models of 'individual optimization and market equilibrium' curtail the ability of economists to understand gender relations (ibid.: 294). She argues that the way in which rationality is depicted in these models is particularly problematic from a feminist perspective. She draws on object relations theory to argue that there is a strong similarity between *Homo economicus* and the separative self identified by feminist scientists, and that this portrayal of human actors is seriously distorted because it 'neglects the embeddedness of individuals (both male and female) in social relationships that shape both our actions and our wants' (ibid.: 295; see also England 1993). To reduce this distortion, economists should continue to weaken the rigid adherence to instrumental rationality of *Homo economicus*; this has already begun through the incorporation of the utility of others in utility functions (see section 3.2 above). Seiz nevertheless states that theory based on the rational actor can still have an important place in feminist economics if human motivation is 'conceived in this more nuanced way'. Indeed, whether 'women's and men's preferences differ systematically is an empirical question that deserves more attention than it receives from economists, but both women and men can usefully be depicted as choosing actions that serve their objectives' (ibid.: 296). Seiz believes that additional problems arise from the neoclassical focus on choice and optimization analysis. Such a focus, she argues, lends itself to the conclusion that the economic position of women is the result of free and rational choices. It also eliminates detailed examinations of 'the social factors [which] are responsible for the existence of systematic differences in individuals' choice sets'. She therefore suggests that economists 'might emphasize that the preferences guiding choice are the products of socialization and social pressure: people are constructed to be the sorts of people who will "choose" to behave in certain ways' (ibid.: 297).

Feminist standpoint theory is the dominant approach in the feminist philosophy of science literature. It is therefore not surprising that feminist economists have drawn on it in their analyses of the neoclassical framework. The feminist standpoint, or perhaps more particularly, its associated psychological underpinnings (object relations theory), has become even more attractive to feminist economists given the anti-empiricist critiques which have become popular even within economics in the last decade (see, for example, McCloskey 1985; Caldwell 1994). However, there is a question as to the extent to which standpoint epistemology is actually being used within feminist economics. This question arises even when considering the work of Seiz, the feminist economist who has been the most explicit in advocating feminist standpoint methodology. The kind of analyses that Seiz has predicted will emerge from the use of this methodology are very similar to those delineated in the previous section. Feminist standpoint theory could therefore be interpreted as an inessential option within her whole vision of feminist economics. Similarly, although Julie Matthaei claims to be drawing upon and extending Harding's argument that 'theories imbued with values generated "from the margins" of society, from the experience or standpoint of oppressed groups, hold special promise for advancing knowledge' (1996:

22), her arguments amount to advocating Marxist economics, rather than standpoint theory.

The lack of feminist work which is in fact underpinned by feminist standpoint theory may simply be due to the immaturity of the field of feminist economics as a whole, practitioners of which are still to a certain extent assessing alternative feminist theoretical frameworks and their implications. There may also be some hesitancy over how actually to implement a research project based on feminist standpoint theory, since, as Rosemary Hennessy has pointed out, the relationship between the socially-constructed feminist standpoint and the empirical referent of 'women's lives' is unclear (1993: 67). Robert Solow, in his commentary on the papers in Ferber and Nelson (1993a), in which feminist economists have drawn heavily upon object relations theory, is himself confused about this relationship, commenting that 'I realize that feminists deny explicitly that they are proposing a "female science". But that may reflect their latent common sense resisting the logic of their own arguments' (1993: 154). Julie Nelson shifts attention away from the problematic relationship between women and a feminist standpoint by focusing on the way in which gender acts as a 'cognitive organizer', and it is to her approach that I now turn.

3.4. Nelson's 'Gender/Value Compass' Approach

Not all feminist economists who draw on the feminist philosophy of science literature argue that knowledge should be reconceptualized from a feminist standpoint. Some argue that those methodological procedures which are valorized as masculine are used to define the traditional scientific domain, while those procedures which are devalued as feminine are used to define the non-scientific domain. Science suffers as a result, and the procedures deemed feminine should therefore be revalued and incorporated within the scientific domain. A specifically female or feminist experience, or standpoint, is not, however, necessary for this reconceptualization. The researcher, male or female, feminist or non-feminist, merely has to realize that there is an additional methodological consideration which will assist her or him to attain a full comprehension of reality. Thus feminist economists argue for a revaluation of some traditionally feminine qualities and the integration of these qualities into economics. As Schiebinger has argued of science, the 'task at hand is to refine the human effort to understand the world by restoring to science a "lost dimension" – the feminine – whose loss has distorted human knowledge' (1987: 34). Julie Nelson has most cogently argued this case within the context of economics (1992a, 1992b, 1993a,

1993b, 1993c, 1994b, 1995a, 1995b, 1996a, 1996b, 1996c). Nelson contends that cognitive facilities are dominated and constrained by hierarchical dualisms which have been metaphorically linked to gender, with the positive or valuable aspect being named as masculine and the negative aspect being named as feminine. She argues that many feminist theorists become caught up in this dualistic way of thinking, and either advocate a rejection of the dualism altogether, or alternatively seek to emphasize the dualism 'in a "feminist" fashion' by revaluing the feminine (1992a: 139). Nelson argues that her 'gender/value compass' or the orthogonal gender/value diagram, a creation of her own making which she developed in detail in Nelson (1992a), will enable feminists to 'break out of the pattern of thinking in terms of an oppositional dualism' (ibid.: 139). She applies this idea to neoclassical economics, and in this section I discuss her work.

The first step in Nelson's argument is that metaphor is essential for understanding and for communication (1992a: 138, 1992b: 104, 1996a: 4). Citing the work of the linguists Lakoff and Johnson (1980) and Johnson (1987), Nelson argues that physical experience is the basis of many metaphoric associations: 'many concepts in the English language . . . have been metaphorically linked to the physical experience of the orientations up-down, in-out, and center-periphery' (1992a: 140).[7] This physical experience is the basis of oppositions such as 'control is up; subjection is down', 'rational is up; emotional is down', 'good is up; bad is down', and 'high status is up; low status is down'. However, Nelson argues that *'opposition is itself only unidimensional in its basis of physical orientation, and not in the realms to which the dualism has been metaphorically applied'* (ibid.; italics in original). In other words, although 'up is good; down is bad' is genuinely a result of the human experience of the body, such extensions of this metaphor to, for example, 'rational is up; emotional is down', are illegitimate, since, in this case, emotional is not unambiguously an antonym for rational, even though the opposite of up is indeed down (ibid.). In short, Nelson argues that metaphor is inevitable, that many metaphors are based on the reality of the human experience of the body but illegitimately extended beyond bodily experience, and that these metaphors take the form of hierarchical dualisms which limit understanding and communication.[8]

The next step in the argument is to establish that these hierarchical dualisms are gendered, and hence to portray gender as a classificatory system. Specifically, Nelson defines gender as 'the cognitive patterning a culture constructs on the base of actual or perceived differences between males and females. Gender is the metaphorical connection of non-biological phenomena with a bodily experience of biological differentiation' (1996a: 5).

Gender, then, is a 'cognitive organizer' (1992a: 138). Dualistic thinking entails associating positive values such as reason and hardness with masculinity, and negative values such as emotion and softness with femininity, and privileging the former over the latter. Nelson's aim, however, is not to rid the world of gender associations,[9] but to create a new metaphor based on a different understanding of opposites. Nelson's new metaphor involves an expansion of the limiting and sexist one-dimensional opposites into two dimensions. Difference is reinterpreted as lack (the traditional sense of opposition), as complementarity (both terms can go together), and as perversion (one term is similar but is a distortion of the other). The three concepts together define difference (1992a: 141), and enable Nelson to replace the straitjacket of unidimensionalist, dualist thinking about gender with multidimensional difference, producing 'a radical break of gender categories from value categories' (1992a: 142).

Nelson names this new cognitive ordering system the gender/value compass. The compass brings together not only the dualistic concepts of positive masculinity (M+) and negative femininity (F−), but also negative masculinity (M−) and positive femininity (F+) (see Figure 3.1 below). Difference as lack – which is the way in which dualism currently operates – is defined by the combinations of (M+, F−) and (F+, M−); difference as complementary is defined by the combinations of (M+, F+) and (M−, F−); and difference as perversion is defined by the combinations (M+, M−) and (F+, F−) (1992a: 142–3). In identifying the different aspects of difference, the compass enables a clearer vision of Nelson's aim. She sees the pairs of positive masculine and feminine characteristics as complementary 'in the sense that one believes that a healthy, balanced, behavior involves both traits or activities', and hence form a synthesis. The negative masculine and feminine characteristics, on the other hand, are perversely complementary (1996a: 11). Thus the dichotomy hard-soft, which is the traditional view of difference as lack (M+, F−), can be reconceptualized within the compass by interpreting each term as composed of both a positive and negative aspect. Hard as strong is M+, while the perversion of hard is rigid, and hence M−. Soft as flexible is F+, while the perversion of soft is weak and hence F−. Difference as perversion is therefore the combinations of strong and rigid (M+, M−), and flexible and weak (F+, F−), and difference as (positive) complementarity is the combination of strong and flexible (M+, F+), a combination which she names with the synthesis term 'durability' (1996a: 13; see Figure 3.1). Sexism entails an ability to see only the combination (M+, F−), and the feminist project therefore entails 'the exploration and valuation of the feminine-positive and the exposing of the masculine-negative' (1992a: 146).

Positive Masculine (M+)	Positive Feminine (F+)
hard–strong	soft–flexible
Negative Masculine (M–)	**Negative Feminine (F–)**
hard–rigid	soft–weak

Figure 3.1 The gender/value compass

The next step in Nelson's analysis is to demonstrate the way in which sexism operates in economics. She argues that the dualistic, hierarchical metaphors which currently dominate understanding of the definition, content and methodology of economics should be replaced by her richer gender/value compass metaphor. Neoclassical economists are hampered by their valuation of the positive aspects of masculine characteristics, without realizing the dangers of the negative aspects, and by their opposition to the negative aspects of feminine characteristics, without recognizing their positive aspects. Nelson argues that economics is seen as hard, rigorous, scientific and masculine in relation to the representation of sociology, for example, as soft, inexact, non-scientific and feminine (1992b: 108–9). She suggests that this is because neoclassical economics is associated with activity, choice, competition and individualism, which are masculine attributes, and sociology is associated with passivity, determinism, cooperation and the collective, which are feminine attributes (ibid.: 110). The solution is not to reject economics because of its valuation of masculinity over femininity. Indeed, Nelson argues that the properties associated with the masculine identity of economics *vis-à-vis* other social sciences have served economics well: 'The emphasis on rigor can be seen as an attempt to avoid sloppiness, the use of mathematical formalism as a way of catching errors that might go unnoticed in ordinary language, and the emphasis on self-interest and competition as a way of avoiding a mushy sentimentality' (ibid.). The solution, then, is not the rejection of the positive aspects of masculine properties, such as hard, logical, scientific and precise, which are masculine-identified and describe legitimate goals of economic practice, but the incorporation of the positive aspects of feminine properties and the rejection of the negative aspects of both masculine and feminine properties in order to improve economics (ibid.: 110–11).

She gives several examples of this change in the metaphor. The positive masculine concept of logical reasoning, which is normally contrasted with the negative feminine concept of illogical, has a negative masculine component which she names 'arithmomania', or the desire to exclude from economics all but those concepts which can be manipulated by formal logic (ibid.: 113). The positive feminine component is dialectical reasoning (F+), which refers to reasoning by analogy, or to the intuition presented alongside formal models. Dialectical reasoning complements logical reasoning, and both are necessary for the achievement of good argument. The exclusion of illogical argument should, of course, be supported by everyone. Similarly, the positive masculine concept of individuation, which is normally contrasted to the negative feminine concept of engulfed, has the negative masculine aspect of radical separation or isolation. The positive feminine complement of individuated is connected. To base economics on the complementary masculine and feminine concepts of individuated and connected is to produce a more realistic picture of selfhood (ibid.: 116–17). Again, all would agree to exclude from economics the (F–) idea that identity dissolves into an undifferentiated nature. Further examples are given by the positive masculine concepts of scientific, individually agenic and active choice, which should be complemented with the positive feminine concepts of humanistic, influenced, and the ability to discern what is needed. The negative masculine concepts of inhuman, radically autonomous and unlimited wants, as well as the negative feminine concepts of unscientific, determined and neediness, are a hindrance to the attainment of truth (see Figure 3.2 below).

Neoclassical economists have therefore done themselves a disservice by failing to recognize positive feminine characteristics: in Nelson's words, by 'eliminating femininity in science, is science made strong in its radical detachment? Or, instead, by going to such extremes to avoid over-attachment, is it left weakened and distorted by insufficient attention to connection?' (Nelson 1993b: 127). The rejection of the metaphor of hierarchical dualisms (signified by M+, F–) and the adoption of the new metaphor of complementarity (signified by M+, F+) will change the way in which economics is practised and the way in which its theoretical relationships are judged. Specifically, the incorporation of all aspects of knowledge which are helpful in understanding a particular problem, regardless of their gender associations, would extend the scope of economics beyond those areas that can be ' "squeezed and moulded" . . . into the form of a mathematically tractable model of an idealized market' (1992b: 123).

Economics will be judged using the positive-negative dualism rather than the masculine-feminine, and it will become a scientific enterprise seeking ever more realistic representations of reality, instead of remaining 'a discipline which concentrates too much on the achievement of masculinity rather than the achievement of good argument' (1992b: 112; see also Nelson 1993c, 1995a, 1995b).

Positive Masculine (M+)	Positive Feminine (F+)
logical reasoning	dialectical reasoning
individuated	connected
scientific	humanistic
individually agenic	influenced
ability to choose actively	ability to discern what is needed
Negative Masculine (M–)	**Negative Feminine (F–)**
arithmomania	illogic
isolated	engulfed
inhuman	unscientific
radically autonomous	determined
unlimited wants	neediness

Source: Nelson (1992b: 113–18)

Figure 3.2 The gender/value compass applied to economics

This project of change is extended to include a revision of the definition of economics, away from the study of choice towards the study of provisioning. Nelson argues that defining the subject of economics 'as individual choice makes the detached cogito, not the material world or real persons in the material world, the center of study. Nature, childhood, bodily needs, and human connectedness, cut off from "masculine" concern in the Cartesian split, remain safely out of the limelight' (1993c: 26). This definition, Nelson contends, explains the discipline's failure to take as its *raison d'être* the 'real economic problems' of poverty, power, unemployment, economic duress, health care and education. Instead, economists undertake research for the purpose of 'the further elaboration of a particular axiomatic theory of human behavior' (ibid.: 33; see also 1994a: 127, 1996c; see also Strassmann 1993a). When economics is practised as a deductive, axiomatic, mathematical and formalized science, it has become too masculine and hence unproductive. Nelson advocates a 'more fully human, rather than distinctly masculine' economics (1992b: 110), one which is both more scientific and more relevant to 'real people's lives'. Such a project moves away from the science of choice and the maximizing of material welfare to a science of the provisioning of human survival, in which needs are distinguished from wants. Once this reorientation has been undertaken, ethical considerations and the above-mentioned 'real economic problems' become the centre of analysis (1993c: 32–3; see also 1996c).

Nelson's account of the gender/value compass is undoubtedly the most developed analysis by an economist to date of the role played by gender in neoclassical theorizing. The central merit of her account rests in the design of a simple device (the gender-value compass) which is readily accessible to non-feminists and which enables the revaluation of 'feminine' methods of theorizing without rejecting the positive results which follow from the 'masculine' methods of theorizing. However, Nelson is perhaps a little over-optimistic in believing that some feminine terms can be revalued as positive merely by emphasizing their usefulness. This optimism may be attributable to her underestimation of the intellectual, and indeed emotional or psychic, investments which accompany binary oppositions, and her view of language as essentially an innocent device by which to convey meaning. For example, she encourages feminists and others to adopt the gender compass and 'break out of the pattern of thinking in terms of an oppositional dualism [which is] endemic in feminist scholarship' (1992a: 139–40). Feminists, it seems, have only themselves to blame for the continuation of dualisms! Nelson's hope for a synthesis of masculine and feminine terms to create a 'human' economics which is still scientific or truthful is in part replicated and in part rejected by the feminist economists discussed in the next section, and it is to their work that I now turn.

3.5. The Gendered Rhetoric of Economics

The feminist economists considered in this section draw on the growing field of the 'rhetoric of economics' to argue that the gendered categories, assumptions and relationships within the neoclassical framework are persuasive to, and accepted by, male economists because they support their interests as men and husbands. The notion that economists employ rhetorical strategies to convince others was popularized by Deirdre (Donald)

McCloskey (1983, 1985). McCloskey contends that the official, modernist methodologies which purportedly establish economics as a science bear no resemblance to the actual, unofficial, 'workaday' methodological procedures followed by economists. The actual procedures employed by economists include a broad array of rhetorical devices which persuade others to accept or reject particular economic theories. Such devices include the citing of historical precedent, exhibitions of mathematical expertise, argument by example, symmetry and philosophical consistency, and, perhaps most importantly, the use of metaphor, since every 'step in economic reasoning, even the reasoning of the official rhetoric, is metaphor' (1983: 502). McCloskey also maintains that economists would have little to say if they did in fact adhere to their own official methodological procedures, since in so doing all economic theory would be rendered non-scientific and the neoclassical paradigm would cease to progress. If, on the other hand, economists were to renounce the official positivist methodology and recognize the actual grounds upon which they were arguing, the theoretical content of economics would remain intact and 'the temper of argument among economists would improve' (ibid.: 482). McCloskey therefore argues that the only methodological principles worth pursuing are honesty, clarity and tolerance, and that economists should revive the art of rhetoric, or 'the art of discovering good reasons, finding what really warrants assent, because any reasonable person ought to be persuaded' (Booth, quoted in McCloskey 1983: 482). Prior to McCloskey's writings, this art had been denigrated by economists with asides about 'empty' or 'mere rhetoric' (ibid.). The recognition and analysis of the unofficial rhetoric actually employed by economists would improve both the writing and teaching of economics; make economists more modest and tolerant; raise the status of economics in other disciplines and hence encourage greater interaction between economics and such disciplines; make economics more 'scientific' (or 'good') by allowing more types of evidence to be included in research; and induce much more productive 'conversations' amongst economists (1983: 512–14, 1985: ch. 10).

In short, McCloskey believes that scholars should draw on the art of rhetoric to select that economic theory which is found to be the most persuasive within a morally-constrained conversation, rather than judge theories on the basis of a narrow set of modernist criteria. However, it should be emphasized that McCloskey does not argue that economists should give up mathematical modelling, statistical testing and other modernist paraphernalia. She instead simply maintains that attention to language would increase the rigour of the disciplinary conversation, since all science is literary in any case, and hypotheses do not in fact stand or fall on tests of significance. McCloskey's pathbreaking work was followed by, amongst others, Klamer (1987, 1988, 1990), Klamer and McCloskey (1988), Klamer, McCloskey and Solow (1988), McCloskey (1988, 1990a, 1990b, 1992, 1994a, 1994b), Mirowski (1988, 1992), Rossetti (1992), Henderson, Dudley-Evans and Backhouse (1993), Brown (1994a) and Henderson (1994) (see also Caldwell and Coats 1984; Mäki 1993, 1995; McCloskey 1995b). Gender was not a focus of, nor rarely even mentioned in, these works. However, a number of scholars have since applied these ideas within a feminist context, namely, Nancy Folbre and Heidi Hartmann (1988), Strassmann (1993a, 1993b, 1994, 1996), Strassmann and Polanyi (1995), McCloskey (1993) and Klamer (1991, 1992, 1993, 1995). In this section, I delineate the arguments articulated in these works.

One of the first published papers to address the gendered rhetoric of economics was written by Nancy Folbre and Heidi Hartmann (1988). They argued that the confinement of self-interest to the public sphere and altruism to the private sphere is used within both the neoclassical and Marxist frameworks to rationalize women's limited opportunities. They described their approach as 'somewhat McCloskeyesque', in that, rather than 'developing an empirical or historical analysis', they 'critically examine the logic and consistency of a set of basic assumptions that have divided the economist's world into two parts, variously designated public and private, market and household, economic and noneconomic, self-interested and altruistic, male and female' (ibid.: 185). They argued that such divisions are gendered, and that they are maintained through a number of theoretical propositions which 'persuade more than others partly because they deliver greater benefits to those who decide the outcome of the debate' (ibid.). Such theoretical propositions include the use of interdependent utility functions in examinations of the family, but the rejection of their use in the public sphere; the assumption that the distribution of income within the family is independent of the source of income; and the claim that women's employment decisions are voluntary. These assumptions idealize the family as a realm in which self-interest is constrained, and in which morality and altruism dominates. In short, the family signifies the 'non-economic'. Since women rather than men are associated with this realm, 'women themselves come to be portrayed as relatively 'non-economic creatures', to whom is allocated the responsibility for altruism (ibid.: 185–6). The outcome of these rhetorical associations is that the concept of the moral, altruistic family has been used to legitimate inequalities between men and women. In the past the idea of the 'benevolent dictator' was used by scholars such as James Mill to argue that women should not be given the vote, and it has since been used by Becker to assume away problems arising from the unequal distribution of resources within the family. Neoclassical theories have also been used to support the idea that women place a higher priority on the welfare of their family than on their own welfare as measured by their wage. Thus women are alleged to choose low-paying jobs in order to remain on call to their family. The interest that men might have in discouraging women's investment in human capital, and hence women's economic independence is ignored (ibid.: 190). Thus Folbre and Hartmann are suspicious of implicit or explicit claims that women are less self-interested than men, arguing that such claims serve as rationalizations for women's lower wages and limited opportunities (ibid.: 195; see also Pujol 1992).

Folbre and Hartmann's (1988) claim that their paper is 'somewhat McCloskeyesque' should be emphasized. Although to some extent they use the art of rhetoric to show that the neoclassical story of self-interest in the marketplace and altruism in the home is persuasive to men but not to feminist economists, they do not self-consciously draw upon any of the tools of rhetoric to argue that their feminist alternative is superior. They instead rely upon traditional empiricist claims to defend their vision of reality, in which women's economic opportunities are constrained and the home is a site of conflict. They cite, for example, a range of empirical literature inconsistent with neoclassical (and Marxist) theoretical work, concluding that contemporary feminist research which focuses on the causes and consequences of unequal power between men and women 'provides a better explanation of economic trends in households and in the labor market than research informed solely by [neoclassical and Marxist] perspectives' (ibid.: 193). Such feminist research is complemented by non-feminist work which undermines the caricature of rational economic man, and both can contribute to 'a more complete theory of economic interests, one that can encompass concepts like cooperation, loyalty, and reciprocity' (ibid.: 197). In short, then, the concept of rhetoric is used only to the extent that it facilitates a critique, but is not used to deny a empiricist vision of the world.

Diana Strassmann (1993a, 1993b, 1994, 1996) and Strassmann and Polanyi (1995) also draw upon the work of McCloskey. Strassmann rejects the idea that the neoclassical paradigm has come to dominate the discipline through competition in the marketplace of ideas, whether the determinant of its success is alleged to be its scientific method or the persuasive force of its superior rhetoric. On the one hand, the positivist method is incapable of distinguishing good from bad theories. On the other hand, even if science is seen as a social process, and 'truth' as the most persuasive account of the world, the marketplace cannot be relied upon to produce 'a "correct" and reliable valuation of ideas' (1994: 154; see also 1993a, 1993b). Strassmann and Polanyi point out that McCloskey's rhetoric of economics entails a shift of allegiance from economic methodology to the marketplace of ideas. McCloskey has faith in the eventual outcome of the rhetorical struggle within the marketplace of ideas because this marketplace is in the hands of thousands upon thousands of honest and intelligent economic scholars (Strassmann and Polanyi 1995: 131). However, it is on this very point that Strassmann points to a blind spot in McCloskey's early or non-feminist work. The scientific community, as a community dominated by white middle-class males, has an important role in consigning some ideas to the scrapheap because they are not persuasive to them. In other words, the 'reasonable person' upon whom McCloskey relies is a 'reasonable man' with all his attendant interests, views and biases, and the community of readers is a community dominated by male perspectives (see McCloskey 1983: 482, 1985: 28–30, 1990b: 72–3; see also McCloskey 1993). Thus, instead of neoclassical economics becoming dominant through competition between ideas via competitive processes of theory verification/falsification or rhetorical ploys, neoclassical economics has come to dominate economics because it has been created and validated by a male-dominated scientific community which legislates on persuasiveness and actively restricts the acceptable rhetoric by which this framework may be challenged.

The predominantly white, middle-class and male members of the economics community produce accounts of the world which reflect their own experiences. The masculine bias of these accounts is, in turn, persuasive to young, male economists of the same background. Thus, 'what counts as "better" is not independent of the demographic composition of an intellectual community' (Strassmann 1994: 154). Feminists and minorities who have had different experiences from the dominant group, on the other hand, experience 'dissonance' with these theoretical claims. However, reflecting the failure of the competitive process in the marketplace of ideas, such people are not able to challenge the economists' standard accounts of reality. They are trained to accept as an invulnerable core the conventional set of assumptions of neoclassical economics, and they are restricted in terms of the forms in which arguments can be made. For example, as Strassmann put it, 'in economics, students quickly learn that it is bad manners to spend too much time questioning the assumptions of a paper' (1993b: 152). Instead, a critique of an economic theory or model must be accompanied by an alternative theory or model, but one which is recognizable, that is, which also conforms to the discipline's requirements of presentation in equations, with mathematically expressed definitions and assumptions (Strassmann 1994: 153).

As Strassmann (1993a, 1993b, 1996) points out, if the marketplace of ideas is to operate competitively, it must be equally open to all accounts. The first step in this solution to the problem of the masculine monopoly is to reveal the existence of a dominant experience underlying economists' accounts of the world. Strassmann and Polanyi (1995) reveal the situated character of currently-accepted accounts by analysing economic texts in terms of the theoretical tools of linguistics and by drawing inferences from a series of 'default assumptions' presumed by the authors of the texts. The first theoretical tool employed is the notion of the 'story-world' or model, the construction of which always leaves out 'extraneous detail' which is filled in by the reader using default assumptions. In other words, the producers of story-worlds and their audiences draw on a background of experience which informs their understanding of the context of the model. Strassmann and Polanyi argue that members of 'intellectual or social communities respond to the information included in texts by making similar default assumptions about the material left out' (ibid.: 135). The second tool is the identification and evaluation of certain key details within the story-world. The evaluator looks for the repetition of certain information, unusual treatment of some details, and the construction of some actors as subjects and others as objects. Strassmann and Polanyi use a conventional labour economics textbook to reveal the class and gender biases within the story-world of economists, and argue that those who do not recognize themselves in the story of the 'enjoyable family' – a white, middle-class, nuclear family – are filtered out of the profession. Thus the perspective of white, middle-class, North American men is reproduced, and the voices of differently situated persons silenced (ibid.: 129, 143–4).

Although situated within the McCloskey tradition of pointing to the importance of language and expression within economics, Strassmann (1993a, 1993b, 1994, 1996) and Strassmann and Polanyi (1995) can also be interpreted as standpoint theorists because of their standpoint-based account of the production of economic truth. For example, Strassmann and Polanyi argue that 'all human knowledge is situated; any account of the world is inevitably shaped by the experiences and human lives of its producers', and, further, that 'the situated character of economic knowledge contradicts the common claim that economic accounts can be constructed independently of the life circumstances of the dominant producers' (1995: 129). Economics as currently constituted is a reflection of an androcentric and Western perspective on selfhood and agency, which means that the construction of economic knowledge is partial (Strassmann 1993a: 55; Strassmann and

Polanyi 1995: 130–2). In response to these problems, Strassmann and Polanyi seek 'to promote economic accounts truer to the lives and experiences of women' (1995: 132). Economists may fear that acknowledging the role of their story-telling will lead to relativism, but this is not the case: 'Making the positioned nature of arguments more visible simply provides more information about arguments and accounts than normally revealed by practicing [*sic*] scientists, and thereby leads to a more reasonable and honest social process for the selection of favored perspectives and accounts – leading in short to better science' (ibid.: 132). Better science is here defined, as in the work of Julie Nelson (see section 3.4), as a more complete economics. Since models are inevitably the product of a partial viewpoint, they will always be biased, and hence a multiplicity of perspectives is required to represent the 'complexity and diversity of economic activities' (Strassmann 1993a: 65). In this sense, then, Strassmann and Strassmann and Polanyi have a strategy similar to that of Folbre and Hartmann: each draws upon the rhetoric of rhetoric, but each ultimately relies upon 'the facts' to support their alternative vision.

McCloskey (1993) has developed her earlier work on the ways in which economists persuade each other by developing a gender analysis of the official and unofficial methodologies of economics. She contends that scientists argue by necessarily using, not just fact and logic, but also metaphor and story. Philosophers of the modernist age have divided this rhetorical 'group of four' or tetrad into two distinct sets: the methodological dyad of fact and logic, and the creative dyad of metaphor and story. McCloskey borrows a diagrammatic parable from Arjo Klamer (1990) to represent the rigorous, axiomatic approach of the methodological dyad as a masculine square and the metaphoric, story approach of the creative dyad as a feminine circle. She criticizes this traditional depiction of science for confining the methodologies of the square and the circle to two non-overlapping spheres, arguing that both the square and the circle are necessary for the successful undertaking of scientific activity, that both shapes are integral to methodology as well as creativity, and that the pervasive role of the circle in the so-called sciences has been overlooked (ibid.: 69–71). Indeed, it 'is not so much that metaphor is an alternative to fact (true though this sometimes is) as that the construction of facts requires metaphors – for example, the metaphor of light as quanta, as against waves, is essential for certain measurements in physics' (ibid.: 74–5). The parable is given a feminist perspective through the contention that the square masculine approach has been valorized and promoted within economics, while the round 'feminine' approach has been denigrated and 'officially' excluded.

Neoclassical economists are particularly prone to this rejection of 'femininity', and McCloskey describes them as 'butch', 'a motorcycle gang among economists, strutting about the camp with clattering matrices and rigorously fixed points, sheathed in leather, repelling affection' (ibid.: 76). In arguing these points, McCloskey is careful to point out that it is irrelevant whether or not women are in fact more disposed to communicate through metaphor and men more inclined to convey information via unnarrated facts: 'Regardless of what men and women actually do statistically speaking, the claims about what they do exist as cultural objects' (ibid.: 69). Thus all that is required for gender bias is that the methodological and creative dyads are produced as stereotypical dispositions of men and women, with the former valued by economists and the latter devalued (ibid.: 69–70). Nevertheless, throughout the paper McCloskey cites numerous examples of the ways in which men have used the masculine square in their delineations of economic activity (see also McCloskey 1997: 22–3). Of course, as in her earlier work, she argues that such delineations inevitably rely upon the unofficial rhetoric of the feminine circle, since metaphors and story-telling are intrinsic to reasoning.

The reliance of 'masculinist economics' upon the feminine half of the tetrad of persuasion is denied because economists suffer from literalism; that is, they mistake stories and metaphors for reality. McCloskey therefore calls upon economists to self-consciously embrace the full tetrad of fact, logic, metaphor and story, and reject the counter-productive modernist distinctions of square/circle and objective/subjective. She contends that, in any case, there is neither objective nor subjective as these terms are usually understood, only the 'conjective': something becomes knowledge or 'objective' when a community with a common language agrees that it constitutes knowledge (ibid.: 76). McCloskey's ultimate aim, then, is not to displace the present masculine form of neoclassical economics, but to enrich it by undertaking a feminine revision. The feminine revision would explode the fantasy of 'literalism' and make researchers self-conscious of their story-telling. The resulting conjective economics would entail a rejection of the masculine fixation with methodological rules, mathematical formalism and the confrontation of highly abstract models with statistical data, and the adoption of a multidimensional approach. There would be a greater use of interactive research practices, such as questionnaires and empathetic investigative techniques (in the tradition of the Nobel Prize-winning geneticist Barbara McClintock mentioned in section 3.3 above), and conversation, story telling, anecdote, listening, cooperation and synthesis would replace the simple-minded falsificationist, verificationist and other modernist corroborationist schemes. These changes 'might humanize economics and enlarge it' (ibid.: 89). Interestingly, however, McCloskey believes that many of the central theoretical tenets of the Chicago version of the neoclassical framework will continue to be accepted as the most persuasive by the majority of those who partake in the conversation (McCloskey 1988: 290, 1992: 1320).

Arjo Klamer (1991, 1992, 1993) has also related the analysis of the disciplinary conversation or discourse of economics to feminist economics. Klamer draws on an unpublished version of McCloskey (1993) entitled 'Some Consequences for [*sic*] a Feminine Economics' to reaffirm the latter's interpretation of his own square/circle diagrammatic parable, in which the square is associated with the masculine and the circle is associated with the feminine. He agrees with McCloskey that the study of the persuasiveness of metaphors, analogies and stories (or what he calls the 'rhetorical perspective') is one means by which to supersede the artificial divide of the square and the circle, and to overcome their improper gender associations (1991: 140–1). He also argues that the rhetorical perspective, in which the researcher interprets the rhetorical devices used in economic texts, makes room for an 'interpretive' approach of the actual economy, in which the researcher sets aside the 'square' analysis of choice-maximizing behaviour and endeavours to understand what people in fact do in their economic activities (see also Klamer 1993). This approach entails entering the 'life worlds' of the economic actors in a similar manner to the way in which the ethnologist enters the life-world of an Indonesian village (1991: 138–40). Klamer believes that the interpretations which result from this close contact would give greater insight into motives and actions. It would also, he argues, 'affect both the discourse about economics and the discourse about the economy', and, importantly, 'meet the feminist subversion of the object-subject split' (ibid.: 141).

Klamer (1991, 1993) acknowledges that his work is not pursued with feminist ends in mind, and that he writes on the basis of connections between his own research programme of 'interpretive' economics and feminist economics rather than pursuing a feminist research programme *per se*. However, although he acknowledges these points, he should be admonished for failing to engage with feminist economics except at a superficial level while simultaneously advocating his interpretive approach to feminist scholars. Indeed, Klamer gives the impression that his application of his programme to feminist issues is an afterthought. In the two papers in which he presents his work as relevant to feminist economics (1991, 1993), he has delineated his interpretive approach in the main body of the text and simply appended a brief introduction and conclusion relating the programme to a small selection of the feminist economics literature. In the latter paper he has merely reprinted, in its entirety, the introduction of the first paper, without further addressing feminist economics. The conclusions which he attributes to feminist economics, and which are consistent with his own approach, are minimal: the 'dismissal' of the Cartesian dualisms which underlie economists' claims that economics is a science, and in particular the subject/object distinction (1991: 140–1), and the need for the development of a discourse in which economists can recognize themselves (Klamer 1993: 2). Nevertheless, Klamer sees value in feminist economics, suggesting that it is feminist economics which may lead the way to a more 'fruitful building ground' in which the economy and economic processes are read as texts (1995: 171).

The feminist economists who use the notion of rhetoric, then, agree with McCloskey that economists persuade each other by employing a diverse range of rhetorical devices, and that economic truths are established by communities of economists drawing upon these rhetorical devices rather than by individual researchers testing theories with positivist or other modernist methodological criteria. They further argue that the male-dominated community of economists has been persuaded to accept various methodological and theoretical aspects of the neoclassical research programme because of their affinity with the interests of masculinity. The market in ideas is therefore not competitive. McCloskey herself has joined the ranks of this branch of feminist economics, and has thus far confined her gender analysis to the way in which methodological procedures and rhetorical techniques have been selected within the marketplace of ideas. Although she has yet to consider explicitly the extent of masculine bias within the theoretical relationships produced by these research approaches, she has repeatedly gone on the record as being generally satisfied with the theoretical notions of the 'good old' Chicago version of the neoclassical framework. Feminist economists such as Hartmann and Folbre, and Strassmann and Polanyi, by contrast, maintain that the general acceptance of both the methodological and theoretical tenets of the neoclassical framework is a product of an imperfect and androcentric market selection process. They follow other heterodox economists in claiming that the marketplace is dominated by social relations (see, for example, Mirowski 1992: 239), but focus specifically on the important role played by gender in restricting open and honest conversation.

In the process of making this appeal, however, the feminist economists considered in this section have tended to rely upon a notion of women's reality, which is in many ways a departure from (or even a contradiction of) the philosophy underlying the rhetoric of economics. This tendency may be attributed to the general reluctance to question the notions of realism and truth. McCloskey, by contrast, explicitly takes a pragmatist position, and indeed states that she would have used the term 'pragmatism' instead of 'rhetoric' but for the possibly confusing usage of the former term (1985: 29, 152–3). Pragmatists contend that truth is relative to a framework of argument and justification: 'Truth consists of propositions that can be justified according to currently accepted modes of justification' (Culler 1983: 152). McCloskey discards the search for 'truth' proper because we do not have a 'path to God's understanding', and commits herself to what she calls 'small-t truth', which is 'the practical knowledge we have of crossing the street or detecting electrons' (1992: 264). Her writings are nevertheless many-layered, and her deliberations on the topics of truth and reality have been the subject of numerous readings, not all of which are compatible (see especially Fish 1988; Mirowski 1988; Backhouse *et al.* 1993; Maki 1993, 1995; McCloskey 1995b).

3.6. Conclusion

The feminist economists considered in this chapter argue that economists' accounts of the world distort women's experiences because they are interpreted through masculine categories, using androcentric methodologies and values (see Thiele 1986: 33–4). It might be argued that many of their objections coincide with those of other critics of neoclassical economics, and hence that their contribution is that of adding gender to an already-existing critical analysis. Indeed, the feminist economists discussed in this chapter usually cite this history of criticism of neoclassical economics in an implicit or explicit acknowledgement of their debt to heterodox economics, and the inability of feminist economists, or any group of theorists, to step outside the history of discourse. These references may also signal feminist economists' belief that their task is one of 'completing' heterodox schools of thought, or, alternatively, their intention to highlight the gender blindness of not only the orthodox school but also of its heterodox critics. Finally, such references to well-known unorthodox critics may be a rhetorical means by which to lend authority and respectability to feminist economics. Whatever the motivation for feminist economists' references to heterodox critics, those references may encourage heterodox critics, as well as orthodox economists themselves, to believe that a feminist analysis simply adds an additional, and perhaps not even very significant, factor to their own analyses.[10] Arjo Klamer and

Solomon Polachek are two examples of this tendency (see sections 3.5 and 2.5 respectively; see also Sen 1990: 123, 1995).

Thus many of the feminist economic analyses discussed in this chapter may appear to be 'domesticated' in Carole Pateman's sense of that term (1986: 5; see section 2.5 above). Within domesticated feminism, sexual power 'is taken to pose no special problems or to have no special status, since it is assumed that relations between men and women can be analysed in the same way, using the same categories, as relations between any other superiors and subordinates' (Pateman 1986: 5). In other words, just as the feminist economists discussed in Chapter 2 appeared simply to be adding women to an existing neoclassical framework, the feminist economists considered in this chapter appear at first sight to be adding women, or at least femininity, to existing unorthodox frameworks. Thus the feminist analyses of this chapter may appear not to be theoretically innovative, but rather derivative of existing critiques. This argument is to some extent justified. For example, some institutionalist feminist economists suggest that they reject neoclassical economics and accept institutionalism because feminism simply slots into its already-existing categories and modes of analysis. However, this argument is also to some extent unjustified. Although feminist economists have acknowledged that unorthodox critics have made similar criticisms, albeit for different reasons, it should be remembered that feminism also arose precisely because of the inadequacies of existing frameworks (unorthodox or otherwise) in relation to feminist issues.[11] For this reason, many feminist economists have not simply adopted existing unorthodox frameworks. They specify particular feminist perspectives and methodologies, such as feminist standpoint theory and the 'gender-compass', which simultaneously operate as an implicit critique of unorthodox frameworks which are unable adequately to incorporate those perspectives. Indeed, much feminist scholarship has been devoted to revealing the ways in which particular disciplinary paradigms have been constituted by their exclusion of such perspectives. Although much of this work remains to be done in the discipline of economics, it is nevertheless the case that many feminist economists have acknowledged that the frameworks of liberal feminism, socialist feminism, radical feminism, and so on, are not adequate to the task, because of the very implication that women or the feminine can simply be added in to those frameworks. In other words, unorthodox critics must not overlook the fact that feminist scholarship produces its own frameworks, and hence feminism is not simply derivative of their perspectives.

I have argued, then, that specifically feminist frameworks should be sharply distinguished from their unorthodox non-feminist counterparts. However, despite this demarcation, most of the feminist economists considered in this chapter share with most of their unorthodox colleagues a commitment to some form of objective knowledge. That is, the majority of the feminist economists discussed in this chapter maintain an allegiance to verisimilitude in theoretical frameworks, while arguing that the basic theoretical assumptions and methodological precepts of neoclassical economics are based upon the standpoint of (non-feminist) men and hence are androcentric. Thus many of these feminist economists also maintain a commitment to science, albeit a reconstituted science, or a science which incorporates the context of discovery, heretofore dominated by a masculine perspective, as intrinsic to knowledge production rather than irrelevant to it. There remains in these works, then, as in the case of feminist empiricism, an appeal to an already-constituted real world and truth, and hence to an already-constituted femininity, to which economics should address itself. Even the feminist standpoint position produces this appeal. Harding, for example, argues that although starting research from the lives of marginalized persons will not produce absolutely falsifiable claims, such claims 'are validly and usefully regarded as "less false" in a limited (not absolute) but meaningful sense' (1995: 27). Other feminist economists discussed in this chapter regard neoclassical economics as bereft of truthful content, and even the possibility of truthful content, and advocate more realistic alternatives, thereby also maintaining a commitment to realism.

It is therefore apparent that the majority of the feminist economists considered in this chapter retain a commitment to the idea that objects of knowledge preexist their discursive construction. Only those feminist economists discussed in the penultimate section of the chapter, such as McCloskey and her colleagues, move toward the poststructuralist position and the associated questioning of an unmediated reality. In any event, the specific feminist poststructuralist approach adopted within this book explicitly treats neoclassical economics as a productive discourse, and this approach should be sharply distinguished from the more realist perspective of those feminist economists discussed in this and the previous chapter, in which an already-constituted femininity is identified and examined. Vivienne Brown, a reviewer of the collection of papers in Ferber and Nelson (1993a), captured the difference between approaches when she suggested that the 'social constructionist' or gender feminist position which can be used to characterize the collection of papers is limited because in places 'the essays seem to entail a somewhat literal acceptance of the argument that masculinist bias has excluded feminine characteristics and in so doing has denied a place for women's experiences. The feminine terms in the system of dualism function not by representing a literal description of women's attributes or even a social construction of women's experience, but by constituting the "other" against which the masculine terms are themselves defined. Thus the feminine terms here denote a constitutive element in a discursively specific definition of masculinity, rather than a literal or universal descriptor of feminine values' (1994b: 303). It is a further discussion of feminist poststructuralism that occupies the next chapter.

Notes

1. The radical implications of a cardinal measure and the consequent ability to make interpersonal utility comparisons were made evident by Pigou (1920), who showed that the law of diminishing marginal utility could be employed to justify a transfer of wealth from poor to rich people. The adoption of ordinal measurement, popularized by Hicks (1934) and Allen (1934), was subsequently welcomed by many economists. Schumpeter, for example, argued that the end-result of the adoption of the notion of ordinal measurement of utility is to 'deprive of their scientific or pseudo scientific foundations many equalitarian articles of faith to which most modern economists are emotionally attached' (1954: 1072). For an overview of the utility measurement problem, see Viner (1925), Alchian (1953), Ozga (1956), Ellsberg (1954) and Arrow (1963).
2. Folbre and Hartmann (1988) and Strassmann and Polanyi (1995: 132) point to the blindspot of this assumption of self-interest in arguing that the self-interest of economists as men has led them to accept androcentric accounts of the world (see section 3.5 below).
3. On non-feminist considerations of altruism, see Zamagni (1995).
4. Jennings and Waller argue that methodological individualism 'denies the reality of culture' (1990: 627). However, to some extent this criticism is out of date. The recent development of new institutionalist economics has given rise to models of institutions ('culture') using traditional neoclassical techniques of individual optimizing.
5. For the domestic labour debate generally, see Kuhn and Wolpe (1978), Sargent (1981a), Hamilton and Barrett (1986: 'Towards Feminist Marxism'); Lovell (1990a: pt 3); Matthaei (1992), Beasley (1994) and Himmelweit (1995). For economists' discussions of domestic labour, see the four special issues of the *Review of Radical Political Economics* on the political economy of women (1970, 1972, 1977, 1980). Feminist economists who contributed to the debate include Fee (1976), Gardiner, Himmelweit and Mackintosh ([1976] 1982), Hartmann (1976, 1981a, 1981b), Himmelweit and Mohun (1977), Humphries (1977), Hartmann and Markusen (1980), Gita Sen (1980), Ferguson and Folbre (1981) and Power (1983).
6. Pujol further contends that women and feminists are actually 'excluded from developing or establishing alternative theoretical approaches' (1995: 29). See also Oakley (1974), who argues that the sexist interests and personalities of the 'founding fathers' are responsible for the male bias in sociology.
7. Nelson argues that the implication of this 'identification of the basis of metaphor as experience, and especially physical experience' is that 'human physical bodies [are] explicitly at the heart of the analysis' (1992a: 148), without, however, explaining why this should be important (see Chapter 4 below for a further discussion of Nelson's use of the body).
8. Nelson uses the term 'metaphor' expansively to encompass the ideas of 'webs of connection', 'patterning', 'cognitive schema', gestalts and analogies (1992b: 104).

9. On this point, Nelson argues that: 'Since complete gender-neutrality requires not only the elimination of sexist gender associations, but also the elimination of gender as a cognitive category, one has to ask what is to be done about sexual dimorphism. If the child and language development story of how gender becomes a cognitive organizer is correct, then gender-neutrality requires the active suppression of sexual difference as a salient aspect of human experience, especially the experience of children' (1994b: 201).

10. Indeed, as Sen points out, unorthodox economists may even be hostile to feminist analysis because of its unnecessary divisiveness in claiming for women a special place within the array of people suffering under some form of inequality (1990: 123). Orthodox economists, on the other hand, may also be hostile to feminists for their attempts to add a gender dimension where they see none existing, or to read gender implications into theoretical propositions where none were intended. Some feminist economists may seem to support the unorthodox interpretation of their works by appearing to assume that because they are feminists, anyone who is disadvantaged, poor or generally 'oppressed' is their responsibility and hence must be addressed within a feminist analysis. This could be called the 'add a feminist and stir' approach.

11. It could be argued that some unorthodox economists have a desire for feminists to remain in the position of the caring, nurturing woman, ready to make the tea and offer support, but not to insist upon a legitimate position to make claims in her own right, as was explicit in the early experiences of women within the radical movements of the 1960s and 1970s (see, for example, Sargent 1981b: xiv–xv; Simms 1981: 229).

4. Women and Knowledge III: Feminist Poststructuralism

4.1. Introduction

The sex/gender distinction (outlined in section 1.2 above) has been of critical importance in the development of feminist theory, and it acts as the foundation for the majority of the criticisms of neoclassical economics by feminist economists delineated in Chapters 2 and 3 of this book. The theorizing of this distinction and its implications has undoubtedly led to improvements in the economic and social positions of women. It has, for example, led to legislative acts which prohibit sex discrimination in most employment situations, which in turn may benefit individual women. Unfortunately, however, the sex/gender distinction derives its analytical power from a number of other distinctions which have been argued by some feminists to be problematic, and to impose limitations upon the ways in which society can be conceptualized. These problematic distinctions include those oppositions, particularly important within liberal humanism, between the mind and the body and culture and nature, as well as the opposition between the 'real' and representations of reality identified within poststructuralist approaches. Such distinctions are necessarily transported into the feminist economic frameworks which implicitly or explicitly rely upon the sex/gender distinction. It is therefore vital to reexamine the sex/gender distinction before developing the feminist poststructuralist position used to structure the analysis in Part Two of the book.

In this chapter, then, I examine the feminist poststructuralist criticisms of the sex/gender distinction and further develop the feminist poststructuralist framework, first considered in Chapter 1 of this book, as an alternative to the various feminist approaches to economics which rely on the sex/gender distinction and which were discussed in the previous two chapters. It is important for the reader to keep in mind, however, that I develop the feminist poststructuralist framework as a coexisting alternative to, rather than a replacement of, the range of feminist economic approaches which rely upon the sex/gender distinction. It is also important to note that, although the feminist poststructuralist framework draws on some ideas similar to those used by the various feminist economists discussed in Chapter 3, there are sufficient differences to warrant a separate analysis. Feminist poststructuralists, for example, deny the possibility of a truly objective stance in relation to some given reality, whereas the majority of the feminist economists considered in previous chapters have retained a commitment to some form of objectivity, whether it be Keller's 'dynamic objectivity', Harding's 'strong objectivity', or Nelson's complementarity approach. Feminist poststructuralists are also centrally concerned with the production of sexed bodies, their cultural significances and relationships to knowledges, whereas this concern is absent in, or at least not a clear focus of, the work of feminist economists discussed in previous chapters because of their implicit adherence to the sex/gender distinction. Indeed, it is an important task of this chapter to elucidate the argument that unless feminist economists theorize the production of sexed bodies, they will retain as unacknowledged foundations of their critique the very same foundations which establish the ability of economists to claim a 'universal', and hence unsexed, individual as the founding premise of neoclassical economics. In other words, I seek to convince the reader that, despite their protestations, feminist economists who rely upon a distinction between sex and gender are at some level supporting the notion that the theoretical and methodological framework of neoclassical economics, rather than being heavily implicated in the production of the economic, social and symbolic position of women and woman or the feminine, and indeed sexual difference itself, is simply a sexually-neutral descriptive and predictive science. This task is undertaken in the following four sections, in which the limitations of the sex/gender distinction and the degendering policy proposal are discussed (section 4.2); the notion of the body as a cultural product is developed (section 4.3); and the relationships between feminist economics and the sex/gender distinction are delineated (section 4.4). Section 4.5 concludes the chapter.

4.2. Limitations of the Sex/Gender Distinction

The conceptual foundations of the sex/gender distinction were discussed in Chapter 1. It was pointed out that this distinction served the feminist cause by providing a way of rejecting those rationalizations of women's social role which are premised upon the allegedly natural or biological basis of women's oppression. According to this approach, the essence of personhood is defined as ungendered or a gender-neutral consciousness, and bodies are viewed as *tabula rasa* and irrelevant to this essence (Gatens 1983: 144). Because women and men have a common consciousness, it is illegitimate to differentiate between them on the basis of their socialized gendered identities. The socialization process entails, in general, the allocation of feminine traits to females and masculine traits to males, but this allocation is viewed as arbitrary, in the sense of being socially produced and hence malleable, rather than biologically necessary. The goal of those who adopt this view of personhood is to adjust the socialization process so that gender as a characteristic of persons either disappears altogether (the 'androgyny' ideal) or gendered characteristics are not unilaterally allocated to the respective sexes, but shared equally by the sexes (the 'human' ideal). The sex/gender distinction, then, can be situated within liberal theory's privileging of consciousness over bodies, in that it is the abstract individual which is the object of projects of gender equality.[1] Such a distinction also underpins the degendered, universal economic agent assumed within the various strands of feminist economics which I considered in the previous chapters of this book. In this section I will examine the problems arising from the use of the sex/gender distinction.

The first problem with the sex/gender distinction is the slippage which occurs between asserting that gender is arbitrary in relation to sexed bodies and simultaneously drawing on an untheorized notion of the female body as a causal agent in women's oppression. This puts gender theorists in somewhat of an impasse, or even in a contradictory position: on the one hand they deploy Stoller's analysis of the sex/gender distinction to argue that gender is the cause of women's oppression and that the sexed body is incidental to gender identity, and on the other hand they maintain that women are oppressed as females. The body, or biological sex, is thereby surreptitiously transported back into the causal mechanism of women's oppression. If indeed the object of society's discriminatory practices is femininity, rather than feminine women, gender feminists are confronted with the strange conclusion that feminine women and feminine men are discriminated against in exactly the same ways, and the even more dubious inference that masculine women are not discriminated against at all. Furthermore, once 'patriarchy' is attributed to masculinity, 'what remains unexamined is men's place in the culture as *men*' (Grosz, quoted in Allen 1990: 38), leading Judith Allen to contend that feminists' use of the sex/gender distinction situates men as the 'dark continent of western knowledge formations' (ibid.). If, on the other hand, the body is re-admitted within the gender framework, gender feminists are confronted with the problem of distinguishing their own theory of oppression, based on the reflection of bodily difference in the social constructs of gender, from a conservative position that the social reflection of sexed bodies is natural and inevitable.

The sex/gender approach is further undermined once it is recognized that the general project of achieving sexual equality through a process of degendering (or re-education) invariably takes male achievements, values and standards as the norms to which women should aspire. Women are therefore implicitly told to strive 'to become the same as men, in a sense, "masculinized"' (Grosz 1994b: 89). In other words, women must fit into a set of structures and meanings which already exist and which are organized around male bodies. A successful career, for example, requires a full-time commitment, competitiveness and ambition. Without in any sense denying that women may be characterized by these attributes, they are nevertheless understood very differently when displayed by women rather than men. A career-oriented woman may be viewed as pushy and aggressive, and hence unnatural; as a sex object who will sleep her way to the top; or as an unreliable mother-to-be who will soon leave the workplace to have children even when behaving in the same ways as career-oriented men. Margaret Thatcher, for example, was vilified in terms such as 'Attila the Hen', despite being praised as a strong leader. As a woman, her quality of strong leadership could be attacked in this way precisely because she was not a man. The point is that 'the very same behaviour which makes a man appear well-adjusted, "attractive" and (socially) appropriate may well make a woman appear maladjusted, "unattractive" and (socially) inappropriate (Gatens 1989: 34; see also Pringle 1988: chs 2 and 3 for a discussion of the different relationships which arise between female secretaries and male and female 'bosses'; Cranny-Francis 1995: ch. 2). When the very same behaviours and traits are understood differently in relation to differently sexed bodies, it is clear that it is not femininity as such which is devalued, but femininity as displayed by women (Gatens 1983: 154). In short, the public sphere is made up of sets of preexisting characteristics and behaviours which are only valorized in relation to male bodies (see Thornton 1986).

Another problem arising from the male norm and the valorization of the male body in the public sphere is that, in reflecting the requirements of this male body, entry into the public sphere requires women to become 'like men' in terms of their needs and wants. Hence women do not have their needs, or at least those needs which are attributed to them within a patriarchal system, met. In Marion Tapper's words, the public sphere 'is organised around the needs of men, conceived as people abstracted from the private, domestic world, assumptions about manliness, and the assumption that it is men who occupy the public world' (1986: 42). Thus it is women rather than men who must deny their sexual specificity in the public sphere (Sullivan 1990: 184). Women who join the public sphere are required to be autonomous individuals who do not have prolonged commitments to childbearing, childcaring and other private sphere matters. They must delegate any requirements in relation to these activities to someone else, just as men have done, or, alternatively, they must perform the many necessary tasks themselves, a solution referred to as the 'double day'. Industrial reforms, such as the provision of maternity leave and childcare, enable women to replicate men's careers in the public sphere. However, this is exactly the point: women are required to adopt the lifestyles of men, in-so-far as men are free of domestic responsibilities, if they are to succeed as men have done in the public sphere (Tapper 1986: 42). Hence reforms which give women equality of opportunity, or the right to compete alongside men in the public sphere, impose a male norm on women. Demands for such reforms, moreover, create a tension within the liberal feminist position: 'The problem for the liberal feminist who recognises that the public is structured so as to favour some people (men) by virtue of their particularity and who argues that it should be changed to allow for sexual differences or to make it more congenial for women is that this is already to bring the theory of abstract individuals into question' (ibid.). In other words, the liberal feminist position contains something of a contradiction. The meaningful implementation of the 'equality of opportunity' concept requires women to be recognized as women, and hence the introduction of supplementary 'special measures'. The equality of presocial individuals with natural rights and freedoms is therefore undermined and the notion of the universal, abstract or ungendered individual is called into question (see Sullivan 1990; Threadgold 1990: 26; Lloyd 1984; Barrett 1988; Cornell 1992).

Still another problem is that legislation designed to achieve sex equality in the public sphere is inherently limited, and may even be counterproductive, because of the problematic recognition of difference which such laws allow. These sex discrimination laws were devised to eliminate gender as a relevant consideration in employment and other decisions by penalizing those who privileged men over women within the public sphere, and, perhaps more importantly, by re-educating or re-socializing others to recognize that discrimination on the basis of sex is unjustifiable. Such legislation, however, has deliberately exempted certain areas of activity and has thereby highlighted in a particularly striking manner the significance of the female body. For example, under the Australian Sex Discrimination Act (1984), the military was permitted to discriminate against women by restricting them to non-combat duties (Sullivan 1990: 180). Such an exemption suggests that the female body exhibiting the masculine trait of aggression, even when that aggression is mediated through modern technological weaponry, is still unacceptable in our society. The female body, it seems, simply cannot be read in this way at the present time. Mandatory maternity leave was also an explicit exclusion of the Act, leading Sullivan to comment that the ' "universality" of the public sphere is maintained only by displacing disruptive factors – such as women when they are pregnant and visibly not the same as men – out of the public sphere and into the private sphere. The efficiency of the public sphere is premised upon the ownership of an "unproblematic" male body' (ibid.: 186). It should of course be emphasized that the gender theorists who advocate this kind of legislation undoubtedly accepted many exemptions as a tactical measure to ensure that the legislation was passed (Sullivan 1990). However, the very need to have recourse to such tactics indicates that there exists a deep unease amongst legislators regarding the possibility that sex discrimination legislation may threaten the boundaries between the public and private spheres. As Sullivan has shown in the Australian case, the deployment of the notion of equality of opportunity, which allows many "private sphere" inequities to be ignored, as well as exemptions such as those of the military, religious bodies, and the operations of the Commonwealth Department of Social Security, served to calm such fears in the face of women's encroachment into the public realm (ibid.: 181; see also Thornton 1991).

It is also apparent that, although the Australian Sex Discrimination Act and similar legislation may offer legal redress to individual women who suffer discrimination, this legal redress also reinforces the male norm of the public sphere. To prove discrimination, the female worker must demonstrate that she can complete a specific job as efficiently as her male counterparts, which amounts to proving that her abilities do not mirror the employer's expectation of the abilities of women in general. If, for example, a job requires the lifting of heavy weights, and a woman capable of lifting such weights is denied the job on the basis of her sex, she has suffered discrimination. She can argue that the stereotype of the physical weakness of women does not apply to her. But to evaluate women in relation to men in this way assumes that the 'standards of an already-established world of work' are valid (Cornell 1992: 283). It also means that 'when women are "truly" different, they cannot claim that they have been discriminated against or treated unequally' (ibid.; see also the discussion of the famous Sears case in Scott 1988a; Schultz 1992; Thornton 1993). In short, then, sex discrimination legislation imposes a male norm because, at the same time as it recognizes difference in order to impose equality, it seeks to repudiate difference: women are equal to men only to the degree that they are like men (see Airo-Farulla 1991 for a discussion of legislation relating to Australian Aboriginal land rights).

Furthermore, although difference is only recognized by gender feminists in order to be effaced in the name of equality or sameness, the enforcement of sameness can produce absurd conclusions. An example of such a conclusion deriving from the rigid adherence to a notion of sameness is the US case of *Geduldig* v *Aiello*, which was a challenge to the exclusion of pregnancy from a disability insurance program. The court concluded that there was no sex discrimination, or, in Ann Scales's words, the court found 'that no discrimination exists if pregnant women and pregnant men are treated the same' (quoted in Graycar and Morgan 1990: 45). Similarly, in a South Australian case, exemption from the Sex Discrimination Act (SA) was denied to a restaurateur who wished to specify that female applicants, only, need apply to his advertisement for topless waiting staff.[2] In upholding the sex-neutrality of the term 'topless waiter/waitress' the South Australian Equal Opportunity Tribunal implied that bare breasts and bare male chests mean the same thing. The female body is to signify nothing – precisely the position advocated by gender feminists.

Finally, sex discrimination legislation based upon this denial of bodily specificity can be used against women as well as for women. This is due to the fact that sex discrimination legislation is, in the words of Renée Leon, 'an uneasy compromise between women's demands for substantive equality and the insistence of liberal individualism on formal equality' (1993: 89). Leon cites a number of Australian cases in which such legislation has been used to deem discriminatory and hence illegal those special measures aimed at offsetting existing inequalities between the sexes (Leon 1993: 89). For example, a badly scarred man argued that a recreation centre which had designated 90 minutes a week as time in which women only were to be able to use the facilities discriminated against men, including those with scars. The court agreed, citing the man's scars as a disadvantage of the same type as the disadvantage suffered by those women who felt they could not use the facilities in the presence of men (ibid.: 96–7). As Leon and others have pointed out, the liberal philosophy upon which sex discrimination legislation is based 'hinders the use of preferential treatment to bring about real equality' (ibid.: 103). Thus 'changing an unequal status quo is discrimination but allowing it to exist is not' (MacKinnon, quoted in Leon 1993: 103; see also Game 1984).

There are clearly a number of problems inherent within the sex/gender dichotomy and associated policy prescriptions. These problems arise for two related reasons. First, the sex/gender dichotomy and its rationalistic view of gendering and degendering draws on the same philosophical foundations as those theoretical systems which exclude and deny woman and the body, and hence leave in place the male norm, in both its gendered and embodied forms (see Caddick 1986). Specifically, this dichotomy draws upon the mind/body and culture/nature dichotomies which structure the public/private division as well as Western knowledges. Second, both gender theorists and the theories they criticize fail to pay due attention to the productivity and materiality of language and knowledges, that is, the production of 'the real' within discourses. Indeed, the sex/gender distinction draws on a distinction between the real and representations of the real (the empiricist view of language), with socially-constructed gender representations representing or re-presencing sex. If the real exists independently of its representations, then a policy of changing the representations (gender) independently of the real (sex) is possible. From a poststructuralist perspective, however, representations of the real produce the experience of the real (Ferrell 1991b: 7). If the real is constituted as meaningful through representations, then sexual difference rather than gender difference, and the sexualized rather than the gendered nature of bodies and knowledges, must be addressed. Elizabeth Grosz has gone so far as to argue that: 'Try as it may, a feminism of equality is unable adequately to theorize sexual and reproductive equality. And this, in turn, results in its inability to adequately theorize women's specific positions within the social and symbolic order' (1994b: 90). The feminist economists considered in Chapters 2 and 3 draw upon the problematic sex/gender distinction, and hence they are, perhaps unwittingly, wedded to the Enlightenment concept of the degendered and universal individual. For this reason, and despite the wealth of valuable work they undertake, they are constrained to argue that women must be 'added in' where previously they had been excluded. Feminist poststructuralism, by contrast, may be interpreted as having arisen from the 'crisis of the subject' which has resulted from the failure of demands by previously excluded groups such as women for inclusion within such subjectivity (Hazel 1994: 95–6). In the next section, I delineate the work of poststructuralist feminists who seek a way out of this impasse.

4.3. Feminist Poststructuralism and the Body as Cultural Product

Feminists who draw on poststructuralist insights have argued that sexual difference and sexed bodies are absolutely central to political, social and historical questions (Threadgold 1990: 30). As argued in the previous section, researchers who retain a commitment to the sex/gender distinction, and hence who fail to analyse embodied subjectivity, are in danger of simply replicating the very construction of the individual which establishes the male as the norm and as the only legitimate form of embodiment. They are therefore in danger of implicitly urging women to become more like men, or, indeed, to 'become men'. In other words, feminists who deny the relevance of sexual difference as an embodied difference construct theoretical systems and disciplinary critiques which are premised upon a one-sex model. The work of the feminist economists discussed in Chapters 2 and 3 is problematic for this reason. A number of poststructuralist feminists, by contrast, theorize the body and investigate the production of embodied, and hence sexed, subjectivity within discourses. Such feminists are sometimes referred to as 'feminists of difference' (Threadgold 1990: 27; Grosz 1994b: 90; Caddick 1986: 63), and as Grosz notes they, in a Derridean move, theorize a 'different difference' from the biological difference implied by the category of sex within the sex/gender distinction. In Grosz's words, within difference feminism, 'difference is seen not as difference from a pre-given norm but as pure difference, difference itself, difference with no identity' (1994b: 91). This means that they do not take the body as an inert biological given, but argue that the body itself is a cultural product. In this section I further criticize the sex/gender distinction by developing the poststructuralist ideas first raised in the introduction of this book, and, more specifically, articulate a poststructuralist 'feminism of difference' position which will be used in Part Two of the book. I seek to convince the reader of the importance of theorizing not only the oppression of women in economic discourse, but also the repression of the feminine and the intimate relationship between these forms of oppression (see Gatens 1991b: ch. 6).

Feminist poststructuralists dispute the notion that 'socially-constructed' gender identities are imposed on 'natural' sexed bodies. Such a notion, they argue, is the product of the mapping of the culture/nature, mind/body, and representation/real or ideology/materiality binary oppositions onto the sex/gender binary opposition. Feminist poststructuralists dispense with this mapping, contending that sexed bodies are products of culture – its discourses and institutional forms – and hence not 'natural'. More specifically, they draw on a post-Saussurian view of language to argue that both sexed bodies and gender identities are brought into being within language, that they are inseparable, and that sexed bodies only gain meaning within a differential relation. Thus the discursively-produced male and female bodies give meaning to their respective inscribed gender traits, and vice versa. This accounts for the claim made in the previous section that the female body exhibiting masculine characteristics is often deemed socially inappropriate, while the male body exhibiting these very same masculine characteristics is invariably deemed appropriate and therefore rewarded (see Gatens 1989: 34). For example, a woman exhibiting the masculine trait of raising her voice during an argument may be labelled hysterical, whereas a man exhibiting the same trait would be seen as forceful. In each case, the gendered characteristic is produced as meaningful only in relation to the body. This view of the relationship between sex and gender has led Grosz to argue that sexed bodies are 'naturally social' (1987: 7) and Moira Gatens to insist that to 'speak of a body as somehow being outside of culture and its influences is nonsensical – already, to speak/write about the body (even the biological body) is to subject it to language, itself a cultural product' (1989: 43). Similarly, Judith Butler contends that 'gender is not to culture as sex is to nature; gender is also the discursive/cultural means by which "sexed nature" or "a natural sex" is produced and established as "prediscursive," prior to culture, a politically neutral surface *on which* culture acts' (1990: 7).

Male and female bodies, then, are not prediscursive and immutable natural entities upon which gender traits are mapped. The meaning of the body, its very experience of itself, its capabilities, traits and characteristics, are products of the discourses in which it is articulated. This philosophical position can be extended by drawing on Irigaray's account of morphology, where 'morphology' is a third or middle term, which disobeys the laws of opposition by inhabiting both sex (body) and gender (mind), and hence breaks down these binary oppositions (Gatens 1991b: 115; see also Grosz 1993b). Note, however, that this third term is not simply a synthesis of the two opposed terms. Each of the terms is a condition of the possibility of the other, and hence they cannot be combined to make a complete whole. Since the opposed terms cannot be summed together, the binary opposition is exceeded rather than collapsed into one term. Feminist economists who seek to combine masculinity and femininity to form a complete whole, a 'human' economics, have failed to recognize this. In a morphological view of the subject, then, the experience of one's body is a lived experience shaped by discourse, rather than a set of universal and unalterable facts. This experience is in no way dictated by a socially-constructed consciousness which is still logically separate from the body. Consciousness or gender

consciousnesses, thereby producing particular kinds of consciousnesses. For example, the disciplinary regimes of the military, the school, the hospital and the prison produce or actively construct particular kinds of corporeal subjectivity: 'The body [of the soldier or the worker, for example] does not automatically align itself into a clockwork composition of actions: it has to be trained to do so. Thus we cannot say that discipline is guided by a "false" or ideological conception of the human body. Rather, it actively seeks to cultivate a certain type of body on the basis of knowledge considered "true" ' (McHoul and Grace 1993: 69; see also Bartky 1988). This process of inscription produces subjectivity by constructing the interior from the outside. For example, Foucault argues that the major effect of the Panopticon, the model prison designed by Jeremy Bentham, is to 'induce in the inmate a state of conscious and permanent visibility that ensures the automatic functioning of power' (1979: 201). This state is brought about by the architecture of the prison, which allows the gaoler to watch the prisoners without himself being observed. Hence, whether or not the gaoler is in fact watching, prisoners become the object of surveillance; they become their own gaolers, and this state of being conscious of observation 'is a sign that the tight, disciplinary control of the body has gotten a hold on the mind as well' (Bartky 1988: 63). Inscription is used in this metaphoric sense, but also in a more 'literal' sense. Hairstyles, makeup and exercise, for example, constitute regimes of discipline to which women, in particular, are subjected (see the discussion in Bartky 1988): 'Food, dieting, exercise, and movement provide meanings, values, norms, and ideals that the subject actively ingests, incorporating social categories into the physiological interior. Bodies *speak*, without necessarily talking, because they become coded with and as signs. They speak social codes. They become *intextuated*, narrativised; simultaneously, social codes, laws, norms and ideals become *incarnated*' (Grosz 1993a: 199). Note, however, that this Foucauldian approach does not entail that 'subjects are passive dupes of the discursive formations that define their subjectivity' (Hekman 1990a: 72). That is, resistance to such inscriptions is possible because the agency/structure dichotomy is disrupted rather than reinforced. Feminism, for example, is a discourse which has been created out of women's resistance to patriarchal discourses of femininity (ibid.: 73).[5]

The second main approach taken by feminists seeking to theorize the body as a cultural product draws on the Freudian view of the subject. In this case, instead of the 'inside' of the body being produced by the 'outside', which is a way of characterizing the Foucauldian approach, the 'outside' is produced by the 'inside'.[6] The 'inside' is the narcissistic ego, which is 'like an internal screen onto which the illuminated images of the body's outer surface are projected . . . The ego is thus an image of the body's *significance* for the subject' (Grosz 1993a: 200). Gatens has developed this position in particular detail. Embodied subjectivity entails not simply the material or anatomical body but an imaginary body, or a body which is organized around introjected images. This psychic image of the body is a product of the culturally specific meanings, values and symbols of the subject's social milieu. More specifically, the body is constructed by a 'shared language; the shared psychical significance and privileging of various zones of the body (e.g. the mouth, the anus, the genitals); and common institutional practices and discourses (e.g. medical, juridical, and educational) on and through the body' (1983: 152). The phenomena of phantom limbs and hysterical paralysis are used to illustrate the way in which it is the imaginary body, rather than the anatomical body *per se*, which is experienced (ibid.; see also Sacks 1985). Such symptoms establish the body as the site of signification, subverting the binary opposition of the real and representations of the real (Ferrell 1991a: 175). Sex and gender, then, are not arbitrarily connected – rather, the former is a product of the latter. It is, however, important to note that these shared values are not immutable and ahistorical. They are historically and culturally specific and may be changed.

Poststructuralist feminists have also drawn on Lacan's re-reading of Freud for an account of embodied subjectivity. According to Lacan ([1949] 1977), the ego comes into existence when the infant identifies with an image of itself, whether reflected in a mirror or in the gaze of its mother (hence, the 'mirror stage'). Thus the inauguration of the ego involves a split between the infant's physical experience of fragmentation and lack of motor coordination, and the coherence and unity of the body image or visual *gestalt* in the mirror: 'The reflection of the body is, then, salutary in that it is unitary and localized in time and space' (Lemaire 1977: 81; see also Grosz 1990b: ch. 2). This identification with something which is not the infant itself is replicated in a second 'splitting' which occurs when the child takes up the speaking position of 'I', at which time the child becomes a (sexed) subject-in-language. To meaningfully use the term 'I' involves a splitting because 'I' represents the subject in language, but, like the image, is not equivalent to the subject. Thus Lacan has argued that 'language speaks us', a position in stark contrast to the empiricist view of language where subjects speak language: 'It is not the subject who speaks; rather, the subject is, as it were, spoken through by discourse, law and culture' (Grosz 1992: 411). It is this second splitting which creates the unconscious; to take up a speaking position requires the repression of anti-social or pleasure-seeking impulses (Rowley and Grosz

1990: 185–7). The unconscious ensures that the subject, or consciousness, can never fully know itself; thus 'consciousness cannot be identified with the whole of subjectivity' (ibid.: 186). Note that the subject is thereby decentred, as in the Foucauldian and Derridean approaches, with radical implications for traditional conceptions of truth, objectivity and knowledge, or, in short, the knowing subject of traditional epistemology.[7]

The third approach to the production of embodied sexual difference draws upon the Derridean strand of poststructuralist philosophy, and, more specifically, Derridean deconstruction. As discussed in Chapter 1, poststructuralism is premised upon the idea that there is no known reality outside the language which constructs it. Meaning, and hence reality, cannot exist outside language. The conception of a reality preexisting language relies on the binary opposition of presence and absence. When language is viewed as a neutral tool of communication, it is supposed to name things and to stand in place of, or represent, or make present, those things in their physical absence. For feminist poststructuralists, this binary opposition of presence/absence, or logocentrism, is itself structured around the binary opposition of man/not-man, or phallocentrism. Indeed, phallocentric representations of woman are part of the very foundations of logocentrism. Such feminist poststructuralists argue that the self-presence and self-identity of masculinity which underpin phallocentric discourses are reliant upon, and derive their privilege from, the exclusion of femininity. In other words, man is the transcendental signifier within phallocentric knowledges: the 'process of evacuating his body from his "objects" requires a space of hierarchised reflection in which the male can look at social, political and conceptual relations from above – the position of God' (Gross 1986b: 79). Other important binary oppositions upon which this phallocentric 'reality' relies are those between culture and nature and between mind and body (and hence sex and gender), with the privileged A term in each binary opposition gaining its meaning through an underlying schema of sexual difference. Sexed subjectivity is therefore discursively produced within a system of binary structures. The way in which these binary oppositions operate to construct embodied subject positions can be further elaborated upon by employing the Derridean idea of deconstruction. It is also important to review this material as it plays an important role in the analysis of Part Two of this book.

Derridean deconstruction is the mechanism or process by which the exclusion of the not-A terms in these binary oppositions – absence, not-man, nature and body – and the interdependence between the A and not-A terms, are identified and disrupted. Deconstruction does not destroy meaning, as is sometimes supposed; rather, meaning is analysed in terms of its constitutive exclusions. In Barbara Johnson's words, 'the word "de-construction" is closely related not to the word "destruction" but to the word "analysis", which etymologically means "to undo" ' (1981: xiv). Thus deconstruction is an analysis of the exclusions which enable a text to make its arguments: 'The critique reads backwards from what seems natural, obvious, self-evident, or universal, in order to show that these things have their history, their reasons for being the way they are, their effects on what follows from them, and that the starting point is not a (natural) given but a (cultural) construct' (ibid.: xv). In other words, deconstruction does not destroy meaning, or demonstrate the flaws, errors or contradictions of texts, nor does it aim to reveal the stupidities of an author (ibid.). It is a process of unravelling the foundations upon which an argument is based: it 'tries to reveal the *necessity* with which what a text says is bound up with what it cannot say' (Grosz 1990a: 97). Just as deconstruction is not the elimination of meaning, it is also not an attempt to create a new truth. Rather, it is an unveiling of the political commitments of discourses (ibid.: 101). For this reason, feminists have found deconstruction a useful concept in terms of revealing and disrupting the self-presence of masculine subjectivity where that subjectivity relies upon the exclusion of the feminine: 'Deconstruction aims to show that the other is always implied in any definition of the self, that is, the self is not identical with itself' (Gatens 1991b: 112). Masculinity, then, relies for its identity upon its own constructions of femininity – there is no essence of either masculinity or femininity. Disrupting the self-presence of masculinity will have important implications for the way femininity and woman, and hence women's lives, may be thought and enacted.

Deconstruction involves three strategies. The first is the identification of the binary opposition, and its constitutive role in a text, and the second is a reversal of the terms so that the subordinate term is placed in the privileged position. These strategies leave in place the binary structure and hence fail to challenge the coercive force or investments which enable the binary opposition to operate. In Grosz's words: 'Simply asserting that difference has primacy over identity, or that the female is privileged over the male, remains merely wishful thinking, unless it can somehow combat the historically accumulated power and dominance that has preserved their hierarchical relation over centuries' (1989: 30). A necessary third step is therefore a displacement of the binary structure through the creation of a third term, 'hinge word' or 'undecidable'. Such terms 'cannot be said to be one or other of the previous terms, either because they are referring to the conditions under which the pair of terms is possible at all, or else because it is not possible to say that they are, or are not, one or other of the two terms'

(Whitford 1991a: 127). The third term therefore confounds the structure of the opposition by simultaneously inhabiting both the A and not-A sides of the binary opposition, displacing it by positioning the not-A term at the core of the A term as its logical condition (ibid.; see also Gross 1986b: 74; Cornell 1991; Diprose 1991a; Whitford 1991a: 126–7).

An example of such a procedure is given by Derrida's (1974) deconstruction of the binary opposition of presence or identity and absence or difference. *Différance* is a third term (a neologism coined by Derrida) which, by invoking both 'difference' and 'deferral', refers to 'the systematic play of differences' and therefore undermines the self-presence of all terms (Derrida 1981: 27). As outlined in Chapter 1 above, no term can be self-present when its meaning relies on an infinite chain of signifiers. The flight of an arrow provides a simple and concrete application of this deconstruction. An arrow is in one particular place at every particular moment during its flight. Thus, although it seems sensible to say that an arrow is in motion throughout its flight, in fact its movement is never present at any particular moment, and to say that its stillness at a particular moment is really movement is to rely upon what has come before. Movement is only present, then, because of the difference between the present and the past (the absence of the present). Thus, in this and (Derrida would argue) in all instances of presence, absence supports and inhabits presence (Culler 1983: 94–5). *Différance*, then, is the very condition of identity (see Derrida 1982a).[8]

Subjectivity is therefore also an effect of *différance*. The fulness of meaning is always deferred, and self-presence itself requires absence (see especially Derrida 1981: 28–9). Feminist poststructuralists who draw on Derrida's work argue specifically that the presence of man is underpinned by the absence of woman. This hierarchical relationship, or phallocentrism, is a result of the way in which sexual difference is represented within (and hence produced by) metaphors, texts, theories and discourses. It is important to note that such representations are not confined to those discourses or theoretical systems which are concerned with sexuality or sexed bodies, such as Freudian psychoanalytic theory in which the male body and sexuality are represented as complete or phallic and the female body and sexuality as lacking (the phallus). Instead, the hierarchical relationship arises in 'all theory which represents women or the feminine in terms dependent on men or the masculine' (Gross 1986b: 71), including those knowledges premised upon an abstract or universal individual. Indeed, phallocentrism necessarily implies the existence of a one-sex model, since it is only man which can claim to be present, self-defining and self-identical. Woman, on the other hand, has meaning only in relation to man, as its lack or absence, and hence has no status as an independent, different or autonomous sex. To refigure Irigaray's (1985) famous formulation, it is 'the sex which is not the one'. Phallocentrism, then, is 'a logic of the Same' (Kirby 1994: 130), in which the masculine occupies both sides of the binary opposition (Butler 1994a: 152). In order for knowledges such as neoclassical economics to function as universally applicable, and for sexual difference to be irrelevant to that functioning, the feminine is excluded. It should be kept in mind, however, that this excluded femininity is not something which pre-exists those knowledges. It is produced within those knowledges as their foundation, and hence feminists cannot simply incorporate it without disturbing those very structures which enable those knowledges to function (see Moi 1989).

Phallocentrism also structures knowledge production and the subject position of the knower. Man connotes the presence of the subject (of knowledge), mind and reason, and the corresponding absence of the object (of knowledge), body and emotions. It is these absences which structure knowledge and enable the production of knowledge as unbiased representations of the 'real world'. The illusion of perspectiveless knowledge requires the fantasy that knowledge producers are 'disembodied', a fantasy supported by the role of woman as body. The feminine must be disavowed because self-presence requires autonomous definition. In the words of Gross: 'the attempts by sciences and knowledges to acquire an "objective", "neutral", "universal", and perspectiveless position is [*sic*] a fantasy possible only because man's "occupation" of and containment in his body are unproblematically assumed and left unavowed' (1986b: 79). Femininity, then, takes on the role of body or nature, performing the bodily functions and tasks which the male body will not perform, to enable masculinity to be free of its body, and able to produce and operate within culture and knowledge (Butler 1994a: 161). The feminine is therefore argued by poststructuralist feminists to be the necessary but disavowed foundation of 'truth'. It is important to keep in mind, however, that the argument is not that the male body preexists phallocentric discourses and operates to structure them in its image – as singular, self-present and disembodied. Rather, there is an isomorphic relation between phallocentric knowledges and masculinity; knowledges structure the male body as present, active and phallic (and the female body as absence). In Vicki Kirby's words, 'Phallocentrism pretends that knowledge is sexually indifferent, that the materiality of the body and the political significance which informs its form as the *lived* morphology of difference, is of no account' (1987: 51–2).

Embodied subjectivity, then, is discursively produced as sexed subjectivity, whether this production is interpreted from a Foucauldian, psychoanalytic or Derridean perspective. The way in which the sexed body is experienced (its morphology) is critically dependent upon the meaning of femininity and masculinity in the socio-symbolic order, the body itself being produced as a discursive effect of discourse (Grosz 1989: xix). This is not to say that we cannot meaningfully speak of women; the real is not eliminated, rather it is produced within discourse. Seemingly natural categories are constructed within discourses, and discourses then appear to recognize, or represent, categories of things which preexist them. Thus the elimination of the unitary category of 'woman' as a preexisting referent which is the source of the meaning of woman implies that particular discourses, texts, practices and institutions must be examined for the way in which 'woman' is produced as a meaningful and natural category. As Carol Smart has noted of feminist analyses of law, it is important that feminist theory 'go beyond analyses of law which stop at the point of "recognition" that men (as a taken-for-granted biological category) make and implement laws whilst women (as a taken-for-granted biological category) are oppressed by them. We need to consider the ways in which law constructs and reconstructs masculinity and femininity, and maleness and femaleness, and contributes routinely to a common-sense perception of difference which sustains the social and sexual practices which feminism is attempting to challenge' (1990: 201). Implementing Smart's challenge in relation to neoclassical economics is the subject of Part Two of this book.

In the next section, this feminist poststructuralist approach will be used to analyse the various strands of feminist economics delineated in Chapters 2 and 3 above in order to distinguish clearly between their projects and the project of this book. However, before proceeding to this task, the implications of this approach for the controversial issue of essentialism must be briefly reviewed. The feminist poststructuralist contention that the 'gendered' body is a discursive production requires a reassessment of the concepts of 'sexual difference' and 'essentialism'. Essentialism 'entails the belief that those characteristics defined as women's essence are shared in common by all women at all times: it implies a limit on the variations and possibilities of change – it is not possible for a subject to act in a manner contrary to her nature' (Grosz 1994b: 84). Those who adopt the sex/gender distinction and the associated degendering policy prescription are compelled to dismiss sexual difference, in the sense of an embodied difference, as an important variable in determining social activity. Indeed, the notion is considered dangerous, since it implies that the position of women in relation to men is a product of biology and hence in some way natural and immutable.

Gender theorists have articulated this position in what may be called the same/difference or equality/difference debate, a debate which hinges on feminists' supposed choice between 'endorsing "equality" or its presumed antithesis "difference" ' (Scott 1988a: 38).

The same/difference debate is about whether women and men are fundamentally the same, the position deriving from an argument that gender is an addition to an otherwise unsexed consciousness, or whether men and women are fundamentally different, the position deriving from the privileging of the sexed body as the essence of a person's humanity. In other words, feminist theorists have debated whether sexual difference is environmental or essential, and these causal mechanisms have been understood such that *either* one *or* the other must be the explanation of women's oppression. In this context, if one does not believe that socialized gender is the cause of women's oppression, then one must be an essentialist. What is objectionable about essentialists, from within the frame of the sex/gender distinction, is that they map femininity onto femaleness, and hence invoke the very mechanisms by which women have been oppressed by men – their biological role in reproduction. However, essentialists of this kind deny that they fall into this trap, since they are affirming the value of the female body rather than repudiating this value as does patriarchal culture: they 'affirm femaleness by bringing "social" gender closer to "natural" sex, in response to the male norm which is thereby unwittingly retained when gender is viewed as "floating free of sex" ' (Lloyd 1989: 15). From the mid-1970s, such an affirmation of the female body has been undertaken within a variant of radical feminism known as 'cultural feminism'. Cultural feminists are committed to preserving rather than challenging gender differences, a preservation which is based on a celebration of a natural or innate femininity. This femininity is opposed to the innate 'rapaciousness or barrenness of male biology' (Echols 1984: 52; see also Alcoff 1989). Cultural feminists therefore argue that, although patriarchy distorts natural femininity, natural masculinity is always misogynist. Essentialists of this kind, then, argue that it is the cultural denigration of femininity and all that it entails – its caring, nurturing and life-affirming nature – which should be the object of feminist intervention, unlike gender theorists, who argue for changes in the gender identities themselves and hence for equality as the object of feminist intervention.

Gender theorists, then, are suspicious of those feminists who take the female body as the central element of their analyses, and it is the sex/gender distinction which imposes this limitation upon them. Specifically, gender theorists assume that only biological accounts of the body are possible

(Grosz 1993b: 195). This is because the sex/gender distinction is itself logocentric: it requires a distinction between the real, 'things in the world' or materiality (sexed bodies), and representations of the real, the interpretations which are made of things in the world or ideology (gender). For precisely this reason bodies are viewed as separate from theory, which, as Ferrell has noted, leads to the paradox that 'the very thing that sexual difference cannot afford to be about, in feminist theory, is the difference between men's and women's bodies' (1991a: 173). However, as Grosz has commented, the gender feminist approach 'is not the answer to essentialism for it conceals its own commitment to essentialism. It says that sex is essential but gender is constructed. Yet, if gender is constructed out of sex then it is as implicated as sex in essentialism' (1994a: 16). The category of gender is often, if not always, referred back to sex (see Butler 1990: ch. 1), producing the 'confused and confusing picture of a body which is independent of all social construction nevertheless exerting a causal force on consciousness' (Lloyd 1989: 20; see also Adams and Minson 1990). The point is that both sex and gender are socially constructed.

Gender feminists who seek to deny the importance of the body are also confronted with the paradox that such a strategy undermines their claim to represent women. As Grosz, commenting on Toril Moi's (1985: 139) well-cited argument that the French poststructuralist feminist Luce Irigaray is essentialist, explains: 'if women cannot be characterized in any general way, if all there is to femininity is socially produced, how can feminism be taken seriously? What justifies the assumption that women are oppressed as a sex? What, indeed, does it mean to talk about women as a category? If we are not justified in taking women as a category, what political grounding does feminism have?' (1994b: 93). Thus the dichotomy between the social construction of gender and the biological given of sex undermines the political grounds of a feminism which seeks to represent the interests of 'women'. Instead such a politics must be based on the representation of feminine persons, or perhaps oppressed persons in general. This, to a certain extent, justifies the claim by non-feminist critics of neoclassical economics that feminist economics is no more than an offshoot of existing unorthodox frameworks which consider exploitation in terms of class and/or race. It is apparent, then, that feminist economists must emphasize the role played by sexual difference in their analyses if they are to demarcate the boundaries of their research in a meaningful way. The feminist poststructuralist position presented here achieves this end by locating femininity and masculinity as embodied, produced within discourse, and constitutive of subjectivity (see Grosz 1993b: 195).[9] It therefore offers a non-essentialist grounding for a feminist politics which opens the body to multiple readings, and hence challenges discourses such as sociobiology which condemn women to patriarchal meanings of bodies, as well as knowledges which claim as their object the 'universal individual', such as neoclassical economics.

There is therefore a clear distinction between essentialists who affirm the female body as if they have found its true meaning (women are loving, nurturing, etc.), and feminists of difference who affirm the importance of the body as constructed in discourse without claiming to know the essence of woman or of sexual difference. The feminist poststructuralists discussed in this section, then, although many times accused of essentialism, are in fact theorizing the way in which the sexed body is produced within phallocentric discourses and are thereby pointing to the possibility of delivering woman from its phallocentric representations. This strategy is a product of the recognition that the referent woman 'is dependent upon the systems of representation in which she is given meaning' (Cornell 1991: 33; see also Irigaray 1985; Gross 1986b, 1986e; Grosz 1987, 1989, 1993a 1993b; Gatens 1983, 1996a: ch. 6; Braidotti 1989; Whitford 1989, 1991a, 1991b; Dallery 1994; Elam 1994; Schor 1994a, 1994b). Such feminists reject both sides of the sex/gender and same/different binary oppositions. They view the ideal of equality, which involves reducing difference to sameness, and the ideal of difference, when reduced to biological difference, as problematic, since both replicate phallocentrism (see Gatens 1991b: 120). At this point, a reappraisal of feminist economics is in order, and is to this task that I now turn.

4.4. Feminist Economics: a Reappraisal

In this section I employ the themes delineated under the rubric of feminist poststructuralism to reappraise the various strands of feminist economics analysed in the previous chapters. The feminist economists considered in Chapters 2 and 3 have, with one or two exceptions, retained a two-fold commitment to achieving the goal of objective knowledge and to analysing the economic position of women within the sex/gender framework. Indeed, the deployment of the sex/gender distinction at some stage in an overall quest for objective knowledge about women in the economy has almost been the defining feature of feminist economics over the last two decades. Ferber and Nelson (1993b) call this approach the 'feminist constructionist' position, and argue that it is the most acceptable position to take in relation to economics. However, as has been emphasized, this approach has its limitations. The sex/gender distinction is intimately connected with the mind/body, culture/nature and real/representations distinctions, and these oppositions undermine, or at least produce limitations for, a feminist economics which ignores their productive effects. Specifically, gender feminists who draw upon these distinctions to improve the position of women in society are complicit in the production of sexual difference as complementarity, lack or opposition. They therefore implicitly or explicitly support the notion of a universal individual, without acknowledging that this individual is always sexed as well as gendered, and that the current economic position of women can be seen to consist in the fact that its sex is male. Feminist poststructuralists, in contrast, contend that discourses and the binary oppositions upon which they rely are productive – their representations of sexual difference have real effects in terms of sexed subjectivity and the possibilities of change. Each strand of feminist economics will now be discussed in turn.

Those feminist economists who have undertaken equity studies to consider the problem of the under-representation of women within the ranks of academic economics have predominately attributed this outcome to socialized gender characteristics (see section 2.2 above). Specifically, women are discouraged from entering the profession both because they are socialized not to have a preference for economics and because employers are socialized to discriminate against women. The solution is a programme of re-education, combined with anti-discrimination legislation. It was for this reason that the American Economic Association formed the Committee on the Status of Women in the Economics Profession. Although the policy prescriptions promoted by those undertaking equity studies have undoubtedly increased women's access to academic positions, there are a number of difficulties with this solution. The main problem is that women are required to become 'like men' in order to gain access to and be incorporated into subject positions structured around the needs and interests of men. In other words, concepts like merit and equality are premised upon a male norm and are not sex-neutral (Thornton 1989; see also Bassi 1990). Women can conform to the requirements of academic careers, but in doing so they take up a subject position already coded as masculine. They do not fit these subject positions in the same way as men because sexed bodies are always signified, and, in a phallocentric society, female bodies are signified as lacking in relation to male bodies. Indeed, to the extent that women have home-related responsibilities which men do not have, they are literally lacking in terms of the structure of a full-time career which assumes the existence of a full-time support staff in the home. To outlaw questions such as 'How do you think you will fulfil your duties when you have children?' and decisions such as failure to hire a qualified woman who is childless but of childbearing years does not in fact change those significations of the female body, although they have undoubtedly helped individual women.

The neoclassical economists who have incorporated women as objects of research through the extension of the discipline's subject matter to the family and related economic decision-making were collectively labelled the 'Chicago school of feminist economists' in section 2.3 above. Such economists implicitly or explicitly draw on the 'sex' side of the sex/gender distinction by attributing women's economic outcomes to brute biological fact and therefore denying the importance of socially-constructed gender identities.[10] On this basis, many feminist economists have argued that such economic work should not be called feminist. In the words of Barbara Bergmann: 'To say that the "new home economists" are not feminist in their orientation would be as much of an understatement as to say that Bengal tigers are not vegetarians' (1987c: 133). However, although I recognize the force of Bergmann's argument, it could be argued that just as cultural feminists are feminist, so the Chicago economists who have undertaken research on women are feminist. There are many feminisms, and those who seek to incorporate women into the neoclassical framework, as the Chicago economists and others have done, are feminist empiricists in the same way as those who criticize their assumptions using the same framework and methodology. Bergmann's evaluation is compelling, however, when she assesses the feminist content of such empiricist research on the basis of outcomes or policy proposals and the degree to which they retain a commitment to 'patriarchal' conceptions of biological sex. She argues that the new home economists do not see any need for change: they declare 'feminists' proposals for the amelioration of women's condition to be devoid of economic sense [and they are] hostile to the suggestion that the economic position of women needs improvement' (ibid.: 132). Bergmann argues that, in contrast to the quietism of the Chicago school, those who she regards as true feminist economists have set for themselves the task of designing a more equitable future. She contends that what 'really distinguishes feminist economists is their view that the present assignment to economic duties based on sex is unfair and should be eliminated' (ibid.: 145).

Those critics of the Chicago feminist approach who retain a commitment to traditional scientific methodology adhere to a liberal feminist framework in which differential economic outcomes across the sexes are viewed as a function of socialized gender roles rather than originating in biology (see section 2.4 above). Such feminists retain the neoclassical agent and model 'women' as 'rational economic men' who face various discriminatory practices which restrict their entry into the public sphere and force their wages below their true marginal product. They argue, for example, that women suffer both direct and indirect discrimination because employers and incumbent workers in the public sphere are socialized to believe that women are either less productive than men or that their 'natural' role is in the home; that women are socialized from a very early age to have preferences for home activities and childbirth, and that these preferences are reinforced in their economic activity; and that parents are socialized to invest less human capital in their daughters compared to their sons. This research has resulted in a number of sophisticated theoretical models and empirical work, which in turn have provided valuable support for legislative acts designed both to 'degender' economic actors and to set in place institutional structures to assist those who have been historically disadvantaged. However, both the 'rational economic man' upon which these models are based and their policy implications are premised upon phallocentric oppositions which would have us believe that the bodies of economic actors are irrelevant. The problems with this failure to grasp the importance of sexually-specific bodies were discussed above in section 4.2.

Those feminist economists who seek to alter the neoclassical framework by adjusting or even displacing the core assumptions of that framework also retain a commitment to the sex/gender distinction (see section 3.2 above). They believe that the core assumptions which construct the centrepiece of neoclassical economics, the rational economic individual, are biased toward masculinity. Hence the rational, selfish and radically separate agent who expresses exogenously-determined preferences in the market is devoid of characteristics traditionally associated with femininity, such as emotion, altruism, caring and connectedness. They also maintain that the neoclassical theorist selectively relaxes the assumptions associated with rational economic man when considering activities traditionally associated with women, such as those in the private sphere (where altruism is made to predominate). The gender-biased neoclassical theory consequently excludes or distorts important aspects of reality, especially those elements which have an important bearing on the position of women in society. Feminists who adhere to these beliefs therefore call for an overhaul of the neoclassical framework, or even for its complete replacement. Theoretical developments of this nature have been made independently of the feminist critique, for example, in experimental work which attempts to theorize unselfish contributions to public good expenditures. Hence, through both this kind of work and the feminist critique, shifts are occurring in neoclassical economics (reminding one of Gatens's suggestion that feminists, and in this case, others, may be disrupting more than they think). However, these suggestions require a degendering of the economic actor at the theoretical level, and hence open up the refigured neoclassical economic individual to the same criticisms as those delineated above.

Feminist economists who draw on object relations theory to argue for a feminist standpoint also rely on the sex/gender distinction (see section 3.3 above). Recall that object relations theory posits the role of women in childrearing as the cause of the development of different types of selves. Men are radically separate and autonomous, while women are more connected and relational, and hence have different views of the world. Men's view of the world and their relationship to it becomes reflected in the form of scientific knowledge. Feminist economists drawing on this theory point out that economics reflects this masculine personality structure, and seek to expand the set of acceptable methods by which knowledge is produced, as well as to open economics up to alternative viewpoints based on other personality structures. They therefore retain a commitment to a prediscursive reality and maintain that masculine bias has skewed male economists' perceptions of this reality. Feminists, particularly those who use psychoanalytic theory, have criticized object relations theory on the basis of its requirement for patriarchal gender differentiation to preexist the mother/father/child relationship in order to explain patriarchal gender differentiation. Gender stereotypes are then absorbed by infants, who reproduce those gender stereotypes (Brennan 1989b: 8). In Jacqueline Rose's words, object relations theory 'sets itself to question sexual *roles*, but only within the limits of an assumed sexual *identity*' (1982: 37n). It can be argued, then, that object relations theory is culturally rather than biologically essentialist. It is unable to account for women who choose not to 'reproduce mothering', or men who do not conform to 'male objectivity', such as Nietzsche, Marx, Freud and Derrida (Moi 1989: 191), and hence, paradoxically, 'the very psychological theory which enables Keller and Bordo to launch their research into the problem of knowledge in the first place, in the end radically prevents them from breaking out of the straitjacket of patriarchal binary thought' (ibid.: 194). Toril Moi argues that Keller's object-relations account of the origins of knowledge, for example, posits *separate* systems of emotion and cognition from the start. But this is precisely the problem which needs to be solved: 'We should also bear in mind the way in which the reason/emotion (or head/heart) split is deeply bound up with the mind/body division (needless to say, both oppositions are read through the male/female paradigm). Feminism needs a theory of knowledge which undoes and displaces *both* dualisms, not one that in a mistaken fear of biologism rejects all efforts to include the body in thought' (ibid.: 199; see also Gatens 1983). Like equality theorists, then, those who adhere to object relations theory seek a transformation of socially-constructed gender traits and characteristics, but without challenging the binary oppositions which construct the phallocentric meaning of sexual difference.

The feminist economics advocated by Nelson also relies on the sex/gender distinction (see section 3.4). Nelson draws upon object relations theory to explain the social denigration of feminine-identified characteristics. This enables her to retain a social rather than a biological explanation of the value attached to masculinity, since, like other gender feminists, Nelson seeks to avoid being accused of essentialism. For example, in explaining the difference between feminist, feminine and female, she denies that 'women somehow "by nature" think differently from men, and would "bring something different" to economics' (1996a: 37). She argues that, in a society characterized by 'sexist expectations', men and women do have different experiences, but this is a result of social rather than biological conditions (ibid.). Her framework is also premised upon a distinction between the real, things in the world, or materiality, and representations of the real, the interpretations which are made of things in the world, or some level of ideology or ideas. The body, its meanings and the value attached to its meanings – up is good, down is bad – are real, while metaphorical linkages between the body and its meanings and gender are representations of the real. Nelson therefore leaves in place a binary structure despite her attempts to displace the structure through the creation of synthesis terms which combine the positive masculine and positive feminine characteristics to form a complete whole. Her work can be interpreted as asserting the primacy of the excluded F+ terms over the privileged M– terms. Although Nelson seeks to integrate the F+ and M+ terms into a complete methodological apparatus and a 'fully human economics', her retention of the binary structure is indicated by condemnation of, and exclusion from economics of, 'mushy sentimentality', 'sloppiness' (1992b: 110) and 'touchy-feely mysticism' (1993b: 142). It is therefore questionable whether she really addresses the coercive force or investments which enabled the binary oppositions to operate and structure economics in the first place. As she argues, 'I propose that we accept that terms like "hard," "logical," "scientific," "precise," are both masculine-identified and describe legitimate goals of economic practice' (1992b: 110–1). As Anni Dugdale has argued of feminist standpoint theory in a different context, Nelson's work 'leaves uncontested the very dichotomies which structure sexual difference and the current practice of science – culture/nature, masculine/feminine, active/passive, objective/subjective, reason/intuition' (1990: 57).

The final group of feminist economists to be considered in light of the sex/gender distinction consists of those scholars who draw upon the 'rhetoric of economics' (McCloskey 1985). These economists also rely on the sex/gender dichotomy, arguing that certain methodological claims made within neoclassical economics are persuasive because they are associated with masculinity as a social formation. Hence their approach can also be criticized along the lines outlined in this chapter. However, unlike the feminist economists considered so far, McCloskey and her colleagues have claimed to be moving toward a postmodernist approach to their subject matter and therefore must be considered in some sense to be aligned to the project of this book. In other words, although they do not focus upon the production of sexed, rather than gendered, subjectivity and the need to displace the sex/gender distinction, they do strive to work within a theory of language where language is viewed as having productive rather than simply descriptive effects. However, it must once again be emphasized that the postmodernism promoted by McCloskey has an American lineage, with origins in the work of philosophers such as Richard Rorty and other pragmatists (Backhouse *et al.* 1993: 6), whereas the poststructuralist approach advocated here has a European lineage with close ties with the work of philosophers such as Jacques Derrida. This lineage has subsequently rendered the 'rhetoric of economics' palatable for American consumption, and hence to a certain extent acceptable to economists trained in the American tradition. The way in which this work has been linked to generally-accepted insights about the philosophy of science, such as those made by Thomas Kuhn, aids this acceptance.[11] The European brand of poststructuralism, and its feminist offshoot, on the other hand, has received a hostile reception, and its use within feminist economics to this date has been limited.

This hostility of feminist economists to feminist poststructuralism and deconstruction is most explicitly expressed in the writings of Nelson. She claims that in her own work, the 'identification of the basis of metaphor as experience, and especially physical experience, . . . puts human physical bodies explicitly at the heart of the analysis' (1992a: 148), without explaining why this might be important. Here one can only guess that the body constitutes the real at the bottom of the (false) representations: in her own words, '*opposition is itself only unidimensional in its basis of physical orientation, and not in the realms to which the dualism has been metaphorically applied*' (ibid.: 140; italics in original). Nelson compares this presence of the body in her own analysis with the contested existence of the body in 'deconstructionist thought', which she suggests is associated with the work of Jacques Derrida as well as Michel Foucault (1996a: 138, 145): 'The extent to which "the body" figures into deconstructionist thought is in dispute' (1992a: 148). Her radical misreading of Foucault, Derrida and feminist work which draws on these theorists is not uncommon (see Chapter 1 above), although few critics would accuse Foucault of a lack of interest in the body. However, Nelson pushes her critique of 'deconstructionist thought' even further to make the following strange claims: 'while deconstructionist thought recognizes that undimensional [*sic*] binary oppositions are basic conceptual building blocks, it does not recognize that we all learn, easily at a young age, to handle more than one dimension at any time. In any movement through space, we have to deal simultaneously with up/down, left/right, and forward/back . . . Moving spatially, we can deal with the fact that "up" and "left" are related but that the relation is not oppositional' (1996a: 146).

This body at the heart of Nelson's analysis, then, is an untheorized, anatomical body that allows unmediated access to its meanings (up is good, down is bad), which then form the basis of the social valuations of a series of dualistic terms metaphorically associated with masculinity and femininity. Nelson fails to recognize that even the seemingly incontestable privileging of 'up' over 'down' draws on a series of divisions which have been constructed upon a human/non-human dichotomy, such as those between human and animal, between culture and nature, and between mind and body or brain and heart (mind and emotion). The body, then, is not an unmediated referent. Thus I contend that Nelson fails to offer an effective critique of 'deconstructionist thought', that her own reliance on the dichotomy between the real and representations of the real is undermined, and that her advocacy of a synthesized, 'more fully human' economics through the incorporation of (positive aspects of) femininity maintains a realm of excluded femininity and hence remains on common ground with the phallocentrism of neoclassical economics. Nevertheless, for these very reasons, her work has been published in prestigious economics journals and may therefore operate to destabilize economists' beliefs in what they see as a gender-neutral disciplinary approach.

The limited work in feminist poststructuralist economics to date, then, is predominantly influenced by the American rather than the European tradition. Publications which draw explicitly upon the European tradition of poststructuralism can be divided into those works which more or less ignore the issue of sexual difference altogether, and those which address the sexually specific nature of economics. Those in the first group include Amariglio (1988, 1990), Amariglio *et al.* (1990), Rossetti (1990, 1992), Ruccio (1991), Samuels (1991) and Dow (1992). The purpose of the remainder of this section is to discuss each of those poststructuralist works which can be considered feminist.

Amariglio and Graham (1993) point out that the reasoning individual, the object of neoclassical economic analysis, has a privileged position as the origin of economic activity and hence of economic theorizing. They point out that neoclassical economics is about the taming of the passions of the body (which is, after all, the source of demands) by the mind, in which the body is historically figured as feminine: 'it can be argued that the blunting of the pure immediacy of the body can . . . be read as a metaphor for the denial, in the space of theory, of women' (ibid.: 5). However, they do not seek to reconstruct the economic agent so as to include women. Using poststructuralist theory, they argue that the economic agent is radically decentred, gendered, fragmented and over- as well as under-determined, a subject 'whose very subjectivity is constituted in the very acts in which he or she are [*sic*] engaged' (ibid.: 16). Hence the economic agent is unable to operate as the exogenous centre or 'totalizing "I" ' for economic discourse (ibid.: 17). Thus to replace rational economic man with a more feminine subject would simply reinstate the centre and reinforce notions of true and false descriptions of an objective reality (ibid.: 5–10). Although they are hopeful of the destabilizing potential of poststructuralism, Amariglio and Graham suggest that, when threatened with the notion of the decentred subject, neoclassical economists will simply 'retreat to the most abstract (but male) notions of subjectivity that allow their theory to remain more or less consistent and coherent'. Thus poststructuralism may simply operate to reinforce the dominance of neoclassical economics in the discipline (ibid.: 15). Graham and Amariglio (1996) are more optimistic for change, arguing that: 'Excluded, repudiated but never entirely negated meanings (the discursive "feminine") exist in a penumbra outside the clear boundaries of the definitive concept and are profoundly destabilizing to the discursive "masculine" when they are foregrounded and brought to light' (ibid.: 4). This hopeful conclusion, incidentally, is also one with which I conclude this book following the analysis of Part Two.

Lee Levin (1995) draws on poststructuralist and postmodernist feminist theory as well as feminist standpoint theory, which he problematically seems to conflate (see 1995: 105–7), to argue that subjectivity is ' "always already" gendered – as well as raced and classed' (ibid.: 106), and to stress the importance of emotion as 'an inherent, everpresent component of perception, understanding and knowledge' (ibid.: 107). He suggests that this view of subjectivity is consistent with the notion of agents' knowledge espoused by certain post-Keynesian theorists such as G.L.S. Shackle. Specifically, such post-Keynesians espouse a radical subjectivism which breaks with the notion of objective knowledge, as well as arguing for the primacy of convention in producing indeterminate and unstable agent expectations (ibid.: 108–9). Further, some post-Keynesians extend these views to the 'post-Keynesian theorist herself' (ibid.: 109). In this scenario, economists should expect, as post-Keynesians predict, an economic system subject to 'bouts of fitful instability' (ibid.: 110). At this point, Levin imports into the discussion of the post-Keynesian view of the economy a number of ideas from sociology 'which emphasize the inherently social nature of agent thought' (ibid.). In particular, he considers the role of rumour, fad and cognitive dissonance, as well as 'social comparison theory' and 'contagion theory', to offer an explanation of the instability of financial markets in the vein of Minsky, in which agents are driven by Keynesian 'sentiment' (emotion) (ibid.: 110–14). Although I think it is useful to consider these elements of financial market operations, Levin appears, like Klamer (see section 3.5), to be tacking comments about feminism, and indeed poststructuralism, on to a preexisting set of ideas. In other words, the feminist theory which Levin delineates does not add anything to the already-developed post-Keynesian view of the instability of financial markets. It is at best consistent with it, despite Levin's declaration that he has raised 'the possibility of *constructing* a theory of investment which takes as its basis a feminist approach to investment theory' (ibid.: 114; emphasis added).

Although feminist economists drawing upon object relations theory have been discussed in section 3.3, Susan Feiner (1995a) applies this theory in a unique way, and hence is more appropriately discussed in this section. She argues that a range of economic objects have symbolic content beyond the comprehension of their authors. Dependence on markets for existence, scarcity versus infinite wants, and perfect markets represent an infant's view of the world: 'the economists' market (quite unlike the market we all know) symbolizes the wish for the empathic mother who not only anticipates all needs, but meets them instantly' (ibid.: 159). Thus 'it is not the market which meets needs but it is rather the neoclassical representation of the market which meets needs' (ibid.: 162). The work is poststructuralist in that it uses this perspective to bring into question the ability of the economist to know himself, and hence his ability to screen out unconscious desires from economic knowledge: 'the texts of neoclassical economics have a symbolic content independent of the conscious intentions of either their authors or consumers' (ibid.: 154). Feiner's argument involves mapping aspects of the mother–baby dyad onto the way in which markets are conceived in neoclassical economics. Specifically, just as a baby is dependent on its mother to fulfil its needs, so individuals within capitalist societies are dependent on markets to fulfil their needs (ibid.: 159; see also Feiner 1995b).

Although Feiner's analysis may strike the average economist as bizarre, from a feminist perspective her work is innovative and deserves attention as the first work to attempt to bring psychoanalytic insights into economics. I strongly advocate the development of more research in this vein, although I suggest that it would benefit from drawing less upon object relations theory and more upon Lacanian theory.

The first task undertaken in this section was the delineation of the reliance of the work of the majority of feminist economists upon the distinction between sex and gender. With few exceptions, these feminist economists argue for a more fully human or complete economics, to be brought about by the inclusion of the excluded feminine, an argument which rests, like neoclassical economics itself, upon self-present identity. Despite my critical appraisal, which acts as motivation for Part Two of this book, the reader should keep in mind that by no means do I advocate an end to all other feminist economics approaches. I also discussed the works of the few exponents of what I have called feminist poststructuralist economics. I have argued that feminist poststructuralism is a better way to examine the masculinity of rational economic man, since this masculinity is embodied, rather than simply a gendered consciousness, and it is women's and men's bodies upon which neoclassical economics operates in its role as a crucially important discourse in Western cultures. The work of Amariglio and Graham (1993) and Graham and Amariglio (1996), in particular, support this contention and the analysis of Part Two of this book.

4.5. Conclusion

In this chapter I have discussed the problems and limitations of the sex/gender distinction, delineated the feminist poststructuralist position which underpins the analyses of the following chapters, summarized feminist economics in relation to the sex/gender distinction and briefly discussed the works of feminist poststructuralist economists. This completes Part One of the book. In Part Two of this book, the ideas of the discursively-produced body, phallocentrism and Derridean deconstruction are employed to critically appraise (and disrupt) the production of the masculinity of the contracting agent of neoclassical economics. The argument proceeds through an examination of the exemplar of rational economic man, Robinson Crusoe, and of the surrogate motherhood exchange. I argue that neoclassical economics relies for its coherence upon the binary oppositions of, amongst others, man/not-man, mind/body and culture/nature. Therefore, by necessity, the female body is excluded from the status of the contracting or exchanging agent. In Chapter 5 I examine the production of the masculinity of the figure of Robinson Crusoe, a teaching device employed by economists to demonstrate the working of a large number of neoclassical principles. I expose the failure of the (white) masculinity of rational economic man to be self-identical through an elaboration of its reliance upon the production of the excluded feminine (as well as non-white masculinity, here positioned as femininity). In Chapter 6 I develop a neoclassical model of the surrogate motherhood exchange. This market had not previously been modelled by economists, although Richard Posner (1989, 1992) had earlier discussed aspects of the exchange. In Chapter 7 I use this model to analyse the surrogate motherhood exchange from a feminist poststructuralist perspective, revealing the operation of the man/not-man, mind/body and culture/nature binary oppositions in the construction of the identity of the contracting agent.[12] I show how the female body is rewritten within neoclassical economics to exclude its specificity as female. Significantly, surrogate motherhood can only be theorized as the rental of human capital, where that human capital is conceptually separate from the contracting agent, circulating as an object of exchange. As Terry Eagleton remarks: 'Woman is the opposite, the "other" of man: she is non-man, defective man, assigned a chiefly negative value in relation to the male first principle. But equally man is what he is only by virtue of ceaselessly shutting out this other or opposite, defining himself in antithesis to it, and his whole identity is therefore caught up and put at risk in the very gesture by which he seeks to assert his unique, autonomous existence' (1983: 132).

The analysis of the following chapters can be viewed as a deconstruction of 'rational economic man'. The first stage of the deconstruction involves the illumination of various binary oppositions which structure the text as meaningful. The second stage involves the reversal of the hierarchies established by the binary structures by showing that the A terms are in fact dependent upon the not-A terms for their identity. Thus, it is not-man, body and nature rather than man, mind and culture which can be treated as the privileged terms: woman establishes the identity of man and her 'natural' role sustains that identity. The deconstruction of rational economic man is completed with the third step, in which I draw upon the notion of morphology (see section 4.3 above). Neoclassical economics relies upon the mind/body split because it requires a neutral body to sustain the myth of the universal individual. Sexual difference, then, must be a social construct, the result of gender differentiation at the level of the mind. This reliance of neoclassical economics on an allegedly universal, disembodied individual is destabilized by the concept of morphology. Embodied subjectivity is everywhere approach supports such a dichotomy. Discourse creates an inside and therefore is not fully outside, while, in psychoanalytic approaches, the introjection of images from outside, and the necessary submission to the preexisting laws of language, mean that the psychic construction of the body relies upon an outside.

7. For discussions of Freud, Lacan and the relationship between psychoanalysis, poststructuralism and feminism, see Lemaire (1977), Mitchell (1982), Jacqueline Rose (1982), Silverman (1983), Henriques *et al.* (1984), Grosz (1987, 1990b), Brennan (1989a, 1989b), Rowley and Grosz (1990), Screen (1992) and Wright (1992).

8. On Derridean deconstruction, see especially Spivak (1974), Derrida (1981), Johnson (1981), Culler (1983), Gross (1986a), Norris (1987: ch. 4), Grosz (1989: xv, 26–38), Selden and Widdowson (1993), Lechte (1994: 105-10) as well as other references cited in notes 13, 15 and 20 in Chapter 1 above. For Derrida's use of the term 'woman' to signify the failure of the self-presence of identity or the 'untruth of truth', see Derrida (1991: pt 4), Grosz (1990a), Braidotti (1991: 98–108), Cornell (1991: ch. 2), Diprose (1991a), Spivak (1991a), Whitford (1991a: 127–35) and Elam (1994: ch. 2).

9. See also Grosz (1987, 1990c), Braidotti (1989), Butler (1990) and Schor and Weed (1994).

10. Note that Becker denies that biology *per se* plays a definitive role in his theoretical system. In his introduction to the second edition of his *Treatise on the Family*, he responds to feminist critics by arguing that: 'Although I do believe that biological differences are very important in explaining why women traditionally have done most of the child rearing, the main lesson from my analysis of an efficient division of labor is not that biology or discrimination causes the traditional division of activities between men and women. Rather . . . the message is that even small amounts of market discrimination against women or small biological differences between men and women can cause huge differences in the activities of husbands and wives' (1991: 4).

11. Acceptance, however, has not led to the kinds of self-conscious practice which McCloskey advocates. The radical implications of McCloskey's work are rarely considered in mainstream work, which largely consists of presenting methodologies and techniques, such as econometric testing and mathematical modelling, as means by which to establish truth.

12. The term 'reveal' may be read as a desire 'to show the text what it "does not know" ' (Spivak 1974: lxxvii). But the text of this book, although it relies upon the assumption that I mean what I say, can always be deconstructed for what it 'doesn't know'.

PART TWO

Deconstructing Rational Economic Man

5. Robinson Crusoe: the Paradigmatic 'Rational Economic Man'

5.1. Introduction[1]

It is evident from my discussion in previous chapters that the empirical, theoretical and methodological basis of neoclassical economics is the individual, and that within this framework entities such as the family, the firm and the economy are no more than aggregations of such individuals. The individual is constructed within neoclassical economics as a universal, and hence unsexed, agent known as rational economic man. This allegedly unsexed individual is commonly represented by the figure of Robinson Crusoe, who is a very important teaching device in undergraduate courses in neoclassical economics (see, for example, Cairncross 1960; Stilwell 1975; Hirshleifer 1980; Pierce 1984; Varian 1984, 1990; and Binger and Hoffman 1988; Crusoe is also used as the representative agent in Plosser 1989). Crusoe as exemplar of rational economic man was used in the founding texts of neoclassical economics, including those written by Jennings, Bastiat, Gossen, Jevons, Menger, Wicksell, Wicksteed, Edgeworth, Clark and Marshall, as well as being found in the writings of Marx ([1867] 1969; see White 1982, 1987; Watt [1951] 1959: 171–2). The Crusoe figure was also important in the 'battle of methods' between the emerging neoclassical school and the historical economists, being used to defend the assumption of the universal applicability of the orthodox economic laws (White 1982, 1987: 218). However, although Crusoe as the universal calculating economic individual was well-established by 1900, and although he is still invoked as the exemplar of the neoclassical economic individual, neoclassical economists would argue that the figure of Robinson Crusoe is unnecessary for economic analysis, an innocent teaching device or metaphor which could easily be excluded from texts (indeed, Robinson Crusoe is not universally employed within economic textbooks). Above all, they would argue that the masculinity of the Crusoe figure is irrelevant, and Crusoe, in-so-far as he is useful to neoclassical economics, is devoid of sexually-specific content.

There has been some discussion by economists of the history and role of Robinson Crusoe in economics (see Hymer [1971] 1980; White 1982, 1987). Literary theorists have also discussed the economics of Daniel Defoe's ([1719] 1945) novel as well as the economic views of the author. These works aim to identify or deny the existence of neoclassical economic behaviour in the Daniel Defoe novel, or to establish the economic views of the author and the way in which these views are portrayed within the novel. The aim of this chapter, on the other hand, is to show that the teaching device of Robinson Crusoe is not some neutral figure, some metaphor of no substance, but a key device by which the masculinity of rational economic man within a one-sex model is produced and sustained. I also demonstrate that economic texts must be viewed intertextually. Thus my argument is not that neoclassical economics is the sole constituent of a phallocentric construction of sexual difference. Rather, it is that neoclassical economics is supportive of, and supported by, a range of other discourses. To this end, I expose the operation of the binary oppositions upon which both the Defoe novel and modern neoclassical texts rely, and reveal how these oppositions construct both Crusoe and the rational economic agent as white men by excluding the feminine and non-white masculinity. I argue that femininity or not-man, nature and body, underpin the construction of the seemingly self-present masculine identity and masculine achievements. I use Irigaray's notion of morphology, discussed in Chapter 4 above, to displace the phallocentric claim that a universal figure such as Robinson Crusoe can represent the two sexes.

This chapter is therefore the first step in the deconstruction of rational economic man, the central task of this book. The chapter has three main sections. In section 5.2 I outline the Defoe tale of Robinson Crusoe, as well as the neoclassical version and the ways in which this version is used to teach economics. I also review the literature on Crusoe as rational economic man, and discuss the intertextuality of this figure. In section 5.3 I use the text of the Defoe novel to argue that Crusoe's white masculinity is constructed in opposition to feminized nature and the feminized native Friday, who, though a male, is denied access to the self-constituting subjectivity of Crusoe. In section 5.4 I draw links between the Defoe character and the neoclassical Crusoe, exposing the masculinity of the neoclassical teaching device and showing that the presence of the male body in the teaching device is significant rather than a mere coincidence, as neoclassical economists have claimed. Section 5.5 concludes the chapter.

5.2. Intertextuality and Robinson Crusoe/*Homo Economicus*

The figure of Robinson Crusoe is the exemplar of the neoclassical model of
the individual. Robinson Crusoe, as Daniel Defoe wrote of him, was a boy of
eighteen when he disobeyed his father's wishes and went to sea. Crusoe
travelled to Brazil, and, following several adventures, including a period of
slavery, he settled there after purchasing a plantation with the proceeds of
theft from his former master. The other plantation owners, all in need of
slave labour, asked Crusoe to travel with them to buy slaves on the African
coast. It is this journey which led to Crusoe's 28 years on the island. His ship
was taken off course by a violent storm and the crew, spotting land, decided
to jump off rather than sink; Crusoe was the only human survivor. He was
able to salvage many useful goods from the wreck of the ship, helping him
survive the next 25 lonely years in relative comfort. After 25 years, Crusoe
saved a native from cannibals who used the island, fortuitously the opposite
side to Crusoe's habitat, to kill and eat their captured enemies. Crusoe named
the native Friday, and they lived harmoniously together in a master–slave
relationship for several years. A mutinous crew then used the island to dump
their captain and others; the mutineers were overcome and taken prisoner.
Finally, Crusoe used this ship to escape the island, now a thriving
'plantation', and return to 'civilized society'.

Economists who have discussed the use of Robinson Crusoe as exemplar
of rational economic man include Stephen Hymer ([1971] 1980), who rejects
the neoclassical reading of Daniel Defoe's *Robinson Crusoe* in favour of a
Marxist interpretation and focuses on the exclusion, from the neoclassical
story of Crusoe, of conquest, slavery, robbery, murder and force, which are
the basis of international trade (ibid.: 29). Michael White (1982) has also
discussed Robinson Crusoe, delineating the nineteenth-century appropriation
of the Robinson Crusoe figure by marginalist economists, and arguing that
this figure derived not from Daniel Defoe's novel but from a particular
nineteenth-century reading of that novel. The story has also been much
studied in literary theory, given that Daniel Defoe's *Robinson Crusoe* is
widely considered the first novel, and as such has an important place within
the literary canon. Discussions of the economics of the *Robinson Crusoe*
story include those by Ian Watt ([1951] 1959; 1957: ch. 3), Diana Spearman
(1966: 166–8) and Maximillian Novak ([1962] 1969; see also Rogers 1979:
77–82). Each of these authors compares the work with Defoe's own beliefs,
in-so-far as they are documented, can be divined from his other writings, or
can be attributed to him from the prominent beliefs of his time. Ian Watt's
(1957: ch. 3) discussion of *Robinson Crusoe*, entitled '*Robinson Crusoe*,

Individualism, and the Novel', places the novel firmly within the conceptual space of neoclassical economics. Individualism depends on 'an economic and political organization which allows its members a very wide range of choices in their actions, and on an ideology primarily based, not on the tradition of the past, but on the autonomy of the individual, irrespective of his particular social status or personal capacity' (ibid.: 62). Watt paints Crusoe as a 'hero of individualism', citing with approval the use made of Robinson Crusoe as the illustration of *Homo economicus* by economic theorists (ibid.: 65), since, in his opinion, Crusoe 'is only a special case of economic man' ([1951] 1959: 170, 174). Novak argues that 'Defoe transmuted his economic theories into fiction in much the same manner as he fictionalized his economic tracts' ([1962] 1969: 102), and that one of the main themes of *Robinson Crusoe* is a utility theory of value (ibid.: 99–100).[2] Spearman, on the other hand, rejects this view of *Robinson Crusoe*, arguing that 'No one in his senses would choose the story of a man cast alone on an uninhabited island to illustrate a theory which only applies to the exchange of goods and services' (1966: 166). She remarks that 'Confusion seems to have been produced by some writers of economic textbooks who have used the situation of Crusoe to illustrate economic activities' (ibid.: 167). *Robinson Crusoe*, she suggests, is simply 'a story of man and nature' (ibid.: 168). Indeed, that the figure of Robinson Crusoe is a story, rather than a truth, of 'man' and 'nature', or the naturalness of man, is the argument of this chapter.

From a feminist poststructuralist perspective, these readings of *Robinson Crusoe* are interesting in their failure to address the issue of sexual difference, except in-so-far as the virtual absence of women is noted (see, for example, Watt 1957: 71). Similarly, no textbook usage of Robinson Crusoe draws attention to his masculinity; his sex is supposed to be irrelevant. Neoclassical economists argue that the Crusoe figure is universally applicable, and that the absence of women from Defoe's text is meaningless. In contrast to these readings, the argument of this chapter is that the apparent absence of femininity from the Crusoe story is central to the text of *Robinson Crusoe* and to its representation in neoclassical economics, rather than a mere footnote to the action, since it is this absence which establishes the self-present masculinity of the Crusoe figure and the exchanging agent of neoclassical economics. Both figures must be understood to be situated intertextually. Intertextuality refers to the creation of meaning between texts rather than between text and 'real world'. Every text refers to a myriad of other texts rather than a so-called 'real world' situated outside language, and hence relies for its intelligibility upon a series of discourses which the texts themselves construct and to which they contribute (Rylance 1987: 112–13;

Culler 1983: 32). In Culler's words:

> 'Intertextuality' . . . has a double focus. On the one hand, it calls our attention to the importance of prior texts, insisting that the autonomy of texts is a misleading notion and that a work has the meaning it does only because certain things have previously been written. Yet in so far as it focuses on intelligibility, on meaning, 'intertextuality' leads us to consider prior texts as contributions to a code which makes possible the various effects of signification. Intertextuality thus becomes less a name for a work's relation to particular prior texts than a designation of its participation in the discursive space of a culture: the relationship between a text and the various languages or signifying practices and its relation to those texts which articulate for it the possibilities of that culture. [Intertextuality refers to] the sum of knowledge that makes it possible for texts to have meaning. (1981: 103–4)

In other words, intertextuality does not indicate a complete 'free for all', but refers us to the politics of the text, the history of its production as meaningful. Examples of the intertextuality of the Crusoe figure include a wide range of discourses in which the figure is situated, such as the genres of 'boy's own classics' and American westerns, the Marlboro Man, narratives of colonization, and, more broadly, Western notions of the lone adventurer and the self-made man.

The neoclassical version of the Crusoe story is likewise situated in these discourses. It has had its own productive effects; for example, it was used by the developing neoclassical school in the late nineteenth century to defend the claim of the universal applicability of economic laws (White 1982: 137–8), and it is used as a teaching device which produces knowledge of neoclassical economics for students in certain ways. Students too are 'produced' as certain types of knowers: in the words of Kay Schaffer, 'narratives engage the reader in a process through which his or her own subjectivity is constructed' (1988: 52). Gross has also pointed to the way in which discourse participates in the phallocentric organisation of society: 'in the isomorphic relation between discourses and male sexuality, discourses do not *reflect* male sexuality and male dominance but actively *participate in the construction* of the meaning, form and experiences of male and female bodies' (1986b: 75). Before turning to the Defoe novel, the novels *Foe* (Coetzee 1986) and *Friday* (Tournier 1969), both of which are subversive readings of the Defoe novel, will be briefly discussed to illustrate the intertextuality of Robinson Crusoe.

J.M. Coetzee's novel *Foe* (1986) is a rewriting of the Robinson Crusoe story in a way which brings to the fore questions of authorship and presence, as well as the silencing of the narratives of women and native others, by situating Susan Barton as the narrator-castaway and Friday as a tongueless native. When Barton is washed up on an island, she finds the Englishman Robinson Cruso and Friday, who have already been there for fifteen-odd years. Cruso's memories are confused and Barton never discovers the truth about the loss of Friday's tongue. The three are rescued, but Cruso dies on the journey to England, leaving Barton to care for Friday. Barton writes her account of 'The Female Castaway. Being a True Account of a Year Spent on a Desert Island. With Many Strange Circumstances Never Hitherto Related' and presents them to the renowned author Daniel Foe, who insists that 'The island is not a story in itself' (ibid.: 117). Barton responds that the story 'doggedly holds its silence. The shadow whose lack you feel is there: it is the loss of Friday's tongue' (ibid.). As Brenda Marshall argues, 'Friday functions in *Foe* as neither presence nor absence, but rather, as the *différance*, the condition of possibility for Barton's stories . . . Friday is not presence (in Barton's frame of reference) because he is speechless and because he is a slave . . . He is not absence because he is that palpable something whose history she tries to name. Friday's own story is not told in *Foe*. Friday is, rather, the condition of possibility for the stories that Barton tries to tell' (1992: 75–6). The novel ends with the entrance of a new narrator who finds Friday's body in 'a place where bodies are their own signs', where Friday's body can speak without talking (Coetzee 1986: 157). The narrator, however, 'is not called upon to provide closure, that is, to interpret Friday's silence into a final meaning, but rather, to listen' (Marshall 1992: 79). Friday, then, cannot be heard in the usual way; he speaks within a different discourse (see also Spivak 1991b).

Michel Tournier's novel *Friday* (1969) is also a rewriting of the Crusoe story, and one of the most interesting aspects of this text is the explicit discussion of Robinson's relationship with the island as a woman. Robinson's production of the femininity of the island, Speranza, takes several forms through the novel, with Robinson's own subjectivity being produced in relation to these forms. Robinson's first period on the island is spent in the construction of a boat, to escape the 'wholly hostile and alien' island (ibid.: 36), a task which, once completed, turns out to have been pointless. This realization is followed by a period of total hopelessness in which he spends most of his time naked in a mire in which his own excrement mixes with the sludge. During this period he knows Speranza as the Island of Despair. He later comments that 'Each man has his slippery slope. Mine leads to the mire. That is where Speranza drives me when she grows evil and shows me her animal face' (ibid.: 51). He realizes that he will succumb to madness unless he begins to work. He rechristens the island Speranza, the Island of Hope, a name which evoked the 'wholly profane memory of a hot-blooded Italian girl'. Moreover, in examining his map of the island, Robinson notes that 'viewed from a certain angle the island resembled a female body, headless but nevertheless a woman' (ibid.: 47–8). At this point, he 'no longer doubted that everything must henceforth depend on his relations with Speranza and his success in ordering their joint affairs' (ibid.: 57). Having ordered the island and imposed on himself a rigid schedule of tasks and ceremonials, guided by his water clock, Robinson has his first glimpse of 'another island', an island, and a metamorphosis within himself, which is hidden from him by his own labour, but revealed when his water clock stopped (ibid.: 90). Now, during periods in which he purposefully 'stops time', he investigates the insides of Speranza, finding his way to a womb-like cavern to which he retreats several times. However, he discovers that this maternal role which he has imposed on Speranza is draining her of energy: '*Being pregnant with myself, Speranza could no longer conceive*' (ibid.: 109; italics in original). This realization leads to the new phase, one in which Robinson becomes Speranza's husband, in every sense (ibid.: 119–30). His marital bliss is shattered, however, when he finds that she has been unfaithful to him with Friday, whom he has in the meantime rescued, ending the phase of the island-wife, and beginning the phase of brotherhood between Crusoe and Friday (ibid.: 167–71). In the brotherhood phase, the island functions as 'something earthly to be superceded [*sic*] by a more mature and fulfilling solar relationship' (Marshall 1992: 98). In Marshall's words, Speranza's role in the novel is to be female, 'as that which is to be cultivated/owned, to function as mother and wife, and then to be outgrown, surpassed by the love of men for each other' (ibid.: 138).

These discussions of *Foe* and *Friday* are illustrations of the inevitable intertextuality of texts rather than a homage to Defoe's work. As mentioned above, in this chapter I do not seek to establish the novel *Robinson Crusoe* as the origin of the neoclassical version, though clearly, if the Defoe novel did not exist, neither would the neoclassical figure of Robinson Crusoe. Crusoe's construction in neoclassical textbooks draws much of its meaning from the Defoe novel; other literary figures such as Jane Austen's *Emma* or Defoe's *Roxana* could not play the role of exemplar, even though both Emma and Roxana faced many a situation of choice. Despite Roxana's positioning as masculine (Wiegman 1989), her female body would create difficulties for neoclassical economics. Male bodies carry meanings, particularly in relation to myths of the self-made or paternal creative force and independence from the mother ('productive' man), which neoclassical economics draws upon when positing Crusoe as the exemplar of utility-maximizing behaviour: both are rational, self-sufficient, independent, active, autonomous, strictly-individuated and atomistic (white) men. It may seem paradoxical to assert on the one hand that the neoclassical Crusoe derives much of its meaning from the Defoe novel, and yet also to assert on the other that the Defoe novel is not the origin of the neoclassical Crusoe. But the point is simply that texts have no origin as such – they always depend on prior codes, and hence each has an 'origin' which can be traced to another 'origin' (Culler 1981: 102–3). However, although intertextuality does not coincide with a project of seeking the source or origins of texts (and therefore closure), what has come before a particular text remains relevant (Marshall 1992: 138–9). Economic texts which use the Crusoe figure, indeed, neoclassical economics as a whole, cannot elude this intertextuality. In the way that *Foe* and *Friday* pick up on certain themes of the Defoe novel, so too does neoclassical economics, but only those themes available within a historically-specific network of discourses. Thus intertextuality must be distinguished from an examination of literary influences; it 'comprises the whole field of contemporary and historical language as reflected within the text' (Nöth 1995: 323; see also Culler 1981: ch. 5; Norris 1987: ch. 2).

5.3. Crusoe's Masculine Identity: the Defoe Case

The figure of Robinson Crusoe from both the Defoe novel and the neoclassical textbook is underpinned by the phallocentric binary oppositions – man/not-man, culture/nature and presence/absence – which have been the object of much feminist poststructuralism. These oppositions construct Crusoe as masculine, autonomous and active, and indeed, procreative, by producing him in relation to feminine others. In this section, I confine my analysis to the operation of these binary oppositions in the Defoe novel.

Robinson Crusoe lost his identity when he was shipwrecked: 'I that was reduced to a meer state of nature' (Defoe [1719] 1945: 87). He must reconstruct himself as a white, male, colonialist Englishman by drawing on a series of binary oppositions which produce a white masculinity founded upon feminine and racial others. In so doing, he demonstrates that the categories which constitute identity are not stable and pre-given, but constructed in language. There are two phases of this project: the first 25 years which Crusoe spends alone on the island, and the following three years during which he shares the island with his 'man Friday'. In the first phase, Crusoe's masculinity is constructed in opposition to the femininity of nature – the island and its animal inhabitants, which he controls and rules. In the second phase, it is Friday who is positioned as the negative feminine upon which the positive masculinity of Crusoe is established, although his black masculinity also plays a key role in establishing the universality of the white man. In each case, a feminine other is necessary for Crusoe's identity. Actual women are absent from the island, but woman is an absent presence; she is present as feminized nature and as the feminized native.

The binary opposition culture/nature is important in building Crusoe's masculinity in the first phase. It is not long before culture (Crusoe and his English heritage) imposes itself on nature (the uninhabited island). Crusoe makes for himself a table and chair, shelving, woven baskets, cooking pots, a pipe, clothing, an umbrella, and so on.[3] Crusoe is so self-sufficient that he states: 'I had a tollerable view of subsisting without any want as long as I liv'd' (ibid.: 48). He *masters* his circumstances with reason, he is resourceful, and though not a trained carpenter, potter or stone mason he is able to produce most of what he desires: 'as reason is the substance and original of the mathematicks, so by stating and squaring every thing by reason, and by making the most rational judgement of things, every man may be in time master of every mechanick art' (ibid.: 51). Crusoe's reason will enable him to overcome the deficiencies of, and thus tame, the island. Crusoe does not forget the role of the ship, though; again invoking the culture/nature binary opposition, he says that had he been unable to salvage goods from the ship he would have been reduced to a 'meer savage', eating food 'with [his] claws like a beast' (ibid.: 96).

Crusoe relates to the island as his dominion – he 'possesses' it and reigns as sovereign over it: 'this was all my own, . . . I was king and lord of all this country indefeasibly, and had a right of possession' (ibid.: 74). He builds two homes: 'I fancy'd now I had my country-house and my sea-coast-house' (ibid.: 76). He constructs himself as the patriarch in other ways, too. He wants to 'husband' the animals on the island (ibid.: 57), finally managing to domesticate a parrot and a goat (ibid: 83). He ends up with a 'family' of animals which gather around the table at meal-times: 'It would have made a stoick smile to have seen me and my little family sit down to dinner; there was my majesty the prince and lord of the whole island; I had the lives of all my subjects at my absolute command; I could hang, draw, give liberty, and take it away, and no rebels among all my subjects. Then to see how like a king I din'd too, all alone, attended by my servants' (ibid.: 109). Thus Crusoe is a male head of household – the patriarch and ruler.[4] He civilizes the island, conquers and possesses it, by cultivating the land, accidentally 'sowing his seed' (ibid.: 58), and then systematically creating fields of barley and rice and fenced-off feeding grounds, imposing a pattern upon the landscape which identifies Crusoe as the master and creator. Crusoe here represents the liberal myth of male procreativity; he actively creates culture, she invisibly supports his endeavours.

Despite his ostensible control of the island, Crusoe reveals his fear of its power to engulf him, and hence his construction of her as, in Barbara Creed's (1993) words, 'the monstrous feminine', the engulfing mother, in his obsession with boundaries. He makes his home in the shelter of a large rock (into which he later carves to make a cave). The boundary of his home is constructed with a double wall of stakes in a semi-circle around the rock indent, a wall which must be scaled with the help of a ladder rather than passed through via a doorway. The ladder does not threaten the completeness of the boundary which divides the inside (and safety) from the unsafe and unknown outside. Eventually Crusoe extends his home back into the cave, and constructs a door on the outside of the hill. He is very nervous about it, even though in the year he has lived on the island the most dangerous creatures he has found are goats: 'I was not perfectly easy at lying so open; for as I manag'd my self befor, I was in a perfect enclosure, whereas now I thought I lay expos'd, and open for any thing to come in upon me' (ibid.: 77). Crusoe experiences a fear of being swallowed up by the island, referring to a distant valley as 'where . . . I almost lost my self once before' (ibid.: 119). He refers ambivalently to his status on the island as 'my reign, or my captivity, which you please' (ibid.: 101). This characterization of the land as the engulfing mother is discussed by Schaffer (1988), who argues that in the Australian tradition the bush is characterized as absorbing and dangerous, robbing its inhabitants of a separate identity, and that this response to the bush constructs it as feminine. Mother Earth is a common construction of the land in Western discourses, but, as in the case of surrogate motherhood (see Chapter 7 below), the mother can 'turn nasty', becoming the powerful and cruel mother who threatens the self-identity of man. The figure of the mother, then, must be controlled and her power diminished, controlled by contract or by the imposition of civilization, hence sustaining the myth of male creativity, the unity and self-presence of man.

Fourteen years later Crusoe's anxiety about boundaries and invasion arises again with his discovery of a footprint in the sand: 'Now I began sorely to repent that I had dug my cave so large as to bring a door through again, which door, as I said, came out beyond where my fortification joyn'd to the rock' ([1719] 1945: 118). Crusoe's response to the footprint was to build a second fortress which extended beyond the original door, thereafter requiring two ladders to enter. Twenty thousand stakes driven into the ground outside the new wall complete the protective barrier. Crusoe's inventions were his way of taming the island and imposing his culture upon it, but when he sees a footprint in the sand this process ends in favour of maximizing his security arrangements. Crusoe's realization that savages are using the island to feast upon their enemy captives precipitates a reconstrual of the island as harmless in comparison to the barbarity and danger associated with cannibals, who may literally 'devour' him and swallow him up. With the threat of engulfment by the mother-land having been overcome, Crusoe's identity is now threatened by human others, and the footprint in the sand spurs him to devote all his time to protecting his self from the savages, creating and reinforcing the boundary between self and, in this case, masculine others. These masculine others are not, however, strictly human; they are 'savage wretches' with a 'wretched inhuman custom of their devouring each other and eating one another up' (ibid.: 121).

The civilized/primitive binary opposition, with its religious resonations in the mind/body and human/divine splits, is an important part of the construction of the native other. Crusoe views the savages and their cannibalistic practices with horror, and plans to kill some of the savages simply for revenge, and to rescue for himself a native slave, to serve as a worker and to provide company. As Watt remarks, when Crusoe notices the lack of 'society' on the island, he does not regret the absence of women but rather prays for the company of a male slave ([1951] 1959: 173). On carrying out his plan to procure a slave, Crusoe obtains Friday, to whom he teaches both his own name and Friday's: 'I made him know his name should be Friday, which was the day I save'd his life; I call'd him so for the memory of the time; I likewise taught him to say Master, and then let him know, that was to be my name' (ibid.: 150). In response, Friday 'lays his head flat upon the ground, close to my foot, and sets my other foot upon his head, as he had done before; and after this, made all the signs to me of subjection, servitude, and submission imaginable, to let me know how he would serve me as long as he liv'd' (ibid.). As Robyn Wiegman argues, 'The fact that Crusoe names this Other not for something intrinsic to the man's nature but for the day on which Crusoe saved Friday's life speaks to the self-reflexive order that Crusoe brings to *his* island. As God created Man on Friday, according to Biblical accounts, so Crusoe replicates his kinship with divine authority by symbolically creating the native other on the same day' (1989: 45). Crusoe constructs Friday as a possession, describing his attributes in great detail:

He was a comely handsome fellow, perfectly well made; with straight strong limbs, not too large; tall and well shap'd, and, as I reckon, about twenty six years of age. He had a very good countenance, not a fierce and surly aspect; but seem'd to have something very manly in his face, and yet he had all the sweetness and softness of an European in his countenance too, especially when he smil'd. His hair was long and black, not curl'd like wool; his forehead very high and large, and a great vivacity and sparkling sharpness in his eyes. The colour of his skin was not quite black, but very tawny; and yet not of an ugly yellow nauseous tawny, as the Brasilians, and Virginians, and other natives of America are; but of a bright kind of a dun olive colour, that had in something very agreeable, tho' not very easy to describe. His face was round and plump; his nose small, not flat like the negroes, a very good mouth, thin lips, and his fine teeth, well set, and white as ivory. (Defoe [1719] 1945: 149–50)

To quote Stephen Hymer, Robinson viewed Friday 'not as a person, but as a sort of pet, a mindless body that is obedient and beautiful' ([1971] 1980: 35). Indeed, Hymer also quotes Crusoe's description of Friday, substituting 'she' for 'he' in the passage just quoted. Of this move, Hymer remarks: 'This is not done to suggest homosexuality but to emphasize how rulers conceive of the ruled only as bodies to minister to their needs' (ibid.: 36). Thus, although Hymer criticized the use of Robinson Crusoe within neoclassical economics because of the way exploitation and violence are ignored, he does so by relying, as does neoclassical economics, upon the existence of a masculine order in which woman is relegated to the realm of nature or body. Masculine others are positioned as feminine, and hence also take up the symbolic space of nature or body underpinning the self-presence of white masculinity. Crusoe's production of the mindless body's subjectivity as inferior to his own continues as he limits Friday's language to pidgin English, and fails to learn Friday's language; converts Friday to Christianity, telling the savage that his people's god is really an evil spirit and their clergy dishonest (Defoe [1719] 1945: 158); and clothes him in a poor version of his own attire: 'I beckon'd to him to come with me, and let him know I would give him some cloaths, at which he seem'd very glad, for he was stark naked . . . I gave him a pair of linnen drawers . . . then I made him a jerkin of goat's-skin, as well as my skill would allow, . . . and I gave him a cap . . . and thus he was cloath'd for the present, tollerably well, and was mighty well pleas'd to see himself almost as well cloath'd as his master (ibid.: 150–1).

Although Friday as a black man is clearly important to the establishment of Crusoe's white masculinity through Crusoe's positioning of him as a 'natural' inferior and subordinate, he is also, as mentioned, positioned as a feminine other. Friday's feminization is clear when we consider the impossibility of a 'boy Friday'. Like the modern 'girl Friday', Friday's role is to be the helpmate and complement of a man. Once Crusoe teaches Friday to speak English, life improves dramatically: 'This was the pleasantest year of all the life I led in this place; Friday began to talk pretty well, and understand the names of almost every thing I had occasion to call for, and of every place I had to send him to' (ibid.: 155). Crusoe teaches Friday to provide the services normally supplied by wives and mothers; he says of Friday, 'I was greatly delighted with him, and made it my business to teach him every thing that was proper to make him useful, handy, and helpful' (ibid.: 153). Crusoe does not vary his routine at all, rather fitting Friday's labour into it: 'I set him to work to beating some corn out, and sifting it in the manner I us'd to do, . . . and he soon understood how to do it as well as I . . . in a little time Friday was able to do all the work for me, as well as I could do it myself' (ibid.: 155). Again, woman is the absent presence. But this feminization of Friday is not independent of his racial otherness. As Wiegman has argued, sexual difference is the founding difference and creates the means by which men are 'hierarchicalized'. Thus not all men have equal access to the process of subjectivity: 'the representational construction of the masculine is contingent not simply on the reiteration of sexual difference but on the simultaneous positing of racial difference, enabling the masculine itself to be hierarchicalized among men' (1989: 34).

As the years go by, the population of the island continues to grow: Friday's father is also rescued from cannibals, several ship-wrecked Spanish sailors move to the island from the mainland, and a mutinied ship is the source of a further increase. Crusoe is able to use this ship to escape the island, leaving behind a host of natives and sailors to tend to what he now calls his 'collony' (Defoe [1719] 1945: 221). In his absence some of the men kidnap five women from the mainland, and when Crusoe arrives back for a visit he finds about twenty children (ibid.). Crusoe himself adds to the population by sending to the island 'more people', 'other supplies', as well as 'seven women, being such as I found proper for service, or for wives to such as would take them', and in addition promises the Englishmen that he will 'send them some women from England' (ibid.: 222). Thus physical women appear in the text only as objects of exchange between the men, and as Ulla Grapard notes, once they appear, women are listed after *people* and other supplies (1995a: 36). But, of course, woman is crucial to the novel – her absence structures the self-presence of Crusoe, and thus woman not only literally but symbolically operates as the facilitation of exchange between self-present white men.

Crusoe's construction of the island as feminine, and his power to name Friday and produce his own subjectivity in relation to that of Friday's black, and hence feminized, masculinity, illustrates the phallocentric construction of white masculine subjectivity. This construction in turn produces the meaning of sexual difference (woman is defined as not-man rather than autonomously different), where sexual difference provides the foundation for the hierarchicalization of man's access to subjectivity ('dark brothers' are defined as non-subjects and hence are positioned as feminine). Thus Crusoe's civilized white masculinity is produced in relation to Friday's primitive black masculinity, an identity which is itself produced and positioned as feminine. Woman, and non-white man, are not represented autonomously, since the 'other' produces white masculine wholeness and the fiction of self-identity. As Schaffer argues: 'Meaning is made possible through reference to a system of differences (of relations between things) within an order of sameness (a white, masculine, heterosexual, middle-class culture)' (1988: 13). The Western culture imposed on Friday illustrates this order of sameness. Crusoe was unable to recognize Friday as different except within this order, and the self-presence of Crusoe's identification constructed Friday as the other, the unacknowledged not-A upon which Crusoe's identity could be founded. However, although Friday's black masculinity is feminized in relation to Crusoe's white masculinity, Friday is nevertheless embodied as a man, and hence can participate in the fantasy of 'sameness' or unversality produced by neoclassical economics. It is to this fantasy that I now turn.

5.4. Crusoe's Masculine Identity: the Neoclassical Case

It is sometimes suggested that a woman would behave no differently from Crusoe were she the one to be shipwrecked. Hence Varian, for example, could simply name the economic individual as Robyn Crusoe, and continue with the analysis, with no changes in meaning. This proves, the argument insinuates, that Robinson Crusoe's masculinity is irrelevant. The point is, however, that Robinson Crusoe already exists as a masculine archetype. Certainly a woman, myself included, would construct shelter and make the other investments required to sustain life. But in doing so she fills the shoes of this male hero, as does the surrogate mother (see Chapter 7 below), and the binary structures which produce sexed subject positions remain in place. As Schaffer has pointed out in her discussion of the mythic figure of the Australian bushman, 'The position of "native son" could . . . in an exceptional circumstance, be filled by a woman. That is, the bushwoman can stand in place of her husband, lover or brother and take on masculine attributes of strength, fortitude, courage and the like in her battle with the environment. But the land as an object virtually always is represented as feminine. It functions as a metaphor for woman – as in father sky to mother earth, colonial master to the plains of promise, native son to the barren bush . . . . All these equations reproduce the "perfect" couple: masculine activity/feminine passivity' (1988: 14). Or again, 'it is not possible to position female-oriented images in place of male ones where the underlying structure accords no specificity to the female' (Grosz, quoted in Whitford 1991a: 62). In this section, I discuss the 'perfect couple' of masculine presence and feminine absence produced within neoclassical economics.

Neoclassical economics can be characterized as a 'science of the individual'. Individuals are motivated by their own self-interest to participate in market and non-market exchanges: this process is known as 'utility maximization', or the maximization of an agent's 'happiness'. Maximization requires the calculation at the margin of the costs and benefits of an exchange, and individuals carry out exchanges until the marginal costs and benefits of doing so are equalized. The core of the neoclassical individual, their 'self-interest', is a set of preferences, the characteristics of which conform to certain assumptions. For example, if an individual prefers A to B and B to C, then that person must prefer A to C; this means that preferences are transitive. Individuals are also instrumentally rational, meaning that they will always choose the least cost means of achieving given ends (defined by their preference bundle) – if they did not, they would not be utility maximizing and hence would not fit the model. Even the 'irrational' inhabitants of mental institutions, who may be assumed by some not to know their own self-interest, are instrumentally rational and have 'well-behaved' preferences. If preferences are well-behaved and the individual maximizes utility, the economic problem faced by individuals can be mathematically described – the problem is to maximize the utility function given that the constraint function (the constraint being income or time and prices) is satisfied. An amazing array of interactions can be constructed as exchanges in this way; indeed, some economists seem to find it difficult to exclude anything, with Gary Becker arguing that 'the economic approach provides a valuable unified framework for understanding *all* human behavior' (1976b: 14).

Although rational economic man can be specified mathematically, and hence exists in algebraic or logical time and in geometric space (White 1982: 117), he is given a concrete identity, but one which is already meaningful as masculine, when the figure of Robinson Crusoe is used to illustrate his activities. Robinson Crusoe as the exemplar of *Homo economicus* is the instrumentally rational, self-interested and radically separate individual who, it is alleged, can be found throughout history and across cultures, alone on an island, or in a society which is conceptualized as the sum of 'isolated' individuals. Crusoe has a set of preferences which drive his utility-maximizing consumption and leisure choices, subject to constraints such as time and resource endowments. Although alone, Crusoe can indulge in a range of illustrative activities and exchanges which exemplify the scope and method of neoclassical economics. He can use his scarce resources – his time, his skills, and his resource endowment – to satisfy competing ends, such as sunbaking, the consumption of coconuts, and building shelter. He can ponder over his rate of time preference – his valuation of current as opposed to future consumption – and thereby determine the optimal division between savings (or investment) and current consumption of grains of corn. He can equate the utility of his 'wage', measured in pineapples per hour, to the disutility he experiences as he collects the pineapples.

Once Crusoe is joined on the island by his 'man Friday', mutually beneficial exchanges can take place. If Friday is better than Crusoe at catching fish, one or both can benefit from specialization in fishing and climbing trees for coconuts respectively, and the voluntary exchange of fish for coconuts. Although Crusoe and Friday are assumed to be self-interested, their interaction in the (implied) market has increased their utilities as an unintended consequence. This is the famous 'invisible hand' at work; society as a whole is better off as a result of self-interested behaviour, since fish and coconuts are available at the lowest possible prices due to the efficient allocation of labour. Any prohibition of mutually beneficial exchanges is inefficient due to the presence of unexploited gains from trade. In fully exploiting the gains from trade, Crusoe and Friday generate an efficient allocation of the island's resources. Crusoe's and Friday's island economy may also be used to illustrate a number of other applications of neoclassical economics, such as international trade where Crusoe and Friday can exploit their comparative advantage and move, as a 'country', to a higher level of utility by trading with 'the rest of the world'.

The neoclassical Crusoe is extracted from his social context without loss of explanatory power; he is a logically asocial being whose relationships, it is alleged, are not constitutive of his identity. Indeed, Crusoe need not even be accompanied by Friday to be meaningful in neoclassical economics. Varian, for example, has eliminated Friday as a necessary component of an exchange model (1990: ch. 28; see also Koopmans 1957). The self-possessive Crusoe forms the firm of Crusoe Inc., of which he is the sole shareholder. Crusoe Inc. works out its production schedule on the basis of profit maximization, and employs labour in order to meet its production targets. Crusoe Inc. employs Crusoe at a particular 'coconut wage'. Crusoe the consumer decides how much labour to offer the firm on the basis of utility maximization (he likes coconuts but also likes leisure). These exchanges take place in 'intra-subject' markets in labour and coconuts. To illustrate comparative advantage, Varian adds Friday to the analysis, and to illustrate Pareto optimality, has

Crusoe and Friday form a new company called Castaways Inc., of which they are the major shareholders, as well as its sole employees and customers. There are now two people on the island, and though each has different natural proficiencies in the production of fish and coconuts, they are the same in every important respect. Their embodiment – their sex as well as Friday's colour – is deemed irrelevant. The lone Robinson Crusoe has therefore simply been replicated. Neoclassical economics relies on this view of the subject: individuals must have fully-constituted, stable and pre-given identities, identities which are not reliant on others for their meaning. Rational economic man must be able to 'abstract [himself] as an agent from the particular social relationships in which [he] exists, from specific others, and even from [his] own activities' (Poole 1990: 54). If not, neoclassical economics may play a role in producing such identities, and the social infrastructure which supports them. In this case, neoclassical economics could no longer lay claim to scientific status, since it would be producing its objects of analysis, rather than simply naming a reality which preexists its theoretical endeavours.

However, the extent to which the neoclassical figure of Robinson Crusoe relies upon but cannot acknowledge 'woman' or the feminine is revealed in his relationship to reproduction, maternity and the private sphere. The Robinson Crusoe economy is a representation of the public (civil) sphere and cannot reproduce itself; it can only be replicated or cloned. In its use of the Crusoe story, neoclassical economics presupposes but renders invisible the reproduction of society. Crusoe simply is. The neoclassical Crusoe is a 'self-made man', but, like Defoe's Crusoe who retrieved a great variety of goods from the wrecked ship, seemingly self-made men are always indebted to society and to others. In particular, there is an unacknowledged debt to femininity; a maternal debt, but also a debt of identity, extracted through exclusion. Without her ability to create humans within her body, man would not exist. Although reproduction also requires a father, the father is not denied; the story of the social contract which created enforceable property rights and the 'body economic' was a story of man's invention. Moreover, without the absent presence of femininity, procreative masculinity would also cease to exist. This story of the creative abilities of man is necessarily assumed and indeed produced in the neoclassical version of Crusoe.

The neoclassical version of the Robinson Crusoe story constructs a one-sex model by drawing upon this myth of the social contract to construct a 'body economic' in which exchanges are between masculine 'sames'. The Robinson Crusoe figure constructs economic relations as relations between (white) male bodies, between self-present, fully-formed 'sames'; exchanges takes place in a hom(m)osexual economy, to use Luce Irigaray's (1985) term. In using the Crusoe story, neoclassical economics transforms the constitutive relationship between Defoe's characters into one of exchange between two fully-formed and self-present equals. An assumption of neoclassical economics and other liberal discourses is that the sex of the body is irrelevant to this 'equality', and hence Robinson Crusoe can stand as a universal figure, representing persons of any kind of embodiment. I have shown that the absent female body is the 'other' upon which rational economic man is premised; like the black man Friday and the 'real mother', the feminine inhabits the body which masculinity must disavow in order to produce objective, universally applicable knowledge. This bodily evacuation allows the objective observations of the economist, the 'Robinson Crusoe scientist', to produce scientific knowledge or universal truth. Hence the masculine denial of corporeality underlies the scientific method and allows the 'universal' to speak for women, while woman is constructed within phallocentric knowledges as the 'corporeal, bodily, material substratum supporting male intellect, reason, theoretical structures – male immateriality' (Gross 1986c: 135–6; see also Irigaray 1985: chs 4, 8 and 9; Grosz 1993a). Woman cannot be the 'universal' individual, then, unless she gives up her sexual specificity. She can only be the subject of exchange if she is the 'same' as man; if she is not, she is relegated either to the place of the object of exchange, or to the place of the mother, the unrecognized but necessary 'infrastructure' of society. The female body has this meaning in neoclassical economics, as its constitutive outside. This cannot be openly acknowledged by neoclassical economics, since this would disrupt its claims to self-present objects of analysis, but can be seen, for example, in Crusoe's radical separation from others (the strictness of his boundaries) which interacts with the assumption of instrumental rationality to produce a being whose 'caring' for others can only be expressed as arguments in his own utility function, so that even altruism can only be the satisfaction of *self*-defined ends; and perhaps too in Nelson's denigration of 'mushy sentimentality', 'sloppiness' and 'touchy-feely mysticism'. The female body represents what can be called the 'irrational (m)other' upon which the rationality of economic man is identified. The female body is the source of all that neoclassical economics cannot deal with and has defined as irrational – specifically, the failure of self-identity (see Chapter 7 below) and the caring and giving provided by the mother.[5] The 'irrational mother' is not calculating in her care, not strictly individuated, not competitive, not able to be extracted from the network of relationships within which she gains her meaning, driven by forces of nature, in short, not rational economic man. Rational economic man cannot be represented by his irrational other, the mother; hence, he must have masculine as opposed to feminine embodiment. The underlying structure of neoclassical economics, then, is a one-sex model. Within its framework, we can only consider the allegedly universal Crusoe, or exchanges between two 'sames', exemplified by the two men Crusoe and Friday, or, using Varian's model of exchange, between the ultimate sames, Crusoe and Crusoe.

Nevertheless, rational economic man is masculine only through the production and exclusion of femininity. If neoclassical economics relies as heavily upon this realm of the feminine as I have argued, then a reversal of the privilege established by each of the binary oppositions of culture/nature, mind/body, man/not-man and maternity/exchange is possible. In other words, the previously devalued terms can now be seen as privileged terms, giving life, meaning, identity and self-presence to masculinity in general and rational economic man in particular. Although neoclassical economics denies an interest in bodies, and Crusoe's personification of the 'universal' individual is therefore viewed as distinct from his embodiment as a man, once sexual difference is understood as a function of the socially constructed, lived experience of the body, it is clear that Crusoe's masculine body is not a meaningless coincidence. Male bodies are already inscribed with meanings, and neoclassical texts cannot disavow these meanings, or somehow exclude them or separate them from the other meanings which are being produced. The male body and masculinity are constructed discursively in opposition to, and valued at the expense of, the feminine, which is understood as irrational, dependent, passive, vulnerable, and self-sacrificing. Thus a female Crusoe would be problematic as an exemplar of rational economic man, and a literally female Friday problematic as a trading partner, but woman is the necessary underpinning of masculine identity.

The binary oppositions which construct the one-sex model must, however, be displaced if this model and its claims to universality are to be challenged, since reversing the oppositions by privileging the feminine does not in fact displace phallocentrism, but merely replicates it. This is because the feminine which is now the privileged determinant of meaning is the feminine as produced within neoclassical economics as the constitutive outside, that is, it is the feminine of the one-sex model. Michèlle Le Doeuff writes of this femininity, 'As soon as we regard this femininity as a fantasy-product of conflicts *within* a field of reason that has been assimilated to masculinity, we can no longer set any store by liberating its voice' (quoted in Moi 1989: 196; see also Derrida 1981: 41–2). As discussed in Chapter 4 above, the concept of morphology provides feminist poststructuralists with a way of conceptualizing the lived and sexed body, or the sexed body as a cultural product, and hence a way of displacing binary oppositions which construct the one-sex model. Sexed bodies are both read and written by discourses, and femininity and masculinity are linked to bodies in sexually-differentiated ways, and morphology is thus a third term able to disrupt phallocentric binary oppositions.

It should be recalled that morphology does not refer to anatomy, but to 'how women's bodies are inscribed, constituted as lacking, but also how this representation (and psychical "reality") serves to underpin and make possible the male evacuation of his corporeality in order to accede to the transcendental position of pure, neutral, "human" knower. These two processes are correlates; the first is the necessary condition of the second: only if women become *the body* for men, can men be free conceptually to dispose of their bodies in this aspiration to the disembodied position of God' (Grosz 1993a: 186). God, of course, is the ultimate symbol of masculine procreativity, and man is created in his image. Specifically, masculine morphology, the morphology of Robinson Crusoe, the contracting agent, is produced as, to borrow the term that Marilyn Lake (1996) used in a related context, 'inviolable'. It is, like Crusoe's fortress, impermeable and unable to be taken by force, and hence utterly independent and self-made. It is also procreative – able to give birth to self, to culture, to contract, and, through its self-presence, to meaning. Neither of these constructions are literally true: the male body can be raped or penetrated, and cannot literally give birth; however, they have powerful truth effects which are played out in numerous contexts. Indeed, phallocentric societies are saturated with the institutional reflections of this masculine morphology. Just as the Greek god Zeus gave birth to Athena from his head, so male productivity establishes mind, culture, contract and production as the dominant and self-present terms which organize society, seemingly able to define their not-A terms or others. Lake (1996) argues, for example, that it was men's imagined inviolability which shaped the nature of men's and women's claims to citizenship in early and mid-twentieth-century Australia. Vicki Schultz (1992) shows how a phallocentric 'rape script' structures men's bodies as inviolable, quasi-invincible and unassailable. Gatens (1991a) points to the difficulty of penetrating Hobbes's male Leviathan. And neoclassical economics uses the myth of Robinson Crusoe to incorporate 'the fantasy of self-sufficiency into economic discourse' (Grapard 1995a: 40), his ultimate self-sufficiency being revealed by Varian's producer/consumer/worker Crusoe. This self-sufficiency is also the source of male procreativity – it is man, not woman, who produces culture, contract, economy.

This masculine morphology has been shown to be produced within a dense web of overlapping discourses within which neoclassical economics is situated. Robinson Crusoe therefore undermines the universality and hence disembodiment of rational economic man, and the concept of morphology, and in particular that of procreative masculinity, undermines the binary structure of body/text upon which neoclassical economics relies to support this disavowal of the masculinity of Robinson Crusoe, since the body *is* a text, one which must be written.

5.5. Conclusion

In this chapter I have argued, using the case study of Robinson Crusoe, that masculinity is not a pregiven identity which simply awaits naming. Rather, it is produced, and within phallocentric knowledges, the meaning of masculinity is constructed through binary oppositions which constitute femininity (and non-white men) as inferior, all that is not-masculine. In section 5.3 I drew on the Defoe text to expose the way in which the masculinity of the novel's Robinson Crusoe was produced. I then argued that the body of the neoclassical Crusoe is inscribed as masculine, both by the way in which Crusoe is used in economics, and by the phallocentric meanings which produce masculinity and femininity and which already exist and cannot be disavowed. However, because masculinity relies upon its feminine other, it is femininity which could be viewed as the privileged term, a response which leaves the binary structure of sexual difference – the one-sex model, in which it is now femininity which is self-present and capable of defining the other sex – in place. Therefore the third term morphology, and specifically, the construction of the masculinity of rational economic man as procreative, was used to undermine the binary structure.

A further theme of the chapter is the procreative masculinity of Robinson Crusoe. The deconstruction shows that to start at the point of a fully-formed male human being makes economics blind to what produces that man as a man. The implications of the blindness of neoclassical economics – to interdependence, to women, and to women's bodies and difference – is that women cannot be incorporated into or represented within neoclassical economics as different (pure difference) from men. Specifically, it is the female body which is excluded from neoclassical economics, and indeed, the contracting agent is male. This analysis is a specific case of the limitations of gender feminism and of the analyses of those feminist economists who seek to incorporate the feminine into neoclassical economics in order to produce a complete, human, content or methodology. Feminist economists using the gender approach argue that rational economic man must be expanded to become 'rational economic human'. My analysis, on the other hand, shows that the masculinity of the economic actor is constitutive of neoclassical economics, and cannot be dislodged or generalized without threatening the coherence of this body of knowledge. It follows from the gender view of sexual difference that a person constructed as feminine may just as easily have a male body as a female body. If this were the case, the sex of Robinson Crusoe's body would in fact be irrelevant. Thus feminist economists who adopt the sex/gender distinction inadvertently consign as irrelevant a key signifier of rational economic man, his masculine embodiment. However, if, as I have argued, the 'universal individual' is procreative man, requiring the exclusion of reproductive woman, the inclusions demanded by gender feminists cannot be effected. Thus, I have, following Irigaray, contested 'the philosophical assumptions, arguments, and methods which infiltrate all other knowledges [and revealed] what remains unspoken and unspeakable in them, to show the debt they owe as their condition of possibility to an unrepresented femininity' (Grosz 1993a: 187).

In the following chapter, I develop a formal neoclassical model of the surrogate motherhood exchange. This involves the assumption of utility maximizing on the part of both parties to the exchange, and the derivation of supply and demand on this basis. The market for contract pregnancies appears at first glance to be one in which the female body plays a significant, and irreducible, role. If this were the case, the above discussion of Robinson Crusoe, and my assertion that neoclassical economics relies upon a particular type of masculine embodiment for rational economic man, would become irrelevant. In Chapter 7 I argue that this is not the case. I undertake a reading of the surrogate motherhood exchange, showing that through the metaphor of the womb-as-capital, a metaphor essential to the neoclassical modelling of the exchange, the female body is rewritten in order to become the masculine figure of the contracting agent.

Notes

1. An earlier version of this chapter was published as Hewitson (1994a).
2. For Defoe's economic works, see Montague ([1925–6] 1963). Montague wrote of Defoe that he was in 'no sense a scientific writer, he has made no contribution to economic theory. But his inventive genius occasionally suggested improvements in the economic mechanism of the nation, and his lively imagination sometimes placed economic truths in a singularly vivid light' (ibid.: 535).

3. One of the few explicit references which Crusoe makes to women arises when Crusoe denigrates himself for making a pot 'as a woman would make pies that had never learned to raise paste' (Defoe [1719] 1945: 90).

4. See Pateman (1988) for a discussion of the links and differences between the 'rule of the father' and the fraternal patriarchy originating in the fiction of the social contract.

5. Note that the self-interested wife-beneficiary in the new home economics stands in the place of rational economic man, and therefore must be considered the 'same' as him (see Becker 1991: chs 2 and 8).

6. The Economics of Surrogate Motherhood

6.1. Introduction

In this chapter I develop a formal neoclassical model of the surrogate motherhood exchange, or the market for contract pregnancies, a task yet to be undertaken by economists, despite the controversy which surrounds the existence of such a market.[1] This chapter is therefore a formal demonstration of the way in which exchanges are modelled within the neoclassical framework, and hence a representation of 'rational economic men' in action. Surrogate motherhood refers to the situation in which a woman gestates a fetus which she subsequently relinquishes to others for raising. The surrogacy process must especially be distinguished from the adoption process. In the surrogacy case, the pregnancy is wholly a contract pregnancy – that is, the contract itself brings the pregnancy into being – while in the case of adoption, the pregnancy preexists any contractual relations which specify the social parents of the child (Posner 1992; National Bioethics Consultative Committee 1990). It also should be noted that there are several variants of this surrogacy process, since each of the three relevant parties – the surrogate mother, the social mother and the social father – may or may not contribute genetic material to the child. The most common case is that in which the fetus is the genetic offspring of the surrogate mother and the biological (and social) father. As the Ethics Committee of the American Fertility Society has spelt out, a surrogate mother in this case is:

> a woman who is artificially inseminated with the sperm of a man who is not her husband; she carries the pregnancy and then turns the resulting child over to the man to rear. In almost all instances, the man has chosen to use a surrogate because his wife is infertile. After the birth, the wife will adopt the child. The primary reason for the use of this technology is to produce a child who is genetically linked to the father. (Quoted in Hirschman 1991: 371)

As this definition makes clear, the most common surrogacy contract is a contract between the biological father and the surrogate mother. It is not a contract between the woman who gestates the child (the 'surrogate' mother) and the woman who subsequently mothers the child (the 'social' mother), as common understanding would have it. The partner of the biological father only becomes a (social) mother by virtue of a second contract which is entered into once the surrogacy contract has been fulfilled. This second contract is an adoption contract, where the partner of the biological father legally takes joint custody of the child.[2]

An examination of the market for surrogacy contracts is important because of the growing demand for and/or use of such arrangements by infertile couples. Posner has identified three factors which explain the growing popularity of the practice of surrogate motherhood: (1) scientific advances which make infertile couples less prone to resign themselves to their infertility; (2) the decline in conventional attitudes towards sex and the family; and (3) the acute shortage of (healthy white) babies for adoption (1989: 22). When these three forces are combined with the innate desire for 'own' children which is central to economists' theorization of the demand for children, in which children are portrayed as valuable consumption and/or investment goods (Becker 1991; Posner 1992), it becomes apparent that adoption is inferior to a surrogacy arrangement as a substitute for 'own' children. This is because, in the former case, neither of the social parents is a genetic parent of the child. As Posner has stated, 'even if there were no shortage of babies for adoption, there would be a demand for surrogate motherhood. People (a biologist would say their genes) desire genetic continuity, and surrogacy enables the man (although not his wife) to satisfy this desire' (1989: 22).

It must be emphasized, however, that the importance of an examination of the surrogacy contract market does not arise solely from the recent growth in such contracts deriving from the demand for 'own' children by couples with fertility problems ('genetic' surrogacy). There is also great potential for fertile couples voluntarily to substitute 'externally-gestated' own children for 'internally-gestated' own children ('gestational' surrogacy).[3] As the theory of the family suggests, a large component of the cost of children is the value of the social mother's time. Thus, as the value of women's time rises, the demand for surrogacy contracts by fertile couples will also rise. If surrogacy arrangements are legal, a fertile woman or couple may commission a surrogate mother to bear their genetic child. Specifically, the surrogate mother would be implanted with the egg of the commissioning woman, where the egg had been fertilized *in vitro* with the sperm of either a donor or the commissioning man.[4]

In this chapter I draw on the economic literature on the market for blood (Stewart 1992), altruistic behaviour (Becker [1974] 1976; Landes and Posner 1978) and the demand for quantity and quality of children (Becker 1991) to develop a neoclassical model of the market for surrogate motherhood contracts. I assume that the surrogate mother and the commissioning party are rational economic agents who seek to maximize their utility subject to constraints. In section 6.2 I derive a supply function for surrogate motherhood contracts under the realistic assumption that commissioning parties are unable to determine the true preferences which govern the behaviour of surrogate mothers during pregnancy. In section 6.3 I derive a demand function for surrogate motherhood contracts in which the commissioning party must undertake monitoring activities, due to the inherent information asymmetry just mentioned, and hence face a tradeoff between the quantity and quality of children. In section 6.4 I examine the interaction of these supply and demand functions, and examine the unusual market outcomes produced by the presence of altruistic preferences. Section 6.5 concludes the chapter.

6.2. The Supply of Surrogacy Contracts

The model for the supply of surrogacy contracts developed in this section is in many ways similar to Stewart's (1992) model of the supply of blood when blood may be both sold and donated. I have made five simplifying assumptions. First, all gestational services are contractual, and these contracts include performance clauses which limit the activities of the surrogate mother to those which benefit, or do not harm, the fetus.[5] It nevertheless should be noted that, as in the case of the labour contract, monitoring of the activities of the surrogate mother may be required to ensure fulfilment of these clauses. Second, there is some optimal level of baby quality, q^*, which is achieved through such monitoring.[6] Third, all surrogacy contracts are enforceable. Fourth, the minimum payment to the surrogate mother is the sum of her medical expenses (including amniocentesis) and associated costs. Fifth, two types of surrogacy contract are available, denoted by Π and A. The surrogacy contract Π is defined as a contract which yields a profit to the gestating mother, while the surrogacy contract A yields no profit, so that the surrogate mother either is, or behaves as, an altruist.

The supply of surrogacy contracts is derived from the (marginal) utility function of potential surrogate mothers.[7] The utility function of a potential surrogate mother is specified for the minimum period required to begin and complete a single pregnancy and commence another (ignoring the unusual case of a surrogate mother who carries multiple fetuses for different commissioning parties), and is therefore the additional utility derived from the performance of a surrogacy contract:

$$U_i = (\alpha_i + \beta_i + \gamma_i)(\Pi_i + A_i) - Mq^* (\theta + \epsilon R)(\Pi_i + A_i) + \delta \mu A_i + P\Pi_i \qquad (6.1)$$

The variable Π takes the value of one if the contract is undertaken and profitable, and zero otherwise (see the Appendix to this chapter for a tabular representation of the following variable definitions). The variable A takes the value one if the contract is undertaken and altruistic, and zero otherwise. It is important to note that altruism is here defined as 'the making of any transfer that is not compensated' (Landes and Posner 1978: 417), and that, under this definition and within this chapter, a person may be denoted as either a 'true' altruist or a 'potential' altruist. A person who is a 'true' altruist receives no utility from compensation, and hence will not accept a profitable contract under any circumstances, due, for example, to a moral commitment to altruism or a moral abhorrence of accepting money for producing a baby (see Sen 1982: 92–4, cited in Stewart 1992: 129), whereas a person who is a 'potential' altruist receives utility from compensation, but will turn down profitable contracts if the utility from completing the exchange free of charge outweighs the utility derived from the offered monetary rewards. Thus, in the context of equation (6.1), some surrogate mothers may switch between A and Π as the level of compensation changes. However, for any given compensation level and particular surrogate mother, A and Π may both be zero, or one of them may be one while the other is zero, but it is not possible for both to be one. In other words, by definition, once compensation is paid ($P > 0$) the contract cannot be altruistic.[8]

The variable α is the utility of gestating the fetus; β is the utility derived from the birth; and γ is the utility from surrendering the baby, or the act of giving up the baby. Each of these three parameters may be positive or negative. Also note that I define the function $F(\alpha + \beta + \gamma)$ as the cumulative distribution function of the uniformly-distributed composite variable $(\alpha + \beta + \gamma)$.[9]

The variable M is the price of a unit of expected baby quality, where the latter is denoted by q. It is assumed that M is the expenditure on the monitoring required to increase expected quality by one unit. The optimal level of expected baby quality, q^*, is established by solving the commissioning party's optimizing problem for D_q, the demand for quality. Thus Mq^* is the commissioning party's expenditure on monitoring the activities of the surrogate mother, and this value is specified in the surrogacy contract. Monitoring expenditures are those expenses incurred over and above the average level of medical expenses associated with the pregnancy of a woman who is not a surrogate mother, and might include the costs of having the surrogate mother live with the commissioning party, a supervisor living with, observing or appraising the surrogate mother, medical examinations of various kinds, blood tests for drugs or alcohol, and/or hospitalization.[10]

The variable θ is the utility which the surrogate mother derives from privacy, and it is assumed to be uniform across all potential surrogate mothers. Since monitoring reduces the surrogate mother's privacy, θ is a negative function of monitoring expenditures Mq, and $Mq^*\theta$ is the utility cost to the surrogate mother of monitoring expenditures Mq^*.

The variable R takes the value 1 if the surrogate mother will indulge, unless monitored, in 'dangerous' activities during pregnancy. Dangerous activities are those which impose actual or potential harm on the fetus; hence quality (q) refers to the expected quality rather than the actual quality of the baby. To make this clear, consider a woman who skis throughout pregnancy. Actual harm may be imposed on the fetus if the woman has a skiing accident, but even if there is no accident the act of skiing lowers the expected quality of the fetus due to a probability of greater than zero of actual harm being imposed. Thus potential harm lowers expected quality. Other dangerous activities include smoking, drinking, drug-taking, strenuous exercise and speeding.

The variable ϵ is the disutility of forsaking 'dangerous' but pleasurable activities during pregnancy, and therefore drops out for those women for whom $R = 0$. For those women for whom $R = 1$, a reduction in these 'dangerous' activities due to monitoring imposes the utility cost of $Mq\epsilon$. For simplicity it is assumed that ϵ is constant across all potential surrogate mothers with $R = 1$. The population of potential surrogate mothers is divided into two groups: those who wish to undertake dangerous activities, and who must therefore expend effort to forgo these activities during pregnancy (a fixed proportion r of the population), and those who do not wish to undertake these activities during pregnancy (the proportion $[1 - r]$). It is assumed that women who have this disposition to undertake such activities cannot be distinguished from those who do not.

The variable μ is the proportion of the population who believe that surrogacy contracts should always be altruistic rather than profitable. I assume that the ability to become a surrogate mother is uncorrelated with beliefs regarding the appropriateness of 'pregnancy for profit' (the same might be argued in the case of beliefs regarding abortion, for example). The variable μ is a 'social pressure' variable, or a measure of the potential social acclaim from providing altruistic surrogacy services. The variable δ is a preference parameter which reflects the utility derived from improving the well-being of others or satisfying social and/or familial pressure (measured by μ) to provide gestational services altruistically (see Becker's [1974] 1976 discussion of altruism in the context of the family and contributions to charity). Assume that δ is uniform across all potential surrogate mothers. The term δμ is therefore the utility derived from altruistically providing surrogate motherhood services.

The variable P is the profit derived from the surrogacy contract, which is equal to the monetary compensation paid to the surrogate mother over and above her maintenance expenses and the costs of establishing a contract (denoted by H in the commissioning party's utility maximizing problem discussed in section 6.3 below). P enters the utility function as the marginal utility of income when income is used as the numeraire. It is this variable which distinguishes between 'true' altruists and 'potential' altruists. 'True' altruists derive no utility from compensation; therefore, the variable P drops out of the 'true' altruist's utility function. 'Potential' altruists, on the other hand, derive utility from compensation, and this utility rises with P.

Let S denote the total population of potential surrogate mothers. There are two major sub-populations of potential surrogate mothers – those who believe that surrogate motherhood contracts should be altruistic, a proportion μ of S, and those who do not, a proportion $(1 - μ)$ of S. Those women who believe that surrogate motherhood contracts should be altruistic are 'true' altruists who make transfers to others but refuse to accept transfers from others (Becker [1974] 1976: 270). These women either undertake surrogacy altruistically or not at all.[11] Those women who do not believe that surrogacy should be altruistic will behave as altruists when the utility payoff from such altruism is greater than the utility payoff from a profitable contract, but they can be induced to switch from altruistic to commercial surrogacy by a 'high enough' price (they are therefore 'potential' altruists).[12]

Each of the two sub-populations of potential surrogate mothers consists of two distinct groups – those who wish to undertake 'dangerous' activities while pregnant ($R = 1$), a proportion r of S, and those who do not ($R = 0$), a proportion $(1 - r)$ of S. Given these divisions, there are four groups of potential surrogate mothers. Population I consists of the proportion μ of S where $R = 1$, giving a proportion $r\mu$ of the total population S. Population II consists of the proportion μ of S where $R = 0$, giving a proportion $(1 - r)\mu$ of the total population S. Population III consists of a proportion $(1 - μ)$ of S where $R = 1$, giving a proportion $r(1 - μ)$ of S. Population IV consists of the proportion $(1 - \mu)$ of S where $R = 0$, giving the proportion $(1 - r)(1 - \mu)$ of S. Note that these four sub-groups exhaust the aggregate population S.

The utility levels available to potential surrogate mothers are as follows:

$$
\begin{aligned}
&\text{If } A = 0, \Pi = 0, U^A = 0 \\
&\text{If } A = 1, \Pi = 0, U^B = \alpha + \beta + \gamma - Mq^*(\theta + \epsilon R) + \delta\mu \\
&\text{If } A = 0, \Pi = 1, U^C = \alpha + \beta + \gamma - Mq^*(\theta + \epsilon R) + P
\end{aligned}
\tag{6.2}
$$

where U^A is the utility from doing nothing, U^B is the utility derived from entering and fulfilling an altruistic contract pregnancy, and U^C is the utility from entering and fulfilling a profitable contract pregnancy.

Consider first population I, the group of altruists who have a propensity to undertake dangerous activities while pregnant, and who therefore have to expend effort to forgo these activities. These women will derive utility U^B and supply altruistic surrogacy services if the following condition holds:

$$
\alpha + \beta + \gamma - Mq^*(\theta + \epsilon) + \delta\mu > 0
\tag{6.3}
$$

If the condition is met, the supply of altruistic contracts from population I is:

$$
A_I = [r\mu\,(1 - F\,[Mq^*(\theta + \epsilon) - \delta\mu]\,)]\,S \text{ when } P \geq 0
\tag{6.4}
$$

It follows that:

$$
\Pi_I = 0
\tag{6.5}
$$

Women in population II, altruists who have no propensity to undertake 'dangerous' activities during pregnancy, yield U^B if the following condition is met:

$$
\alpha + \beta + \gamma - Mq^*\theta + \delta\mu > 0
\tag{6.6}
$$

If this condition is met, the supply of altruistic contracts from population II is:

$$
A_{II} = [r\mu\,(1 - F\,[Mq^*\theta - \delta\mu])]S \text{ when } P > 0
\tag{6.7}
$$

It follows that:

$$
\Pi_{II} = 0
\tag{6.8}
$$

Women in population III derive U^B and behave as altruists if the following conditions are met:

1. $\alpha + \beta + \gamma - Mq^* (\theta + \epsilon) + \delta\mu > 0$
2. $\delta\mu - P > 0$ (6.9)

The supply of altruistic surrogacy contracts from this group is therefore:

$$A_{III} = [r(1 - \mu)(1 - F[Mq^* (\theta + \epsilon) - \delta\mu])]S \text{ when } P < \delta\mu$$
$$0 \text{ when } P \geq \delta\mu \qquad (6.10)$$

$(1 - F[Mq^*(\theta + \epsilon) - \delta\mu])$ is the proportion of the population proportion $r(1 - \mu)$ who are willing to enter altruistic surrogacy contracts despite the fact that they do not have a commitment to altruistic surrogacy. This group will supply their services for profit if the following conditions are met:

1. $\alpha + \beta + \gamma - Mq^* (\theta + \epsilon) + P > 0$
2. $P - \delta\mu > 0$ (6.11)

The supply of profitable contract pregnancies from this group is therefore:

$$\Pi_{III} = [r(1 - \mu)(1 - F[Mq^* (\theta + \epsilon) - P])]S \text{ when } P \geq \delta\mu$$
$$0 \text{ when } P < \delta\mu \qquad (6.12)$$

Finally, women in population IV derive U^B and hence supply their services altruistically if the following conditions are met:

1. $\alpha + \beta + \gamma - Mq^* \theta + \delta\mu > 0$
2. $\delta\mu - P > 0$ (6.13)

The supply of altruistic surrogacy contracts from this group is therefore:

$$A_{IV} = [(1 - r)(1 - \mu)(1 - F[Mq^* \theta - \delta\mu])]S \text{ when } P < \delta\mu$$
$$0 \text{ when } P \geq \delta\mu \qquad (6.14)$$

$(1 - F[Mq^*\theta - \delta\mu])$ is the proportion of the population proportion $(1 - r)(1 - \mu)$ who are willing to enter altruistic surrogacy contracts despite the fact that they do not have a commitment to altruistic surrogacy. This group will supply their services for profit, and hence yield U^C, if the following conditions are met:

1. $\alpha + \beta + \gamma - Mq^* \theta + P > 0$
2. $P - \delta\mu > 0$ (6.15)

The supply of profitable contract pregnancies from this group is therefore:

$$\Pi_{III} = [(1 - r)(1 - \mu)(1 - F[Mq^* \theta - P])]S \text{ when } P \geq \delta\mu$$
$$0 \text{ when } P < \delta\mu$$ (6.16)

The supply curve of surrogacy contracts is derived by summing the individual components. Summing the supply of altruistic contracts yields:

$$A = [\, r\mu(1 - F[Mq^* (\theta + \epsilon) - \delta\mu])$$
$$+ (1 - r)\mu(1 - F[Mq^* \theta - \delta\mu])$$
$$+ r(1 - \mu)(1 - F[Mq^* (\theta+\epsilon) - \delta\mu])$$
$$+ (1 - r)(1 - \mu)(1 - F[Mq^* - \delta\mu])]\, S \text{ when } P < \delta\mu$$ (6.17)

$$[\, r\mu(1 - F[Mq^* (\theta + \epsilon) - \delta\mu])$$
$$+ (1 - r)\mu(1 - F[Mq^* \theta - \delta\mu])]\, S \text{ when } P \geq \delta\mu$$

Summing the supply of profitable contracts yields:

$$\Pi = 0 \text{ when } P < \delta\mu$$ (6.18)

$$[\, r(1 - \mu)(1 - F[Mq^* (\theta + \epsilon) - P])$$
$$+ (1 - r)(1 - \mu)(1 - F[Mq^* \theta - P])]\, S \text{ when } P \geq \delta\mu$$

The total supply of surrogacy contracts is therefore:

$$T = [\, r\mu(1 - F[Mq^* (\theta + \epsilon) - \delta\mu])$$
$$+ (1 - r)\mu(1 - F[Mq^* \theta - \delta\mu])$$
$$+ r(1 - \mu)(1 - F[Mq^* (\theta + \epsilon) - \delta\mu])$$
$$+ (1 - r)(1 - \mu)(1 - F[Mq^* \theta - \delta\mu])\,]\, S \text{ when } P < \delta\mu$$ (6.19)

$$[\, r\mu(1 - F[Mq^* (\theta + \epsilon) - \delta\mu])$$
$$+ (1 - r)\mu(1 - F[Mq^* \theta - \delta\mu])$$
$$+ r(1 - \mu)(1 - F[Mq^* (\theta + \epsilon) - P])$$
$$+ (1 - r)(1 - \mu)(1 - F[Mq^* \theta - P\,])\,]\, S \text{ when } P \geq \delta\mu$$

Figure 6.1 below illustrates the supply curve. Note that the origin of the vertical axis is not zero but $H + Mq^*$ (where H, as mentioned, is the surrogate mother's maintenance expenses and the costs of establishing the contract), in order to represent diagrammatically both demand and supply in section 6.4 below. The four elements of total supply can now be summarized.

(1) Altruistic contracts when $P = 0$, denoted $n(A)$, which is made up of the supply of altruistic contracts $n(S_0)$ from population I women and $n(S_1) - n(S_0)$ from population II women, as well as contracts forthcoming from women in populations III and IV $(n(A) - n(S_1))$. All suppliers are monitored because there is no way to distinguish between those women for whom $R = 1$ and those for whom $R = 0$.

Note that when the price rises to $0 < P < \delta\mu$, the supply of altruistic contracts drops to $n(S_1)$, since women from populations III and IV will refuse to offer any surrogacy services at all over this price range. This is because over this price range these women fail both to capture utility from behaving altruistically – and hence withdraw their altruistic services – and to reach the switchpoint $P = \delta\mu$ – at which point they will offer profitable contracts. The reasoning here is that it is implausible that women from populations III and IV offer commissioning parties the following deal: 'Pay me either nothing or some fee which yields (marginal) utility greater than $\delta\mu$.' Such a deal eliminates any possibility of achieving a utility level higher than $\delta\mu$, the utility from behaving altruistically, since all commissioning parties will prefer the zero fee option. Therefore I assume that such women take the price as given and offer their services or not accordingly. Women from populations I and II, on the other hand, simply refuse to accept a fee at any time, supplying their services altruistically whatever the price being offered. Thus, whenever the price falls within the range $H + Mq^* < P < \delta\mu$, price will be driven to zero (this is discussed further in relation to Figure 6.2 below).

(2) Altruistic contracts when $P \geq \delta\mu$. When P is greater than $\delta\mu$ and profitable contracts are being established, the supply of altruistic contracts is derived solely from population I and II women, denoted $n(S_1)$.

(3) Profitable contracts when $P < \delta\mu$. When $P < \delta\mu$, no profitable contracts are undertaken, since women from populations I and II never accept a fee, and women from populations III and IV either enter altruistic contracts (when $P = 0$), or withdraw their services completely (when $0 < P < \delta\mu$).

(4) Profitable contracts when $P \geq \delta\mu$. The supply of profitable contracts when $P \geq \delta\mu$ is a positive function of P and is derived from women in populations III and IV, who switch from altruistic to profitable contracts when the price rises from zero to $P \geq \delta\mu$.

An interesting point to note is that this supply curve is consistent with the widely-held view on blood donation, which is that once blood donation becomes profitable, the supply of blood falls (Titmuss 1970). In the surrogacy contract case, once the utility value of the price outweighs the

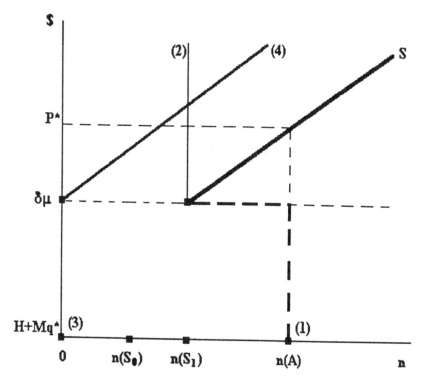

Figure 6.1   The supply of surrogacy contracts

utility derived from acting altruistically, the supply - falls because the 'potential' altruists from populations III and IV switch from altruistic to profitable contracts. P must reach P^* before the total number of profitable and altruistic contracts exceeds the number of altruistic contracts on offer when $P = 0$.

6.3.   The Demand for Surrogacy Contracts

In this section I consider the demand for surrogacy contracts or externally-gestated 'own' children. This demand may arise from fertile men married to infertile women or women who cannot bear children, or those female partners who are able to induce them to enter into a surrogacy contract,[13] gay couples, single men or single women. The term 'commissioning party' may therefore refer to a male, a female or to male/female-couple combinations.

Following Becker (1991: 137), the commissioning party's utility function is of the form:

$$U = U(n, q, Z_i) \tag{6.20}$$

The variable n is the number of surrogacy contracts, q is the expected quality per baby, and Z_i refers to all other goods. Note that this demand is specified for one period, and, since many contracts can be initiated for that period, there is an enlarged set of choices relative to the case of 'own' children. In other words, unlike Becker's (1991) model, the commissioning party can choose to have more than one child per period.

The budget constraint facing the commissioning party is as follows:

$$H n + P n + M n q + \zeta_i Z_i = I \tag{6.21}$$

where H is the surrogate mother's maintenance expenses and the costs of establishing a contract, P is the surrogacy contract price, M is the (constant) price of monitoring, and hence is the cost of a unit of quality, ζ_i is the set of prices of commodities, and I is income. H, M and ζ_i are assumed to be competitively determined elsewhere.

The first order conditions for a maximum are:

$$L(n,q,Z_i)=U(n,q,Z_i)+\lambda(I-Hn-Pn-Mnq-\zeta_i Z_i)$$

$$\frac{\delta L}{\delta n} = MU_n - \lambda(H+P+Mq) = 0$$

$$\frac{\delta L}{\delta q} = MU_q - \lambda Mn = 0$$

$$\frac{\delta L}{\delta Z_i} = MU_{Z_i} - \lambda \zeta_i = 0 \tag{6.22}$$

$$\frac{\delta L}{\delta \lambda} = I - Hn - Pn - Mqn - \zeta_i Z_i = 0$$

The first-order conditions yield:

$$\frac{MU_n}{(H+P+Mq)} = \frac{MU_q}{Mn} = \frac{MU_{Z_i}}{\zeta_i} \tag{6.23}$$

That is, the ratios of the marginal utilities to (shadow) prices are equal across all 'commodities'.

Let the shadow price of quantity equal Φ_n; the shadow price of quality equal Φ_q; the price of other goods equal Φ_Z; and shadow income equal X. Then solve the utility maximizing problem for the following demand functions:[14]

$$D_n = D_n\,(\Phi_n,\,\Phi_q,\,\Phi_Z,\,X)$$
$$D_q = D_q\,(\Phi_n,\,\Phi_q,\,\Phi_Z,\,X) \qquad\qquad (6.24)$$
$$D_Z = D_Z\,(\Phi_n,\,\Phi_q,\,\Phi_Z,\,X)$$

The variables n and q interact through Φ_n, Φ_q and X. An increase in H or P raises Φ_n, lowers the demand for quantity D_n, which lowers Φ_q and raises the demand for quality D_q; the increase in q then raises Φ_n, and so on. As long as n and q are not close substitutes, this process will end in a new equilibrium n and q.[15] An increase in M lowers both n and q, *ceteris paribus*.[16]

6.4. Interaction of Supply and Demand

In this section, I discuss the interaction of the demand and supply for surrogacy contracts. The demand and supply functions are represented in Figure 6.2 below. The origin of the vertical axis is $H+Mq$ (since $H+P+Mq = \Phi_n$). The equilibrium price and quantity depend, as usual, on the positions of the demand and supply curves. I examine five possible outcomes.

Consider first a demand curve in the position of $D = D_0$. The equilibrium price is zero, and there is an excess supply of altruistic surrogacy contracts of $n(A) - n0$. Given that there is an excess demand for adoptable babies in Australia, the US and Britain, and given the absence of a glut of surrogate mothers in the US surrogacy market (the most developed of such markets), the outcome D_0 is an unlikely outcome. However, it may be the case that the Australian demand for surrogacy contracts is currently reflected by $D = D_0$, due to lack of experience with such exchanges, the illegality of such contracts in a large proportion of the country relative to the US, and/or the smaller market and hence the absence of intermediaries. This argument may in turn be challenged on the grounds that the Australian, US and other markets should be treated as one market, since, as Ragoné reports, commissioning parties travel from all over the world to the US in order to undertake surrogacy contracts (1994: 193n).

Consider now a demand curve in the position of $D = D_1$. At $P = 0$, there is

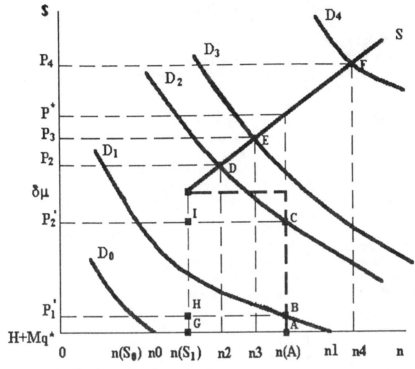

Figure 6.2   The demand and supply of surrogacy contracts

an excess demand for surrogacy contracts. This excess demand drives the price up to P_1 (point B), the price which appears to clear the market. However, women from populations III and IV prefer to withdraw their services completely rather than accept a price of P_1. As explained above, this is because $H + Mq^* < P < \delta\mu$ is insufficient to compensate such women for the loss of the utility they derive from behaving altruistically, and they therefore supply neither altruistic nor profitable contract pregnancies (point H). However, women from populations I and II refuse the fee and continue to supply altruistic contract pregnancies. The quasi-equilibrium therefore moves from point B to point H to point G. Once the price falls to zero, women from populations III and IV are again prepared to offer altruistic contract pregnancies and hence the quasi-equilibrium moves back to point A. At point A, the excess demand pushes up the price toward point B. For a demand curve $D = D_1$, then, an unstable situation arises and the market fails to settle at any particular price–quantity combination, circulating from point

A to point B to point H to point G and back to A.

If the demand curve lies in a position such as $D = D_2$, the equilibrium depends on whether a Dutch or an English auction determines the price (see Smith 1989). If a Dutch auction prevails, the initial offer is above P_2 and price is reduced until an equilibrium is established at point D. The question then arises as to how the altruistic contracts are distributed. As in the case of credit rationing, it could be assumed that altruistic contracts are distributed randomly amongst observationally equivalent commissioning parties (Stiglitz and Weiss 1981). However, it is clear that not all commissioning parties are observationally equivalent: it seems reasonable to assume that at least a certain proportion of these contracts are entered into for the benefit of family members or friends, and, given the importance to many surrogate mothers of the sense of 'giving the gift of a baby' (Parker 1983), a further proportion may, consistent with the surrogate mothers' wishes, be entered into for the sake of those commissioning parties who are the least well off, as measured, for example, by the time spent on adoption waiting lists.

If, however, an English auction determines the price, the initial offer is very low (I assume below P_2'), and is bid up to P_2'. This is not an equilibrium price, however, since if $0 < P < \delta\mu$, the altruistic supply from populations III and IV drops out. The market then moves to point I, 'true' altruists refuse the fee, the price drops to zero (point G). Once price is zero, the altruistic supply from populations III and IV reappears (point A), and once again the price is pushed up by excess demand. Therefore an English auction will produce an unstable market which oscillates between points A, C, I and G.

In the case of $D = D_3$, there is only one possible outcome – equilibrium at point E – which will be reached whether a Dutch or an English auction system prevails. This is because the excess demand at $P = 0$ is sufficient to raise the price past the switchpoint $\delta\mu$. What is interesting about this situation is that at the equilibrium P is less than P^*, so that point E is characterized by a lower level of exchanges relative to the purely altruistic case. This is consistent with the literature on blood, in which the existence of a positive price (in this case, $P \geq \delta\mu$) can reduce the quantity exchanged due to the reduction in altruistic supply (Stewart 1992). Finally if $D = D_4$, equilibrium is at point F, and $P_4 > P^*$ so that the forthcoming supply is greater than that when $P = 0$, and apart from the issue of the distribution of altruistic surrogacy contracts, the market operates in the usual way.

The available evidence of transactions in surrogate motherhood contracts reveals, however, that the market may, in the current social environment, be subject to additional cultural factors which produce rigidity in the fee paid to surrogate mothers undertaking profitable surrogacy contracts. These cultural factors are associated with the commercialization of motherhood, and an indication of their importance is given by the existence of legal regimes in which the commercial aspects of surrogacy are banned but altruistic surrogacy is legal. In the US, where the surrogate motherhood market is most developed, there are eight established surrogacy programmes, and a number of small part-time businesses in which lawyers, doctors, adoption agents and others arrange surrogate motherhood contracts (Ragoné 1994: 4). Surrogate mothers who fulfil contracts mediated by the programmes are actively encouraged to identify with the needs and desires of the commissioning party, both to ensure that they fulfil the contract, and to avoid casting 'reproduction in a materialistic light [which] would contradict a number of cultural norms, not the least of which is that reproduction is traditionally undertaken out of "love" and not out of a desire for "money" ' (1994: 41). Ragoné quotes a psychologist working for one of the surrogacy programmes who suggested that, although the fee of $10,000 might usefully be increased to cover cost-of-living increases, it should not be increased beyond $15,000 since this may result in a 'woman denying her true feelings and doing it just for the money' (1994: 29; see also Ragoné 1994: ch. 1; Morgan 1986, 1994; Anderson 1990; Field 1990; Anleu 1992; Satz 1992; Wertheimer 1992; Trebilcock 1993: ch. 2). Thus these cultural factors are of a similar nature to the variable μ in the model, but now operating to censure not surrogate mothers who make profitable contracts, but surrogate mothers who seek to profit beyond a socially-sanctioned level. For example, in 1994 the fee paid to surrogate mothers by the eight surrogacy programmes in the USA had remained at the standard of between $10,000 and $12,000 for ten years (Ragoné 1994: 29). However, excess demand in the market raises the potential for private contracting, and such offers have been made by both commissioning parties and surrogate mothers, with Katz reporting that in the mid-1980s $50,000 was offered to a 22–35 year old surrogate mother who 'was tall, trim, intelligent and stable', and that a surrogate mother offered to 'produce a beautiful child especially for you' for a fee of $125,000 (1986: 3). Media reports give evidence of the simultaneous existence of altruistic arrangements. The surrogate motherhood market, then, appears to be characterized by Dutch and English auction components in non-programme contracting as well as a fixed price component, with the fixed price being somewhere below the equilibrium price but above the switchpoint, which determines the number of altruistic contracts. In terms of Figure 6.2, the market may be characterized by the following: demand is represented by D_4, the standard fee by a price such as P_2, non-programme contractual offers in the regions of $P > P_4$ (from potential surrogate mothers) and $P_2 < P < P_4$

6.6. Appendix: Definitions of Variables

Variable	Definition	Value
Π	Profitable surrogacy contract	0 or 1
A	Altruistic surrogacy contract	0 or 1
α	Utility of gestating the foetus	+ or −
β	Utility derived from the birth	+ or −
γ	Utility of surrendering the baby to the commissioning party	+ or −
M	Price of a unit of baby quality (q) obtained through monitoring	$M \geq 0$
Mq^*	Expenditure on monitoring the surrogate mother	$Mq^* \geq 0$
θ	Utility derived from privacy	$\theta > 0$
$Mq^*\theta$	Surrogate mother's disutility from loss of privacy due to monitoring	$Mq^*\theta > 0$
R	Propensity for dangerous activities during pregnancy (takes the value 1 if the propensity is present)	0 or 1
r	Proportion of potential surrogate mother population for whom $R = 1$	$r + (1 - r) = S$
$(1 - r)$	Proportion of potential surrogate mother population for whom $R = 0$	
ϵ	Disutility of forsaking 'dangerous' but pleasurable activities during pregnancy	$\epsilon \geq 0$

Variable	Definition	Value
$Mq*\epsilon$	Surrogate mother's disutility from giving up 'dangerous' but pleasurable activities due to monitoring	$Mq*\epsilon > 0$ if $R = 1$, 0 otherwise
μ	Proportion of population who believe surrogacy should be altruistic	$\mu \geq 0$
δ	Utility from improving well-being of others or satisfying social/familial pressure	
$\delta\mu$	Utility of altruistically supplying surrogate mother services	$\delta\mu \geq 0$
P	Profit from surrogacy contract	$P \geq 0$
H	Surrogate mother's maintenance expenses and the costs of establishing the contract	$H \geq 0$
S	Total population of potential surrogate mothers	$r\mu + (1-r)\mu + r(1-\mu) + (1-r)(1-\mu) = S$
Pop. I	Potential surrogate mothers for whom $R = 1$ and who believe that contracts should be altruistic	$(r\mu)S$
Pop. II	Potential surrogate mothers for whom $R = 0$ and who believe that contracts should be altruistic	$[(1 - r)\mu]S$
Pop. III	Potential surrogate mothers for whom $R = 1$ and who believe contracts should be altruistic	$[r(1 - \mu)]S$
Pop. IV	Potential surrogate mothers for whom $R = 0$ and who do not believe that contracts should be altruistic	$[(1 - r)(1 - \mu)]S$

Notes

1. The controversial nature of contract pregnancy is shown by the fact that its practice has been outlawed in several states of both the United States and Australia. Both commercial and altruistic surrogacy contracts are illegal in South Australia and Queensland, while in Tasmania and the ACT these contracts are unenforceable. In Victoria, altruistic but not commercial surrogacy is legal. The status of surrogacy is uncertain in New South Wales, Western Australia and the Northern Territory (Stuhmcke 1994). In the USA, the practice is banned in four states, payments to surrogate mothers, apart from living expenses, are banned in a further five states, and in eight states payments to intermediaries are banned (Ragoné 1994: 37).

2. As Anderson (1990: 74) points out, if a woman who is genetically unrelated to the fetus is a party to the surrogacy contract, the surrogacy contract is transformed into an illegal contract for baby-selling, or the offering of a financial reward to a woman for giving up her parental rights. This excludes from the potential expansion of the surrogacy market those contracts in which a surrogate mother gestates a fetus which has no biological connection to the commissioning party.

3. The technology for such an expansion of the market for surrogacy services exists. The first child of a gestational surrogate mother using *in vitro* fertilization was born in 1987, the first child of a gestational surrogate mother using a frozen embryo was born in 1989, and, in 1991, a frozen embryo was shipped from England to the USA and implanted in the womb of an American gestational surrogate mother (Ragoné 1994: 6). Ragoné, who has undertaken a study of the majority of the US surrogate mother programmes, reports that over the period 1988–90 to 1992–94 gestational surrogacy had increased from 5 per cent to over 50 per cent of the surrogate motherhood contracts arranged by two of these programmes (1994: 196). Ragoné attributes the 'meteoric rise in the number of couples seeking gestational surrogacy' to the increased success rate of IVF procedures, which, incidentally, add an estimated $7,000 per procedure to the costs borne by the commissioning party (ibid.: 34).

4. 'Gestational' surrogate mothers may choose to carry more than one fetus at a time, each with different genetic parents. I would like to thank John King for bringing a case of this kind to my attention.

5. Examples of such behavioural restrictions include the following: the surrogate mother may not engage in intercourse during the period, which may be a number of months, over which she is being artificially inseminated; she must not smoke cigarettes, drink any alcoholic beverages, or use any illegal drugs, non-prescription medications or prescribed medications without written consent from her physician; she must not allow an emotional bond between herself and the fetus to develop; she may have to give up her employment in the interests of the fetus; she must attend any and all appointments – with doctors, lawyers, psychiatrists, and so on – required by the commissioning party or its agent, the intermediary; and she must abort the fetus should the commissioning party so desire (see Keane and Breo 1981: ch. 13; Ince 1984). These contractual clauses may or may not be legally enforceable, and, in particular, the clause which requires the surrogate mother to abort the fetus should the commissioning party so desire is not an enforceable clause in the United States, where abortion is a woman's constitutional right. It should be kept in mind, however, that the tendency within US courts to create fetal rights and hence establish the fetus as a legal person may make many behaviours of pregnant women, and perhaps in particular, surrogate mothers, the subject of legal intervention.

6. This assumption significantly simplifies the analysis. In this chapter I wish only to consider the market for surrogacy contracts, leaving for another work the analysis of the market for 'baby quality'.

7. The population of potential surrogate mothers excludes infertile women as well as those women who would not undertake a surrogacy contract under any conditions, due, for example, to a moral abhorrence of the practice. It is possible that a very large price would induce such women to offer their services. I have chosen to simply ignore this group, however, since they complicate the utility function without adding additional interesting insights. I would like to thank an anonymous referee of *Economic Record* for this point.

8. Various factors which motivate surrogate mothers have been identified. Hirschman, for example, reports that surrogate mothers are variously motivated by a need to redress past 'reproductive crimes', such as abortion, and/or the desires to reenact their own childhood abandonment, to re-experience pregnancy and childbirth, to be altruistic, to make a contribution to society, to gain a feeling of self-fulfilment and accomplishment, and to help others attain a family (1991: 374–5; see also Ragoné 1994). Parker's widely-cited examination of the motivations of surrogate mothers revealed that the decision to become a surrogate mother was influenced by a number of complementary factors, including, in his words: '1) the perceived need and desire for money, 2) the perceived degree of enjoyment and desire to be pregnant, and 3) the perception that the advantages of relinquishment outweighed the disadvantages'. The advantages of relinquishment were 'the gift of a baby to a parent who needed a child' and a (possibly unconscious) need to overcome unresolved feelings about their reproductive past. Of Parker's sample of 122 women, 89 per cent said they required a fee for their participation, but the fee was never the sole reason for entering a surrogacy contract; the other factors were also important to a greater or lesser extent (1983: 118). Landes and Posner's (1978: 418) question as to 'why [a person] derives *any* utility from the welfare of a complete stranger' is relevant to the case of surrogate mothers. Reciprocal altruism would appear to be as irrelevant in the case of surrogate motherhood as in the case of the altruistic rescue of strangers (see the discussion in Landes and Posner 1978: 419). The 'recognition factor' – the publicity or recognition which flows from the performance of an altruistic act such as rescuing a stranger (ibid.) – may be simply an alternative way of expressing the above-named motivations of surrogate mothers. In any case, as Landes and Posner conclude, while 'the basis for altruistic impulses towards strangers . . . may be obscure, the existence of the impulse is verified by . . . numerous instances' (ibid.).

9. The previous note indicated that, although many surrogate mothers would refuse to undertake a contract without monetary compensation, they nevertheless satisfy a range of other motivations, some of which are altruistic, as well. The utility derived from satisfying such motives is reflected in the variables α, β and γ. For example, the utility derived from repairing past 'reproductive crimes' is picked up by α, β and/or γ, and the utility from giving the 'gift of a child' is picked up by γ. Thus the dichotomy between Π and A contracts does not eliminate the existence of a range of utility-producing aspects within a surrogacy arrangement. In light of the tendency, at least within the US surrogate motherhood market, for surrogate mothers entering profitable contracts to be paid a set fee, the satisfaction of such utility-producing motivations raises the producer surplus from such exchanges.

10. Ragoné has estimated the fee paid by commissioning parties to the agency which arranges the contract at around $23,000, which includes the agency's retainer and contract fees, initial screening of the surrogate mother, and psychological fees (1994: 34). In such programmes, the commissioning party in effect passes the responsibility for monitoring to the agency, and the agency discourages the commissioning party from undertaking its own monitoring activities. In privately-arranged contracts, the commissioning party would take on the responsibility of such monitoring.

11. I ignore the complication implied by Becker's discussion of charity: 'an increase in the incomes of both recipients and givers should not increase giving by as much as an increase in the incomes of givers alone' ([1974] 1976: 274). In the case of surrogate motherhood, this result indicates that as alternatives to surrogacy contracts improve, for example, through an increase in the supply of adoptable babies or in the availability or efficiency of

other 'new reproductive technologies', the supply of altruistic surrogate contracts will fall (the supply curve in Figure 6.1 below shifts to the left). Note that I also exclude the case of an altruistic surrogate mother entering a profitable contract in order to donate the proceeds to a charity. The effect of this would be to fill in the discontinuity of the supply curve (see Figure 6.1 below). However, since the empirical evidence suggests that a discontinuity exists, the exclusion seems reasonable.

12. The results of Parker (1983) and Hirschman (1991) indicate that the proportion of 'potential' altruists $(1 - \mu)$ is likely to be quite large relative to the proportion of 'true' altruists μ. It may also be the case that μ varies with the legal regime. For example, a woman may be a 'true' altruist in relation to childless couples unable to adopt, but a 'potential' altruist in relation to commissioning parties, such as fertile career women, deemed less deserving. Similarly, δ may be a function of legal regimes, so that as the market expands both μ and δ fall (see Ragoné 1994: ch. 2 who examines a number of particular cases).

13. In this context, Posner has argued that if surrogacy were not available, it is possible that 'the husband will abandon his wife for a woman who is fertile' (1989: 24). Note that Mrs Stern, the wife of the commissioning party in the 'Baby M' case, was fertile but for medical reasons did not wish to conceive and carry her own child to term.

14. Shadow income, X, is the sum of the shadow amounts spent on different commodities (see Becker 1991: 145–6):

$$(Mn)q + (H + P + Mq)n + \zeta_i Z_i = I + Mnq = X$$

15. Note that, if n and q are close substitutes, equilibrium will not be possible, for n and q continue to interact following an exogenous increase in either, until one or other of their values reaches zero and the other approaches infinity. See Becker (1991: 145–50).

16. As in the case of the supply of contracts, the demand for contracts can be bifurcated into the demand for altruistic contracts and the demand for commercial contracts. I would like to thank an anonomous referee of *Economic Record* for this point. The implication of the existence of commissioning parties who demand altruistic contracts is that the demand curves in Figure 6.2 below shift to the right, and each demand curve includes a section of the horizontal axis beginning at the origin. A further complication on the demand side of the surrogacy contract market is suggested by Ragoné, who argues that improvements in women's education and employment opportunities would mean that 'fewer women [adoptive mothers] would elect to participate in surrogacy as a means by which to attain satisfaction and fulfillment' (1994: 3). However, offsetting this tendency for women to find fulfilment outside the home may be a simultaneous rise in the demand for gestational surrogacy, as the opportunity cost of women's time in the home increases. A quantitative study should incorporate these variables on the demand side.

7. Surrogate Motherhood and the Work of a Metaphor

7.1. Introduction

Feminist poststructuralism allows a distinction to be made between a person, say a woman, who undertakes economic activities such as work and other exchanges, and the subject position which is constructed for women in such exchanges by the discourse of neoclassical economics. This is the distinction between economics as a literal, although abstract, representation of women's activities, and economics as a productive discourse which constructs the meaning of these activities in particular ways. Many feminist economists read economics literally, and find it lacking in terms of its representations of women. For example, it has been argued on the basis of object relations theory that women are more relationally defined and connected to others than are men (see Chapter 3 above). A feminist undertaking a literal reading of neoclassical economics through object relations theory would argue that neoclassical economics, in its tendency to theorize individuality as fiercely independent and competitive, is a representation of the way that men experience the world. The conclusion which follows is that neoclassical economics is a poor representation of the real world, in which both men and women participate in economic activity. This leads some feminist economists to challenge those who claim that neoclassical assumptions are universally applicable, and to argue for a broader framework, one which encompasses representations of both men and women. Thus a 'true woman' is opposed to the false representations (or lack thereof) which dominate neoclassical theories. Using feminist poststructuralism, I question this implicit assumption that neoclassical theory is simply a mirror of society, albeit one which heretofore has reflected only a partial view of society, and instead attempt to draw out the way that neoclassical economics constructs subject positions and may actually rely upon the exclusion of the feminine for its truth effects.

I argue that it is not possible simply to add the feminine without examining the way in which the feminine, rather than being overlooked or left out, as it were, is actually the constitutive outside of neoclassical economics.

The production of embodied subject positions within discourses, and the importance of the excluded feminine for the production of masculine subjectivity within the discourse of neoclassical economics, has been discussed in relation to Robinson Crusoe in Chapter 5 above. In the present chapter, I read the neoclassical interpretation of the surrogate motherhood exchange developed in Chapter 6 above through the metaphor of the womb-as-capital in order to reveal the way in which the binary opposition of man/not-man supports the claims of economists that neoclassical economics is a universally applicable and sexually-indifferent knowledge. I argue that the womb-as-capital metaphor is essential for the neoclassical conception of the surrogate motherhood exchange, and I situate it within a range of discourses which support the notion of the universal individual and hence a one-sex model. When considering these issues, it is important to recall that to argue that a particular discourse constructs sexual difference or femininity in particular ways is not to essentialize sexual difference or femininity, since, as Drucilla Cornell argues, 'Woman "is" only in language, which means that her "reality" can never be separated from the metaphors and fictions in which she is presented' (1991: 18). I argue, then, that the neoclassical account of the surrogate motherhood exchange produces the female body as meaningful in particular ways, but I do not simultaneously assert another true meaning which I would then compel neoclassical economists to add to their analyses. The purpose of this chapter is neither to advocate nor to oppose surrogate motherhood contracts. Rather, this is a specific case study of the problematic status of 'woman' within the neoclassical account of exchange in general. It is therefore a feminist poststructuralist reading of the neoclassical modelling of the exchange for its production of meaning, but not, I again stress, for the purpose of producing a specific position in relation to surrogate motherhood contracts *per se*. It is also important to keep in mind that, although I draw upon the extant economic texts on surrogate motherhood (Posner 1989, 1992; Chapter 6 above), the analysis to follow requires neither consistency with the conscious intentions of authors, nor verification from the experience of women and men who have been involved in surrogacy. On this latter point, I endorse Pateman's argument that the existence of smoothly completed surrogacy contracts (as well as, in the context of the 'sexual contract', happy marriages or satisfied prostitutes) is irrelevant to the productive work of the discourse of the contract or exchange itself (1988: 215).

My contention is that the phallocentric nature of neoclassical economics can be seen within the surrogate motherhood exchange in two ways. First, as discussed in section 7.3, the pregnant woman's body is rewritten through the womb-as-capital metaphor to enable her to take up the masculine subject position of contracting agent. Hence, 'woman' is constructed as the 'same' as 'man' within a one-sex model. Second, as discussed in section 7.4, the 'natural' place of 'woman' as the material foundation of rational economic man is re-established in the face of the breakdown of the boundary between the natural and the social (signified by the 'mercenary' mother) through the elimination of the surrogate mother's status as 'mother'. Thus I contend that the metaphor of the womb-as-capital is the key means by which neoclassical economics maintains the range of binary oppositions which support the one-sex model and hence the 'universal' individual in the face of the embodied difference brought into the realm of exchange through surrogate motherhood. Before embarking on this argument, however, the nature of metaphor in a poststructuralist account of meaning production must be examined. It is to this task that section 7.2 is devoted.

7.2. The Productive Work of Metaphor

The womb-as-capital is of vital importance to the following analysis of the neoclassical modelling of the surrogate motherhood exchange. It is therefore of some importance briefly to review the nature and significance of metaphor in the production of meaning. The claim that metaphor and figurative language are important in the production of economic truth is already familiar to many economists through the work of McCloskey, which was briefly considered in section 3.5 of this book. A metaphorical relationship is a relationship of similarity. In conventional understanding, a metaphor reveals the similarity between things, and hence allows one thing to stand for or represent another. Metaphors therefore appear to draw on preexisting and self-present similarities between things, and hence simply to bring into view these similarities. In most philosophical or scientific discourse, metaphor is viewed as an inessential addition to the literal meaning of the text, since although metaphor draws attention to similarities, those similarities are self-present rather than a creation of the metaphor. Thus a metaphor may 'save time' by making present a similarity, but it is inessential in that it can be dropped without loss. Metaphors are therefore seen as 'innocent'. They simply name or make present that which is already there, and it is only in that sense that they are productive. For example, to use one of McCloskey's illustrations, in the Chicago feminist literature, children are like durable goods, where the similarities, if one were to undertake a literal translation, are that a child 'is costly to acquire initially, lasts for a long time, gives flows of pleasure during that time, is expensive to maintain and repair, has an imperfect second-hand market' (1985: 76). Once the empiricist view of language is rejected, however, metaphors are viewed quite differently.

Poststructuralists reject this traditional interpretation of metaphor. In a poststructuralist view, metaphor is an example of the deferral of meaning, since one signified is substituted for another signified, and each signified is also a signifier. Thus, in a poststructuralist framework, metaphor must be seen as the site of the construction of similarities which only appear to be preexisting. Both the metaphor and the signified to which it is applied are produced as meaningful within a particular system of differences or discourse. Much of Derrida's work has been concerned with the binary oppositions of the non-metaphorical and the metaphorical. This appears in his analyses of the oppositions between the literal and the figurative, and, as mentioned in Chapter 1 above, between speech and writing, as they operate within philosophical texts (see especially Derrida 1974, 1982c). Metaphor is opposed to the literal in philosophical writing which asserts the primacy of speech over writing and hence the access of the subject to self-present truth, in short, within texts which rely upon the empiricist view of language. Self-presence is ensured when metaphor is ornamental, a deviation from the literal, or a removable supplement. In Derrida's words, 'Metaphor, therefore, is determined by philosophy as a provisional loss of meaning, an economy of the proper without irreparable damage, a certainly inevitable detour, but also a history with its sights set on, and within the horizon of, the circular reappropriation of the literal, proper meaning' (1982c: 270; see also Ferrell 1993). The central project of Derrida and other deconstructionists is to reveal the ways in which such dichotomies operate to produce certain unquestionable foundations within knowledges. In this chapter, I am particularly concerned with the way in which the productive work of the metaphor of the womb-as-capital supports the notion of the universal individual and hence the one-sex model of neoclassical economics.

This poststructuralist interpretation of metaphor is in many ways similar to McCloskey's, and as such is familiar to many economists. McCloskey argues that metaphor is not simply ornamental, but is integral to the creation of meaning. Economists who interpret metaphors 'literally' are blinkered, and the 'unexamined metaphor is a substitute for thinking – which is a recommendation to examine metaphors, not to attempt the impossible by banishing them' (McCloskey 1983: 507). However, there is a danger in taking certain readings of the McCloskey position too far. If economics *is* literature, as McCloskey implies when she argues that each step in 'economic reasoning, even the reasoning of the official rhetoric, is metaphoric' (1985: 75), and that even 'mathematical theorizing in economics is metaphorical, and literary' (ibid.: 79), then metaphor is positioned as the origin or source of meaning, and hence acts as a foundation for economic truths. The danger here, and one to which Derrida points, is that metaphor itself displaces the previously privileged term 'science' or the literal within a binary structure, and the binary structure is itself retained. Metaphor becomes a transcendental signified; it is self-present, and ensures the self-presence of all other terms. It should therefore be noted that to read an economic text through metaphors relating to woman or femininity is not to privilege metaphor and hence implicitly to retain a commitment to logocentrism, but to call into question the very mechanisms by which woman is 'known' within economics. Indeed, as will be argued below, to model the womb as capital is not only metaphorical but also metonymical, and both aspects have implications for the symbolic place of woman as constructed within neoclassical economics. Here I follow Irigaray (1985) in taking women's symbolic place as integral to her social/economic place. To quote Margaret Whitford on this point, 'the symbolic contract (that is, the possibility of exchange in general, in whatever register: linguistic, interpersonal, mercantile and so on) and the social contract (the passage from "nature" to "culture") are inseparable' (1991a: 173).

Neoclassical economics should therefore not be seen as either purely literal, as the majority of economists would have it, or as purely metaphorical. Neoclassical economics is a productive discourse, producing rational economic man as a particular type of man: the self-made, procreative man, or the independent choosing agent. Metaphors play an important role in this construction. Poststructuralists generally argue that they operate to produce and reinforce binary oppositions which structure Western knowledges. Feminist poststructuralists argue that they operate in particular to produce and reinforce phallocentric binary oppositions; namely, those which produce woman as the 'other' of man and hence construct a one-sex model. In the sections to follow, I argue that the womb-as-capital metaphor plays an important role in the production of a one-sex model in neoclassical economics.

7.3. The Womb-as-Capital and the One-Sex Model

The one-sex model upon which 'rational economic man' relies is the product of the binary opposition of man/not-man. The surrogate mother is constructed as the calculating, choosing agent who owns capital in the neoclassical model of the surrogacy exchange delineated in Chapter 6 above. The womb-as-capital metaphor plays a key role in this transformation of a pregnant woman into 'rational economic man'. The pregnant woman is seemingly 'unsexed' within the neoclassical framework by the representation of the womb as capital. The womb stands in an external relationship to the woman, and she uses it instrumentally to produce services which can be sold on the market and hence to maximize her utility. In this sense, surrogate motherhood is the same as the case of a man renting out his factory. Indeed, the surrogate motherhood exchange is no different to other exchanges which involve bodies, such as labour market exchanges. In each case, the sexed body is disavowed by the transformation of the marketable aspects of the body into capital which is possessed by the mind. Despite this disavowal, necessary for the fantasy of a 'universal' individual, the man/not-man opposition remains, and it is only the female body which disappears. As argued in Chapter 5, the personification of 'rational economic man' in the figure of Robinson Crusoe reveals this masculine embodiment. In this section, then, I examine the way in which the metaphor of the womb-as-capital underpins the one-sex model.

As has been mentioned, neoclassical economists are yet to model the new, but rapidly growing, phenomenon of the surrogate motherhood exchange. This fact motivated the delineation of the formal neoclassical model of this exchange in Chapter 6 above, since the central features of the neoclassical interpretation of the exchange needed to be highlighted before a poststructuralist investigation could be undertaken. The essence of this model, as in neoclassical models in general, is the rational calculating agent. The market was constructed on the basis of the utility-maximizing choices of the surrogate mother and the commissioning party. As in any exchange in which the services of the body are the object of the exchange, such as exchanges of labour, sexual services and blood, the exchanger is assumed to own the objects of exchange, which are therefore metaphorically separate or detached from the personhood of the agent. The transformation of the body into capital, and the depiction of exchanges involving the body as the sale of the services derived from this capital, is the central means by which this externalization is achieved. The womb-as-capital metaphor is therefore no more than a specific example of the general underlying metaphor of own-body ownership which is required for any exchange to take place at all. Without own-body ownership, the services of the body cannot be sold. The social contract itself, which produces the conditions in which voluntary exchange replaces the rule of the strongest, requires that, in John Locke's words, 'Over himself, his own body and mind, the individual is sovereign' (quoted in Diprose 1996b: 261n; see Pateman 1988 for a discussion of social contract theorists). Thus, in order to be part of a surrogate motherhood exchange, a woman must be in a relationship of possession with her body, and, more specifically, with her womb.

The metaphor of the womb-as-capital therefore constructs the body of the surrogate mother as a possession, the services of which can be sold or given away according to the utility-maximizing calculus. Indeed, if it were not the case that a surrogate mother were renting her womb, she would be selling a baby, an illegal transaction since babies are also own-body owners (Pateman 1988: 212).[1] Richard Posner concurs with this point, arguing that women rent their reproductive services: 'Fertility is just another asset, like a professional degree or other job-market human capital' (1992: 425, see also 1989: 27). The surrogate motherhood exchange must therefore be understood to be the exchange of a service, specifically, the service of gestation ('biological housing', as Becker 1991: 3 called pregnancy in another context), for which the biological father may or may not pay. In this formulation, surrogacy is 'a process which transforms the commissioning parents' goods, that is their gametes, through the service of incubation provided by the surrogate' (Secomb 1995: 20). Hence it is no different from the employment contract, in which the worker's labour transforms the employer's material inputs into products over which the worker has no claim (Pateman 1988: 213).[2] The idea of the body and its parts as capital, then, not only allows exchanges to take place, but also eliminates the possibility of trades in self-possessing persons and therefore overcomes the threat to civil society which such trades, i.e. 'baby-selling' and its attendant denial of the self-possession of certain individuals, would invoke .

The metaphor of the womb-as-capital also divides the surrogate mother into two individuals. This is because the womb-as-capital takes the form of a rentable space which can be made available for hire – no different from a warehouse or factory floor, or a room in the woman's house. The biological father combines the semen with a rented womb to produce his child.[3] The fetus therefore stands in relation to the surrogate mother in the same way that commodities produced by hired machinery under the direction of an entrepreneur stand in relation to the owners of this machinery. It is evident that the owners of the machinery have no rights to the commodities being produced through the rented services of their capital, assuming the contractual obligations are fulfilled, and that they are certainly not somehow inseparable from the commodities for the period of the production process. Thus, just as the metaphor of the womb-as-capital transforms the womb into something separate and inessential to personhood, it also transforms the fetus housed within that womb into a separate entity. This means that the sexed body is disavowed within the neoclassical framework. An exchange which appears to involve sexed bodies is rewritten through the metaphor of the womb-as-capital as one involving self-possessing capital owners. Neither the womb nor the fetus is essential to the personhood of the surrogate mother, who has been recast as a rational economic agent fortunate enough to own capital of a particular kind. Women as embodied, and hence sexed, subjects are eliminated, and all that is left is the 'universal' individual sometimes known as Robinson Crusoe.

There are an immense number of representations which support this neoclassical depiction of the surrogacy exchange and its division of the pregnant body into two persons. These representations shed further light on the problematic status of the female body in economic relations, and once again point to the intertextuality of neoclassical economics which I considered in relation to the figure of Robinson Crusoe in Chapter 5 above. The conceptual separation of the mother from the fetus is especially prominent in the biomedical discourse surrounding technological developments in fetal surgery, ultrasound and fetal photography.[4] Such developments have made the fetus both accessible and visible, providing an image of the fetus as separate from the mother (Secomb 1995: 20). In her discussion of such imagery and its links to the film *2001: A Space Odyssey* and satellite photography, Rosalind Petchesky has argued that 'the autonomous, free-floating fetus merely extends to gestation the Hobbesian view of born human beings as disconnected, solitary individuals' (1994: 406; see also Sofia 1984; Young 1993). The resulting simultaneous construction of the image of the fetus as 'space-hero' and the pregnant woman as 'empty space' points to the 'disappearance' of the pregnant woman herself within these new technologies (ibid.: 414, 416). Linnell Secomb has argued that the view of surrogacy as a service also makes the pregnant woman disappear, since 'she becomes an incubator or "the nurse who tends the growth of the young seed planted by the true parent, the male . . ." rather than a woman or a mother' (1995: 20).

Roxanne Mykitiuk has used the term 'manthropomorphizing' to refer to the process in which 'the importance of the contribution of pregnancy, gestation and birth have vanished with regard to the creation of a child' (1994: 93). Common understanding supports this minimal role of the gestating woman: 'The dominant culture projects pregnancy as a time of quiet waiting. We refer to the woman as "expecting", as though this new life were flying in from another planet and she sat in her rocking chair by the window,

occasionally moving the curtain aside to see whether the ship is coming'
(Young 1990: 167). Indeed, in modern 'fetology' the fetus is even ascribed
the role of active partner within the pregnancy process, with a will of its own
and an ability to dictate the terms of its environment. It is defined, in short, as
'an individual agent, who is separate from the mother and has its own distinct
interests of which it is both aware and capable of acting on' (Franklin 1991:
193). Interestingly a fetologist describes the fetus as an egoist, the aim of
whom 'is to see that its own needs are served' (quoted in Franklin 1991:
194). This portrait of fetal independence implies a pregnant woman at the
biological 'beck and call' of her fetus. It is therefore apparent that certain
medical discourses support the neoclassical interpretation of the surrogate
mother's womb as capital producing an independent fetus.

The neoclassical interpretation of the surrogate mother also has many
similarities with the depiction of the pregnant woman within the various legal
and political discourses which have emerged from the abortion debate in the
United States. The 'fetal rights' discourse, for example, constructs the fetus
as a legal person, and the pregnant body as two self-possessing individuals,
who, due to the location of the fetus, are within an antagonistic relationship.
The US anti-abortionists construct the fetus as a person 'housed' by another
whenever they equate the beginning of life (the moment the fertilized egg
comes into existence) with personhood, or whenever a person is equated with
their genetic inputs. To argue that 'the individual *is whoever he is going to
become from the moment of impregnation*' (Ramsey, quoted in Petchesky
1990: 340; italics in original) is to argue that a fetus *is* a person.[5] The
potentially victimized but mute fetus is given voice in the classic anti-
abortionist film, *Silent Scream*. Here technologies which 'reveal' the life of
the fetus are shown also to be used as instruments of its death, before which
it responds with a physically-enacted 'silent scream'. As Isabel Karpin
remarks, the 'fetus unable to be heard from inside the womb, gains a right to
speech when it is technologically given a text' (1994: 57; see the detailed
discussion of this film in Petchesky 1994; on fetal rights see also Fyfe 1991;
McNeil 1991; Randles 1991; Steinberg 1991). Anti-abortionists, then, tend to
depict the fetus as simultaneously an independent legal person and a
biological dependent, constructing the pregnant woman as the potentially
hostile 'fetal environment'. A bumper sticker used in the USA depicts
precisely this view, stating that 'The Most Dangerous Place in America to
Live is in a Mother's Womb' (Karpin 1994: 36).

Yet another discourse in which the separate personhood of the pregnant
woman and the fetus is constructed is the corpus of legal cases in which
pregnant women play a role. For example, those cases in which women have

been brought to account regarding their behaviour and actions during pregnancy, at least those which 'fail to respect the rights of the fetus', contribute to the construction of the fetus as (legal) person (even if the cases fail). One of the first of these cases was the charging of a woman with criminal neglect for failing to follow medical advice during pregnancy (see Bordo 1993: 81–8; Anleu 1994: 24; Karpin 1994; Haberfield 1996; Keane 1996). In those cases in which the fetal environment is viewed as having actually imposed harm, a child born alive has been given leave to sue. In one case, a child was given leave to sue doctors who had performed surgery on its mother (which subsequently had been held responsible for causing brain damage to the fetus) before it was even conceived (Poovey 1992a: 248). In addition, cases in which women are legally required to undergo such treatments as Caesarian section pit the rights, or even the life, of the pregnant woman against those of the fetus (see Young 1993; Bordo 1993: 71–97). These cases rely, as has the US legal debate over abortion, upon the notion of fetal viability. This notion, as Alison Young argues, 'asserts the "livingness" of the fetus and its independence from the woman. As such, the woman's necessity is diminished: if the fetus is viable it can leave the uterus and live happily ever after outside it' (1993: 292). In each of these cases, the courts or the terms of a contract control and punish the potentially or actually hostile fetal environment in the name of the fetus, thus construed as an individual with rights (for the developing legal status of the fetus in the USA, see the discussion in Poovey 1992a). This construction of the pregnant woman and the fetus as separate, conflicting entities is also evident in the typical surrogacy contract. Whether or not the specific provisions of such a contract are enforceable, numerous obligations are imposed upon the 'fetal environment' (see note 6 in Chapter 6 above; Keane and Breo 1981: ch. 13; Ince 1984). The self-interest of the surrogate mother is thereby mitigated by contractual provisions and monitoring which force her to maintain her capital so that the health of the fetus is ensured.

Perhaps the most important support of the womb-as-capital metaphor and its associated division of the pregnant body into two discrete persons is the liberal paradigm of the self as a self-present rational consciousness with individualized rights and freedoms, basic to which is his ownership of his own body (see Pateman 1988; Johnson 1991; Diprose 1992, 1994, 1996a; Poovey 1992a; Mykitiuk 1994). Indeed, Sarah Franklin has described 'patriarchal individualism' as the 'meta-discourse' which 'holds together the construction of fetal personhood in a number of respects, including how it is constructed through power/knowledge or discourse, how it is described through language and metaphor, how it is represented visually, how it is narrated and how it is positioned as a masculine subject' (1991: 201). As pointed out above, this positioning of the body as property owned by the liberal individual is central to the surrogate motherhood exchange. The liberal individual, the essence of which is unsexed consciousness, possesses the body, ruling over it and using it instrumentally to meet its ends. Susan Dodds and Karen Jones point out that accepting that each person has a property right in their own person means accepting a model of an entity which stands in an external relationship with that which it owns, including its own mental capacities, leaving only 'a purely deliberative capacity: a thing which weights and ranks options and preferences . . . The agent, thus conceived, has no identity' (1992: 13). This is precisely a description of rational economic man, as neoclassical economists would like to view him: he is disembodied, he has no (sexed) identity, he is universally applicable, in short, he is instrumental reason in control of body. In the tradition of Western philosophy as well as neoclassical economics there is therefore a denial that embodiment is critical to personhood, and simultaneously a denial that the specificity of this body is integral to subjectivity.

These discourses show that the neoclassical interpretation of the surrogate mother is not independent of the ways in which Western cultures are structured. Specifically, pregnant women are represented within non-economic discourses as separate persons from the fetuses they house. The surrogate mother is similarly represented within the neoclassical model as separate from the product of the capital she rents out. The womb-as-capital metaphor is instrumental in constructing this representation, which amounts to producing the surrogate mother as a possessive, or liberal, individual. This sheds considerable light on the way in which 'woman' can be incorporated into models of exchange. Representing the womb-as-capital eliminates the specificity of the female body from the economic analysis, it converts the surrogate mother into a rational economic agent, and it produces a one-sex model. This one-sex model is the basis of the neoclassical claim that its object of analysis, rational economic man, is a universal figure. What actually occurs, however, is that the male body is established as the embodiment of the rational economic agent. As first discussed in Chapter 1 above, the female body acts as the foundation for the construction of the masculinity of the economic agent through its exclusion. Woman is incorporated into the subject position of exchanging agent as the same as man: her specificity (in this case, her pregnant embodiment) is eliminated, in the name of the universal contracting agent, but actually in the service of the man/not-man binary opposition. It should be kept in mind that these conclusions rely not only upon a view of neoclassical economics as a productive discourse (a non-empiricist view of language), but also upon a specific focus upon sexed embodiment, and it is these joint considerations which have in the main been missing from other feminist economic accounts of the masculinity of economics.

Feminist poststructuralists have already examined the way in which the exclusion of the female body acts as a foundation for various non-economic discourses, and my analysis in this chapter should be considered as an extension of this scholarship. The exclusion of the female body in the construction of the political agent which is central to liberal discourse has particularly close parallels with the exclusion of the female body in the construction of the neoclassical agent. Feminists have argued that the liberal individual is never simply abstract, disembodied or absent, but 'a particular body – one who is white, male, heterosexual, able bodied, young, adult, and it is this body which has been generalized as the normative body of liberal discourse' (Mykitiuk 1994: 80). Other bodies are constructed in reference to this white male body. This power to construct other bodies is elided by the liberal logic of individuals as prior to society, in which 'society has no power to constitute or inscribe itself on embodied subjects' (ibid.). Thus the seemingly absent body at the centre of liberal discourse serves to disguise the reality of the particular body which actually operates as the normative body in modern Western societies, positioning other types of bodies only in relation to its own form (ibid.: 80–1; see also Eisenstein 1988; Pateman 1988; Gatens 1988, 1991a, 1991b).

This phallocentric construction of sexual difference is central to the myth of the origin of modern liberal states, and although the rights and freedoms of the civil sphere have now largely been extended to women in Western nations,[6] women have not taken up these rights unproblematically, since this seemingly universal subject position was premised upon, and continues to be symbolically linked to, (white) masculinity alone. As in the case of neoclassical economics, the incorporation of sexed (and raced) bodies into the universality of the subject position of the liberal individual has problematized that alleged universality. To maintain the fantasy of universality, such bodies must be incorporated as 'the same' as those of white men. Although the surrogate mother is a contracting agent, then, her taking up of this subject position involves a rewriting of the meaning of her body, a rewriting which must exclude pregnant embodiment. This is because women, and pregnant women in particular, do not fit the liberal paradigm of the individual. As Franklin points out, the 'very term "individual", meaning *one who cannot be divided*, can only represent the male, as it is precisely the process of one individual becoming two which occurs through a woman's pregnancy' (1991: 203).

In her discussion of the role of the law in maintaining the boundaries of 'the proper' (as analysed by Derrida), Secomb has similarly pointed out that pregnancy 'is problematic, in part, because the laws of propriety and property relations become ungainly and inadequate in adjudicating on the question of foetal and infant ownership and control. The law must treat that product of pregnancy either as a thing available for exchange on the market like other things or as a human subject which as human is not available for exchange. The neither/nor status of the pregnant woman and foetus confounds the humanistic dichotomy of subject/object, self-conscious/incognizant, human/non-human, and free/predetermined' (1995: 34; see also Dodds and Jones 1992; Poovey 1992a; Diprose 1994: ch. 1). In her discussion of the abortion debate in the USA, Mary Poovey (1992a) also argues that the concept of the liberal individual can be taken to its *reductio ad absurdum* when applied to pregnant women, rather than independent men. She contends that the *Roe* v *Wade* decision, which set the scene for the discourse of fetal rights, problematized the notion of legal personhood. It 'implicitly granted the fetus some of the properties of a gendered subject even though this subject does not have an autonomous, sexed body' (ibid.: 248–9). Poovey points out that this logic would mean that personhood could be granted to an egg or a sperm. On the other hand, if the fetus is not given the status of legal personhood, a neonate would similarly have to be deprived of this status, since it is no more physically independent than a fetus (ibid.: 249). Thus pregnant embodiment is inconsistent with the realm of the contracting individual.

In this section it was argued that the metaphor of the womb-as-capital is essential for the establishment of the pregnant body as a self-possessive individual, and hence one capable of sustaining contractual relations with other 'sames'. This manoeuvre relies upon the mind/body and the man/not-man dichotomies. By converting the surrogate mother into two persons, the fetus and the capital-owning contracting agent, the metaphor of the womb-as-capital eliminates the specificity of female embodiment and constructs a one-sex model within the neoclassical paradigm. The surrogate mother becomes the contracting liberal individual, 'rational economic man'. Both the fetus and the surrogate mother are awarded masculine subject positions as self-possessive individuals. The surrogate mother, conceptually separate from the fetus, becomes a 'universal', seemingly disembodied, rational agent with the property rights of a citizen of the civil sphere, who is therefore able to undertake voluntary exchanges in that sphere: she exchanges the rights to her rentable space for a utility gain. Pregnant women, however, remain problematic, especially when they enter contracts to exchange 'sexed body property' (the term is due to Diprose 1996b: 254). In the next section, I discuss the ways in which the impropriety of the pregnant body's presence within the civil realm of contract is reined in.

7.4. Maintaining the Propriety of Motherhood

The deployment of the womb-as-capital metaphor and the associated construction of the surrogate mother as a contracting agent allows the pregnant body, stripped of its sexed specificity, to be incorporated within neoclassical economics. However, this incorporation simultaneously endangers neoclassical economics and other phallocentric knowledges by disrupting the divisions between the natural and the contractual. The impropriety of the presence of the pregnant body within the realm of contract – specifically, the mother as rational economic man – is due to the fundamental conflict between motherhood and contract which is established by the reliance of the liberal and neoclassical paradigms upon a division between the natural and the social/contractual. In order to preserve the phallocentric oppositions upon which neoclassical economics relies, the realm of the natural must be re-established. In other words, the propriety or the proper place of the pregnant body must be maintained, and this occurs through the production of a 'real mother' who is distinct from the surrogate mother and who is therefore not a contracting agent. In this section, then, I argue that neoclassical economics relies upon a division between the realms of the natural and exchange, and discuss the ways in which the transgression of this boundary by the surrogate motherhood exchange is contained in order to maintain a phallocentric construction of sexed identity in which man can function as the universal. To this end I begin with a brief overview of the way in which the opposition between the natural and the social, and the associated opposition between motherhood and contract, are central to Western discourses.

Feminists have argued that the supposedly unsexed contracting agent within the social or civil sphere, together with the associated rights and freedoms which that agent derives from the social contract which brings that sphere into existence, are meaningful only because of the existence of a realm of nature in which such rights and freedoms do not exist (see Tapper 1986; Pateman 1988; Poole 1990; Gatens 1991a). That is, the mythical origin of a civil domain and the agents who inhabit that domain (the 'social contract') is not simply a displacement of the 'state of nature'. Rather, the state of nature continues to reside within a binary structure as that which is excluded from the civil realm in order to give the civil realm its meaning. To frame it in a way more familiar to economists, the rights and freedoms of contracting or exchanging agents in the market arena are premised upon another arena, where the so-called natural work of reproduction and care takes place. Under the social contract, these 'natural' functions were allocated to women, who were legally as well as symbolically denied the rights and freedoms of men. In addition to the mind/body binary opposition, then, the identity of the liberal individual relies upon the exclusion of 'nature' from the realm of contract, and hence an opposition between the mother and the contracting agent, where motherhood connotes nature, body and not-man. This means that social practices which shift motherhood into the realm of contract threaten the coherence of this pyramid of oppositions and hence the phallocentric construction of sexual difference which allows the fantasy of the universal individual. The contracting and self-interested mother becomes such a threat if she is introduced into the liberal and neoclassical discourses without first being divested not only of her sexually-specific embodiment, but also of her connections to 'real motherhood'. To preserve the binary opposition between motherhood and contract, then, the incorporation of markets for reproductive services or motherhood into the realm of contract must proceed in a way which excludes 'real motherhood', represented by women who are virtuous, natural and good mothers.

Feminists have drawn upon a range of discourses to reveal the importance of the boundary between contract and motherhood, and the ways in which representations of 'real motherhood' or the virtuous, natural mother, and self-interested motherhood, or the selfish, unnatural mother, uphold this boundary. In other words, feminists have shown that it has been essential to the coherence of such discourses to represent mothers who enter the civil sphere as contracting agents as bad mothers, and hence not mothers at all. The identification of woman with virtuous, natural motherhood has long been central to Western discourses.[7] The constitution of maternity as the essence of the female subject was elaborated and institutionalized in the late seventeenth and eighteenth centuries, and has since been central to an 'entire battery' of social practices (Poovey 1992a: 243; see Foucault 1981b; Laqueur 1990b, 1990c; Poovey 1990a; Scott 1993). Such practices include all those premised upon the nuclear family in which the man is the breadwinner while the woman is the wife and mother, such as 'full-time' work; the idea that married women displace other, more legitimate workers (see Alford 1981); dependent spouse allowances and other tax and welfare policies (see Edwards 1985b; Pateman 1992); 'fetocentric' employment regulations (see Thomson 1996); in short, the whole apparatus of the division between the public realm of work and exchange and the private realm of family. These practices support the notion that the essence of woman is motherhood: women are either already mothers or they will become mothers. This equation of woman and mother is particularly prominent in representations of pregnant women as already mothers. The discourses of fetal rights, fetal viability and the fetus as a potential or actual person construct the fetus as an unborn *child*, and operate to exclude all possible outcomes of the pregnancy except that the fetus will be brought to term. Thus the pregnant woman is denoted as a mother before she has given birth (see Poovey 1992a: 245–6).

The essence of woman, however, is not simply assumed to be maternity. As already indicated, it is the representation of woman as the self-sacrificing mother which operates to preserve the boundary between contract and motherhood. This is particularly evident in medical and legal discourses which focus on the pregnant body. For example, in a judgment dealing with the case of a Caesarian section having been imposed upon an unwilling and dying woman who was 26 weeks pregnant, and who died shortly after the procedure, it was asserted that 'the welfare of the fetus is of the utmost importance to the majority of women; thus only rarely will a conflict arise . . . The vast majority of women will accept significant risk, pain and inconvenience to give their babies the best chance possible. One obstetrician states that most of the women he sees would "cut off their heads" to save their babies' (quoted in Young 1993: 293). Similarly, King Solomon found the 'real mother' to be the woman prepared to make the greatest sacrifice for the baby. Moreover, woman as the self-sacrificing, indeed, self-less, mother is supported by those representations of women as 'mere bodies' (Bordo 1993: 72). For example, when courts refuse to violate the bodily integrity of individuals on the one hand, and fail to uphold this vision of bodily integrity when the subject at issue is a pregnant woman, they construct women as a non-citizen and hence a body without a mind.

Susan Bordo (1993) has discussed these cases at length, comparing those in which bodily integrity is upheld by courts and those in which it is not. Courts have refused to order individuals to make donations such as bone marrow even when those donations could save the lives of others. Similarly, a court likened the forced regurgitation of two capsules swallowed by a suspected drug dealer to medieval torture. On the other hand, courts have failed to uphold the bodily integrity of women when ordering them to undergo major surgery, such as sterilization and Caesarian sections, against their wills (ibid.: 73–88). Bordo points to the logical inconsistencies apparent in these bodies of case law. That pregnant women are 'a special class of persons' due to the 'total dependence' of the fetus fails to explain these contradictions, since 'total dependence' for life occurs in other cases where the bodily integrity of, for example, bone marrow donors has been upheld (ibid.: 312n). Bordo argues that such decisions 'are mediated by normative conceptions of the pregnant woman's role and function' (ibid.: 78). When women fail to be 'good mothers', when they fail completely to subordinate their own subjectivity to that of the fetus, they are construed by courts as 'excessive [and] wicked': 'The cultural archetype of the cold, selfish mother – the evil goddesses, queens, and stepmothers of myth and fairy tale – clearly lurks in the imaginations of many judges issuing court orders for obstetrical intervention' (ibid.: 79). Thus the pregnant woman has been constructed as the opposite 'of the abstract subject whose bodily integrity the law is so determined to protect . . . The essence of the pregnant woman . . . is her biological, purely mechanical role in preserving the life of another.' When her subjectivity conflicts with her 'life-support function', her life-support function is privileged (ibid.). In short, the pregnant woman is the subject of metonymic as well as metaphoric transformation. Part of her – her body or womb – replaces the whole of her. Thus the pregnant woman as such is excluded from the social contract; she is simply body, with a will that courts have often failed to recognize when this means supporting the woman's subjectivity or right to bodily integrity at the expense of the fetus.

The identification of woman with the self-sacrificing mother is also extended to an identification of this mother with family and nature. This identity is supported by those Western political theories which require a natural counterpoint to the cultural and political endeavours of man. Examples of feminist investigations of such constructions of the nature/culture opposition are numerous. John Rawls's theory of justice, despite his pronouncement that the family is part of the subject-matter of such a theory, actually excludes the family from such a consideration by assuming that persons in the original position are not single individuals but heads or representatives of families (Okin 1991). Marx also banished the mother from his account of social relations (Stefano 1991). As Pateman and Shanley remark, 'Notwithstanding all the differences between theorists from Plato to Habermas, the tradition of Western political thought rests on a conception of the "political" that is constructed through the exclusion of women and all that is represented by femininity and women's bodies' (1990b: 3; see also Lloyd 1984; Pateman 1988; Pateman and Shanley 1990a; Gatens 1991b; Lake 1992a).[8] Mary Poovey has emphasized the danger of undermining this concept of 'mother-nature' in her discussion of the abortion debate. She states that: 'if the normative woman is a mother, then the mother-nature of woman is one of the linchpins of sexed identity and therefore, by the oppositional logic of gender, one ground of the intelligible masculinity of men. If women are allowed to question or to reject their maternity, then not only is the natural (sexed) basis of rights in jeopardy, but so is the natural basis of female identity, and, by implication, of masculine identity as well' (1992a: 243; see also Secomb 1995). Poovey concludes that the abortion debate – and, I would argue, debates about women's reproductive authority in general – is about what it means to accept (or reject) 'the notion that there is a "natural" basis for individual identity and therefore for individual rights and sexual identity' (1992a: 243; see also Secomb 1995 for a discussion of the intense policing, in light of new reproductive technologies, of the boundaries around the 'proper' family by the law).[9]

The identification of woman with motherhood and motherhood with nature, and hence the binary constructions of culture/nature and motherhood/exchange, is also important within the discourse of neoclassical economics. It is particularly evident in the neoclassical model of the surrogate motherhood exchange. The introduction of the surrogate mother as a contracting agent is an obvious threat to the natural, virtuous mother, and hence, if the binary oppositions which support the identity of rational economic man are to be preserved, the surrogate mother must somehow be divested of her motherhood. The rewriting of the female body, necessary for its incorporation within the realm of masculine subjectivity, destroys the very feminine characteristics which give meaning to the economic sphere. Specifically, despite the transformation of the surrogate mother into a rational economic individual, she remains a woman, and, as a contracting woman, she is unnatural (see Pateman 1988: 217). This is one reason for the controversy and public attention which accompany exchanges of 'sexed body property' (Diprose 1996b: 254; see also Anleu 1992). A woman who profits from her womb is a mercenary mother who rejects her maternal instinct by contracting to part with her baby. She therefore threatens the figure of the nurturing/caring mother so essential for the retention of the culture/nature divide and its support of masculine subjectivity. As Sharon Anleu points out, critics of commercial surrogacy 'castigate these women for entering a contractual agreement to give up a baby, thereby violating assumed maternal instincts and abrogating "natural" motherhood. In contrast, many of these critics present surrogacy without payment as an appropriate and acceptable solution to infertility [arguing] that such an arrangement involves gift giving and the demonstration of love and sacrifice rather than rational self-interest' (1992: 32). The general condemnation of 'pregnancy for profit' is reflected in the most common legal regime imposed on the surrogacy market; namely, the banning of commercial surrogacy and the authorization of altruistic surrogacy (National Bioethics Consultative Committee 1990). The surrogate mother, then, is the reverse side of the notion of maternal self-sacrifice which is constructed alongside the notion of fetal personhood and the right of the fetus to protection from the state (see Bordo 1993: 312n). She is the 'cold, selfish mother' prepared to contract away her natural identity, and hence antithetical to 'real' motherhood.

This vision of a calculating, avaricious mother who sells her own offspring for profit is kept at bay in a number of ways by representing the womb as rentable space. As already mentioned, such a metaphor operates to produce the object of the exchange as the service rather than the baby. Carole Pateman, for example, argues that a woman 'who enters a surrogacy contract is not being paid for (bearing) a child; to make a contract of that kind *would* be tantamount to baby-selling' (1988: 212).[10] The contract price, then, is the market-determined price which would be paid for storing an item in a house, which recompenses the owner for the disutility experienced from not being able to use the space themselves, and from having the item in the house. Judge Sorkow, the judge in the (original) Baby M case, stated this clearly in his decision: 'the money to be paid to the surrogate is not being paid for the surrender of the child to the father . . . The biological father pays the surrogate for her willingness to be impregnated and carry his child to term. At birth, the father does not purchase the child. It is his own biologically genetically related child. He cannot purchase what is already his' (quoted in Pateman 1988: 213). The surrogate mother, then, provides a service to men who desire biologically-related children (Posner 1989, 1992: 422), and this representation or construction of the exchange mitigates the threat to the binary opposition between motherhood and contract by eliminating the spectre of mothers selling their babies.

The metaphor of the womb-as-capital also reduces the threat to social order by facilitating the reconstruction of the surrogacy contract as a service provided by one woman to another – one who desperately wants a child but who cannot conceive or gestate one herself, the 'real mother', and one who is prepared to provide the services of her uterus for the sake of this other woman. The term 'surrogate mother', as well as 'contract pregnancy', contributes to this rewriting of the woman entering a contract as 'not a mother', since a surrogate mother is a substitute mother or a representative of a mother, not really a mother at all, or rather, not a 'real' mother at all. Indeed, the term arose from the use of an inanimate object to study the effect of newborn monkeys being separated from their real mothers (Annas 1988: 28). Posner urges his readers not to forget that 'the surrogates are not the only women in the picture' (1989: 27). In the context of the Baby M case, he argued that the 'purpose of the contract [which produced Baby M] was not to extinguish a mother's rights but to induce a woman to become a mother for the sake of another woman' (1992: 426). He points out that occasionally a surrogate mother feels 'intense regret at having to give up "her" child' (ibid.: 424), a statement in which Posner simultaneously relieves the contracting woman of any parental connection and therefore puts her motherhood into question, as well as supports the neoclassical understanding of the contract, specifically, the commissioning party's contractual 'ownership' of the product. Posner also argues that the surrogate mother is a 'surrogate' for the father's wife. She acts as a marital corrective since 'under modern permissive divorce law [a husband] is always free to "walk," and seek a fertile woman to marry' (1989: 27). The father's wife, however, becomes a mother only after a separate (adoption) contract is enacted. Linda Singer's words, 'In the context of the [Baby M] case, Mrs Stern's claim to maternity is entirely dependent upon and has status only in terms of her husband's desire to claim paternity. Had Mr Stern for some reason chosen not to exercize his paternal claim, the question of Mrs Stern's maternity would never come up' (1989: 60–1). But although Mrs Stern had no contractual claim to Baby M, she is vitally important as the person in the position of the 'real mother'. She is the 'real mother' because the womb-as-capital is employed in her service, and she is the one with the 'natural' desire to nurture a child.

Thus the term 'surrogate mother' installs at centre stage the 'normal' mother, a woman who does not reject motherhood, but rather desires a child – the wife of the commissioning male – rather than the mercenary mother. This covers over the gestating mother's rejection of motherhood (in favour of the contracted price, or the utility benefit) which is actually at the heart of the surrogacy contract, as well as the tenuous grasp which the wife of the commissioning male actually has on the child. That the surrogate mother is not a 'real mother' is even clearer in the case of gestational surrogacy, in which the commissioning party consists of both a male and a female. Nearly as famous as the Baby M case, at least in the USA, is the case of Baby Johnson, in which Anna Johnson, a black woman, was employed for gestational surrogacy by a white couple. Six months into the pregnancy Anna Johnson filed suit for parental rights to the child-to-be. A blood test was used to establish the fact that she was not genetically related to the child, and hence that she was not the mother and had no custody rights. Although this seems to be in contradiction to the finding in the Baby M case (that the genetic relationship between Mary Beth Whitehead and Baby M did not constitute her as the mother), in fact, both cases come to the same conclusion: that the intention to procreate is sufficient to establish the identity of the 'natural mother' (see Horstmeyer 1993–4; Douglas 1994; Morgan 1994). The term 'surrogate', then, or contract pregnancy in general, depends on the existence of a 'real', other, mother.

The motherhood status of the surrogate mother is further undermined by locating the source of the new life within the commissioning male. The male intention to parent (an act of will) and the concomitant surrogacy contract is credited with the creation of the child: ' "But for the intention to parent", the argument goes, "the child would never have existed" ' (Mykitiuk 1994: 86; see also Pateman 1988: 216). Posner concurs: 'no contract, no child' (1992: 426). He also argues, in discussing the Baby M case, that 'What is at stake is an infertile woman's right to compensate a fertile woman for the cost . . . of assisting the former to overcome the consequences of her infertility' (ibid.: 424). But the other woman was not a party to the contract, and, in Posner's own words, no contract, no child. The productive energy, then, is not that of the 'other woman' but of the man (see also Rothman 1988; Roof 1992; Secomb 1995). Thus the pregnancy is subject to or controlled by contract, eliminating the 'maternal instinct' of the contracting agent while elevating the maternal instinct of the wife of the commissioning party, crediting the contract and hence the father with generative or reproductive power, and, most importantly, maintaining the boundaries between the mother and contract, nature and culture, man and not-man. This idea of paternal or masculine procreative force and the concomitant repression of the mother is a major myth in phallocentric cultures (see Gatens 1991a; Lake 1992a). It also plays an important but disavowed role in economics, as Susan Feiner (1995a) identified, and is played out in the story of Robinson Crusoe.

It is therefore evident that the metaphor of the uterus as rentable space not only acts as the mechanism by which surrogate motherhood is incorporated in the neoclassical framework as a rational contracting agent, but is also the central means by which the threat to the binary opposition of motherhood and culture posed by this incorporation is mitigated. The metaphor constructs the surrogate mother as a contracting agent and as a non-mother, thereby disavowing the problem of sexual difference, and allowing the unproblematized retention of the fantasy of the universal individual. This is important because pregnancy is 'a site of rupture which threatens the humanistic rational all-knowing world view which is founded on [a] dichotomous organisation that separates man from animal, reason from non-reason, culture from nature, and the social from the biological' (Secomb 1995: 28). The conversion of a pregnancy into two distinct individuals, one of whom's temporary abode is the other's capital, resolves this threat. Thus the surrogate mother is rendered an 'embryo carrier', an 'incubator', a 'biological entrepreneur', a 'manufacting plant', a 'gestator', a 'receptacle', 'a kind of hatchery', a 'surrogate uterus', 'a uterine hostess', in short, a 'rented womb', and anything but a mother (these expressions are quoted in Andrews 1988: 74 and Woliver 1995: 358). The metaphor of the womb-as-capital, then, permits the extension of the neoclassical discourse into the realm of nature – pregnancy and motherhood – yet without endangering its coherence as a discourse describing exchange relations between disembodied autonomous contracting agents.

7.5. Conclusion

In this chapter I have argued that the surrogate motherhood exchange, in which the female body appears to play an irreducible role, is constructed within the neoclassical paradigm as one between two autonomous individuals. I have pointed to the ways in which the discourse of neoclassical economics supports, and indeed is premised upon, a phallocentric construction of sexual difference (the one-sex model), which (symbolically) forces women to enter the economic sphere with the specificity of their bodies, and their associated meanings, erased. This insight has some important implications. It indicates that surrogate motherhood poses something of a double bind for women. On the one hand, if surrogate motherhood contracts are declared illegal or unenforceable, women are excluded from the realm of exchange by virtue of their particular (gestational) embodiment. They are not allowed to be individuals who own their own bodies and have the right to dispose of the services of that body as they see fit, because of that particular body and that particular service. In short, the pregnant body is excluded from the realm of contract. In Carmel Shalev's words, 'the refusal to acknowledge the legal validity of surrogacy agreements implies that women are not competent, by virtue of their biological sex, to act as rational, moral agents regarding their reproductive activity' (1989: 11–12; see also Andrews 1988).

On the other hand, if such contracts are legal and enforceable and the one-sex model of sexual difference is thereby reproduced, then what is excluded from the realm of exchange is again the female body and its most infamous capacity, the simultaneous one-ness and two-ness of that female body in its reproductive mode: its *différance*. In this case, the pregnant body is excluded on a symbolic level, and woman is included in the realm of contract only in-so-far as she becomes the 'same' as man. The pregnant body – which under a different discourse is both one and two, and hence not separable, both the same as and different from itself, and hence not an individual – is now a rentable space.[11] Femininity is reinstated as maternal, natural and outside the realm of instrumental rationality, and masculinity retained as independent, rational and social; in short, real woman must remain the 'other' of the contracting agent. This ensures that the female body is maintained, within a series of binary oppositions, as the unacknowledged foundation of the economic and social spheres. Difference continues to be excluded from neoclassical economics, and racial and sexual others are incorporated into the realm of the social, political and economic only if they take up white masculine subject positions.

Another implication of the analysis presented in this chapter, as well as that of earlier chapters, is that surrogate motherhood is not a special case in which the specificity of women's bodies is eliminated from the scene of exchange. It is a case of 'the exception proving the rule'. The surrogate motherhood contract involves the exchange of, using Diprose's term, 'sexed body property', and this is precisely what is exchanged in many other forms of implicit or explicit contracting as well. If bodies are always sexed bodies, then the employment contract, for example, is also for the exchange of sexed body property. Women are positioned as men in entering the social contract, whether as surrogate mothers or as workers of other kinds, in that they participate in the fantasy of sexually indifferent or neutral bodies owned by minds which are the essence of personhood. Hence many feminist economic approaches, as well as sex discrimination and equal opportunity laws which follow as remedial strategies from the gender approach, and which are informed by assumptions of disembodiment, are problematic. They fail to recognize, and hence begin to shift the meaning of, difference at the level of embodiment.

Finally, the analysis of this chapter has also undermined the claim by neoclassical economists that their analyses are descriptive and not productive of reality. Discourses, even those which are premised upon disembodied individualism, produce meanings beyond the conscious intentions of its authors. Specifically, the neoclassical economist implies that his or her analysis is independent of questions of sexual difference and the production of subjectivity by invoking a preexisting, universal individual. However, I have argued, using a feminist poststructuralist reading of the surrogate motherhood exchange, that this is not the case. Sexual difference is of key significance when neoclassical economics produces sexed body exchanges in particular ways. I suggest that neoclassical economics cannot deny its integral role in both producing and supporting phallocentric constructions of that difference. However, by delineating the binary opposition of maternity and contract within neoclassical economics and its productive effects, I am not suggesting that the paradigm of autonomous and disembodied individuals interacting in markets should, or indeed, could, be replaced with a different central figure. Above all, I do not advocate the mother–child relation as the paradigmatic relation to which all others should conform, as did the sociologist Virginia Held (provisionally) in her paper 'Mothering versus Contract', and as some feminist economists have done. Held advocates this point of view on the basis that, before the social contract, men were children and hence the mother–child relation could logically be seen as the founding relation of society (ibid.: 288–9). It is nevertheless evident that before men were born and became children, there was a sexual relation between the sexes. It is the status of the sexual relation with which this book is concerned, that is, the issue of sexual difference, and how difference is excluded by a one-sex model.

Notes

1. The question of whether the surrogate motherhood exchange involves womb-rental or baby-selling has often been raised in the feminist literature on surrogate motherhood. Those who maintain that it is womb-rental include Andrews (1988) and Shalev (1989). Katz (1986) reviews US legislation and concludes that surrogacy is fundamentally different from baby-selling. Those who argue that surrogate motherhood is the sale of babies include Zelizer (1988) and Wright (1990). Mary Shanley argues that a distinction must be made between what were identified in Chapter 6 as genetic and gestational surrogacy contracts. In the former case, Shanley suggests, the surrogate mother is not simply renting her womb, but is also selling her genetic material, and in this case 'it becomes difficult to see how the exchange escapes the charge of baby selling' (1993: 624–5). From the perspective of neoclassical economics, the genetic input of the surrogate mother is only a minor complication which, contrary to Shanley's view, does not imply that the surrogate mother is selling a baby. Surrogate mothers implicitly compete in a market for attractive genetic attributes in which access to those attributes are indeed sold, but the womb itself, in which the input of genetic attributes are put to work along with the father's genetic attributes, remains rented capital.

2. Feminists have also considered the question of whether gestating a fetus is the same kind of work as employment of other kinds. Lisa Newton, who is a director of the Program of Applied Ethics at Fairfield University, has argued that surrogacy is a service that is 'simply an extension . . . of baby-sitting and other child-care arrangements which are very widely practiced [*sic*]' (quoted in Shanley 1993: 623). Similarly, the judge in the 'Baby Johnson' case argued that Anna Johnson had been paid for 'pain and suffering' analogous to the physical and psychological demands of other kinds of labour (Shanley 1993: 625). The variables α and β in the neoclassical model of surrogate motherhood delineated in Chapter 6 above also reflect this reasoning. Feminists who argue that the work of pregnancy is fundamentally different from other types of work include Pateman (1988), Anderson (1990), Satz (1992) and Shanley (1993). Shanley argues that contract pregnancy is so different from other forms of employment that it should be considered analogous to consensual slavery (1993: 629).

3. In certain situations, as pointed out in the previous chapter, the exchange may take the form of a gift, leading to a utility gain from an altruistic act rather than a utility gain from pecuniary return.

4. Fetal images first appeared in the public space in 1965 as a feature of *Life* magazine entitled 'Drama of Life Before Birth'. These images were of embryos autopsied rather than embryos *in utero* as was claimed by the photographer (Young 1993: 291).

5. For a critique of this notion, see Petchesky (1990: 338–42). See Poovey (1992a) for a discussion of the problematic use of the individual rights framework by both pro- and anti-abortionists. See Mykitiuk (1994: 92–3) for a discussion of a judge who based his decision to use the 'best interests of the child' test to determine 'custody' over frozen embryos upon the notion that an embryo is a completely-constituted person.

6. The exception being those states where rape within marriage is not a criminal offence, since this obviously denies a woman rights over her own body.

7. Note, however, that sanctified motherhood is, in particular in the USA and Australia, an ideal constructed especially around white middle-class women. That is, not all women are 'good mothers'. This is shown by the history of appropriation of the children of non-white women (see Collins 1994; Grimshaw *et al.* 1994; Lake 1994; Roberts 1995). More recently, young women likely to bear and raise children at the expense of the state were the specific target of an anti-natalist advertising campaign in the USA (Singer 1989: 58–9; see also Fineman 1995). Also, those women in the USA who are subjected to forced sterilization or other reproductive interventions, such as the use of a surgically implanted contraceptives, are more likely to be on welfare and of non-European descent. For example, in 1987 in the USA 81 per cent of those women subjected to court-ordered obstetrical interventions were black, Asian or Hispanic (Bordo 1993: 76; see also Roberts 1991, Pateman 1992: 25–6; Ashe 1995).

8. On feminists' demand for recognition as the 'citizen mother', see Lake (1992a, 1993, 1996) and Pateman (1992).

9. An interesting analysis of the transgressions of the boundary between the public and private within the Baby M case is given by Doane and Hodges (1989). Mary Beth Whitehead argued her case that she was entitled to 'natural maternal rights', in the media, and hence 'left the private sphere that is her appropriate place as a mother' (ibid.: 69). The media were not entirely sympathetic to her situation. Indeed, Doane and Hodges argue that 'In the face of a practice, surrogacy, that challenges the ideology of the naturalness of the bourgeois nuclear family, the Baby M Case became an occasion for the media and the courts to celebrate an "ideal" family in which the mother is a natural caretaker, the father a kindly provider, and the child an object of selfless attention' (ibid.). They also describe how Mary Beth Whitehead's use of the media to publicize her plight led Judge Sorkow to describe her as exhibitionist, narcissistic and manipulative, 'qualities antithetical to those required in a "good" mother' (ibid.: 68). Doane and Hodges disagree with the sentiment that, since the subject at issue was the contract and not Mrs Whitehead, the judge's attack upon Mrs Whitehead was 'entirely gratuitous'. They point out that the contract cannot be separated from attacks on Mrs Whitehead as an individual, arguing that 'The judge's attack on Mary Beth Whitehead, so essential to preserving traditional notions of the good family, is intimately bound up with a defense of the bourgeois individual. The traditional family creates this individual, and contract law protects *his* rights. Indeed, the ideology of contract and the ideology of familialism both define and defend him' (ibid.: 71).

10. As mentioned in note 2 above, not all commentators agree that the surrogate motherhood exchange is one of a service. Janet Wright (1990), for example, contends that a woman who gestates a fetus and gives birth to a child, whether or not a genetic link exists, is that child's mother, and argues that 'if you start from the premise that a woman isn't necessarily the mother of the child she gives birth to, it becomes easier to break down public opposition to child-selling. It's not being sold, you see. It's being given to its rightful owners or "commissioning parents" ' (1990: 12).

11. A feminist discourse is an example of one in which the pregnant body is posed as different in kind to that of the contracting 'individual'. Pateman (1988), Anderson (1990) and Shanley (1993), for example, argue that the very selfhood of the pregnant woman is undermined when the labour of pregnancy is viewed in the same light as other types of labour, since the fetus is not alienated in the same way as other products of work. Note that some feminists and others also seek to outlaw surrogacy for a range of other reasons to do with the morality of such exchanges and/or the potential for exploitation which is inherent within such exchanges (see Dodds and Jones 1989a; Arneson 1992; Wertheimer 1992; Horsburgh 1993).

8. Conclusion

8.1. The Main Theme of the Book

In this book I have drawn upon feminist poststructuralism to deconstruct rational economic man and to reveal the myth of the procreative man which is at the heart of neoclassical economics. Feminist poststructuralists draw upon Saussure's structuralist linguistics and Derrida's deconstruction of the presence/absence dichotomy to argue that reality is produced within language or discourses, and that self-presence, including that of the subject, is always deferred. They argue that claims to self-presence are not only logocentric but also phallocentric, since such claims rely upon the man/not-man binary opposition, and those oppositions which support this one-sex model, such as culture/nature and mind/body. These oppositions situate and define woman as the other of self-present man, in which she is understood only in reference to man; she is either the same as him, his complement or his opposite. Feminist poststructuralists argue that although phallocentric knowledges constantly seek to fix in place this meaning of the feminine and hence man's self-presence, such texts can never succeed in closing off the deferral of meaning. Thus the self-presence of man is always deferred, just as in the case of meaning in general. Phallocentric theoretical systems, then, cannot fix sexual difference, and similarly, neither can feminists themselves. However, although feminist poststructuralists do not seek to replace the phallocentric definition of sexual difference with some other fixed definition, they are nevertheless able to disrupt this definition by exposing its production. Hence I used a textual process of Derridean deconstruction to read neoclassical economics for its production of sexual difference as a one-sex model of masculine procreativity from which femininity is excluded.

Before turning to the task of delineating the particular contributions made by this analysis, however, it is important to note, once again, that the project of this book is not to disable all other feminist economic approaches, since, as has been argued, each has its strengths as well as its weaknesses, and in some sense, the approaches can complement each other. Deconstruction itself reveals that work may proceed simultaneously on more than one front. In Derrida's words, a strategy of deconstruction avoids 'both simply *neutralizing* the binary oppositions of metaphysics and simply *residing* within the closed field of these oppositions, thereby confirming it. Therefore we must proceed using a double gesture' (1981: 41; see also Culler 1983: 172-4). Feminists must demonstrate that women are as able as men in those privileged sites of masculine activity from which women have traditionally been excluded, and in which their current achievements may be undervalued, so that women too can share in society's rewards. This strategy attempts to neutralize the male/female opposition, but, as Derrida remarks, 'the hierarchy of the binary opposition always reconstitutes itself' (1981: 42). Thus it is also vital to go beyond a gender feminist approach, not by attributing a given identity to woman or the feminine, thereby 'countering myths of the male with new myths of the female' (Culler 1983: 174), but by undermining the phallocentric constructions of the feminine.

8.2. Contribution to the Literature

In this book I have made a number of contributions to the literature. One of the most important is the delineation of the boundaries of a new and growing sub-discipline of economics known as feminist economics. Although there have been some substantial reviews of the literature on women and economics, for example, women and the labour market (such as Kahne and Kohen 1975; Shields *et al.* 1975; Ferber 1987), and some article-length and hence relatively sketchy reviews of feminist economics (such as Ferber and Nelson 1993b; Hyman 1994a, 1994b; Grapard 1995b; Humphries 1995b; Nelson 1995b), a comprehensive and wide-ranging survey of the feminist economics literature has not before been undertaken. In particular, there has been no systematic development of the ways in which feminist theory interacts with and positions particular feminist economics projects. I have focused on two main categories of feminist economists: those who wish to add women or the feminine to economic theories or methodologies where they are previously absent, and those who approach economics as a productive discourse and who aim to illuminate the subject, neoclassical economics, rather than women or the feminine.

I have also revealed the ways in which the assumptions made by feminist economists about women influence their approach to neoclassical economics as knowledge. The way in which woman is understood, whether as a biological entity, a socially-gendered individual, or as a discursively-produced sexed subjectivity, influences the approach made to the question of women and knowledge. In other words, a feminist economist will identify neoclassical economics as problematic in ways which are directly related to what she or he understands woman to be. If, for example, woman is understood to be a self-present individual, in essence the same as man, as she is conceived within the gender approach, then the problem of women and knowledge is solved through the production of realistic accounts of the activities of women. If, on the other hand, knowledges are understood to be productive and to actively construct sexed subjectivities and the feminine as that which is excluded, then the question of realistic representations is not one upon which feminists should concentrate exclusively. As Graham and Amariglio argue: 'Representation, conventionally seen as a secondary and therefore subordinate and ultimately dispensable "imitation" of reality, has been repositioned by deconstructive feminism in the role of cause or constituent, thereby relocating reality as the outcome or "effect" ' (1996: 5). However, although different understandings of woman produce different accounts of the masculinity of neoclassical economics, I have argued throughout the book that there is room, and indeed the necessity, for a range of alternative projects within feminist economics.

Another major contribution is my delineation of a variant of feminist poststructuralism or a feminism of difference and its use for reading neoclassical texts. This book is the only piece of work explicitly to address and reveal the production of sexed bodies in neoclassical economics. I have demonstrated the way in which phallocentric binary oppositions operate within neoclassical economics to construct a one-sex model. Specifically, I have used Derridean deconstruction to argue that the man/not-man opposition underpins the masculinity of rational economic man, focusing on the teaching device of Robinson Crusoe and the neoclassical model of the surrogate motherhood exchange. This is the first time that such an analysis has been undertaken within the field of feminist economics, and, I believe, the first time that the notion of masculine morphology has been addressed by a feminist economist. I have therefore demonstrated that feminist poststructuralism offers a quite different perspective on neoclassical economics from those available from other feminist frameworks. However, it is only the beginning of the general feminist project of having men 'take back the body that is theirs', so that 'women will have access to and recognition of a body that is in fact *women's* and not an imperfect variant or projection of men's needs and wishes' (Gross 1986b: 77).

A further contribution has been to reveal the importance of the Robinson Crusoe story in constructing the masculinity of 'rational economic man'. Although the role played by this teaching device in neoclassical economics had been examined by other economists, such as White (1982, 1987) and Hymer ([1971] 1980), Crusoe's masculinity was not an issue in their accounts. That this was a glaring omission is evident from the fact that two feminist economists influenced by poststructuralism, myself (1994a) and Ulla Grapard (1995a), simultaneously and independently wrote papers on the significance of Robinson Crusoe as a man. In the process of showing the way in which Robinson Crusoe is critical in producing the economic agent as procreative man, my analysis revealed the importance of situating neoclassical economics intertextually. Neoclassical economics is not a discourse independent of all others; its theoretical concepts are meaningful only in relation to a particular historically situated set of discourses. This is particularly evident in the case of the Robinson Crusoe story, since Robinson Crusoe is an icon of Western masculinity.

Still another contribution is the development of the first formalized neoclassical model of the surrogate motherhood exchange. There is a growing interest in and controversy surrounding surrogate motherhood exchanges in the United States, Britain and Australia, but a formal neoclassical model of these exchanges had not previously been developed, although Posner (1989, 1992: 420-9) had earlier appraised the arguments for and against such contracts using traditional neoclassical reasoning. Depicting surrogate motherhood within the neoclassical framework entailed the modelling of rational economic man optimizing subject to constraints and the effects of changes in those constraints. The development of the model was a necessary underpinning of my analysis of rational economic man in Chapter 7, but has the additional advantage of demonstrating to those readers not formally trained in economics the way in which new knowledge is understood to develop within the discipline.

8.3. Future Directions

The question arises as to whether future work based on this book and other feminist poststructuralist economic work should be aimed at constructing an alternative to neoclassical economics, or a 'new feminist economics'. The construction of an alternative is often cited as a prerequisite for a critique to be useful, as if criticisms itself were unproductive. Criticism of feminist economics has also been focused upon its failure, or indeed its inability, to produce a fully-fledged alternative to neoclassical economics (see, for example, Blank 1993; Solow 1993; Vaughn 1994). Indeed, two works which have heralded the emergence of a 'new feminist economics' have perhaps been over-optimistic. Marilyn Waring, a New Zealand politician and activist, named her book *If Women Counted: A New Feminist Economics* (1988), and Chris Beasley, an academic feminist trained in political theory, has more recently published *Sexual Economyths: Conceiving a Feminist Economics* (1994). Waring's book is a polemical work, using no firm theoretical basis, the aim of which is to exhort policy-makers to value the environment and the unpaid labour of women. Beasley's, on the other hand, is a scholarly work in which she criticizes conventional and feminist Marxism as well as the approach used by Waring and others who privilege the market in their examinations of unpaid labour, and seeks to establish a materialist feminism as the basis of a new feminist economics. Beasley's work is nevertheless only a tentative beginning and not a fully-developed research programme which could compete with the neoclassical orthodoxy. However, as should be clear from the preceding chapters, the central aim of this book is to read neoclassical economics as a discourse, not to produce a new orthodoxy.

My aim, then, is not to produce a new feminist economics; indeed, this would be contradictory given the feminist poststructuralist approach used here. Rather, I suggest that localized 'skirmishes' around meanings generated in particular contexts may be more useful than advocating a wholesale alternative to neoclassical economics, perhaps one which reifies rather than contests the oppressive meaning of sexual difference produced by neoclassical economics itself. To quote McHoul and Grace, 'if discourses don't merely represent "the real", and if in fact they are part of its production, then which discourse is "best" can't be decided by comparing it with any real object. The "real" object simply isn't available *for* comparison outside its discursive construction. Instead, discourses (forms of representation) might be tested in terms of how they can actually intervene in local struggles' (1993: 35). So, for example, revealing the symbolic implications of the surrogate motherhood exchange as conceived of by neoclassical economics is critical in effecting shifts in women's economic position. Changes such as the legalization of surrogacy contracts may well improve the lives of women who enter into such contracts, but at the cost of a continuing failure to challenge the masculinity of subject positions available in the economic realm, with obvious implications for women in terms of work, childcare and family responsibilities.

Similar feminist poststructuralist analyses could and should be undertaken of the range of exchanges involving female bodies now being modelled by neoclassical economists. The neoclassical economist's interpretation of the market for sex services is a particularly obvious candidate for a feminist deconstruction. In addition, those concepts and problems which within neoclassical economics appear to be 'natural', such as the sexual division of labour, the worker and discrimination, should also be examined for the ways in which they are produced as concepts or problems, not to deny their reality but to consider their production and hence to promote change (see, for example, Schultz 1992; Scott 1993). Investigations of this type could also be employed to expose the way in which phallocentric binary oppositions operate within the powerful discourse of the family offered by the new home economics, an area of study which is undoubtedly one of the main points of entry into neoclassical economics for women as objects of research. Historians of economic thought could also draw upon feminist poststructuralist ideas in their readings of particular foundational texts in the neoclassical and other economic traditions in order to reveal the ways in which sexual difference operated as a sub-text to the main arguments. Furthermore, it would be useful for historians of thought to examine the changing ways in which certain binary oppositions have operated in economics through time. In each case, rather than seeking to displace the neoclassical framework with an alternative, the theorist's goal is to fight a localized skirmish over meaning with the purpose of revealing the ways in which discourse produces and limits the meaning of woman and her economic persona. Such an exercise is the first step in the feminist poststructuralist aim of encouraging resistance to dominant discourses. In the near future, neoclassical economics is more likely to remain entrenched in our institutions than to be displaced, and, as shown in section 2.3 of this book, neoclassical economists of the 'Chicago feminist school' may in fact continue to shed light on economic relationships which other feminist economists may draw upon and develop, with useful policy outcomes for women. Feminists must nevertheless continue ceaselessly to expose the phallocentric commitments of this school, and thereby promote resistance and unsettle scholars who unquestioningly accept its conclusions.

I therefore believe that economists will learn from feminist poststructuralism by becoming aware that meanings of sexual difference are continually being unintentionally produced by the authors of knowledges which claim to be universally applicable. That is, neoclassical economists will learn that neoclassical economics is a sexually-specific discourse. Economists must learn to consider, within their theorizing, the broader social significations of female bodies as natural rather than social, emotional rather than rational, reproductive rather than productive, and look for the ways in which their own discourse supports these significations. If economists are to acknowledge and give up the role of their discourse in the oppression of women and the repression of the feminine, they must acknowledge the materiality of language and the real effects of their discourse; in short, they must acknowledge their own political positioning. And as Drucilla Cornell has pointed out, to view language as constitutive of reality is also to view language as able to shift that reality (1991: 104). Hence works such as this book might also have real effects.

Bibliography

Adams, Parveen and Jeff Minson (1990), 'The "subject" of feminism', in Parveen Adams and Elizabeth Cowie (eds), *The Woman in Question: m/f*, Cambridge, Mass.: MIT Press, pp. 81–101.

Airo-Farulla, Geoff (1991), ' "Dirty deeds done dirt cheap": deconstruction, Derrida, discrimination and difference/ance in (the High) Court', in Ian Duncanson (ed.), *Legal Education and Legal Knowledge (Special Issue of Law in Context)*, Bundoora: La Trobe University Press, pp. 102–16.

Albelda, Randy (1995), 'The impact of feminism in economics – beyond the pale? A discussion and survey results', *Journal of Economic Education*, **26** (3), 253–73.

Alchian, Armen A. (1953), 'The meaning of utility measurement', *American Economic Review*, **43** (1), 26–50.

Alcoff, Linda (1989), 'Cultural feminism versus post-structuralism: the identity crisis in feminist theory', in Micheline R. Malson, Jean F. O'Barr, Sarah Westphal-Wihl and Mary Wyer (eds), *Feminist Theory in Practice and Process*, Chicago: University of Chicago Press, pp. 295–326.

Alcoff, Linda and Elizabeth Potter (1993), 'Introduction: When feminisms intersect epistemology', in *Feminist Epistemologies*, New York: Routledge, pp. 1–14.

Aldrich, Michelle L. (1978), 'Women in science', *Signs*, **4** (1), 126–35.

Alexander, Judith A. (1995), 'Our ancestors in their successive generations', *Canadian Journal of Economics*, **28** (1), 205–24.

Alford, Katrina (1981), 'Academic and media views of married women's employment', in Norma Grieve and Patricia Grimshaw (eds), *Australian Women: Feminist Perspectives*, Melbourne: Oxford University Press, pp. 205–12.

Alford, Katrina (1986), 'Colonial women's employment as seen by nineteenth-century statisticians and twentieth-century economic historians', *Labour History*, **51**, 1–10.

Alford, Katrina (1993), '"What is a nice girl like you doing in a place like this?": gender and economics', paper presented at the *Out of the Margin: Feminist Perspectives on Economic Theory* Conference, Amsterdam, June.

Alford, Katrina (1996), 'Gender and economics', *Academy of the Social Sciences in Australia Newsletter*, **15** (4), 21–6.

Allen, Judith (1986), 'Evidence and silence: feminism and the limits of history', in Carole Pateman and Elizabeth Gross (eds), *Feminist Challenges: Social and Political Theory*, Sydney: Allen & Unwin, pp. 173–89.

Allen, Judith (1990), '"The wild ones": the disavowal of *men* in criminology', in Regina Graycar (ed.), *Dissenting Opinions: Feminist Explorations in Law and Society*, Sydney: Allen & Unwin, pp. 21–39.

Allen, Judith and Elizabeth Grosz (1987), 'Editorial: Feminism and the body', *Australian Feminist Studies*, **5** (Summer), vii–xi.

Allen, R.D.G. (1934), 'A reconsideration of the theory of value. Part II', *Economica*, n.s
1 (2), 196–219.

Amariglio, Jack (1988), 'The body, economic discourse, and power: an economist's
introduction to Foucault', *History of Political Economy*, **20** (4), 583–613.

Amariglio, Jack (1990), 'Economics as a postmodern discourse', in Warren J. Samuels
(ed.), *Economics as Discourse: An Analysis of the Language of Economists*, Boston,
Mass.: Kluwer, pp. 15–46.

Amariglio, Jack and Julie Graham (1993), 'Gendering and fragmenting the economic
subject', paper presented at the *Out of the Margin: Feminist Perspectives on
Economic Theory* Conference, Amsterdam, June.

Amariglio, Jack, Stephen Resnick and Richard Wolff (1990), 'Division and difference
in the "discipline" of economics', *Critical Inquiry*, **17**, 108–37.

American Economic Association (1972), Minutes of the Annual Meeting December 28,
1971, *American Economic Association Papers and Proceedings*, **62**, 470–4.

Amsden, Alice H. (ed.) (1980a), *The Economics of Women and Work*, Harmondsworth,
Middx: Penguin Books.

Amsden, Alice H. (1980b), 'Introduction', in *The Economics of Women and Work*,
Harmondsworth, Middx: Penguin Books, pp. 11–38.

Anderson, Elizabeth S. (1990), 'Is women's labor a commodity?', *Philosophy and Public
Affairs*, **19**, 71–92.

Andrews, Lori (1988), 'Surrogate motherhood: the challenge for feminists', *Law,
Medicine and Health Care*, **16** (1–2), 72–80.

Anleu, Sharyn Roach (1990a), 'New procreative technologies, donor gametes and the
law's response: developments in Australia', *Australian Journal of Social Issues*, **25**
(1), 40–51.

Anleu, Sharyn Roach (1990b), 'Reinforcing gender norms: commercial and altruistic
surrogacy', *Acta Sociologica*, **33** (1), 63–74.

Anleu, Sharyn Roach (1992), 'Surrogacy: for love but not for money?', *Gender and
Society*, **6** (1), 30–48.

Anleu, Sharyn Roach (1994), 'Reproductive autonomy: infertility, deviance and
conceptive technology', *Law in Context (Law and Medicine)*, **11** (3), 17–40.

Annas, George J. (1988), 'Fairy tales surrogate mothers tell', *Law, Medicine and Health
Care*, **16**, (1–2), 27–33.

Appleby, Joyce, Elizabeth Covington, David Hoyt, Michael Latham and Allison Sneider
(eds) (1996), *Knowledge and Postmodernism in Historical Perspective*, New York:
Routledge.

Arneson, Richard J. (1992), 'Commodification and commercial surrogacy', *Philosophy
and Public Affairs*, **21** (2), 132–64.

Arrow, Kenneth J. (1963), *Social Choice and Individual Values*, New Haven, Conn.:
Yale University Press.

Arrow, Kenneth J. (1972), 'Models of job discrimination', in A.H. Pascal (ed.), *Race
Discrimination in Economic Life*, Lexington, Mass.: D.C. Heath, pp. 83–102.

Arrow, Kenneth J. (1976), 'Comment I', *Signs*, **1** (3, pt 2), 233–7.

Ashe, Marie (1995), 'Postmodernism, legal ethics, and representation of "bad mothers"',
in Martha Albertson Fineman and Isabel Karpin (eds), *Mothers in Law: Feminist
Theory and the Legal Regulation of Motherhood*, New York: Columbia University
Press, pp. 142–66.

Ashraf, Javed (1996), 'The influence of gender on faculty salaries in the United States,

1969–89', *Applied Economics*, **28**, 857–64.

Australian Bureau of Statistics (1990), *Measuring Unpaid Work: Issues and Experimental Estimates*, Catalog No. 5236.

Bacchi, Carol Lee (1990), *Same Difference: Feminism and Sexual Difference*, Sydney: Allen & Unwin.

Backhouse, Roger, Tony Dudley-Evans and Willie Henderson (1993), 'Exploring the language and rhetoric of economics', in Willie Henderson, Tony Dudley-Evans and Roger Backhouse (eds), *Economics and Language*, London: Routledge, pp. 1–20.

Badgett, M.V. Lee (1995), 'Gender, sexuality, and sexual orientation: all in the feminist family?', *Feminist Economics*, **1** (1), 121–40.

Badgett, M.V. Lee and Rhonda M. Williams (1992), 'The economics of sexual orientation: establishing a research agenda', *Feminist Studies*, **18** (3), 649–57.

Bahr, Stephen J. (ed.) (1980), *Economics and the Family*, Lexington, Mass.: Lexington Books.

Bailey, Elizabeth E. (1981), Report of the Committee on the Status of Women in the Economics Profession, *American Economic Review*, **71** (2), 470–7.

Bailey, Elizabeth E. (1982), Report of the Committee on the Status of Women in the Economics Profession, *American Economic Review*, **72** (2), 431–41.

Bailey, Elizabeth E. (1983), Report of the Committee on the Status of Women in the Economics Profession, *American Economic Review*, **73** (2), 419–26.

Barker, Drucilla K. (1994), 'Mushroom men and classical physics: an analysis of economic imperialism', paper presented at the *Fourth Annual Conference of the International Association for Feminist Economics*, Milwaukee, July.

Barker, Drucilla K. (1995), 'Economists, social reformers, and prophets: a feminist critique of economic efficiency', *Feminist Economics*, **1** (3), 26–39.

Barrett, Michèle (1988), 'Introduction to the 1988 edition', in *Women's Oppression Today: The Marxist/Feminist Encounter*, rev. edn, London: Verso, pp. v–xxxiv.

Barrett, Michèle (1992), 'Words and things: materialism and method in contemporary feminist analysis', in Michèle Barrett and Anne Phillips (eds), *Destabilizing Theory: Contemporary Feminist Debates*, Cambridge: Polity Press, pp. 201–19.

Barrett, Michèle and Anne Phillips (1992), 'Introduction', in *Destabilizing Theory: Contemporary Feminist Debates*, Cambridge: Polity Press, pp. 1–9.

Barrett, Nancy S. (1981), 'How the study of women has restructured the discipline of economics', in Elizabeth Langland and Walter Gove (eds), *A Feminist Perspective in the Academy: The Difference it Makes*, Chicago: University of Chicago Press, pp. 101–9.

Bartky, Sandra Lee (1988), 'Foucault, femininity, and the modernization of patriarchal power', in Irene Diamond and Lee Quinby (eds), *Feminism and Foucault: Reflections on Resistance*, Boston, Mass.: Northeastern University Press, pp. 61–86.

Bartlett, Robin L. and Susan F. Feiner (1992), 'Balancing the economics curriculum: content, method and pedagogy', *American Economic Review*, **82** (2), 559–64.

Bassi, Laurie J. (1990), 'Confessions of a feminist economist: why I haven't taught an economics course on women's issues', *Women's Studies Quarterly*, **17** (3 & 4), 42–5.

Beasley, Chris (1994), *Sexual Economyths: Conceiving a Feminist Economics*, St Leonards: Allen & Unwin.

Beasley, Chris (1996), 'Charting an/other direction? Sexual economyths and suggestions for a feminist economics', *Australian Feminist Studies*, **11** (23), 99–114.

Becker, Gary S. (1957), *The Economics of Discrimination*, Chicago: University of

Chicago Press.

Becker, Gary S. (1964), *Human Capital*, New York: Columbia University Press.

Becker, Gary S. (1965), 'A theory of the allocation of time', *Economic Journal*, **75** (299), 493–517.

Becker, Gary S. (1971), *The Economics of Discrimination*, 2nd edn, Chicago: University of Chicago Press.

Becker, Gary S. (1973), 'A theory of marriage: part I', *Journal of Political Economy*, **81** (4), 813–16.

Becker, Gary S. (1974a), 'A theory of marriage', in Theodore W. Shultz (ed.), *Economics of the Family: Marriage, Children, and Human Capital*, Chicago: NBER and University of Chicago Press, pp. 299–344.

Becker, Gary S. (1974b), 'A theory of marriage: part II', *Journal of Political Economy*, **82** (2, pt 2), S11–26.

Becker, Gary S. ([1974] 1976), 'A theory of social interactions', reprinted in *The Economic Approach to Human Behavior*, Chicago: University of Chicago Press, pp. 253–81.

Becker, Gary S. (1975), *Human Capital*, 2nd edn, New York: Columbia University Press.

Becker, Gary S. (1976a), 'Altruism, egotism and genetic fitness: economics and sociobiology', *Journal of Economic Literature*, **14**, 817–26.

Becker, Gary S. (1976b), *The Economic Approach to Human Behavior*, Chicago: University of Chicago Press.

Becker, Gary S. (1981a), *A Treatise on the Family*, Cambridge, Mass.: Harvard University Press.

Becker, Gary S. (1981b), 'Altruism in the family and selfishness in the market place', *Economica*, **48** (1), 1–15.

Becker, Gary S. (1985), 'Human capital, effort, and the sexual division of labor', reprinted in Jane Humphries (ed.) (1995), *Gender and Economics*, Aldershot, Hants.: Edward Elgar, pp. 153–78.

Becker, Gary S. (1987), 'Family', in John Eatwell, Murray Milgate and Peter Newman (eds), *The New Palgrave: A Dictionary of Economics*, vol. 2, New York: Stockton, pp. 281–6.

Becker, Gary S. (1988), 'A theory of rational addiction', *Journal of Political Economy*, **96** (4), 675–700.

Becker, Gary S. (1991), *A Treatise on the Family*, 2nd enl. edn, Cambridge, Mass.: Harvard University Press.

Becker, Gary S. and H. Gregg Lewis (1973), 'On the interaction between quantity and quality of children', *Journal of Political Economy*, **81** (2, pt 2), S279–88.

Becker, Gary S. and Kevin Murphy (1988), 'The family and the state', *Journal of Law and Economics*, **31**, 1–18.

Becker, Gary S., E.M. Landes and R.T. Michael (1977), 'An economic analysis of marital instability', *Journal of Political Economy*, **85** (6, pt 2), 1141–87.

Bell, Carolyn Shaw (1973a), Report of the Committee on the Status of Women in the Economics Profession, *American Economic Review*, **63** (2), 508–11.

Bell, Carolyn Shaw (1973b), 'Age, sex, marriage, and jobs', *Public Interest*, **30** (Winter), 76–87.

Bell, Carolyn Shaw (1974a), 'Economics, sex, and gender', *Social Science Quarterly*, **55** (3), 615–31.

Bell, Carolyn Shaw (1974b), Report of the Committee on the Status of Women in the Economics Profession, *American Economic Review*, **64** (2), 519–23.

Benería, Lourdes (1981), 'Conceptualizing the labor force: the underestimation of women's economic activities', *Journal of Development Studies*, **17**, 11–28.

Benería, Lourdes (1992), 'Accounting for women's work: the progress of two decades', *World Development*, **20** (11), 1547–60.

Ben-Porath, Yoram (1982), Review of *A Treatise on the Family*, by Gary S. Becker. *Journal of Economic Literature*, **20**, 52–64.

Berg, Helen M. and Marianne A. Ferber (1983), 'Men and women graduate students: who succeeds, and why?', *Journal of Higher Education*, **54** (6), 629–48.

Bergmann, Barbara R. (1971), 'The effect on white incomes of discrimination in employment', *Journal of Political Economy*, **79** (2), 294–313.

Bergmann, Barbara R. (1973), 'The economics of women's liberation', *Challenge*, May/June, 11–17.

Bergmann, Barbara R. (1974), 'Occupational segregation, wages and profits when employers discriminate by race or sex', reprinted in Jane Humphries (ed.) (1995), *Gender and Economics*, Aldershot: Edward Elgar, pp. 309–16.

Bergmann, Barbara R. (1981), 'The economic risks of being a housewife', *American Economic Review*, **71** (2), 81–6.

Bergmann, Barbara R. ([1983] 1990), 'Feminism and economics', *Women's Studies Quarterly*, **18** (3 & 4), 68–74.

Bergmann, Barbara R. (1984a), 'Feminism and economics', *Challenge*, July-August, 46–9.

Bergmann, Barbara R. (1984b), Report of the Committee on the Status of Women in the Economics Profession, *American Economic Review*, **74** (2), 457–62.

Bergmann, Barbara R. (1985), Report of the Committee on the Status of Women in the Economics Profession, *American Economic Review*, **75** (2), 448–53.

Bergmann, Barbara R. (1986), *The Economic Emergence of Women*, New York: Basic Books.

Bergmann, Barbara R. (1987a), '"Measurement" or finding things out in economics', *Journal of Economic Education*, **18** (2), 191–203.

Bergmann, Barbara R. (1987b), 'Women's roles in the economy: teaching the issues', *Journal of Economic Education*, **18** (4), 393–407.

Bergmann, Barbara R. (1987c), 'The task of a feminist economics: a more equitable future', in Christie Farnham (ed.), *The Impact of Feminist Research on the Academy*, Bloomington: Indiana University Press, pp. 131–47.

Bergmann, Barbara R. (1989), 'Does the market for women's labor need fixing?', *Journal of Economic Perspectives*, **3** (1), 43–60.

Bergmann, Barbara R. (1990), 'Reading lists on women's studies in economics', *Women's Studies Quarterly* **18** (3 & 4), 75–86.

Bergmann, Barbara R. (1996a), 'Becker's theory of the family: preposterous conclusions', *Feminist Economics* **1** (1), 141–50.

Bergmann, Barbara R. (1996b), 'Becker's theory of the family: preposterous conclusions', *Challenge*, January/February, 9–12.

Bergmann, Barbara R. and Irma Adelman (1973), 'The 1973 Report of the President's Council of Economic Advisors: the economic role of women', *American Economic Review*, **63** (4), 509–14.

Berk, Richard A. (1987), 'Household production', in John Eatwell, Murray Milgate and

Peter Newman (eds), *The New Palgrave: A Dictionary of Economics*, vol. 2, New York: Stockton, pp. 675–8.

Best, Steven and Douglas Kellner (1991), *Postmodern Theory: Critical Interrogations*, London: Macmillan.

Bielby, Denise and William Bielby (1988), 'She works hard for the money: household responsibilities and the allocation of work effort', *American Journal of Sociology*, **93**, 1031–59.

Binger, Brian and Emily Hoffman (1988), *Microeconomics with Calculus*. Glenview, Ill.: Scott, Foresman.

Bittman, Michael (1991), *Juggling Time: How Australian Families Use Time*, Canberra: Office of the Status of Women, Department of Prime Minister and Cabinet.

Black, Maria and Rosalind Coward (1990), 'Linguistic, social and sexual relations: a review of Dale Spender's *Man-made Language*', in Deborah Cameron (ed.), *The Feminist Critique of Language*, London: Routledge, pp. 111–33.

Black, R.D. Collison (1987), 'Utility', in John Eatwell, Murray Milgate and Peter Newman (eds), *The New Palgrave: A Dictionary of Economics*, vol. 4, New York: Stockton, pp. 776–9.

Blank, Rebecca M. (1991), 'The effects of double-blind versus single-blind reviewing: experimental evidence from *The American Economic Review*', *American Economic Review*, **81** (5), 1041–67.

Blank, Rebecca M. (1993), 'What should mainstream economists learn from feminist theory?', in Marianne A. Ferber and Julie A. Nelson (eds), *Beyond Economic Man: Feminist Theory and Economics*, Chicago: University of Chicago Press, pp. 133–42.

Blank, Rebecca M. (1994), Report of the Committee on the Status of Women in the Economics Profession, *American Economic Review*, **84** (2), 491–5.

Blank, Rebecca M. (1995), Report of the Committee on the Status of Women in the Economics Profession, *American Economic Review*, **85** (2), 492–6.

Blank, Rebecca M. (1996), Report of the Committee on the Status of Women in the Economics Profession, *American Economic Review*, **86** (2), 502–6.

Blau, Francine D. (1976), 'Comment on Mueller's "Economic determinants of volunteer work by women"', *Signs*, **2** (1), 251–4.

Blau, Francine D. (1981), 'On the role of values in feminist scholarship', *Signs* **6** (3), 538–40.

Blau, Francine D. (1984), 'Occupational segregation and labor market discrimination', in Barbara Reskin (ed.), *Sex Segregation in the Workplace*, Washington D.C.: National Academy Press, pp. 117–43.

Blau, Francine D. (1987), 'Gender', in John Eatwell, Murray Milgate and Peter Newman (eds), *The New Palgrave: A Dictionary of Economics*, vol. 2, New York: Stockton, pp. 492–8.

Blau, Francine D. and Marianne A. Ferber (1989), 'Economics determines gender roles', in Neal Bernards and Terry O'Neill (eds), *Male/Female Roles*, San Diego, Cal.: Greenhaven, pp. 40–6.

Blau, Francine D. and Marianne A. Ferber (1992), *The Economics of Women, Men and Work*, 2nd edn, Englewood Cliffs, N.J.: Prentice-Hall.

Blau, Francine D. and Carol L. Jusenius (1976), 'Economists' approaches to sex segregation in the labor market: an appraisal', *Signs*, **1** (3, pt 2), 181–200.

Blaxall, Martha and Barbara B. Reagan (eds) (1976), *Women and the Workplace: The Implications of Occupational Segregation*, special issue of *Signs*, **1** (3, pt 2).

Bleier, Ruth (ed.) (1986a), *Feminist Approaches to Science*, New York: Pergamon.

Bleier, Ruth (1986b), 'Introduction', in *Feminist Approaches to Science*, New York: Pergamon, pp. 1–17.

Boettke, Peter J. (1995), 'Good economics – bad sex (and even worse philosophy): a review essay', *Review of Political Economy*, **7** (3), 360–73.

Bordo, Susan (1987a), 'The cartesian masculinization of thought', in Sandra Harding and Jean F. O'Barr (eds), *Sex and Scientific Inquiry*, Chicago: University of Chicago Press, pp. 247–64.

Bordo, Susan (1987b), *The Flight to Objectivity: Essays on Cartesianism and Culture*. Albany, N.Y.: State University of New York Press.

Bordo, Susan (1990), 'Feminism, postmodernism, and gender-scepticism', in Linda J. Nicholson (ed.), *Feminism/Postmodernism*, New York: Routledge, pp. 133–56.

Bordo, Susan (1993), *Unbearable Weight: Feminism, Western Culture, and the Body*, Berkeley, Cal.: University of California Press.

Boserup, Esther (1987), 'Inequality between the sexes', in John Eatwell, Murray Milgate and Peter Newman (eds), *The New Palgrave: A Dictionary of Economic Theory*, vol. 2, New York: Stockton, pp. 824–7.

Boulding, Kenneth (1972), 'The household as Archilles' heel', *Journal of Consumer Affairs*, **6** (Winter), 110–19.

Bowles, Samuel and Herbert Gintis (1993), 'The revenge of homo economicus: contested exchange and the revival of political economy', *Journal of Economic Perspectives*, **7** (1), 83–102.

Braidotti, Rosi (1989), 'The politics of ontological difference', in Teresa Brennan (ed.), *Between Feminism and Psychoanalysis*, London: Routledge, pp. 89–105.

Braidotti, Rosi (1991), *Patterns of Dissonance: A Study of Women in Contemporary Philosophy*, Cambridge: Polity Press.

Brennan, Teresa (ed.) (1989a), *Between Feminism and Psychoanalysis*, London: Routledge.

Brennan, Teresa (1989b), 'Introduction', in *Between Feminism and Psychoanalysis*, London: Routledge, pp. 1–23.

Brodribb, Seyla (1992), *Nothing Ma(T)ters: A Feminist Critique of Postmodernism*, Melbourne: Spinifax.

Brown, Clair (Vickery) (1982), 'Home production for use in a market economy', in Barrie Thorne (ed.), *Rethinking the Family: Some Feminist Questions*, New York: Longman, pp. 151–67.

Brown, Clair and Amelia Preece (1987), 'Housework', in John Eatwell, Murray Milgate and Peter Newman (eds), *The New Palgrave: A Dictionary of Economics*, vol. 2, New York: Stockton, pp. 678–80.

Brown, Doug (1994), 'Radical institutionalism and postmodern feminist theory', in Janice Peterson and Doug Brown (eds), *The Economic Status of Women Under Capitalism: Institutional Economics and Feminist Theory*, Aldershot: Edward Elgar, pp. 35–52.

Brown, Murray (1992), 'Optimal marriage contracts', *Journal of Human Resources*, **27** (3), 534–50.

Brown, Vivienne (1993), 'Decanonizing discourses: textual analysis and the history of economic thought', in Willie Henderson, Tony Dudley-Evans and Roger Backhouse (eds), *Economics and Language*, London: Routledge, pp. 64–84.

Brown, Vivienne (1994a), 'The economy as text', in Roger E. Backhouse (ed.), *New

Directions in Economic Methodology, London: Routledge, pp. 368–82.

Brown, Vivienne (1994b), Review of *Beyond Economic Man: Feminist Theory and Economics*, edited by Marianne A. Ferber and Julie A. Nelson, *Journal of Economic Methodology*, **1** (2), 301–6.

Browning, Martin, Francois Bourguignon, Pierre-Andre Chiappori and Valerie Lechene (1994), 'Income and outcomes: a structural model of intrahousehold allocation', *Journal of Political Economy*, **102** (6), 1067–96.

Burke, Carolyn, Naomi Schor and Margaret Whitford (eds) (1994), *Engaging with Irigaray: Feminist Philosophy and Modern European Thought*, New York: Columbia University Press.

Butler, Judith (1990), *Gender Trouble: Feminism and the Subversion of Identity*, New York: Routledge.

Butler, Judith (1992), 'Contingent foundations: feminism and the question of "postmodernism"', in Judith Butler and Joan W. Scott (eds), *Feminists Theorize the Political*, New York: Routledge, pp. 3–21.

Butler, Judith (1994a), 'Bodies that matter', in Carolyn Burke, Naomi Schor and Margaret Whitford (eds), *Engaging with Irigaray: Feminist Philosophy and Modern European Thought*, New York: Columbia University Press, pp. 141–74.

Butler, Judith (1994b), 'Gender as performance: an interview with Judith Butler', *Radical Philosophy*, **67** (Summer), 32–9.

Butler, Judith and Joan W. Scott (eds) (1992a), *Feminists Theorize the Political*, New York: Routledge.

Butler, Judith and Joan W. Scott (1992b), 'Introduction', in *Feminists Theorize the Political*, New York: Routledge, pp. xiii–xvii.

Caddick, Alison (1986), 'Feminism and the body', *Arena*, **74**, 60–88.

Cain, Glen G. (1966), *Married Women in the Labor Force*, Chicago: University of Chicago Press.

Cain, Glen G. (1991), 'The uses and limits of statistical analysis in measuring economic discrimination', in Emily P. Hoffman (ed.), *Essays on the Economics of Discrimination*, Kalamazoo, Mich.: W.E. Upjohn Institute for Employment Research, pp. 115–44.

Caine, Barbara (1994), 'Feminism and political economy in Victorian England – or John Stuart Mill, Henry Fawcett and Henry Sidgwick ponder the "woman question"', in Peter Groenewegen (ed.), *Feminism and Political Economy in Victorian England*, Aldershot: Edward Elgar, pp. 25–45.

Cairncross, Alec (1960), *Introduction to Economics*, 3rd edn, London: Butterworth.

Caldwell, Bruce J. (1994), *Beyond Positivism: Economic Methodology in the Twentieth Century*, rev. edn, London: Routledge.

Caldwell, Bruce J. and A.W. Coats (1984), 'The rhetoric of economists: a comment on McCloskey', *Journal of Economic Literature*, **22**, 575–8.

Campbell, Kate (1992), 'Introduction: Matters of theory and practice – *or*, we'll be coming out the harbour', in *Critical Feminism: Argument in the Disciplines*, Buckingham: Open University Press, pp. 3–24.

Campioni, Mia and Elizabeth Gross (1983), 'Love's labours lost: marxism and feminism', *Intervention (Beyond Marxism)*, **20**, 113–41.

Carter, Anne P. (1976), Review of *Sex, Discrimination, and the Division of Labor*, edited by Cynthia B. Lloyd, *Signs*, **1** (3, pt 1), 738–42.

Carter, John and Michael Irons (1991), 'Are economists different, and if so, why?',

Journal of Economic Perspectives, **5** (2), 171–7.

Chalmers, A.F. (1976.),*What is This Thing Called Science?*, St Lucia: University of Queensland Press.

Chapman, Jane Roberts (1975), 'Economics', *Signs*, **1** (1), 139–46.

Cheah, Pheng (1991), 'The law of/as rape – poststructuralism and the framing of the legal text', in Ian Duncanson (ed.), *Legal Education and Legal Knowledge (Special Issue of Law in Context)*, Bundoora: La Trobe University Press, pp. 117–29.

Chodorow, Nancy (1978), *The Reproduction of Mothering: Psychoanalysis and the Sociology of Gender*, Berkeley: University of California Press.

Chodorow, Nancy (1994), 'Gender, relation and difference in psychoanalytic perspective', in *The Polity Reader in Gender Studies*, Cambridge: Polity Press, pp. 41–9.

Christian, Barbara (1988), 'The race for theory', *Feminist Studies*, **14** (1), 67–79.

Ciancanelli, Penelope and Bettina Berch (1987), 'Gender and the GNP', in Beth B. Hess and Myra Marx Ferree (eds), *Analyzing Gender: A Handbook of Social Science Research*, Newbury Park, Cal.: Sage, pp. 244–66.

Cigno, Alessandro (1991), *Economics of the Family*, Oxford: Clarendon Press.

Cixous, Hélène and Catherine Clément (1986), *The Newly Born Woman*, trans. Betsy Wing, Minneapolis: University of Minnesota Press.

Clark, Colin (1958), 'The economics of housework', *Quarterly Bulletin of the Oxford University Institute of Statistics*, **20** (1), 205–11.

Coetzee, J.M. (1986), *Foe*, London: Secker & Warburg.

Cohen, Marjorie (1982), 'The problem of studying "economic man"', in Angela Miles and Geraldine Finn (eds), *Feminism: From Pressure to Politics*, Montreal: Black Rose Books, pp. 147–59.

Cohen, Marjorie (1985), 'The razor's edge invisible: feminism's effect on economics', *International Journal of Women's Studies*, **8** (3), 286–98.

Collins, Patricia Hill (1994), 'Shifting the center: race, class, and feminist theorizing about motherhood', in Donna Bassin, Margaret Honey and Maryle Mahrer Kaplan (eds), *Representations of Motherhood*, New Haven, Conn.: Yale University Press, pp. 56–74.

Conrad, Cecilia A. (1992), 'Evaluating undergraduate courses on women in the economy', *American Economic Review*, **82** (2), 565–9.

Cooper, Brian (1993), 'Harriet Martineau's "embodied principles": whose bodies, what principles?', paper presented at the *Out of the Margin: Feminist Perspectives on Economic Theory* Conference, Amsterdam, June.

Cornell, Drucilla (1991), *Beyond Accommodation: Ethical Feminism, Deconstruction, and the Law*, New York: Routledge.

Cornell, Drucilla (1992), 'Gender, sex, and equivalent rights', in Judith Butler and Joan W. Scott (eds), *Feminists Theorize the Political*, New York: Routledge, pp. 280–96.

Cranny-Francis, Anne (1995), *The Body in the Text*, Melbourne: Melbourne University Press.

Creed, Barbara (1993), *The Monstrous Feminine: Film, Feminism, and Psychoanalysis*, London: Routledge.

Culler, Jonathan (1974), 'Introduction', in *Course in General Linguistics*, by Ferdinand de Saussure, trans. Wade Baskin, London: Fontana, pp. xi–xxv.

Culler, Jonathan (1976), *Saussure*, London: Fontana Paperbacks.

Culler, Jonathan (1981), *The Pursuit of Signs: Semiotics, Literature, Deconstruction*,

London: Routledge & Kegan Paul.

Culler, Jonathan (1983), *On Deconstruction: Theory and Criticism after Structuralism*, London: Routledge & Kegan Paul.

Dallery, Arleen B. (1994), 'The politics of writing (the) body: écriture féminine', in Anne C. Herrmann and Abigail J. Stewart (eds), *Theorizing Feminism: Parallel Trends in the Humanities and Social Sciences*, Boulder, Col.: Westview Press, pp. 288–300.

Davies, Bronwyn (1991), 'The concept of agency: a feminist poststructuralist approach', *Social Analysis*, **30** (December), 42–53.

Day, Tanis (1995), 'Symposium on feminist economics: introduction', *Canadian Journal of Economics*, **28** (1), 139–42.

Deacon, Desley (1985), 'Political arithmetic: the nineteenth-century Australian census and the construction of the dependent woman', *Signs*, **11** (1), 27–47.

Defoe, Daniel ([1719] 1945), *Robinson Crusoe*, London: J.M. Dent.

Derrida, Jacques (1974), *Of Grammatology*, trans. Gayatri Chakravorty Spivak, Baltimore, Md: Johns Hopkins University Press.

Derrida, Jacques (1978), 'Structure, sign and play in the discourse of the human sciences', in *Writing and Difference*, London: Routledge & Kegan Paul, pp. 278–93.

Derrida, Jacques (1981), *Positions*, Chicago: University of Chicago Press.

Derrida, Jacques (1982a), 'Différance', in *Margins of Philosophy*, trans. Alan Bass, New York: Harvester Wheatsheaf, pp. 1–28.

Derrida, Jacques (1982b), 'Signiture event context', in *Margins of Philosophy*, trans. Alan Bass, New York: Harvester Wheatsheaf, pp. 307–30.

Derrida, Jacques (1982c), 'White mythology: metaphor in the text of philosophy', in *Margins of Philosophy*, trans. Alan Bass, New York: Harvester Wheatsheaf, pp. 207–71.

Derrida, Jacques (1984), 'Dialogue with Jacques Derrida', in Richard Kearney (ed.), *Dialogues with Contemporary Continental Thinkers: The Phenomenological Heritage*, Manchester: Manchester University Press, pp. 105–26.

Derrida, Jacques (1991), *A Derrida Reader: Between the Blinds*, Peggy Kamuf (ed.), New York: Columbia University Press.

Diamond, Irene (1988), 'Medical science and the transformation of motherhood: the promise of reproductive technologies', in Ellen Bonepart and Emily Stoper (eds), *Women, Power and Policy: Toward the Year 2000*, New York: Pergamon, pp. 155–67.

Diamond, Irene and Lee Quinby (eds) (1988a), *Feminism and Foucault: Reflections on Resistance*, Boston, Mass.: Northeastern University Press.

Diamond, Irene and Lee Quinby (1988b), 'Introduction', in *Feminism and Foucault: Reflections on Resistance*, Boston, Mass.: Northeastern University Press, pp. ix–xx.

Dimand, Mary Ann (1996), 'Gilman as polemicist', paper presented at the *Allied Social Sciences Association Annual Meetings*, San Francisco, January.

Diprose, Rosalyn (1991a), 'Foucault, Derrida and the ethics of sexual difference', *Social Semiotics*, **1** (2), 1–21.

Diprose, Rosalyn (1991b), 'In excess: the body and the habit of sexual difference', *Hypatia*, **6** (3), 156–71.

Diprose, Rosalyn (1992), 'The body which biomedical ethics forgets', in Stephen Darling (ed.), *Cross Currents: Philosophy in the Nineties*, Adelaide: Flinders University Press, pp. 147–62.

Diprose, Rosalyn (1994), *The Bodies of Women: Ethics, Embodiment and Sexual Difference*, London: Routledge.

Diprose, Rosalyn (1996a), 'The gift, sexed body property and the law', in Pheng Cheah, David Fraser and Judith Grbich (eds), *Thinking Through the Body of the Law*, St. Leonards: Allen & Unwin, pp. 120–35.

Diprose, Rosalyn (1996b), 'Giving corporeality against the law', *Australian Feminist Studies*, **11** (24), 253–62.

Doane, Janice and Devon Hodges (1987), *Nostalgia and Sexual Difference: The Resistance to Contemporary Feminism*, New York: Methuen.

Doane, Janice and Devon Hodges (1989), 'Risky business: familial ideology and the case of Baby M', *differences*, **1** (1), 67–81.

Dodds, Susan and Karen Jones (1989a), 'Surrogacy and autonomy', *Bioethics*, **3** (1), 1–17.

Dodds, Susan and Karen Jones (1989b), 'A response to Purdy', *Bioethics*, **3** (1), 35–9.

Dodds, Susan and Karen Jones (1992), 'Surrogacy and the body as property', in Stephen Darling (ed.), *Cross Currents: Philosophy in the Nineties*, Adelaide: Flinders University Press, pp. 119–33.

Douglas, Gillian (1994), 'The intention to be a parent and the making of mothers', *Modern Law Review*, **57** (July), 636–41.

Dow, Sheila (1992), 'Postmodernism and economics', in Joe Doherty, Elspeth Graham and Mo Malek (eds), *Postmodernism and the Social Sciences*, London: Macmillan, pp. 148–61.

Driscoll, Kathy and Joan McFarland (1989), 'The impact of a feminist perspective on research methodologies: social sciences', in Winnie Tomm (ed.), *The Effects of Feminist Approaches on Research Methodologies*, Waterloo: Wilfrid Laurier University Press, pp. 185–203.

Dugdale, Anni (1990), 'Beyond relativism: moving on – feminist struggles with scientific/medical knowledges', *Australian Feminist Studies*, **12** (Summer), 51–63.

Dugger, William M. (1994), 'Institutionalism and feminism', in Janice Peterson and Doug Brown (eds), *The Economic Status of Women Under Capitalism: Institutional Economics and Feminist Theory*, Aldershot: Edward Elgar, pp. 3–18.

Eagleton, Terry (1983), *Literary Theory: An Introduction*, Minneapolis: University of Minnesota Press.

Echols, Alice (1984), 'The taming of the id: feminist sexual politics, 1968–83', in Carole S. Vance (ed.), *Pleasure and Danger: Exploring Female Sexuality*, Boston, Mass.: Routledge & Kegan Paul, pp. 50–72.

Edwards, Anne (1989), 'The sex/gender distinction: has it outlived its usefulness?', *Australian Feminist Studies*, **10** (Summer), 1–12.

Edwards, Meredith (1984), 'The distribution of income within households', in Dorothy H. Broom (ed.), *Unfinished Business: Social Justice for Women in Australia*, Sydney: Allen & Unwin, pp. 120–36.

Edwards, Meredith (1985a), 'Individual equity and social policy', in Jacqueline Goodnow and Carole Pateman (eds), *Women, Social Science and Public Policy*, Sydney: Allen & Unwin, pp. 95–103.

Edwards, Meredith (1985b), 'The relevance of economic analysis for feminists', *Australian Feminist Studies*, **1** (Summer), 55–66.

Eisenstein, Hester (1984), *Contemporary Feminist Thought*, London: Unwin Paperbacks.

Eisenstein, Zillah R. (1988), *The Female Body and the Law*, Berkeley: University of

California Press.

Eisner, Robert (1988), 'Extended accounts for national income and product', *Journal of Economic Literature*, **26**, 1161–85.

Eisner, Robert, Emily R. Simons, Paul J. Pieper and Steven Bender (1982), 'Total incomes in the United Sates, 1946–1976: a summary report', *Review of Income and Wealth*, **28** (2), 133–74.

Elam, Diane (1994), *Feminism and Deconstruction: Ms. en Abyme*, London: Routledge.

Elliot, Patricia (1994), 'More thinking about gender: a response to Julie A. Nelson', *Hypatia*, **9** (1), 195–8.

Ellsberg, D. (1954), 'Classic and current notions of measurable utility', *Economic Journal*, **64** (255), 528–56.

Elshtain, Jean Bethke (1987), 'Against androgyny', in Anne Phillips (ed.), *Feminism and Equality*, New York: New York University Press, pp. 139–59.

Elson, Diane (1995), 'The empowerment of women: comments on chapters by Trzcinski, Hopkins and Agarwal', in Edith Kuiper and Jolande Sap (eds), *Out of the Margin: Feminist Perspectives on Economics*, London: Routledge, pp. 295–9.

England, Paula (1982), 'The failure of human capital theory to explain occupational sex segregation', *Journal of Human Resources*, **17** (3), 358–70.

England, Paula (1984), 'Wage appreciation and depreciation: a test of neoclassical economic explanations of occupational sex segregation', *Social Forces*, **62** (3), 726–49.

England, Paula (1989), 'A feminist critique of rational-choice theories: implications for sociology', reprinted in Jane Humphries (ed.) (1995), *Gender and Economics*, Aldershot: Edward Elgar, pp. 42–56.

England, Paula (1993), 'The separative self: androcentric bias in neoclassical economics', in Marianne A. Ferber and Julie A. Nelson (eds), *Beyond Economic Man: Feminist Theory and Economics*, Chicago: University of Chicago Press, pp. 37–53.

England, Paula and Barbara Stanek Kilbourne (1990), 'Feminist critiques of the separative model of the self: implications for rational choice theory', *Rationality and Society*, **2** (2), 156–71.

England, Paula and Lori McCreary (1987), 'Gender inquality in paid employment', in Beth B. Hess and Myra Marx Ferree (eds), *Analyzing Gender: A Handbook of Social Science Research*, Newbury Park, Cal.: Sage, pp. 286–320.

Equal Opportunity Commission (South Australia) (1987), In the matter of an application for exemption by Nieham Pty Ltd and Ors Working Women's Centre Inc, *Australian and New Zealand Equal Opportunity Cases*, Sydney: CCH, pp. 92–101.

Farganis, Sondra (1989), 'Feminism and the reconstruction of social science', in Alison M. Jaggar and Susan R. Bordo (eds), *Gender/Body/Knowledge: Feminist Reconstructions of Being and Knowing*, New Brunswick: Rutgers University Press, pp. 207–23.

Fee, Elizabeth (1986), 'Critiques of modern science: the relationship of feminism to other radical epistemologies', in Ruth Bleier (ed.), *Feminist Approaches to Science*, New York: Pergamon, pp. 42–56.

Fee, Terry (1976), 'Domestic labor: an analysis of housework and its relation to the production process', *Review of Radical Political Economics*, **8** (1), 1–8.

Feiner, Susan F. (1995a), 'Reading neoclassical economics: toward an erotic economy of sharing', in Edith Kuiper and Jolande Sap (eds), *Out of the Margin: Feminist*

Perspectives on Economics, London: Routledge, pp. 151–66.

Feiner, Susan F. (1995b), 'A portrait of homo economicus as a young man', paper presented at the *Modern Language Association of America Meetings*, St Louis.

Feiner, Susan F. and Barbara A. Morgan (1987), 'Women and minorities in introductory economics textbooks: 1974 to 1978', *Journal of Economic Education*, **18** (4), 376–92.

Feiner, Susan F. and Bruce B. Roberts (1990), 'Hidden by the invisible hand: neoclassical economic theory and the textbook treatment of race and gender', *Gender and Society*, **4** (2), 159–81.

Ferber, Marianne A. (1982), 'Women and work: issues of the 1980s', *Signs*, **8** (2), 273–95.

Ferber, Marianne A. (1984), 'Suggestions for improving the classroom climate for women in the introductory economics course: a review article', *Journal of Economic Education*, **15** (2), 160–8.

Ferber, Marianne A. (1986), 'Citations: are they an objective measure of scholarly merit?', *Signs*, **11** (2), 381–9.

Ferber, Marianne A. (1987), *Women and Work, Paid and Unpaid: A Selected, Annotated Bibliography*, New York: Garland.

Ferber, Marianne A. (1988), 'Citations and networking', *Gender and Society*, **2** (1), 82–8.

Ferber, Marianne A. (1993), 'A feminist treatise on the family', paper presented at the *Out of the Margin: Feminist Perspectives on Economic Theory* Conference, Amsterdam, June.

Ferber, Marianne A. and Bonnie G. Birnbaum (1977), 'The "new home economics": retrospects and prospects', *Journal of Consumer Research*, **4** (1), 19–28.

Ferber, Marianne A. and Bonnie G. Birnbaum (1980a), 'Housework: priceless or valueless?', *Review of Income and Wealth*, **26** (4), 387–400.

Ferber, Marianne A. and Bonnie G. Birnbaum (1980b), 'Economics of the family: who maximises what?', *Family Economics Review,* Summer/Fall, pp. 13–16.

Ferber, Marianne A. and Carole A. Green (1983), 'Housework vs. marketwork: some evidence of how the decision is made', *Review of Income and Wealth,* **29** (2), 147–59.

Ferber, Marianne A. and Carole Green (1991), 'Occupational segregation and the earnings gap: further evidence', in Emily P. Hoffman (ed.), *Essays on the Economics of Discrimination*, Kalamazoo, Mich.: W.E. Upjohn Institute for Employment Research, pp. 145–65.

Ferber, Marianne A. and Helen M. Lowry (1976), 'The sex differential in earnings: a reappraisal', reprinted in Jane Humphries (ed.) (1995), *Gender and Economics*, Aldershot: Edward Elgar, pp. 429–39.

Ferber, Marianne A. and Julie A. Nelson (eds) (1993a), *Beyond Economic Man: Feminist Theory and Economics*, Chicago: University of Chicago Press.

Ferber, Marianne A. and Julie A. Nelson (1993b), 'Introduction: The social construction of economics and the social construction of gender', in *Beyond Economic Man: Feminist Theory and Economics*, Chicago: University of Chicago Press, pp. 1–22.

Ferber, Marianne A. and Michelle L. Teiman (1980), 'Are women economists at a disadvantage in publishing articles?', *Eastern Economics Journal*, **6**, 189–94.

Ferber, Marianne A. and Michelle L. Teiman (1981), 'The oldest, the most established, the most quantitative of the social sciences – and the most dominated by men', in Dale Spender (ed.), *Men's Studies Modified*, New York: Pergamon, pp. 125–39.

Ferber, Marianne A., Bonnie G. Birnbaum and Carole A. Green (1983), 'Gender differences in economic knowledge: a reevaluation of the evidence', *Journal of Economic Education*, **14** (2), 24–37.

Ferber, Marianne A., Carole A. Green and Joe L. Spaeth (1986), 'Work power and the earnings of women and men', *American Economic Review*, **76** (2), 53–6.

Ferguson, Ann (1977), 'Androgyny as an ideal for human development', in Mary Vetterling-Braggin, Frederick A. Elliston and Jane English (eds), *Feminism and Philosophy*, Totowa, N.J.: Rowman & Allanheld, pp. 45–69.

Ferguson, Ann and Nancy Folbre (1981), 'The unhappy marriage of patriarchy and capitalism', in Lydia Sargent (ed.), *Women and Revolution: A Discussion of the Unhappy Marriage of Marxism and Feminism*, Boston, Mass.: South End, pp. 313–38.

Ferrell, Robyn (1991a), 'The passion of the signifier and the body in theory', *Hypatia*, **6** (3), 172–84.

Ferrell, Robyn (1991b), 'Richard Rorty and the poet's utopia', in Rosalyn Diprose and Robyn Ferrell (eds), *Cartographies: Poststructuralism and the Mapping of Bodies and Spaces*, Sydney: Allen & Unwin, pp. 3–12.

Ferrell, Robyn (1993), 'Why bother? Defending Derrida and the significance of writing', *Australasian Journal of Philosophy*, **71** (2), 121–31.

Field, Martha A. (1990), *Surrogate Motherhood: The Legal and Human Issues*, exp. edn, Cambridge, Mass.: Harvard University Press.

Findlay, Jeanette and Robert E. Wright (1996), 'Gender, poverty and the intra-household distribution of resources', *Review of Income and Wealth,* **42** (3), 335–51.

Fineman, Martha A. (1995), 'Images of mothers in poverty discourse', in Martha Albertson Fineman and Isabel Karpin (eds), *Mothers in Law: Feminist Theory and the Legal Regulation of Motherhood*, New York: Columbia University Press, pp. 205–23.

Fish, Mary and Jean Gibbons (1989), 'A comparison of the publications of female and male economists', *Journal of Economic Education*, **20** (1), 93–105.

Fish, Stanley (1988), 'Comments from outside economics', in Arjo Klamer, Donald N. McCloskey and Robert M. Solow (eds), *The Consequences of Economic Rhetoric*, Cambridge: Cambridge University Press, pp. 21–30.

Fiumara, Gemma Corradi (1994), 'The metaphoric function and the question of objectivity', in Kathleen Lennon and Margaret Whitford (eds), *Knowing the Difference: Feminist Perspectives on Epistemology*, London: Routledge, pp. 31–44.

Flax, Jane (1983), 'Political philosophy and the patriarchal unconscious: a psychoanalytic perspective on epistemology and metaphysics', in Sandra Harding and Merrill B. Hintikka (eds), *Discovering Reality: Feminist Perspectives on Epistemology, Metaphysics, Methodology and Philosophy of Science*, Dordrecht: Reidel, pp. 245–82.

Flax, Jane (1987), 'Postmodernism and gender relations in feminist theory', *Signs*, **12** (4), 621–43.

Folbre, Nancy (1982), 'Exploitation comes home: a critique of the marxian theory of family labour', *Cambridge Journal of Economics*, **6**, 317–29.

Folbre, Nancy (1983), 'Of patriarchy born: the political economy of fertility decisions', *Feminist Studies*, **9** (2), 269–84.

Folbre, Nancy (1984), 'The pauperization of motherhood: patriarchy and public policy in the United States', *Review of Radical Political Economics*, **16** (4), 72–88.

Folbre, Nancy (1986), 'Hearts and spades: paradigms of household economics', *World Development*, **14** (2), 245–55.

Folbre, Nancy (1991), 'The unproductive housewife: her evolution in nineteenth-century economic thought', *Signs*, **16** (3), 463–84.

Folbre, Nancy (1992), 'The improper arts: sex in classical political economy', *Population and Development Review*, **18** (1), 105–21.

Folbre, Nancy (1993a), 'Socialism, feminist and scientific', in Marianne A. Ferber and Julie A. Nelson (eds), *Beyond Economic Man: Feminist Theory and Economics*, Chicago: University of Chicago Press, pp. 94–110.

Folbre, Nancy (1993b), 'How does she know? Feminist theories of gender bias in economics', *History of Political Economy*, **25** (1), 167–84.

Folbre, Nancy (1995), '"Holding hands at midnight": the paradox of caring labor', *Feminist Economics*, **1** (1), 73–92.

Folbre, Nancy and Marjorie Abel (1989), 'Women's work and women's households: gender bias in the US Statistics', *Social Research*, **56** (3), 545–70.

Folbre, Nancy and Heidi Hartmann (1988), 'The rhetoric of self-interest: ideology and gender in economic theory', in Arjo Klamer, Donald N. McCloskey and Robert M. Solow (eds), *The Consequences of Economic Rhetoric*, Cambridge: Cambridge University Press, pp. 184–203.

Foucault, Michel (1972), *The Archaeology of Knowledge and the Discourse on Language*, New York: Pantheon Books.

Foucault, Michel (1979), *Discipline and Punish: The Birth of the Prison*, New York: Vintage Books.

Foucault, Michel (1980a), 'Body/power', in Colin Gordon (ed.), *Power/Knowledge: Selected Interviews and Other Writings of Michel Foucault, 1972-1977*, trans. Colin Gordon, Leo Marshall, John Mepham and Kate Soper, New York: Pantheon Books, pp. 55–62.

Foucault, Michel (1980b), 'Truth and power', in Colin Gordon (ed.), *Power/Knowledge: Selected Interviews and Other Writings of Michel Foucault, 1972-1977*, trans. Colin Gordon, Leo Marshall, John Mepham and Kate Soper, New York: Pantheon Books, pp. 109–33.

Foucault, Michel (1981a), 'The order of discourse', in Robert Young (ed.), *Untying the Text: A Post-structuralist Reader*, Boston, Mass.: Routledge & Kegan Paul, pp. 48–78.

Foucault, Michel (1981b), *The History of Sexuality: An Introduction*, vol. 1, trans. Robert Hurley, London: Penguin.

Frank, Robert H. (1990), 'Rethinking rational choice', in Roger Friedland and A.F. Robertson (eds), *Beyond the Marketplace: Rethinking Economy and Society*, New York: Aldine de Gruyter, pp. 53–88.

Frank, Robert H., Thomas Gilovich and Dennis T. Regan (1993), 'Does studying economics inhibit cooperation?', *Journal of Economic Perspectives*, **7** (2), 159–71.

Franklin, Sarah (1991), 'Fetal fascinations: new dimensions to the medical-scientific construction of fetal personhood', in Sarah Franklin, Celia Lury and Jackie Stacey (eds), *Off-Centre: Feminism and Cultural Studies*, London: HarperCollins Academic, pp. 190–205.

Fraser, Nancy and Linda J. Nicholson (1990), 'Social criticism without philosophy: an encounter between feminism and postmodernism', in Linda J. Nicholson (ed.), *Feminism/Postmodernism*, New York: Routledge, pp. 19–38.

Fricker, Miranda (1994), 'Knowledge as construct: theorizing the role of gender in knowledge', in Kathleen Lennon and Margaret Whitford (eds), *Knowing the Difference: Feminist Perspectives on Epistemology*, London: Routledge, pp. 95–109.

Friedlaender, Ann F. (1979), Report of the Committee on the Status of Women in the Economics Profession, *American Economic Review*, **69** (2), 414–21.

Friedlaender, Ann F. (1980), Report of the Committee on the Status of Women in the Economics Profession, *American Economic Review*, **70** (2), 466–74.

Fuchs, Victor R. (1971), 'Differences in hourly earnings between men and women', *Monthly Labor Review*, **94** (5), 9–15.

Fuchs, Victor R. (1988), *Women's Quest for Economic Equality*, Cambridge, Mass.: Harvard University Press.

Fuchs, Victor R. (1989), 'Women's quest for economic equality', *Journal of Economic Perspectives*, **3** (1), 25–41.

Fuss, Diana (1989), *Essentially Speaking: Feminism, Nature and Difference*, New York: Routledge.

Fuss, Diana (1994), 'Reading like a feminist', in Naomi Schor and Elizabeth Weed (eds), *The Essential Difference*, Bloomington: Indiana University Press, pp. 98–115.

Fyfe, Wendy (1991), 'Abortion acts: 1803 to 1967', in Sarah Franklin, Celia Lury and Jackie Stacey (eds), *Off-Centre: Feminism and Cultural Studies*, London: HarperCollins Academic, pp. 160–74.

Gallagher, Catherine and Thomas Laqueur (1987), 'Introduction', in *The Making of the Modern Body: Sexuality and Society in the Nineteenth Century*, Berkeley: University of California Press, pp. vii–xv.

Game, Ann (1984), 'Affirmative action: liberal rationality or challenge to patriarchy?', *Legal Services Bulletin*, **9** (6), 253–7.

Gardiner, Jean (1993), 'Domestic labour revisited: a feminist critique of neoclassical and marxist economics', paper presented at the *Out of the Margin: Feminist Perspectives on Economic Theory* Conference, Amsterdam, June.

Gardiner, Jean, Susan Himmelweit and Maureen Mackintosh (1976), 'Women's domestic labour', reprinted in Ellen Malos (ed.) (1982), *The Politics of Housework*, London: Allison & Busby, pp. 198–216.

Gatens, Moira (1983), 'A critique of the sex/gender distinction', *Intervention (Beyond Marxism?)*, **17**, 143–60.

Gatens, Moira (1986), 'Feminism, philosophy and riddles without answers', in Carole Pateman and Elizabeth Gross (eds), *Feminist Challenges: Social and Political Theory*, Sydney: Allen & Unwin, pp. 13–29.

Gatens, Moira (1988), 'Towards a feminist philosophy of the body', in Barbara Caine, E.A. Grosz and Marie de Lepervanche (eds), *Crossing Boundaries: Feminisms and the Critique of Knowledges*, Sydney: Allen & Unwin, pp. 59–70.

Gatens, Moira (1989), 'Woman and her double(s), sex, gender and ethics', *Australian Feminist Studies*, **10** (Summer), 33–47.

Gatens, Moira (1991a), 'Corporeal representation in/and the body politic', in Rosalyn Diprose and Robyn Ferrell (eds), *Cartographies: Poststructuralism and the Mapping of Bodies and Spaces*, Sydney: Allen & Unwin, pp. 79–87.

Gatens, Moira (1991b), *Feminism and Philosophy: Perspectives on Difference and Equality*, Cambridge: Polity Press.

Gatens, Moira (1992), 'Power, bodies and difference', in Michèle Barrett and Anne Phillips (eds), *Destabilizing Theory: Contemporary Feminist Debates*, Cambridge:

Polity Press, pp. 120–37.

Gatens, Moira (1994), 'The dangers of a woman-centred philosophy', in *The Polity Reader in Gender Studies*, Cambridge: Polity Press, pp. 93–107.

Gatens, Moira (1995), 'Between the sexes: care or justice?', in Brenda Almond (ed.), *Introducing Applied Ethics*, Oxford: Blackwell, pp. 42–57.

Gatens, Moira (1996a), *Imaginary Bodies: Ethics, Power and Corporeality*, London: Routledge.

Gatens, Moira (1996b), 'Spinoza, law and responsibility', in Pheng Cheah, David Fraser and Judith Grbich (eds), *Thinking Through the Body of the Law*, St. Leonards: Allen & Unwin, pp. 26–42.

Gauger, William (1973), 'Household work: can we add it to the GNP?', *Journal of Home Economics*, **65** (10), 12–15.

Gilman, Charlotte Perkins ([1898] 1966), *Women and Economics: The Economic Factor Between Men and Women as a Factor in Social Evolution*, New York: Harper Torchbooks.

Goldschmidt-Clermont, Luisella (1982), *Unpaid Work in the Household: A Review of Economic Evaluation Methods*, Geneva: International Labour Organisation.

Goldschmidt-Clermont, Luisella (1983), 'Does housework pay? A product-related microeconomic approach', *Signs*, **9** (1), 108–19.

Goldschmidt-Clermont, Luisella (1990), 'Economic measurement of non-market household activities: is it useful and feasible?', *International Labour Review*, **129** (3), 279–99.

Goodnow, Jacqueline J. (1989), 'Work in households: an overview and three studies', in Duncan Ironmonger (ed.), *Households Work*, Sydney: Allen & Unwin, pp. 38–58.

Gordon, Nancy M. (1988), Report of the Committee on the Status of Women in the Economics Profession, *American Economic Review*, **78** (2), 422–5.

Gordon, Nancy M. (1989), Report of the Committee on the Status of Women in the Economics Profession, *American Economic Review*, **79** (2), 422–5.

Gordon, Nancy M. (1990), Report of the Committee on the Status of Women in the Economics Profession, *American Economic Review*, **80** (2), 520–1.

Gordon, Nancy M. (1991), Report of the Committee on the Status of Women in the Economics Profession, *American Economic Review*, **81** (2), 409–12.

Graham, Julie and Jack Amariglio (1996), 'What difference does difference make? Gender, sexuality, and economic theory', paper presented at the *American Economic Association Annual Meetings*, San Francisco, January.

Grapard, Ulla (1995a), 'Robinson Crusoe: the quintessential economic man?', *Feminist Economics*, **1** (1), 33–52.

Grapard, Ulla (1995b), 'Feminist economics: let me count the ways', paper presented at the *Eastern Economics Association Meetings*, New York, March.

Grapard, Ulla (1996), 'Sexual danger in economics: a consequence of feminist postmodernism?', paper presented at the *American Economic Association Meetings*, San Francisco, January.

Gray, Tara (1992), 'Women in labor economics textbooks', *Journal of Economics Education*, **23** (4), 362–73.

Graycar, Regina and Jenny Morgan (1990), *The Hidden Gender of Law*, Leichhardt: Federation Press.

Grbich, Judith (1992), 'The body in legal theory', *University of Tasmania Law Review*, **11**, 26–58.

Grbich, Judith (1996), 'The taxpayer's body: genealogies of exertion', in Pheng Cheah, David Fraser and Judith Grbich (eds), *Thinking Through the Body of the Law*, St Leonards: Allen & Unwin, pp. 136–60.

Greenwood, Daphne (1984), 'The economic significance of "woman's place" in society: a new-institutionalist view', *Journal of Economic Issues*, **18** (3), 663–80.

Grimshaw, Patricia, Marilyn Lake, Ann McGrath and Marian Quartly (1994), *Creating a Nation: 1788–1990*, Melbourne: McPhee Gribble.

Groenewegen, Peter (ed.) (1994a), *Feminism and Political Economy in Victorian England*, Aldershot: Edward Elgar.

Groenewegen, Peter (1994b), 'Introduction: Women in political economy and women as political economists in victorian England', in *Feminism and Political Economy in Victorian England*, Aldershot: Edward Elgar, pp. 1–24.

Groenewegen, Peter (1994c), 'Alfred Marshall – women and economic development: labour, family and race', in *Feminism and Political Economy in Victorian England*, Aldershot: Edward Elgar, pp. 79–109.

Groenewegen, Peter (1994d), 'A neglected daughter of Adam Smith: Clara Elizabeth Collet (1860–1948)', in *Feminism and Political Economy in Victorian England*, Aldershot: Edward Elgar, pp. 147–73.

Gronau, Reuben (1973), 'The intrafamily allocation of time: the value of the housewives' time', *American Economic Review*, **63** (4), 634–51.

Gronau, Reuben (1980), 'Home production: a forgotten industry', *Review of Economics and Statistics*, **62** (3), 408–16.

Gross, Elizabeth (1986a), 'Derrida and the limits of philosophy', *Thesis Eleven*, **14**, 26–43.

Gross, Elizabeth (1986b), 'Derrida, Irigaray and deconstruction', *Intervention (Leftwright)*, **20**, 70–81.

Gross, Elizabeth (1986c), 'Philosophy, subjectivity and the body: Kristeva and Irigaray', in Carole Pateman and Elizabeth Gross (eds), *Feminist Challenges: Social and Political Theory*, Sydney: Allen & Unwin, pp. 125–43.

Gross, Elizabeth (1986d), 'What is feminist theory?', in Carole Pateman and Elizabeth Gross (eds), *Feminist Challenges: Social and Political Theory*, Sydney: Allen & Unwin, pp. 190–204.

Gross, Elizabeth (1986e), 'Irigaray and sexual difference', *Australian Feminist Studies*, **2** (Autumn), 63–77.

Grosz, E.A. (1986), 'Introduction', in E.A. Grosz, Terry Threadgold, David Kelly, Alan Cholodenko and Edward Colless (eds), *Futur*fall: Excursions into Post-Modernity*, Sydney: Power Institute of Fine Arts, University of Sydney, pp. 7–17.

Grosz, E.A. (1987), 'Notes towards a corporeal feminism', *Australian Feminist Studies*, **5** (Summer), 1–16.

Grosz, E.A. (1988a), 'The in(ter)vention of feminist knowledges', in Barbara Caine, E.A. Grosz and Marie de Lepervanche (eds), *Crossing Boundaries: Feminisms and the Critique of Knowledges*, Sydney: Allen and Unwin, pp. 92–104.

Grosz, E.A. (1988b), 'Desire, the body and recent French feminisms', *Intervention (Flesh)* **21/22**, 28–33.

Grosz, Elizabeth (1989), *Sexual Subversions: Three French Feminists*, Sydney: Allen & Unwin.

Grosz, Elizabeth (1990a), 'Contemporary theories of power and subjectivity', in Sneja Gunew (ed.), *Feminist Knowledge: Critique and Construct*, London: Routledge, pp.

59–120.

Grosz, Elizabeth (1990b), *Jacques Lacan: A Feminist Introduction*, Sydney: Allen & Unwin.

Grosz, Elizabeth (1990c), 'A note on essentialism and difference', in Sneja Gunew (ed.), *Feminist Knowledge*, London: Routledge, pp. 332–44.

Grosz, Elizabeth (1990d), 'Philosophy', in Sneja Gunew (ed.), *Feminist Knowledge: Critique and Construct*, London: Routledge, pp. 147–74.

Grosz, Elizabeth (1990e), 'Inscriptions and body maps: representations and the corporeal', in Terry Threadgold and Anne Cranny-Francis (eds), *Feminine/Masculine and Representation*, Sydney: Allen & Unwin, pp. 62–74.

Grosz, Elizabeth (1992), 'The subject', in Elizabeth Wright (ed.), *Feminism and Psychoanalysis: A Critical Dictionary*, Oxford: Blackwell, pp. 409–16.

Grosz, Elizabeth (1993a), 'Bodies and knowledges: feminism and the crisis of reason', in Linda Alcoff and Elizabeth Potter (eds), *Feminist Epistemologies*, New York: Routledge, pp. 187–216.

Grosz, Elizabeth (1993b), 'Irigaray's notion of sexual morphology', in Shirley Neuman and Glennis Stephenson (eds), *Reimagining Women: Representations of Women in Culture*, Toronto: University of Toronto Press, pp. 182–95.

Grosz, Elizabeth (1994a), 'Theorising corporeality: bodies, sexuality and the feminist academy. An interview with Elizabeth Grosz', *Melbourne Journal of Politics*, **22**, 3–29.

Grosz, Elizabeth (1994b), 'Sexual difference and the problem of essentialism', in Naomi Schor and Elizabeth Weed (eds), *The Essential Difference*, Bloomington: Indiana University Press, pp. 82–97.

Grosz, E.A. and Marie de Lepervanche (1988), 'Feminism and science', in Barbara Caine, E.A. Grosz and Marie de Lepervanche (eds), *Crossing Boundaries: Feminisms and the Critique of Knowledges*, Sydney: Allen and Unwin, pp. 5–27.

Gunderson, Morley (1989), 'Male–female wage differentials and policy responses', *Journal of Economic Literature*, **27**, 46–72.

Gunew, Sneja (1990a), 'Introduction', in *Feminist Knowledge: Critique and Construct*, London: Routledge, pp. 1–10.

Gunew, Sneja (1990b), 'Feminist knowledge: critique and construct', in *Feminist Knowledge: Critique and Construct*, London: Routledge, pp. 13–35.

Gustafsson, Siv S. (1995), 'Economic measurement: comments on chapters by MacDonald, Perrons and Redmount', in Edith Kuiper and Jolande Sap (eds), *Out of the Margin: Feminist Perspectives on Economics*, London: Routledge, pp. 223–7.

Haberfield, Les (1996), 'Foetal health risks – whose body is it?', *Law Institute Journal*, **70**, 50–2.

Haddad, Lawrence and Ravi Kanbur (1990), 'How serious is the neglect of intra-household inequality?', *Economic Journal*, **100** (September), 866–81.

Haltiwanger, John and Michael Waldman (1993), 'The role of altruism in economic interaction', *Journal of Economic Behavior and Organization*, **21**, 1–15.

Hamilton, Roberta and Michèle Barrett (eds) (1986), *The Politics of Diversity: Feminism, Marxism and Nationalism*, London: Verso.

Hammond, Claire H. (1993), 'American women and the professionalization of economics', *Review of Social Economy*, **51** (3), 347–70.

Hammond, Peter J. (1987), 'Altruism', in John Eatwell, Murray Milgate and Peter Newman (eds), *The New Palgrave: A Dictionary of Economics*, vol. 1, New York:

Stockton, pp. 85–7.

Harding, Sandra (1986a), *The Science Question in Feminism*, Ithaca, N.Y.: Cornell University Press.

Harding, Sandra (1986b), 'The instability of the analytical categories of feminist theory', reprinted in Sandra Harding and Jean F. O'Barr (eds) (1987), *Sex and Scientific Inquiry*, Chicago: University of Chicago Press, pp. 283–302.

Harding, Sandra (1987a), 'Epistemological questions', in *Feminism and Methodology*, Bloomington: Indiana University Press, pp. 181–90.

Harding, Sandra (1987b), 'Is there a feminist method?', in *Feminism and Methodology*, Bloomington: Indiana University Press, pp. 1–14.

Harding, Sandra (1989), 'Feminist justificatory strategies', in Ann Garry and Marilyn Pearsall (eds), *Women, Knowledge, and Reality: Explorations in Feminist Philosophy*, Boston, Mass.: Unwin Hyman, pp. 189–201

Harding, Sandra (1992), 'How the women's movement benefits science: two views', in Gill Kirkup and Laurie Smith Keller (eds), *Inventing Women: Science, Technology and Gender*, Cambridge: Polity Press, pp. 57–72.

Harding, Sandra (1993a), 'Rethinking standpoint epistemology: "what is strong objectivity?" ', in Linda Alcoff and Elizabeth Potter (eds), *Feminist Epistemologies*, New York: Routledge, pp. 49–82.

Harding, Sandra (1993b), 'Feminist philosophy of science: the objectivity question', paper presented at the *Out of the Margin: Feminist Perspectives on Economic Theory* Conference, Amsterdam, June.

Harding, Sandra (1995), 'Can feminist thought make economics more objective?', *Feminist Economics*, **1** (1), 7–32.

Harding, Sandra and Merrill Hintikka (1983), 'Introduction', in *Discovering Reality: Feminist Perspectives on Epistemology, Metaphysics, Methodology and Philosophy of Science*, Dordrecht: Reidel, pp. ix–xix.

Hargreaves-Heap, Sean and Martin Hollis (1987), 'Economic man', in John Eatwell, Murray Milgate and Peter Newman (eds), *The New Palgrave: A Dictionary of Economics*, vol. 1, New York: Stockton, pp. 54–5.

Hartmann, Heidi I. (1976), 'Capitalism, patriarchy, and job segregation by sex', *Signs*, **1** (3, pt 2), 137–70.

Hartmann, Heidi I. (1981a), 'The family as the locus of gender, class and political struggle: the example of housework', *Signs*, **6** (3), 366–94.

Hartmann, Heidi I. (1981b), 'The unhappy marriage of marxism and feminism: towards a more progressive union', in Lydia Sargent (ed.), *Women and Revolution: A Discussion of the Unhappy Marriage of Marxism and Feminism*, Boston, Mass.: South End, pp. 1–42.

Hartmann, Heidi I. and Ann R. Markusen (1980), 'Contemporary marxist theory and practice: a feminist critique', *Review of Radical Political Economics*, **12** (2), 87–99.

Hartmann, Heidi I., Ellen Bravo, Charlotte Bunch, Nancy Hartsock, Roberta Spalter-Roth, Linda Williams and Maria Blanco (1996), 'Bringing together feminist theory and practice: a collective interview', *Signs*, **21** (4), 917–51.

Hartsock, Nancy C.M. (1983), *Money, Sex and Power: Towards a Feminist Historical Materialism*, Boston, Mass.: Northeastern University Press.

Hartsock, Nancy C.M. (1987), 'The feminist standpoint: developing the ground for a specifically feminist historical materialism', in Sandra Harding (ed.), *Feminism and Methodology*, Bloomington: Indiana University Press, pp. 157–80.

Hawkesworth, Mary E. (1989), 'Knowers, knowing, known: feminist theory and claims of truth', in Micheline R. Malson, Jean F. O'Barr, Sarah Westphal-Wihl and Mary Wyer (eds), *Feminist Theory in Practice and Process*, Chicago: University of Chicago Press, pp. 327–52.

Hawrylyshun, Oli (1976), 'The value of household services: a survey of empirical estimates', *Review of Income and Wealth*, **22**, 101–31.

Hazel, Valerie (1994), 'The in-transi(gen)t subject of feminist theory', *Melbourne Journal of Politics*, **22**, 89–104.

Heath, J.A. (1989), 'An econometric model of the role of gender in economic education', *American Economic Review*, **79** (2), 226–30.

Hekman, James J. (1978), 'A partial survey of recent research on the labor supply of women', *American Economic Review*, **68** (2), 200–7.

Hekman, Susan J. (1990a), *Gender and Knowledge: Elements of a Postmodern Feminism*, Cambridge: Polity Press.

Hekman, Susan (1990b), 'Comment on Hawkesworth's "Knowers, knowing, known: feminist theory and claims to truth" ', *Signs*, **15** (2), 417–19.

Hekman, Susan J. (1991), 'Reconstituting the subject: feminism, modernism, and postmodernism', *Hypatia*, **6** (2), 45–63.

Held, Virginia (1990), 'Mothering versus contract', in Jane J. Mansbridge (ed.), *Beyond Self-Interest*, Chicago: University of Chicago Press, pp. 287–304.

Henderson, Willie (1994), 'Metaphor and economics', in Roger E. Backhouse (ed.), *New Directions in Economic Methodology*, London: Routledge, pp. 343–67.

Henderson, Willie, Tony Dudley-Evans and Roger Backhouse (eds) (1993), *Economics and Language*, London: Routledge.

Hennessy, Rosemary (1993), *Materialist Feminism and the Politics of Discourse*, New York: Routledge.

Henriques, Julian, Wendy Hollway, Cathy Urwin, Couze Venn and Valerie Walkerdine (eds) (1984), *Changing the Subject: Psychology, Social Regulation and Subjectivity*, London: Methuen.

Hewitson, Gillian (1994a), 'Deconstructing Robinson Crusoe: a feminist interrogation of "rational economic man" ', *Australian Feminist Studies*, **20** (Summer), 131–49.

Hewitson, Gillian (1994b), 'Neoclassical economics: a feminist perspective', in Norma Grieve and Aylsa Burns (eds), *Australian Women: Contemporary Feminist Thought*, Melbourne: Oxford University Press, pp. 142–50.

Hewitson, Gillian (1994c), 'Rational economic man: a feminist evaluation', School of Economics, Discussion Paper 1/94, La Trobe University.

Hewitson, Gillian (1996a), 'The body of economic theory: a feminist poststructuralist investigation', Schools of Economics and Commerce, Series A Discussion Paper No. 96.15, La Trobe University.

Hewitson, Gillian (1997), 'The market for surrogate motherhood contracts', *Economic Record*, **73** (222): 212–24.

Hicks, John R. (1934), 'A reconsideration of the theory of value. Part I', *Economica* (n.s.), **1** (1), 52–76.

Hill, Marianne (1996), 'Gilman's *Women in Economics*', paper presented at the *Allied Social Sciences Association Meetings*, San Francisco, January.

Himmelweit, Susan (1987), 'Domestic labour', in John Eatwell, Murray Milgate and Peter Newman (eds), *The New Palgrave: A Dictionary of Economics*, vol. 1, New York: Stockton, pp. 914–16.

Himmelweit, Susan (1995), 'The discovery of "unpaid work": the social consequences of the expansion of work', *Feminist Economics*, **1** (2), 1–19.

Himmelweit, Susan and Simon Mohun (1977), 'Domestic labour and capital', *Cambridge Journal of Economics*, **1**, 15–31.

Hirschfeld, Mary, Robert L. Moore and Eleanor Brown (1995), 'Exploring the gender gap on the GRE subject test in economics', *Journal of Economic Education*, **26** (1), 3–15.

Hirschman, Elizabeth C. (1991), 'Babies for sale: market ethics and the new reproductive technologies', *Journal of Consumer Affairs*, **25** (2), 358–90.

Hirshleifer, Jack (1980), *Price Theory and Applications*, 2nd edn, London: Prentice-Hall.

Hoffman, Elizabeth (1992), Report of the Committee on the Status of Women in the Economics Profession, *American Economic Review*, **82** (2), 610–14.

Hoffman, Elizabeth (1993), Report of the Committee on the Status of Women in the Economics Profession, *American Economic Review*, **83** (2), 508–11.

Hollis, Martin and Edward J. Nell (1975), *Rational Economic Man: A Philosophical Critique of Neo-classical Economics*, London: Cambridge University Press.

Hopkins, Barbara E. (1995), 'Women and children last: a feminist redefinition of privatization and economic reform', in Edith Kuiper and Jolande Sap (eds), *Out of the Margin: Feminist Perspectives on Economics*, London: Routledge, pp. 249–63.

Horsburgh, Beverly (1993), 'Jewish women, black women: guarding against the oppression of surrogacy', *Berkeley Women's Law Journal*, **8**, 29–62.

Horstmeyer, Eric S. (1993–4), 'Gestational surrogacy', *Journal of Family Law*, **32**, 953–60.

Horwitz, Steven (1995), 'Feminist economics: an Austrian perspective', *Journal of Economic Methodology*, **2** (2), 259–79.

Humm, Maggie (1995), *The Dictionary of Feminist Theory*, 2nd edn, Hemel Hempstead, Herts.: Prentice-Hall/Harvester Wheatsheaf.

Humphries, Jane (1977), 'Class struggle and the persistence of the working-class family', *Cambridge Journal of Economics*, **1**, 241–58.

Humphries, Jane (1982), Review of *A Treatise on the Family*, by Gary S. Becker, *Economic Journal*, **92** (September), 739–40.

Humphries, Jane (1987), 'Women and work', in John Eatwell, Murray Milgate and Peter Newman (eds), *The New Palgrave: A Dictionary of Economics*, vol. 4, New York: Stockton, pp. 925–8.

Humphries, Jane (1992), 'Method, materialism, and marxist-feminist: a comment on Matthaei', in Bruce B. Roberts and Susan F. Feiner (eds), *Radical Economics*, Boston, Mass.: Kluwer, pp. 145–54.

Humphries, Jane (ed.) (1995a), *Gender and Economics*, Aldershot: Edward Elgar.

Humphries, Jane (1995b), 'Introduction', in *Gender and Economics*, Aldershot: Edward Elgar, pp. xiii–xxxix.

Humphries, Jane and Jill Rubery (1984), 'The reconstitution of the supply side of the labour market', *Cambridge Journal of Economics*, **8**, 331–46.

Huston, Nancy (1985), 'The matrix of war: mothers and heroes', in Susan Rubin Suleiman (ed.), *The Female Body in Western Culture: Contemporary Perspectives*, Cambridge, Mass.: Harvard University Press, pp. 119–36.

Hutcheon, Linda (1989), *The Politics of Postmodernism*, London: Routledge.

Hutchinson, Frances (1995), 'A heretical view of economic growth and income distribution', in Edith Kuiper and Jolande Sap (eds), *Out of the Margin: Feminist*

Perspectives on Economics, London: Routledge, pp. 35–50.

Huyssen, Andreas (1990), 'Mapping the postmodern', in Linda J. Nicholson (ed.), *Feminism/Postmodernism*, New York: Routledge, pp. 234–77.

Hyman, Prue (1992), 'The use of economic orthodoxy to justify inequality: a feminist critique', in Rosemary Du Plessis (ed.), *Feminist Voices: Women's Studies Texts for Aotearoa/New Zealand*, Auckland: Oxford University Press, pp. 252–65.

Hyman, Prue (1994a), 'Feminist critiques of orthodox economics: a survey', *New Zealand Economic Papers*, **28** (1), 53–80.

Hyman, Prue (1994b), *Women and Economics: A New Zealand Perspective*, Wellington: Bridget Williams Books.

Hymer, Stephen (1971), 'Robinson Crusoe and the secret of primitive accumulation', reprinted in Edward J. Nell (ed.) (1980), *Growth, Profits, and Property*, Cambridge: Cambridge University Press, pp. 29–40.

Ince, Susan (1984), 'Inside the surrogate industry', in Rita Arditti, Renate Duelli Klein and Shelley Minden (eds), *Test-Tube Women*, Boston, Mass.: Pandora, pp. 99–116.

Irigaray, Luce (1985), *This Sex Which is Not One*, trans. Catherine Porter, Ithaca, N.Y.: Cornell University Press.

Irigaray, Luce (1989), 'The language of man', *Cultural Critique*, **9** (Fall), 191–202.

Ironmonger, Duncan (ed.) (1989a), *Households Work: Productive Activities, Women and Income in the Household Economy*, Sydney: Allen & Unwin.

Ironmonger, Duncan (1989b), 'Households and the household economy', in *Households Work: Productive Activities, Women and Income in the Household Economy*, Sydney: Allen & Unwin, pp. 3–13.

Ironmonger, Duncan and Evelyn Sonius (1989), 'Household productive activities', in Duncan Ironmonger (ed.), *Households Work: Productive Activities, Women and Income in the Household Economy*, Sydney: Allen & Unwin, pp. 18–32.

Jackson, Vicki C. (1988), '*Baby M* and the question of parenthood', *Georgetown Law Journal*, **76** (5), 1811–28.

Jacobsen, Joyce P. (1994), *The Economics of Gender*, Oxford: Blackwell.

Jacobus, Mary (1990), 'In parenthesis: immaculate conceptions and feminine desire', in Mary Jacobus, Evelyn Fox Keller and Sally Shuttleworth (eds), *Body/Politics: Women and the Discourses of Science*, New York: Routledge, pp. 11–28.

Jacobus, Mary, Evelyn Fox Keller and Sally Shuttleworth (1990), 'Introduction', in *Body/Politics: Women and the Discourses of Science*, New York: Routledge, pp. 1–10.

Jaggar, Alison M. (1983), *Feminist Politics and Human Nature*, Chichester: Harvester.

Jaggar, Alison M. and Susan R. Bordo (1989), 'Introduction', in *Gender/Body/Knowledge: Feminist Reconstructions of Being and Knowing*, New Brunswick: Rutgers University Press, pp. 1–10.

Jay, Nancy (1991), 'Gender and dichotomy', in Sneja Gunew (ed.), *A Reader in Feminist Knowledge*, London: Routledge, pp. 89–106.

Jefferson, Terese (1995), 'Measuring household production and economic growth', paper presented at the Economics Department Seminar Series, Murdoch University, May.

Jefferson, Terese (1997), *Some Implications of the Commodification of Activities Previously Carried Out Within Households*, unpublished Master of Economics Thesis, School of Business, La Trobe University.

Jennings, Ann L. (1993), 'Public or private? Institutional economics and feminism', in Marianne A. Ferber and Julie A. Nelson (eds), *Beyond Economic Man: Feminist*

Theory and Economics, Chicago: University of Chicago Press, pp. 111–30.

Jennings, Ann L. (1994), 'Feminism', in Geoffrey M. Hodgson, Warren J. Samuels and Marc R. Tool (eds), *The Elgar Companion to Institutional and Evolutionary Economics, A–K*, Aldershot: Edward Elgar, pp. 225–9.

Jennings, Ann L. and William Waller (1990), 'Constructions of social hierarchy: the family, gender, and power', *Journal of Economic Issues*, **24** (2), 623–31.

Johnson, Barbara (1981), 'Translator's introduction to *Dissemination*, by Jacques Derrida', in Barbara Johnson (ed.), *Dissemination*, Chicago: University of Chicago Press, pp. vii–xxxiii.

Johnson, George E. and Frank P. Stafford (1974), 'The earnings and promotion of women faculty', *American Economic Review*, **64** (5), 888–903.

Johnson, Mark (1987), *The Body in the Mind: The Bodily Basis of Meaning, Imagination, and Reason*, Chicago: University of Chicago Press.

Johnson, Pauline (1991), 'Feminism and liberalism', *Australian Feminist Studies*, **14** (Summer), 57–68.

Jones, Jennifer M. and Frances H. Lovejoy (1980), 'Discrimination against women academics in Australian universities', *Signs*, **5** (3), 518–26.

Kahn, Shulamit (1995), 'Women in the economics profession', *Journal of Economic Perspectives*, **9** (4), 193–206.

Kahne, Hilda and Andrew I. Kohen (1975), 'Economic perspectives on the roles of women in the American economy', *Journal of Economic Literature*, **13**, 1249–92.

Kamuf, Peggy (1991a), 'Editor's preface', in *A Derrida Reader: Between the Blinds*, New York: Columbia University Press, pp. vii–xii.

Kamuf, Peggy (1991b), 'Sexual difference in philosophy', in *A Derrida Reader: Between the Blinds*, New York: Columbia University Press, pp. 313–14.

Karpin, Isabel (1994), 'Reimagining maternal selfhood: transgressing body boundaries and the law', *Australian Feminist Law Journal*, **2** (March), 36–62.

Katz, Avi (1986), 'Surrogate motherhood and the baby-selling laws', *Columbia Journal of Law and Social Problems*, **20** (1), 1–54.

Keane, Helen (1996), 'The toxic womb: fetal alcohol syndrome, alcoholism and the female body', *Australian Feminist Studies*, **11** (24), 263–76.

Keane, Noel and Dennis L. Breo (1981), *The Surrogate Mother*, New York: Everest House Publishers.

Keller, Evelyn Fox (1978), 'Gender and science', reprinted in Sandra Harding and Merrill B. Hintikka (eds) (1983), *Discovering Reality: Feminist Perspectives on Epistemology, Metaphysics, Methodology and Philosophy of Science*, Dordrecht: Reidel, pp.187–205.

Keller, Evelyn Fox (1983), *A Feeling for the Organism: The Life and Work of Barbara McClintock*, New York: W.H. Freeman.

Keller, Evelyn Fox (1985), *Reflections on Gender and Science*, New Haven, Conn.: Yale University Press.

Keller, Evelyn Fox (1986), 'How gender matters: or, why it's so hard for us to count past two', in Jan Harding (ed.), *Perspectives on Gender and Science*, London: Farmer, pp. 168–83.

Keller, Evelyn Fox (1989a), 'Feminism and science', in Ann Garry and Marilyn Pearsall (eds), *Women, Knowledge, and Reality: Explorations in Feminist Philosophy*, Boston, Mass.: Unwin Hyman, pp. 175–88.

Keller, Evelyn Fox (1989b), 'Women scientists and feminist critics of science', in Jill K.

Conway, Susan C. Bourque and Joan W. Scott (eds), *Learning About Women: Gender, Politics, and Power*, Ann Arbor: University of Michigan Press, pp. 77–91.

Kendrick, John W (1979), 'Expanding imputed values in the national income and product accounts', *Review of Income and Wealth*, **25** (4), 349–64.

Kirby, Vicki (1987), 'On the cutting edge: feminism and clitoridectomy', *Australian Feminist Studies*, **5** (Summer), 35–55.

Kirby, Vicki (1991a), 'Corporeal habits: addressing essentialism differently', *Hypatia*, **6** (3), 4–24.

Kirby, Vicki (1991b), '*Corpus delicti*: the body at the scene of writing', in Rosalyn Diprose and Robyn Ferrell (eds), *Cartographies: Poststructuralism and the Mapping of Bodies and Spaces*, Sydney: Allen & Unwin, pp. 88–100.

Kirby, Vicki (1993), ' "Feminisms, reading, postmodernisms": rethinking complicity', in Sneja Gunew and Anna Yeatman (eds), *Feminism and the Politics of Difference*, St Leonards: Allen & Unwin, pp. 20–34.

Kirby, Vicki (1994), 'Viral identities: feminisms and postmodernisms', in Norma Grieve and Aylsa Burns (eds), *Australian Women: Contemporary Feminist Thought*, Melbourne: Oxford University Press, pp. 120–32.

Klamer, Arjo (1987), 'As if economists and their subjects were rational', in John S. Nelson, Allan Megill and Donald N. McCloskey (eds), *The Rhetoric of the Human Sciences: Language and Argument in Scholarship and Public Affairs*, Madison: University of Wisconsin Press, pp. 163–83.

Klamer, Arjo (1988), 'Negotiating a new conversation about economics', in Arjo Klamer, Donald N. McCloskey and Robert M. Solow (eds), *The Consequences of Economic Rhetoric*, Cambridge: Cambridge University Press, pp. 265–79.

Klamer, Arjo (1990), 'The textbook presentation of economic discourse', in Warren J. Samuels (ed.), *Economics as Discourse: An Analysis of the Language of Economists*, Boston, Mass.: Kluwer, pp. 129–54.

Klamer, Arjo (1991), 'On interpretive and feminist economics', in G.K. Shaw (ed.), *Economics, Culture and Education: Essays in Honour of Mark Blaug*, Aldershot: Edward Elgar, pp. 133–41.

Klamer, Arjo (1992), 'Commentary on "Gender and economic research" by Janet A. Seiz', in Neil de Marchi (ed.), *Post-Popperian Methodology of Economics: Recovering Practice*, Boston, Mass.: Kluwer, pp. 321–6.

Klamer, Arjo (1993), 'The return to interpretive economics, or: everyday versus academic rhetoric in economics', paper presented at the *Out of the Margin: Feminist Perspectives on Economic Theory* Conference, Amsterdam, June.

Klamer, Arjo (1995), 'Feminist interpretive economics: comments on chapters by Strassmann and Polanyi, and Feiner', in Edith Kuiper and Jolande Sap (eds), *Out of the Margin: Feminist Perspectives on Economics*, London: Routledge, pp. 167–71.

Klamer, Arjo and Donald N. McCloskey (1988), 'Economics in the human conversation', in Arjo Klamer, Donald N. McCloskey and Robert M. Solow (eds), *The Consequences of Economic Rhetoric*, Cambridge: Cambridge University Press, pp. 3–20.

Klamer, Arjo, Donald N. McCloskey and Robert Solow (eds) (1988), *The Consequences of Economic Rhetoric*, Cambridge: Cambridge University Press.

Koopmans, Tjalling C. (1957), *Three Essays on the State of Economic Science*, New York: McGraw-Hill.

Krueger, Anne O., Kenneth J. Arrow, Olivier Jean Blanchard, Alan S. Blinder, Claudia

Goldin, Edward E. Leamer, Robert Lucas, John Panzar, Rudolph G. Penner, T. Paul Schultz, Joseph E. Stiglitz and Lawrence H. Summers (1991), Report of the Commission on Graduate Education in Economics, *Journal of Economic Literature*, **29**, 1035–53.

Kuhn, Annette and AnnMarie Wolpe (eds) (1978), *Feminism and Materialism: Women and Modes of Production*, London: Routledge & Kegan Paul.

Kuiper, Edith and Jolande Sap (eds) (1995a), *Out of the Margin: Feminist Perspectives on Economics*, London: Routledge.

Kuiper, Edith and Jolande Sap (1995b), 'Introduction', in *Out of the Margin: Feminist Perspectives on Economics*, London: Routledge, pp. 1–13.

Lacan, Jacques ([1949] 1977), 'The mirror stage as formative of the function of the I', in *Ecrits: A Selection*, trans. Alan Sheridan, New York: W.W. Norton, pp. 1–7.

Lake, Marilyn (1986), 'The politics of respectability: identifying the masculinist context', *Historical Studies*, **22** (86), 116–31.

Lake, Marilyn (1988), 'Women, gender and history', *Australian Feminist Studies*, **7 & 8** (Summer), 1–9.

Lake, Marilyn (1992a), 'Mission impossible: how men gave birth to the Australian nation – nationalism, gender and other seminal acts', *Gender and History*, **4** (3), 305–22.

Lake, Marilyn (1992b), 'The independence of women and the brotherhood of man: debates in the labor movement over equal pay and motherhood endowment in the 1920s', *Labour History*, **63** (November), 1–24.

Lake, Marilyn (1993), 'A revolution in the family: the challenge and contradictions of maternal citizenship in Australia', in Seth Koven and Sonya Michel (eds), *Mothers of a New World: Maternalist Politics and the Origins of Welfare States*, New York: Routledge, pp. 378–95.

Lake, Marilyn (1994), 'Between old world "barbarism" and stone age "primitivism": the double difference of the white Australian feminist', in Norma Grieve and Aylsa Burns (eds), *Australian Women: Contemporary Feminist Thought*, Melbourne: Oxford University Press, pp. 80–91.

Lake, Marilyn (1996), 'The inviolable woman: feminist conceptions of citizenship in Australia, 1900–1945', *Gender and History*, **8** (2), 197–211.

Lakoff, George and Mark Johnson (1980), *Metaphors We Live By*, Chicago: University of Chicago Press.

Landes, William M. and Richard A. Posner (1978), 'Altruism in law and economics', *American Economic Review*, **68** (2), 417–21.

Laqueur, Thomas W. (1990a), 'The facts of fatherhood', in Marianne Hirsch and Evelyn Fox Keller (eds), *Conflicts in Feminism*, New York: Routledge, pp. 205–21.

Laqueur, Thomas W. (1990b), *Making Sex: Body and Gender from the Greeks to Freud*, Cambridge, Mass.: Harvard University Press.

Laqueur, Thomas W. (1990c), 'Orgasm, generation, and the politics of reproductive biology', in Catherine Gallagher and Thomas Laqueur (eds), *The Making of the Modern Body: Sexuality and Society in the Nineteenth Century*, Berkeley: University of California Press, pp. 1–41.

Lawson, Hilary (1989a), 'Stories about stories', in Hilary Lawson and Lisa Appignanesi (eds), *Dismantling Truth: Reality in the Post-Modern World*, London: Weidenfeld & Nicolson, pp. xi–xxviii.

Lawson, Hilary (1989b), 'Introduction: stories about truth', in Hilary Lawson and Lisa

Appignanesi (eds), *Dismantling Truth: Reality in the Post-Modern World*, London: Weidenfeld & Nicolson, pp. 3–5.

Lawson, Hilary (1989c), 'Introduction: stories about science', in Hilary Lawson and Lisa Appignanesi (eds), *Dismantling Truth: Reality in the Post-Modern World*, London: Weidenfeld & Nicolson, pp. 79–81.

Lawson, Hilary (1989d), 'Introduction: stories about representation', in Hilary Lawson and Lisa Appignanesi (eds), *Dismantling Truth: Reality in the Post-Modern World*, London: Weidenfeld & Nicolson, pp. 129–30.

Lazear, Edward P. (1991), 'Discrimination in labor markets', in Emily P. Hoffman (ed.), *Essays on the Economics of Discrimination*, Kalamazoo, Mich.: W.E. Upjohn Institute for Employment Research, pp. 9–24.

Lechte, John (1994), *Fifty Contemporary Thinkers: From Structuralism to Post-modernity*, London: Routledge.

Leder, Drew (1992), 'The tale of two bodies', in *The Body in Medical Thought and Practice*, Dordrecht: Kluwer, pp. 17–35.

Leghorn, Lisa and Katherine Parker (1981), *Woman's Worth: Sexual Economics and the World of Women*, Boston, Mass.: Routledge & Kegan Paul.

Lemaire, Anika (1977), *Jacques Lacan*, trans. David Macey, London: Routledge.

Leon, Renée (1993), 'W(h)ither special measures? How affirmative action for women can survive sex discrimination legislation', *Australian Feminist Law Journal*, **1** (August), 89–113.

Levin, Lee B. (1995), 'Toward a feminist, post-Keynesian theory of investment: a consideration of the socially and emotionally constituted nature of agent knowledge', in Edith Kuiper and Jolande Sap (eds), *Out of the Margin: Feminist Perspectives on Economics*, London: Routledge, pp. 100–19.

Lloyd, Cynthia B. (ed.) (1975a), *Sex, Discrimination, and the Division of Labor*, New York: Columbia University Press.

Lloyd, Cynthia B. (1975b), 'The division of labor between the sexes: a review', in *Sex, Discrimination, and the Division of Labor*, New York: Columbia University Press, pp. 1–24.

Lloyd, Cynthia B. (1975c), 'Preface', in *Sex, Discrimination, and the Division of Labor*, New York: Columbia University Press, pp. ix–xi.

Lloyd, Cynthia B., Emily S. Andrews and Curtis L. Gilroy (1979), 'Introduction', in *Women in the Labor Market*, New York: Columbia University Press, pp. xi–xxi.

Lloyd, Genevieve (1984), *The Man of Reason: 'Male' and 'Female' in Western Philosophy*, London: Methuen.

Lloyd, Genevieve (1986), 'Selfhood, war and masculinity', in Carole Pateman and Elizabeth Gross (eds), *Feminist Challenges: Social and Political Theory*, Sydney: Allen & Unwin, pp. 63–76.

Lloyd, Genevieve (1989), 'Woman as other: sex, gender and subjectivity', *Australian Feminist Studies*, **10** (Summer), 13–22.

Longino, Helen E. (1988), 'Science, objectivity, and feminist values', *Feminist Studies*, **14** (3), 561–74.

Longino, Helen E. (1989), 'Can there be a feminist science?', in Ann Garry and Marilyn Pearsall (eds), *Women, Knowledge, and Reality: Explorations in Feminist Philosophy*, Boston, Mass.: Unwin Hyman, pp. 203–16.

Longino, Helen E. (1993a), 'Economics for whom?', in Marianne A. Ferber and Julie A. Nelson (eds), *Beyond Economic Man: Feminist Theory and Economics*, Chicago:

University of Chicago Press, pp. 158–68.

Longino, Helen E. (1993b), 'Subjects, power, and knowledge: description and prescription in feminist philosophies of science', in Linda Alcoff and Elizabeth Potter (eds), *Feminist Epistemologies*, New York: Routledge, pp. 101–20.

Longino, Helen E. (1993c), 'Feminist standpoint theory and the problems of knowledge', *Signs*, **19** (11), 201–12.

Longino, Helen E. and Ruth Doell (1983), 'Body, bias, and behavior: a comparative analysis of reasoning in two areas of biological science', reprinted in Sandra Harding and Jean F. O'Barr (eds) (1987), *Sex and Scientific Inquiry*, Chicago: University of Chicago Press, pp. 165–86.

Longino, Helen E. and Evelynn Hammonds (1990), 'Conflicts and tensions in the feminist study of gender and science', in Marianne Hirsch and Evelyn Fox Keller (eds), *Conflicts in Feminism*, New York: Routledge, pp. 164–83.

Lorber, Judith, Rose Laub Coser, Alice S. Rossi and Nancy Chodorow (1981), 'On *The Reproduction of Mothering*: a methodological debate', *Signs*, **6** (3), 482–514.

Lovell, Terry (ed.) (1990a), *British Feminist Thought: A Reader*, Oxford: Basil Blackwell.

Lovell, Terry (1990b), 'Introduction to part III', in *British Feminist Thought: A Reader*, Oxford: Basil Blackwell, pp. 71–7.

Lovibond, Sabina (1989), 'Feminism and postmodernism', *New Left Review*, **178**, 5–28.

Lucy, Niall (1995), *Debating Derrida*, Melbourne: Melbourne University Press.

Lumsden, K.G. and A. Scott (1987), 'The economics student reexamined: male–female differences in comprehension', *Journal of Economic Education*, **18** (Fall), 365–75.

Lundberg, Shelly and Robert A. Pollak (1993), 'Separate spheres bargaining and the marriage market', *Journal of Political Economy*, **10** (6), 988–1010.

Lundberg, Shelly and Robert A. Pollak (1994), 'Noncooperative bargaining models of marriage', *American Economic Review*, **84** (2), 132–7.

Lundberg, Shelly and Robert A. Pollack (1996), 'Bargaining and distribution in marriage', *Journal of Economic Perspectives*, **10** (4), 139–58.

MacDonald, Martha (1982), 'Implications for understanding women in the labour force of labour market segmentation analysis: the unanswered questions', in Naomi Hersom and Dorothy E. Smith (eds), *Women and the Canadian Labour Force*, Ottawa: Supply and Services Canada, pp. 167–207.

MacDonald, Martha (1984), 'Economics and feminism: the dismal science?', *Studies in Political Economy*, **15** (Fall), 151–78.

MacDonald, Martha (1993), 'Becoming visible: women and the economy', in Geraldine Finn (ed.), *Limited Edition: Voices of Women, Voices of Feminism*, Halifax, N.S.: Fernwood Publishing, pp. 157–70.

MacDonald, Martha (1994), 'What is feminist economics?', in *Papers on Economic Equality Prepared for the Economic Equality Workshop*, Ottawa: Status of Women, pp. 109–24.

MacDonald, Martha (1995a), 'Feminist economics: from theory to research', *Canadian Journal of Economics*, **28** (1), 159–76.

MacDonald, Martha (1995b), 'The empirical challenges of feminist economics: the example of economic restructuring', in Edith Kuiper and Jolande Sap (eds), *Out of the Margin: Feminist Perspectives on Economics*, London: Routledge, pp. 175–97.

Macdonell, Diane (1986), *Theories of Discourse: An Introduction*, Oxford: Basil Blackwell.

Madden, Janice Fanning (1972), 'The development of economic thought on the "woman problem" ', *Review of Radical Political Economics*, **4** (3), 21–39.

Madden, Janice Fanning (1973), *The Economics of Sex Discrimination*, Lexington, Mass.: D.C. Heath, Lexington Books.

Madden, Janice Fanning (1975), 'Discrimination – a manifestation of male market power?', in Cynthia B. Lloyd (ed.), *Sex, Discrimination, and the Division of Labor*, New York: Columbia University Press, pp. 146–74.

Madden, Janice Fanning (1979), 'Comment', in Cynthia B. Lloyd, Emily S. Andrews and Curtis L. Gilroy (eds), *Women in the Labor Market*, New York: Columbia University Press, pp. 158–67.

Mäki, Uskali (1993), 'Two philosophies on the rhetoric of economics', in Willie Henderson, Tony Dudley-Evans and Roger Backhouse (eds), *Economics and Language*, London: Routledge, pp. 23–50.

Mäki, Uskali (1995), 'Diagnosing McCloskey', *Journal of Economic Literature*, **33**, 1300–18.

Malkiel, Burton G. and Judith A. Malkiel (1973), 'Male–female pay differentials in professional employment', *American Economic Review*, **63** (4), 693–705.

Mandelbaum, Dorothy Rosenthal (1978), 'Women in medicine', *Signs*, **4** (1), 136–45.

Manser, Marilyn and Murray Brown (1979), 'Bargaining analyses of household decisions', in Cynthia B. Lloyd, Emily S. Andrews and Curtis L. Gilroy (eds), *Women in the Labor Market*, New York: Columbia University Press, pp. 3–26.

Manser, Marilyn and Murray Brown (1980), 'Marriage and household decision-making: a bargaining analysis', *International Economic Review*, **21** (1), 31–44.

Marcus, Sharon (1992), 'Fighting bodies, fighting words: a theory and politics of rape prevention', in Judith Butler and Joan W. Scott (eds), *Feminists Theorize the Political*, New York: Routledge, pp. 385–403.

Marecek, Jeanne (1995), 'Psychology and feminism: can the relationship be saved?', in Domna C. Stanton and Abigail J. Stewart (eds), *Feminisms in the Academy*, Ann Arbor: University of Michigan Press, pp. 101–32.

Markusen, Ann R (1977), 'Feminist notes on introductory economics', *Review of Radical Political Economics*, **9** (3), 1–6.

Marshall, Brenda K. (1992), *Teaching the Postmodern: Fiction and Theory*, New York: Routledge.

Marwell, Gerald and Ruth Ames (1981), 'Economists free ride, does anyone else? Experiments on the provision of public goods IV', *Journal of Public Economics*, **15** (3), 295–310.

Marx, Karl (1867), 'Excerpt from *Das Kapital*, vol. 1', in Frank H. Ellis (ed.) (1969), *Twentieth Century Interpretations of Robinson Crusoe*, Englewood Cliffs, N.J.: Prentice-Hall, pp. 90–2.

Matthaei, Julie (1992), 'Marxist-feminist contributions to radical economics', in Bruce B. Roberts and Susan F. Feiner (eds), *Radical Economics*, Boston, Mass.: Kluwer, pp. 117–44.

Matthaei, Julie (1996), 'Why feminist, marxist and anti-racist economists should be feminist-marxist-anti-racist economists', *Feminist Economics*, **2** (1), 22–42.

McCloskey, Deirdre (1997), 'Interview with Deirdre McCloskey', *Challenge*, January/February, pp. 16–29.

McCloskey, Donald N. (1983), 'The rhetoric of economics', *Journal of Economic Literature*, **21**, 481–517.

McCloskey, Donald N. (1985), *The Rhetoric of Economics*, Madison: University of Wisconsin Press.

McCloskey, Donald N. (1988), 'The consequences of rhetoric', in Arjo Klamer, Donald N. McCloskey and Robert M. Solow (eds), *The Consequences of Economic Rhetoric*, Cambridge: Cambridge University Press, pp. 280–93.

McCloskey, Donald N. (1990a), *If You're So Smart: The Narrative of Economic Expertise*, Chicago: University of Chicago Press.

McCloskey, Donald N. (1990b), 'Storytelling in economics', in Don Lavoie (ed.), *Economics and Hermeneutics*, New York: Routledge, pp. 61–75.

McCloskey, Donald N. (1992), 'Commentary', in Neil de Marchi (ed.), *Post-Popperian Methodology of Economics: Recovering Practice*, Boston, Mass.: Kluwer-Nijhoff, pp. 261–71.

McCloskey, Donald N. (1993), 'Some consequences of a conjective economics', in Marianne A. Ferber and Julie A. Nelson (eds), *Beyond Economic Man: Feminist Theory and Economics*, Chicago: University of Chicago Press, pp. 69–93.

McCloskey, Donald N. (1994a), 'How to do a rhetorical analysis, and why', in Roger E. Backhouse (ed.), *New Directions in Economic Methodology*, London: Routledge, pp. 319–42.

McCloskey, Donald N. (1994b), *Knowledge and Persuasion in Economics*, Cambridge: Cambridge University Press.

McCloskey, Donald N. (1995a), 'The discrete charm of the bourgeoisie', *Feminist Economics*, 1 (3), 119–24.

McCloskey, Donald N. (1995b), 'Modern epistemology against analytic philosophy: a reply to Mäki', *Journal of Economic Literature*, 33, 1319–23.

McCrate, Elaine (1983), 'Comment on Ferber's "Women and work: issues of the 1980s" ', *Signs*, 9 (2), 326–30.

McCrate, Elaine (1987), 'Trade, merger and employment: economic theory of marriage', *Review of Radical Political Economics*, 19 (1), 73-89.

McCrate, Elaine (1988), 'Gender difference: the role of endogenous preferences and collective action', *American Economic Review*, 78 (2), 235–9.

McElroy, Marjorie and Mary Jane Horney (1981), 'Nash-bargained household decisions: toward a generalization of the theory of demand', *International Economic Review*, 22 (2), 333–49.

McFarland, Joan (1976), 'Economics and women: a critique of the scope of traditional analysis and research', *Atlantis*, 1, 26–41.

McHoul, Alec and Wendy Grace (1993), *A Foucault Primer: Discourse, Power and the Subject*, Melbourne: Melbourne University Press.

McNeil, Maureen (1991), 'Putting the Alton Bill in context', in Sarah Franklin, Celia Lury and Jackie Stacey (eds), *Off-Centre: Feminism and Cultural Studies*, London: HarperCollins Academic, pp. 149–59.

Mehta, Judith (1993), 'Meaning in the context of bargaining games: Narratives in opposition', in Willie Henderson, Tony Dudley-Evans and Roger Backhouse (eds), *Economics and Language*, London: Routledge, pp. 85–99.

Merchant, Carolyn (1980), *The Death of Nature: Women, Ecology and the Scientific Revolution*, San Francisco: Harper & Row.

Miller, Edythe S. (1972), 'Veblen and women's lib: a parallel', *Journal of Economic Issues*, 6 (3), 75–96.

Millett, Kate ([1969] 1977), *Sexual Politics*, London: Virago.

Milner, Andrew (1991), *Contemporary Cultural Theory: An Introduction*, Sydney: Allen & Unwin.

Mincer, Jacob ([1962] 1993), 'Labor-force participation of married women: a study of labor supply', reprinted in *Studies in Labor Supply: Collected Essays of Jacob Mincer*, vol. 2, Aldershot: Edward Elgar, pp. 3–35.

Mincer, Jacob (1993), 'Introduction', in *Studies in Labor Supply: Collected Essays of Jacob Mincer*, vol. 2, Aldershot: Edward Elgar, pp. ix–xxv.

Mincer, Jacob and Solomon Polachek ([1974] 1993), 'Family investments in human capital: earnings of women', reprinted in *Studies in Labor Supply: Collected Essays of Jacob Mincer*, vol. 2, Aldershot: Edward Elgar, pp. 105–39.

Mincer, Jacob and Solomon Polachek (1974), 'Women's earnings reexamined', *Journal of Human Resources*, **13** (1), 118–34.

Ministry of Employment and Training (1984), *From Margin to Mainstream: A National Conference About Women and Employment*, Melbourne.

Mirowski, Philip (1988), 'Shall I compare thee to a Minkowski–Ricardo–Leontief–Metzler matrix of the Mosak–Hicks type?', in Arjo Klamer, Donald N. McCloskey and Robert M. Solow (eds), *The Consequences of Economic Rhetoric*, Cambridge: Cambridge University Press, pp. 117–45.

Mirowski, Philip (1992), 'Three vignettes on the state of economic rhetoric', in Neil de Marchi (ed.), *Post-Popperian Methodology of Economics: Recovering Practice*, Boston, Mass.: Kluwer-Nijhoff, pp. 235–59.

Mitchell, Juliet (1982), 'Introduction – I', in Juliet Mitchell and Jacqueline Rose (eds), *Feminine Sexuality: Jacques Lacan and the école freudienne*, New York: W.W. Norton, pp. 1–26.

Moi, Toril (1985), *Sexual/Textual Politics: Feminist Literary Theory*, London: Routledge.

Moi, Toril (1989), 'Patriarchal thought and the drive for knowledge', in Teresa Brennan (ed.), *Between Feminism and Psychoanalysis*, London: Routledge, pp. 189–205

Montague, F.C. (1925–26), 'Defoe', in Henry Higgs (ed.) (1963), *Dictionary of Political Economy*, New York: Augustus M. Kelley, pp. 535–6.

Morgan, Derek (1986), 'Who to be or not to be: the surrogacy story', *Modern Law Review*, **49** (May), 358–68.

Morgan, Derek (1994), 'A surrogacy issue: who is the other mother?', *International Journal of Law and the Family*, **8**, 386–412.

Mueser, Peter (1987), 'Discrimination', in John Eatwell, Murray Milgate and Peter Newman (eds), *The New Palgrave: A Dictionary of Economics*, vol 1, New York: Stockton, pp. 856–8.

Murphy, Martin (1978), 'The value of non-market household production: opportunity cost versus market cost estimates', *Review of Income and Wealth*, **24** (3), 243–55.

Murphy, Martin (1982), 'Comparative estimates of household work in the United States for 1976', *Review of Income and Wealth*, **28** (1), 29–43.

Mykitiuk, Roxanne (1994), 'Fragmenting the body', *Australian Feminist Law Journal*, **2** (March), 63–98.

Naffine, Ngaire (1990), *Law and the Sexes: Explorations in Feminist Jurisprudence*, Sydney: Allen & Unwin.

National Bioethics Consultative Committee (1990), *Surrogacy, Report 1*, Canberra: Commonwealth of Australia.

Nelson, Julie A. (1992a), 'Thinking about gender', *Hypatia*, **7** (3), 138–54.

Nelson, Julie A. (1992b), 'Gender, metaphor, and the definition of economics', *Economics and Philosophy*, **8**, 103–25.

Nelson, Julie A. (1993a), 'Gender and economic ideologies', *Review of Social Economy*, **51** (3), 287–301.

Nelson, Julie A. (1993b), 'Value-free or value-less? Notes on the pursuit of detachment in economics', *History of Political Economy*, **25** (1), 121–45.

Nelson, Julie A. (1993c), 'The study of choice or the study of provisioning? Gender and the definition of economics', in Marianne A. Ferber and Julie A. Nelson (eds), *Beyond Economic Man: Feminist Theory and Economics*, Chicago: University of Chicago Press, pp. 23–36.

Nelson, Julie A. (1994a), 'I, thou, and them: capabilities, altruism, and norms in the economics of marriage', *American Economic Review*, **84** (2), 126–31.

Nelson, Julie A. (1994b), 'More thinking about gender: reply', *Hypatia*, **9** (1), 199–205.

Nelson, Julie A. (1995a), 'Economic theory and feminist theory: comments on chapters by Polachek, Ott, and Levin', in Edith Kuiper and Jolande Sap (eds), *Out of the Margin: Feminist Perspectives on Economics*, London: Routledge, pp. 120–5.

Nelson, Julie A. (1995b), 'Feminism and economics', *Journal of Economic Perspectives*, **9** (2), 131–48.

Nelson, Julie A. (1996a), *Feminism, Objectivity and Economics*, London: Routledge.

Nelson, Julie A. (1996b), 'What is feminist economics all about?' *Challenge*, January/February, pp. 4–8.

Nelson, Julie A. (1996c), 'The masculine mindset of economic analysis', *Chronicle of Higher Education*, **42** (42), B3.

Nicholson, Linda J. (ed.) (1990a), *Feminism/Postmodernism*, New York: Routledge.

Nicholson, Linda J. (1990b), 'Introduction', in *Feminism/Postmodernism*, New York: Routledge, pp. 1–16.

Nicholson, Linda J. (1992), 'Feminism and the politics of postmodernism', *Boundary 2*, **19** (2), 53–69.

Norris, Christopher (1982), *Deconstruction: Theory and Practice*, London: Routledge.

Norris, Christopher (1987), *Derrida*, London: Fontana Paperbacks.

Norris, Christopher (1990), 'Further thoughts on *Deconstruction: Theory and Practice* (critical postscript and a user's guide)', *Southern Review*, **23** (November), 233–50.

Nöth, Winfried (1995), *Handbook of Semiotics*, Bloomington: Indiana University Press.

Novak, Maximillian E. (1962), 'The economic meaning of *Robinson Crusoe*', reprinted in Frank H. Ellis (ed.) (1969), *Twentieth Century Interpretations of Robinson Crusoe*, Englewood Cliffs, N.J.: Prentice-Hall, pp. 97–102.

Nye, Andrea (1988), *Feminist Theory and the Philosophies of Man*, New York: Routledge.

Nyland, Chris (1993a), 'John Locke and the social position of women', *History of Political Economy*, **25** (1), 39–63.

Nyland, Chris (1993b), 'Adam Smith, stage theory, and the status of women', *History of Political Economy*, **25** (4), 617–40.

Nyland, Chris and Gaby Ramia (1994), 'The Webbs and the rights of women', in Peter Groenewegen (ed.), *Feminism and Political Economy in Victorian England*, Aldershot: Edward Elgar, pp. 110–46.

Oakley, Ann (1972), *Sex, Gender and Society*, Melbourne: Sun Books.

Oakley, Ann (1974), *The Sociology of Housework*, London: Martin Robinson.

O'Donnell, Carol (1984), 'Major theories of the labour market and women's place within it', *Journal of Industrial Relations*, **26** (June), 147–65.

O'Donnell, Margaret G. (1994), 'Early analysis of the economics of family structure: Charlotte Perkins Gilman's *Women and Economics*', *Review of Social Economy*, **52** (2), 86–95.

Okin, Susan Moller (1991), 'John Rawls: justice as fairness – for whom?', in Mary Lyndon Shanley and Carole Pateman (eds), *Feminist Interpretations and Political Theory*, Cambridge: Polity Press, pp. 181–98.

Olson, Paulette (1990), 'Mature women and the rewards of domestic ideology', *Journal of Economic Issues*, **24** (2), 633–43.

Olson, Paulette (1994), 'Feminism and science reconsidered: insights from the margins', in Janice Peterson and Doug Brown (eds), *The Economic Status of Women Under Capitalism: Institutional Economics and Feminist Theory*, Aldershot: Edward Elgar, pp. 77–94.

Ott, Notburga (1995), 'Fertility and division of work in the family: a game theoretic model of household decisions', in Edith Kuiper and Jolande Sap (eds), *Out of the Margin: Feminist Perspectives on Economics*, London: Routledge, pp. 80–99.

Oxman, R. Brian (1993), 'Maternal–fetal relationships and nongenetic surrogates', *Jurimetrics Journal*, **33** (Spring), 387–425.

Ozga, S.A. (1956), 'Measurable utility and probability: a simplified rendering', *Economic Journal*, **66** (263), 419–30.

Paludi, Michelle A. and William Bauer (1983), 'Goldberg revisited: what's in an author's name?', *Sex Roles*, **9** (3), 387–90.

Paludi, Michelle A. and Lisa A. Strayer (1985), 'What's in an author's name? Differential evaluations of performance as a function of author's name', *Sex Roles*, **12** (3–4), 353–61.

Parker, Philip J. (1983), 'Motivation of surrogate mothers: initial findings', *American Journal of Psychiatry*, **140** (1), 117–18.

Pateman, Carole (1986), 'Introduction: The theoretical subversiveness of feminism', in Carole Pateman and Elizabeth Gross (eds), *Feminist Challenges: Social and Political Theory*, Sydney: Allen & Unwin, pp. 1–10.

Pateman, Carole (1987), 'Feminist critiques of the public/private dichotomy', in Anne Phillips (ed.), *Feminism and Equality*, New York: New York University Press, pp. 103–26.

Pateman, Carole (1988), *The Sexual Contract*, Cambridge: Polity Press.

Pateman, Carole (1992), 'Equality, difference, subordination: the politics of motherhood and women's citizenship', in Gisela Bock and Susan James (eds), *Beyond Equality and Difference: Citizenship, Feminist Politics and Female Subjectivity*, London: Routledge, pp. 17–31.

Pateman, Carole and Elizabeth Gross (eds) (1986), *Feminist Challenges: Social and Political Theory*, Sydney: Allen & Unwin.

Pateman, Carole and Mary Lyndon Shanley (eds) (1990a), *Feminist Interpretations and Political Theory*, Cambridge: Polity Press.

Pateman, Carole and Mary Lyndon Shanley (1990b), 'Introduction', in Mary Lyndon Shanley and Carole Pateman (eds), *Feminist Interpretations and Political Theory*, Cambridge: Polity Press, pp. 1–10.

Perrons, Diane (1995), 'Measuring equality in opportunity 2000', in Edith Kuiper and Jolande Sap (eds), *Out of the Margin: Feminist Perspectives on Economics*, London: Routledge, pp. 198–215.

Petchesky, Rosalind Pollack (1990), *Abortion and Women's Choice: The State, Sexuality and Reproductive Freedom*, rev. edn, Boston, Mass.: Northeastern University Press.

Petchesky, Rosalind Pollack (1994), 'Fetal images: the power of visual culture in the politics of reproduction', in Anne C. Herrmann and Abigail J. Stewart (eds), *Theorizing Feminism: Parallel Trends in the Humanities and the Social Sciences*, Boulder, Col.: Westview, pp. 401–23.

Phelps, Edmund S. (1972), 'The statistical theory of racism and sexism', *American Economic Review*, **62** (4), 659–61.

Phillips, Anne (1994), 'The representation of women', in *The Polity Reader in Gender Studies*, Cambridge: Polity Press, pp. 195–204.

Phillips, Anne and Barbara Taylor (1980), 'Sex and skill: notes towards a feminist economics', reprinted in Feminist Review (ed.) (1986), *Waged Work: A Reader*, London: Virago, pp. 54–66.

Phipps, Shelley A. and Peter S. Burton (1995), 'Sharing within families: implications for the measurement of poverty among individuals in Canada', *Canadian Journal of Economics*, **28** (1), 177–204.

Pierce, J. (1984), *Monetary and Financial Economics*, New York: John Wiley.

Pigou, Arthur C. (1920), *The Economics of Welfare*, London: Macmillan.

Plosser, Charles I. (1989), 'Understanding real business cycles', *Journal of Economic Perspectives*, **3** (3), 51–77.

Polachek, Solomon W. (1975), 'Discontinuous labor force participation and its effect on women's market earnings', in Cynthia B. Lloyd (ed.), *Sex, Discrimination, and the Division of Labor*, New York: Columbia University Press, pp. 90–122.

Polachek, Solomon W. (1979), 'Occupational segregation among women: theory, evidence, and a prognosis', in Cynthia B. Lloyd, Emily S. Andrews and Curtis L. Gilroy (eds), *Women in the Labor Market*, New York: Columbia University Press, pp. 137–57.

Polachek, Solomon W. (1981), 'Occupational self-selection: a human capital approach to sex differences in occupational structure', *Review of Economics and Statistics*, **63** (1), 60–9.

Polachek, Solomon W. (1995), 'Human capital and the gender earnings gap: a response to feminist critiques', in Edith Kuiper and Jolande Sap (eds), *Out of the Margin: Feminist Perspectives on Economics*, London: Routledge, pp. 61–79.

Pollak, Robert A. (1985), 'A transaction cost approach to families and households', *Journal of Economic Literature*, **23**, 581–608.

Pollak, Robert A. (1988), 'Tied transfers and paternalistic preferences', *American Economic Review*, **78** (2), 240–4.

Pollak, Robert A. (1994), 'For better or worse: the roles of power in models of distribution within marriage', *American Economic Review*, **84** (2), 148–52.

Pollak, Robert A. and Michael L. Wachter (1975), 'The relevance of the household production function and its implications for the allocation of time', *Journal of Political Economy*, **83** (2), 255–77.

Poole, Ross (1990), 'Modernity, rationality and "the masculine"', in Terry Threadgold and Anne Cranny-Francis (eds), *Feminine/Masculine and Representation*, Sydney: Allen & Unwin, pp. 48–61.

Poovey, Mary (1988), 'Feminism and deconstruction', *Feminist Studies*, **14** (1), 51–65.

Poovey, Mary (1990a), ' "Scenes of an indelicate character": the medical "treatment" of Victorian women', in Catherine Gallagher and Thomas Laqueur (eds), *The Making of the Modern Body: Sexuality and Society in the Nineteenth Century*, Berkeley: University of California Press, pp. 137–68.

Poovey, Mary (1990b), 'Speaking of the body: mid-Victorian constructions of female desire', in Mary Jacobus, Evelyn Fox Keller and Sally Shuttleworth (eds), *Body/Politics: Women and the Discourses of Science*, New York: Routledge, pp. 29–46.

Poovey, Mary (1992a), 'The abortion question and the death of man', in Judith Butler and Joan W. Scott (eds), *Feminists Theorize the Political*, New York: Routledge, pp. 239–56.

Poovey, Mary (1992b), 'Feminism and postmodernism – another view', *Boundary 2*, **19** (2), 34–52.

Poovey, Mary (1995), 'The differences of women's studies: the example of literary criticism', in Domna C. Stanton and Abigail J. Stewart (eds), *Feminisms in the Academy*, Ann Arbor: University of Michigan Press, pp. 135–56.

Posner, Richard (1989), 'The ethics and economics of enforcing contracts of surrogate motherhood', *Journal of Contemporary Health Law and Policy*, **5** (1), 21–31.

Posner, Richard (1992), *Sex and Reason*, Cambridge, Mass.: Harvard University Press.

Power, Margaret (1984), 'Writing women out of the economy: economic theory and its effects', in *From Margin to Mainstream: A National Conference About Women and Employment*, Melbourne: Ministry of Employment and Training.

Power, Marilyn (1983), 'From home production to wage labor: women as a reserve army of labor', *Review of Radical Political Economics*, **15** (1), 71–91.

Pringle, Rosemary (1988), *Secretaries Talk: Sexuality, Power and Work*, Sydney: Allen & Unwin.

Pringle, Rosemary (1995), 'Destabilising patriarchy', in Barbara Caine and Rosemary Pringle (eds), *Transitions: New Australian Feminisms*, St Leonards: Allen & Unwin, pp. 198–211.

Pujol, Michèle A. (1984), 'Gender and class in Marshall's *Principles of Economics*', reprinted in Jane Humphries (ed.) (1995), *Gender and Economics*, Aldershot: Edward Elgar, pp. 59–76.

Pujol, Michèle A. (1992), *Feminism and Anti-Feminism in Early Economic Thought*, Aldershot: Edward Elgar.

Pujol, Michèle A. (1995), 'Into the margin!', in Edith Kuiper and Jolande Sap (eds), *Out of the Margin: Feminist Perspectives on Economics*, London: Routledge, pp. 17–34.

Purdy, Laura M. (1989a), 'Surrogate mothering: exploitation or empowerment?', *Bioethics*, **3** (1), 18–34.

Purdy, Laura M. (1989b), 'A response to Dodds and Jones', *Bioethics*, **3** (1), 40–4.

Quade, Ann (ed.) (1994), *The Feminist Economics Curriculum Project*, Pedagogy Committee of the International Association for Feminist Economics, California State University at Sacramento.

Ragoné, Helena (1994), *Surrogate Motherhood: Conception in the Heart*, Boulder, Col.: Westview Press.

Ramazanoğlu, Caroline (ed.) (1993a), *Up Against Foucault: Explorations of Some Tensions Between Foucault and Feminism*, London: Routledge.

Ramazanoğlu, Caroline (1993b), 'Introduction', in *Up Against Foucault: Explorations of Some Tensions Between Foucault and Feminism*, London: Routledge, pp. 1–25.

Randles, Tessa (1991), 'The Alton Bill and the media's "consensual" position', in Sarah Franklin, Celia Lury and Jackie Stacey (eds), *Off-Centre: Feminism and Cultural*

Studies, London: HarperCollins Academic, pp. 206–13.

Rapport, Sara (1985), 'An incomplete picture: the debate about surrogate motherhood', *Harvard Women's Law Journal*, **8**, 230–46.

Reagan, Barbara B. (1975a), Report of the Committee on the Status of Women in the Economics Profession, *American Economic Review*, **65** (2), 490–501.

Reagan, Barbara B. (1975b), 'Two supply curves for economists? Implications of mobility and career attachment of women', *American Economic Review*, **65** (2), 100–7.

Reagan, Barbara B. (1976), Report of the Committee on the Status of Women in the Economics Profession, *American Economic Review*, **66** (2), 509–20.

Reagan, Barbara B. (1977), Report of the Committee on the Status of Women in the Economics Profession, *American Economic Review*, **67** (1), 460–4.

Reagan, Barbara B. (1978), Report of the Committee on the Status of Women in the Economics Profession, *American Economic Review*, **68** (2), 484–99.

Reagan, Barbara B. and Martha Blaxall (1976), 'Occupational segregation in international women's year', *Signs*, **1** (3, pt 2), 1–5.

Redmount, Esther (1995), 'Towards a feminist econometrics', in Edith Kuiper and Jolande Sap (eds), *Out of the Margin: Feminist Perspectives on Economics*, London: Routledge, pp. 216–22.

Reid, Margaret (1934), *Economics of Household Production*, New York: John Wiley.

Review of Radical Political Economics (1970), Special issue on the political economy of women, **2** (1).

Review of Radical Political Economics (1972), Special issue on the political economy of women, **4** (3).

Review of Radical Political Economics (1977), Special issue on women, class and the family, **9** (3).

Review of Radical Political Economics (1980), Special issue on the political economy of women, **12** (2).

Richardson, Sue (1996), 'Why women make lousy economists', *Academy of the Social Sciences in Australia Newsletter*, **15** (4), 19–20.

Riley, Denise (1988), *Am I that Name? Feminism and the Category of 'Women' in History*, Minneapolis: University of Minnesota Press.

Riley, Denise (1992), 'A short history of some preoccupations', in Judith Butler and Joan W. Scott (eds), *Feminists Theorize the Political*, New York: Routledge, pp. 121–9.

Rimmer, Sheila M. (1991), 'Occupational segregation, earnings differentials and status among Australian workers', *Economic Record*, **67** (198), 205–16.

Robbins, Lionel ([1935] 1948), *An Essay on the Nature and Significance of Economic Science*, 2nd edn, London: Macmillan.

Roberts, Bev (1981), 'Notes on women and literature: the case of poetry', in Norma Grieve and Patricia Grimshaw (eds), *Australian Women: Feminist Perspectives*, Melbourne: Oxford University Press, pp. 95–106.

Roberts, Dorothy E. (1991), 'Punishing drug addicts who have babies: women of color, equity, and the right to privacy', *Harvard Law Review*, **104** (7), 1419–82.

Roberts, Dorothy E. (1995), 'Racism and patriarchy in the meaning of motherhood', in Martha Albertson Fineman and Isabel Karpin (eds), *Mothers in Law: Feminist Theory and the Legal Regulation of Motherhood*, New York: Columbia University Press, pp. 224–49.

Rogers, Pat (1979), *Robinson Crusoe*, London: Allen & Unwin.

Roof, Judith (1992), 'The ideology of fair use: xeroxing and reproductive rights', *Hypatia*, **7** (2), 63–73.

Rorty, Richard (1989), 'Science as solidarity', in Hilary Lawson and Lisa Appignanesi (eds), *Dismantling Truth: Reality in the Post-Modern World*, London: Weidenfeld & Nicolson, pp. 6–22.

Rose, Carol M. (1990), 'Property as storytelling: perspectives from game theory, narrative theory, feminist theory', *Yale Journal of Law and the Humanities*, **2**, 37–57.

Rose, Hilary (1983), 'Hand, brain, and heart: a feminist epistemology for the natural sciences', reprinted in Sandra Harding and Jean F. O'Barr (eds) (1987), *Sex and Scientific Inquiry*, Chicago: University of Chicago Press, pp. 265–82.

Rose, Hilary (1986), 'Beyond masculine realities: a feminist epistemology for the sciences', in Ruth Bleier (ed.), *Feminist Approaches to Science*, New York: Pergamon, pp. 57–76.

Rose, Jacqueline (1982), 'Introduction – II', in Juliet Mitchell and Jacqueline Rose (eds), *Feminine Sexuality: Jacques Lacan and the école freudienne*, New York: W.W. Norton, pp. 27–58.

Rosewarne, Stuart and Gabrielle Meagher (1994), 'Homo economicus: the gendering of economics', paper presented at the *Conference of the Economic Society of Australia*, Queensland, September.

Rossetti, Jane (1990), 'Deconstructing Robert Lucas', in Warren J. Samuels (ed.), *Economics as Discourse: An Analysis of the Language of Economists*, Boston, Mass.: Kluwer, pp. 225–43.

Rossetti, Jane (1992), 'Deconstruction, rhetoric, and economics', in Neil de Marchi (ed.), *Post-Popperian Methodology of Economics: Recovering Practice*, Boston, Mass.: Kluwer, pp. 211–34.

Rothfield, Philipa (1990), 'Feminism, subjectivity, and sexual difference', in Sneja Gunew (ed.), *Feminist Knowledge: Critique and Construct*, London: Routledge, pp. 121–44.

Rothfield, Philipa (1991a), 'Alternate epistemologies, politics and feminism', *Social Analysis*, **30** (December), 54–67.

Rothfield, Philipa (1991b), 'Introduction', in Sneja Gunew (ed.), *A Reader in Feminist Knowledge*, London: Routledge, pp. 109–13.

Rothfield, Philipa (1994), 'A conversation between bodies', *Melbourne Journal of Politics*, **22**, 30–44.

Rothfield, Philipa (1995), 'Beyond the brain: towards an alternative economy of the body', *Hysteric: Body, Medicine, Text*, **1**, 33–9.

Rothman, Barbar Katz (1988), 'Cheap labor: sex, class, and race – and "surrogacy" ', *Society*, March/April, pp. 21–3.

Rowley, Hazel and Elizabeth Grosz (1990), 'Psychoanalysis and feminism', in Sneja Gunew (ed.), *Feminist Knowledge: Critique and Construct*, London: Routledge, pp. 175–204.

Rubery, Jill (1987), 'Women's wages', in John Eatwell, Murray Milgate and Peter Newman (eds), *The New Palgrave: A Dictionary of Economics*, vol. 4, New York: Stockton, pp. 929–32.

Ruccio, David R. (1991), 'Postmodernism and economics', *Journal of Post Keynesian Economics*, **13** (4), 495–510.

Ryan, Michael (1988), 'Postmodern politics', *Theory Culture and Society*, **5** (2–3), 559–76.

Rylance, Rick (ed.) (1987), *Debating Texts: Readings in 20th Century Literary Theory and Method*, Toronto: University of Toronto Press.

Sacks, Oliver (1985), *The Man Who Mistook his Wife for a Hat*, London: Pan Books.

Samson, Melanie (1995), 'Towards a "Friday" model of international trade: a feminist deconstruction of race and gender bias in the Robinson Crusoe trade allegory', *Canadian Journal of Economics*, **28** (1), 143–58.

Samuels, Warren J. (1991), ' "Truth" and "discourse" in the social construction of economic reality: an essay on the relation of knowledge to socioeconomic policy', *Journal of Post Keynesian Economics*, **13** (4), 511–24.

Samuelson, Paul A. (1955), *Economics*, 3rd edn, New York: McGraw-Hill.

Samuelson, Paul A. (1956), 'Social indifference curves', *Quarterly Journal of Economics*, **70** (1), 1–22.

Samuelson, Paul A. (1976), *Economics*, 10th edn, Montreal: McGraw-Hill.

Sanborn, Henry (1964), 'Pay differences between men and women', *Industrial and Labor Relations Review*, **17** (July), 534–50.

Sandler, Bernice R. (1988), 'The classroom climate for women', in Susan F. Feiner (ed.) (1994), *Race and Gender in the American Economy: Views from Across the Spectrum*, New York: Prentice-Hall, pp. 166–8.

Sappideen, Carolyn (1983), 'The surrogate mother – a growing problem', *University of New South Wales Law Journal*, **6**, 79–102.

Sargent, Lydia (ed.) (1981a), *Women and Revolution: A Discussion of the Unhappy Marriage of Marxism and Feminism*, Boston, Mass.: South End.

Sargent, Lydia (1981b), 'New left women and men: the honeymoon is over', in *Women and Revolution: A Discussion of the Unhappy Marriage of Marxism and Feminism*, Boston, Mass.: South End, pp. xi–xxxii.

Sarup, Madan (1993), *An Introductory Guide to Post-Structuralism and Postmodernism*, 2nd edn, Athens: University of Georgia Press.

Satz, Debra (1992), 'Markets in women's reproductive labor', *Philosophy and Public Affairs*, **21** (2), 107–31.

Saussure, Ferdinand de ([1916] 1974), *Course in General Linguistics*, trans. Wade Baskin, London: Fontana.

Sawhill, Isabel V. (1973), 'The economics of discrimination against women: some new findings', *Journal of Human Resources*, **8** (3), 383–96.

Sawhill, Isabel V. (1977), 'Economic perspectives on the family', reprinted in Alice H. Amsden (ed.) (1980), *The Economics of Women and Work*, Harmondsworth, Middx: Penguin, pp. 125–39.

Sawhill, Isabel V. (1986), Report of the Committee on the Status of Women in the Economics Profession, *American Economic Review*, **76** (2), 452–7.

Sawhill, Isabel V. (1987), Report of the Committee on the Status of Women in the Economics Profession, *American Economic Review*, **77** (2), 400–3.

Schaffer, Kay (1988), *Women and the Bush*, Cambridge: Cambridge University Press.

Scheman, Naomi (1983), 'Individualism and the objects of psychology', in Sandra Harding and Merrill B. Hintikka (eds), *Discovering Reality: Feminist Perspectives on Epistemology, Metaphysics, Methodology and Philosophy of Science*, Dordrecht: Reidel, pp. 225–44.

Schick, Irvin Cemil (1990), 'Representing Middle Eastern women: feminism and colonial discourse', *Feminist Studies*, **16** (2), 345–80.

Schiebinger, Londa (1987), 'The history and philosophy of women in science: a review essay', in Sandra Harding and Jean F. O'Barr (eds), *Sex and Scientific Inquiry*, Chicago: University of Chicago Press, pp. 7–34.

Schor, Naomi (1994a), 'Introduction', in Naomi Schor and Elizabeth Weed (eds), *The Essential Difference*, Bloomington: Indiana University Press, pp. vii–xiv.

Schor, Naomi (1994b), 'This essentialism which is not one: coming to grips with Irigaray', in Naomi Schor and Elizabeth Weed (eds), *The Essential Difference*, Bloomington: Indiana University Press, pp. 40–62.

Schor, Naomi and Elizabeth Weed (eds) (1994), *The Essential Difference*, Bloomington: Indiana University Press.

Schultz, Theodore W. (1960), 'Capital formation by education', *Journal of Political Economy*, **68** (6), 571–83.

Schultz, Theodore W. (ed.) (1973), Special issue of *Journal of Political Economy*, **81** (2, pt 2).

Schultz, Theodore W. (ed.) (1974a), *Economics of the Family: Marriage, Children and Human Capital*, Chicago: Chicago University Press.

Schultz, Theodore W. (ed.) (1974b), Special issue of *Journal of Political Economy*, **82** (2, pt 2).

Schultz, Vicki (1992), 'Women "before" the law: judicial stories about women, work, and sex segregation on the job', in Judith Butler and Joan W. Scott (eds), *Feminists Theorize the Political*, New York: Routledge, pp. 297–338.

Schumpeter, Joseph A. (1954), *History of Economic Analysis*, London: Allen & Unwin.

Scott, Joan W. (1988a), 'Deconstructing equality-versus-difference: or, the uses of poststructuralist theory for feminism', *Feminist Studies*, **14** (1), 33–50.

Scott, Joan W. (1988b), *Gender and the Politics of History*, New York: Columbia University Press.

Scott, Joan W. (1992), ' "Experience" ', in Judith Butler and Joan W. Scott (eds), *Feminists Theorize the Political*, New York: Routledge, pp. 22–40.

Scott, Joan W. (1993), 'The woman worker', in Geneviève Fraisse and Michelle Perrot (eds), *A History of Women in the West: Emerging Feminism from Revolution to World War*, Cambridge, Mass.: Harvard University Press, pp. 399–426.

Screen (ed.) (1992), *The Sexual Subject: A Screen Reader in Sexuality*. London: Routledge.

Secomb, Harry (1974), 'The housewife and her labour under capitalism', reprinted in Michael Anderson (ed.) (1980), *Sociology of the Family*, Harmondsworth, Middx: Penguin, pp. 370–95.

Secomb, Linnell (1995), 'IVF: reproducing the "proper [family] of man" ', *Australian Feminist Law Journal*, **4** (March), 19–38.

Seguino, Stephanie, Thomas Stevens and Mark A. Lutz (1996), 'Gender and cooperative behavior: economic man rides alone', *Feminist Economics*, **2** (1), 1–21.

Seidman, Steven (1994), 'Introduction', in *The Postmodern Turn: New Perspectives on Social Theory*, Cambridge: Cambridge University Press, pp. 1–23.

Seiz, Janet A. (1990), 'Comment on "The textbook presentation of economic discourse" ', in Warren J. Samuels (ed.), *Economics as Discourse: An Analysis of the Language of Economists*, Boston, Mass.: Kluwer, pp. 155–65.

Seiz, Janet A. (1991), 'The bargaining approach and feminist methodology', *Review of Radical Political Economics*, **23** (1/2), 22–9.

Seiz, Janet A. (1992), 'Gender and economic research', in Neil de Marchi (ed.), *Post-Popperian Methodology of Economics: Recovering Practice*, Boston, Mass.:

Kluwer, pp. 273–319.

Seiz, Janet A. (1993), 'Feminism and the history of economic thought', *History of Political Economy*, **25** (1), 185–201.

Seiz, Janet A. (1995a), 'Epistemology and the tasks of feminist economics', *Feminist Economics*, **1** (3), 110–18.

Seiz, Janet A. (1995b), 'Bargaining models, feminism, and institutionalism', *Journal of Economic Issues*, **29** (2), 609–18.

Selden, Raman and Peter Widdowson (1993), *A Reader's Guide to Contemporary Literary Theory*, 3rd edn, New York: Harvester Wheatsheaf.

Sen, Amartya K. (1977), 'Rational fools: a critique of the bahavioral foundations of economic theory', reprinted in Jane J. Mansbridge (ed.) (1990), *Beyond Self-Interest*, Chicago: University of Chicago Press, pp. 25–43.

Sen, Amartya K. (1983), 'Economics and the family', *Asian Development Review*, **1** (2), 14–26.

Sen, Amartya K. (1990), 'Gender and cooperative conflicts', in Irene Tinker (ed.), *Persistent Inequalities*, New York: Oxford University Press, pp. 123–49.

Sen, Amartya K. (1995), 'Varieties of deprivation: comments on chapters by Pujol and Hutchinson', in Edith Kuiper and Jolande Sap (eds), *Out of the Margin: Feminist Perspectives on Economics*, London: Routledge, pp. 51–8.

Sen, Gita (1980), 'The sexual division of labor and the working-class family: towards a conceptual synthesis of class relations and the subordination of women', *Review of Radical Political Economics*, **12** (2), 76–86.

Senior, Nassau W. ([1836] 1965), *An Outline of the Science of Political Economy*, New York: Augustus M. Kelley.

Shackleford, Jean (1992), 'Feminist pedagogy: a means for bringing critical thinking and creativity to the economics classroom', *American Economic Review*, **82** (2), 570–6.

Shalev, Carmel (1989), *Birth Power: The Case for Surrogacy*, New Haven, Conn.: Yale University Press.

Shanley, Mary Lyndon (1993), ' "Surrogate mothering" and women's freedom: a critique of contracts for human reproduction', *Signs*, **18** (3), 618–39.

Shapiro, Judith (1981), 'Anthropology and the study of gender', in Elizabeth Langland and Walter Gove (eds), *A Feminist Perspective in the Academy: The Difference it Makes*, Chicago: University of Chicago Press, pp. 110–29.

Sharp, Rhonda and Ray Broomhill (1988), *Short-Changed: Women and Economic Policies*, Sydney: Allen & Unwin.

Sharp, Rhonda and Susan Donath (1995), Review of *Sexual Economyths: Conceiving a Feminist Economics*, by Chris Beasley and *Portrait of the Family Within the Total Economy: A Study of Longrun Dynamics, Australia 1788–1990*, by Graeme D. Snooks, *Feminist Economics*, **1** (3), 128–34.

Shelburn, Marsha R. and Patsy G. Lewellyn (1995), 'Gender bias in doctoral programs in economics', *Journal of Economic Education*, **26** (4), 373–82.

Shields, S., S. Breinich and A. Kohen (1975), *Women and the Economy: A Bibliography and a Review of the Literature on Sex Differentiations in the Labor Market*, Centre for Human Resource Research, Ohio State University

Siegfried, John J. (1979), 'Male–female differences in economic education: a survey', *Journal of Economic Education*, **10** (2), 1–11.

Siegfried, John J. and S.H. Strand (1977), 'Sex and the economics student', *Review of Economics and Statistics*, **59** (2), 247–9.

Silverman, Kaja (1983), *The Subject of Semiotics*, New York: Oxford University Press.

Simms, Marian (1981), 'The Australian feminist experience', in Norma Grieve and Patricia Grimshaw (eds), *Australian Women: Feminist Perspectives*, Melbourne: Oxford University Press, pp. 227–39.

Singer, Linda (1989), 'Bodies-pleasures-powers', *differences*, **1** (1), 45–65.

Singer, Linda (1992), 'Feminism and postmodernism', in Judith Butler and Joan W. Scott (eds), *Feminists Theorize the Political*, New York: Routledge, pp. 464–75.

Smart, Carol (1986), 'Feminism and the law: some problems of analysis and strategy', *International Journal of the Sociology of Law*, **14**, 109–23.

Smart, Carol (1987), ' "There is of course the distinction dictated by nature": law and the problem of paternity', in Michelle Stanworth (ed.), *Reproductive Technologies: Gender, Motherhood and Medicine*, Cambridge: Polity Press, pp. 98–117.

Smart, Carol (1989), 'Power and the politics of child custody', in Carol Smart and Selma Sevenhuijsen (eds), *Child Custody and the Politics of Gender*, London: Routledge, pp. 1–26.

Smart, Carol (1990), 'Law's power, the sexed body, and feminist discourse', *Journal of Law and Society*, **17**, 194–210.

Smart, Carol (1992), 'Disruptive bodies and unruly sex: the regulation of reproduction and sexuality in the nineteenth century', in *Regulating Womanhood: Historical Essays on Marriage, Motherhood and Sexuality*, London: Routledge, pp. 7–32.

Smith, Dorothy E. (1974), 'Women's perspective as a radical critique of sociology', *Sociological Inquiry*, **44**, 7–13.

Smith, Dorothy E. (1987), *The Everyday World as Problematic*, Boston, Mass.: Northeastern University Press.

Smith, George P. (1988), 'The case of Baby M: love's labor lost', *Law, Medicine and Health Care*, **16** (1–2), 121–30.

Smith, James P. and Michael Ward (1989), 'Women in the labor market and in the family', *Journal of Economic Perspectives*, **3** (1), 9–23.

Smith, Paul Julian (1992), 'Phallogocentrism', in Elizabeth Wright (ed.), *Feminism and Psychoanalysis: A Critical Dictionary*, Oxford: Blackwell, pp. 316–18.

Smith, Vernon L. (1989), 'Auctions', in John Eatwell, Murray Milgate and Peter Newman (eds), *The New Palgrave: Allocation, Information, and Markets*, New York: W.W. Norton, pp. 39–53.

Snooks, Graeme D. (1994), *Portrait of the Family Within the Total Economy: A Study of Longrun Dynamics, Australia 1788–1990*, Cambridge: Cambridge University Press.

Sofia, Zoë (1984), 'Exterminating fetuses: abortion, disarmament, and the sexo-semiotics of extraterrestrialism', *Diacritics*, **14** (2), 47–59.

Solow, Robert M. (1993), 'Feminist theory, women's experience, and economics', in Marianne A. Ferber and Julie A. Nelson (eds), *Beyond Economic Man: Feminist Theory and Economics*, Chicago: University of Chicago Press, pp. 153–7.

Spearman, Diana (1966), *The Novel and Society*, London: Routledge & Kegan Paul.

Spender, Dale (ed.) (1981), *Men's Studies Modified: The Impact of Feminism on the Academic Disciplines*, Oxford: Pergamon.

Spivak, Gayatri Chakravorty (1974), Translator's preface to *Of Grammatology*, by Jacques Derrida, in *Of Grammatology*, trans. Gayatri Chakravorty Spivak, Baltimore, Md: Johns Hopkins University Press, pp. ix–lxxxvii.

Spivak, Gayatri Chakravorty (1991a), 'Feminism and deconstruction, again: negotiating with unacknowledged masculinism', in Teresa Brennan (ed.), *Between Feminism and Psychoanalysis*, London: Routledge, pp. 206–23.

Spivak, Gayatri Chakravorty (1991b), 'Theory in the margin: Coetzee's *Foe* reading Defoe's *Crusoe/Roxanna*', in Jonathan Arac and Barbara Johnson (eds), *Consequences of Theory: Selected Papers from the English Institute, 1987-1988*, Baltimore, Md: Johns Hopkins University Press, pp. 154–80.

Stanton, Domna and Abigail J. Stewart (eds) (1995a), *Feminisms in the Academy*, Ann Arbor: University of Michigan Press.

Stanton, Domna C. and Abigail J. Stewart (1995b), 'Remodeling relations: women's studies and the disciplines', in *Feminisms in the Academy*, Ann Arbor: University of Michigan Press, pp. 1–16.

Stanworth, Michelle (1987), 'Reproductive technologies and the threat to motherhood', in *Reproductive Technologies: Gender, Motherhood and Medicine*, Cambridge: Polity Press, pp. 10–35.

Stanworth, Michelle (1990), 'Birth pangs: contraceptive technologies and the threat to motherhood', in Marianne Hirsch and Evelyn Fox Keller (eds), *Conflicts in Feminism*, New York: Routledge, pp. 288–304.

Stefano, Christine Di (1990), 'Dilemmas of difference: feminism, modernity, and postmodernism', in Linda J. Nicholson (ed.), *Feminism/Postmodernism*, New York: Routledge, pp. 63–82.

Stefano, Christine Di (1991), 'Masculine Marx', in Mary Lyndon Shanley and Carole Pateman (eds), *Feminist Interpretations and Political Theory*, Cambridge: Polity Press, pp. 146–63.

Steinberg, Deborah Lynn (1991), 'Adversarial politics: the legal construction of abortion', in Sarah Franklin, Celia Lury and Jackie Stacey (eds), *Off-Centre: Feminism and Cultural Studies*, London: HarperCollins Academic, pp. 175–89.

Steinbock, Bonnie (1988), 'Surrogate motherhood as prenatal adoption', *Law, Medicine and Health Care*, **16** (1–2), 44–50.

Stevenson, Mary H. (1975), 'Relative wages and sex segregation by occupation', in Cynthia B. Lloyd (ed.), *Sex, Discrimination, and the Division of Labor*, New York: Columbia University Press, pp. 175–200.

Stewart, Hamish (1992), 'Rationality and the market for human blood', *Journal of Economic Behavior and Organization*, **19**, 125–43.

Stichter, Sharon (1990), 'Women, employment and the family: current debates', in Sharon Stichter and Jane L. Parpet (eds), *Women, Employment and the Family in the International Division of Labour*, London: Macmillan, pp. 11–61.

Stiglitz, Joseph E. and Andrew Weiss (1981), 'Credit rationing in markets with imperfect information', *American Economic Review*, **71** (3), 393–410.

Stilwell, Frank (1975), *Normative Economics*, Sydney: Pergamon.

Stolcke, V. (1988), 'New reproductive technologies: the old quest for fatherhood', *Reproductive and Genetic Engineering*, **1**, 5–20.

Stoller, Robert (1968), *Sex and Gender*, London: Hogarth.

Strassmann, Diana (1993a), 'Not a free market: the rhetoric of disciplinary authority in economics', in Marianne A. Ferber and Julie A. Nelson (eds), *Beyond Economic Man: Feminist Theory and Economics*, Chicago: University of Chicago Press, pp. 54–68.

Strassmann, Diana (1993b), 'The stories of economics and the power of the storyteller', *History of Political Economy*, **25** (1), 147–65.

Strassmann, Diana (1994), 'Feminist thought and economics; or, what do the visigoths know?', *American Economic Review*, **84** (2), 153–8.

Strassmann, Diana (1996), 'How economists shape their tales', *Challenge*, January/February, pp. 13–20.

Strassmann, Diana and Livia Polanyi (1995), 'The economist as storyteller: what the texts reveal', in Edith Kuiper and Jolande Sap (eds), *Out of the Margin: Feminist Perspectives on Economics*, London: Routledge, pp. 129–50.

Strickland, Susan (1994), 'Feminism, postmodernism and difference', in Kathleen Lennon and Margaret Whitford (eds), *Knowing the Difference: Feminist Perspectives on Epistemology*, London: Routledge, pp. 265–74.

Strober, Myra H. (1972), 'Lower pay for women: a case of economic discrimination?', *Industrial Relations*, **11** (2), 279–84.

Strober, Myra H. (1975), 'Women economists: career aspirations, education and training', *American Economic Review*, **65** (2), 92–9.

Strober, Myra H. (1987), 'The scope of microeconomics: implications for economic education', *Journal of Economic Education*, **18** (2), 135–49.

Strober, Myra H. (1993), 'Feminist economics and the improvement of women's economic condition', paper presented at the *Out of the Margin: Feminist Perspectives on Economic Theory* Conference, Amsterdam, June.

Strober, Myra H. (1994), 'Rethinking economics through a feminist lens', *American Economic Review*, **84** (2), 143–7.

Strober, Myra H. (1995), 'Feminist economics: what's it all about?', *Downing Oration*, University of Melbourne.

Strober, Myra H. and Barbara B. Reagan (1976), 'Sex differences in economists' fields of specialization', *Signs*, **1** (3, pt 2), 303–17.

Stuhmcke, Anita (1994), 'Surrogate motherhood: the legal position in Australia', *Journal of Law and Medicine*, **2** (November), 116–24.

Sturrock, John (1986), *Structuralism*, London: Paladin Grafton.

Sullivan, Barbara (1990), 'Sex equality and the Australian body politic', in Sophie Watson (ed.), *Playing the State: Australian Feminist Interventions*, Sydney: Allen & Unwin, pp. 173–90.

Sullivan, Barbara (1995), 'Rethinking prostitution', in Barbara Caine and Rosemary Pringle (eds), *Transitions: New Australian Feminisms*, St Leonards: Allen & Unwin, pp. 184–97.

Tapper, Marion (1986), 'Can a feminist be a liberal?', *Australasian Journal of Philosophy*, **64** (June), S37–47.

Taub, Nadine (1989/90), 'Surrogacy: sorting through the alternatives', *Berkeley Women's Law Journal*, **4**, 285–99.

Taubman, Paul J. (1991), 'Discrimination within the family', in Emily P. Hoffman (ed.), *Essays on the Economics of Discrimination*, Kalamazoo, Mich.: W.E. Upjohn Institute for Employment Research, pp. 25–42.

Tauchen, Helen V., Ann Dryden Witte and Sharon K. Long (1991), 'Domestic violence: a nonrandom affair', *International Economic Review*, **32** (2), 491–511.

Thiele, Beverly (1986), 'Vanishing tricks in social and political thought: tricks of the trade', in Carole Pateman and Elizabeth Gross (eds), *Feminist Challenges: Social and Political Theory*, Sydney: Allen & Unwin, pp. 30–42.

Thom, Deborah (1992), 'A lop-sided view: feminist history or the history of women', in Kate Campbell (ed.), *Critical Feminism: Argument in the Disciplines*, Buckingham:

Open University Press, pp. 25–51.

Thompson, Denise (1989), 'The "sex/gender" distinction: a reconsideration', *Australian Feminist Studies*, **10** (Summer), 23–31.

Thomson, Dorothy Lampen (1973), *Adam Smith's Daughters*, New York: Exposition.

Thomson, Michael (1996), 'Employing the body: the reproductive body and employment exclusion', *Social and Legal Studies*, **5**, 243–67.

Thornton, Margaret (1989), 'Hegemonic masculinity and the academy', *International Journal of the Sociology of Law*, **17**, 115–30.

Thornton, Margaret (1991), 'The public/private dichotomy: gendered and discriminatory', *Journal of Law and Society*, **18** (4), 448–63.

Thornton, Margaret (1993), 'The indirection of sex discrimination', *University of Tasmania Law Review*, **12** (1), 88–101.

Thornton, Merle (1986), 'Sex equality is not enough for feminism', in Carole Pateman and Elizabeth Gross (eds), *Feminist Challenges: Social and Political Theory*, Sydney: Allen & Unwin, pp. 77–98.

Thornton, Merle (1994), *Gender in the Economics Curriculum*, Melbourne: University of Melbourne.

Threadgold, Terry (1988), 'Language and gender', *Australian Feminist Studies*, **6** (Autumn), 41–70.

Threadgold, Terry (1990), 'Introduction', in Terry Threadgold and Anne Cranny-Francis (eds), *Feminine/Masculine and Representation*, Sydney: Allen & Unwin, pp. 1–35.

Thurow, Lester (1975), *Generating Inequality*, New York: Basic Books.

Titmuss, Richard (1970), *The Gift Relationship: From Human Blood to Social Policy*, London: Allen & Unwin.

Tong, Rosemarie (1989), *Feminist Thought: A Comprehensive Introduction*, London: Unwin Hyman.

Tournier, Michel (1969), *Friday*, trans. Norman Denny, New York: Pantheon Books.

Trebilcock, Michael J. (1993), *The Limits of Freedom of Contract*, Cambridge, Mass.: Harvard University Press.

Trebilcot, Joyce (1977), 'Two forms of androgynism', in Mary Vetterling-Braggin, Frederick A. Elliston and Jane English (eds), *Feminism and Philosophy*, Totowa, N.J.: Rowman & Allanheld, pp. 70–8.

Troup, Maggie (1993), 'Rupturing the veil: feminism, deconstruction and the law', *Australian Feminist Law Journal*, **1** (August), 63–88.

Trzcinski, Eileen (1995), 'The use and abuse of neoclassical theory in the political arena: the example of family and medical leave in the United States', in Edith Kuiper and Jolande Sap (eds), *Out of the Margin: Feminist Perspectives on Economics*, London: Routledge, pp. 231–48.

United Nations (1993), *Methods of Measuring Women's Economic Activity*, New York: United Nations.

Varian, Hal (1984), *Microeconomic Analysis*, 2nd edn, New York: W.W. Norton.

Varian, Hal (1990), *Intermediate Microeconomics*, 2nd edn, New York: W.W. Norton.

Vaughn, Karen (1994), Review of *Beyond Economic Man: Feminist Theory and Economics*, edited by Marianne A. Ferber and Julie A. Nelson, *Journal of Economic Methodology*, **1** (2), 307–13.

Viner, Jacob (1925), 'The utility concept in value theory and its critics', *Journal of Political Economy*, **33**, 369–87.

Wagman, Barnet and Nancy Folbre (1996), 'Household services and economic growth in the United States, 1870–1930', *Feminist Economics*, **2** (1), 43–66.

Wajcman, Judy (1981), 'Work and the family: who gets "the best of both worlds"?', in Cambridge Women's Studies Group (ed.), *Women in Society: Interdisciplinary Essays*, London: Virago, pp. 9–24.

Waldby, Catherine (1995), 'Feminism and method', in Barbara Caine and Rosemary Pringle (eds), *Transitions: New Australian Feminisms*, St Leonards: Allen & Unwin, pp. 15–28.

Waller, Louis (1984), 'Borne for another', *Monash University Law Review*, **10** (June), 113–30.

Waller, William (1994), 'Technology and gender in institutional economics', in Janice Peterson and Doug Brown (eds), *The Economic Status of Women Under Capitalism: Institutional Economics and Feminist Theory*, Aldershot: Edward Elgar, pp. 55–76.

Waller, William and Ann Jennings (1990), 'On the possibility of a feminist economics: the convergence of institutional and feminist methodology', *Journal of Economic Issues*, **24** (2), 613–22.

Waller, William and Ann Jennings (1991), 'A feminist institutionalist reconsideration of Karl Polanyi', *Journal of Economic Issues*, **25** (2), 485–97.

Walters, Suzanna Danuta (1995), *Material Girls: Making Sense of Feminist Cultural Theory*, Berkeley: University of California Press.

Waring, Marilyn (1988), *If Women Counted: A New Feminist Economics*, New York: HarperCollins.

Watt, Ian (1951), '*Robinson Crusoe* as a Myth', in James L. Clifford (ed.) (1959), *Eighteenth-Century English Literature: Modern Essays in Criticism*, New York: Oxford University Press, pp. 158–79.

Watt, Ian (1957), *The Rise of the Novel: Studies in Defoe, Richardson, and Fielding*, Harmondsworth, Middx: Penguin Books in assoc. with Chatto & Windus.

Weed, Elizabeth (1989), 'Introduction: Terms of reference', in *Coming to Terms: Feminism, Theory, Politics*, New York: Routledge, pp. ix–xxxi.

Weedon, Chris (1987), *Feminist Practice and Poststructuralist Theory*, Oxford: Basil Blackwell.

Weinreich-Haste, Helen (1986), 'Brother sun, sister moon: does rationality overcome a dualistic world view?', in Jan Harding (ed.), *Perspectives on Gender and Science*, London: Farmer, pp. 113–31.

Weintraub, E. Roy (1993), 'Editor's introduction', *History of Political Economy*, **25** (1), 117–19.

Weisskoff, Francine Blau (1972), ' "Women's place" in the labor market', *American Economic Review*, **62** (2), 161–6.

Wendt, Paul (1990), 'Comment on "Economics as a postmodern discourse" ', in Warren J. Samuels (ed.), *Economics as Discourse: An Analysis of the Language of Economists*, Boston, Mass.: Kluwer, pp. 47–64.

Wertheimer, Alan (1992), 'Two questions about surrogacy and exploitation', *Philosophy and Public Affairs*, **21** (3), 211–39.

Whalen, Charles and Linda Whalen (1994), 'Institutionalism: a useful foundation for feminist economics?', in Janice Peterson and Doug Brown (eds), *The Economic Status of Women Under Capitalism: Institutional Economics and Feminist Theory*, Aldershot: Edward Elgar, pp. 19–33.

White, Margaret A. (1984), 'Breaking the circular hold: taking on the patriarchal and ideological biases in traditional economic theory', Centre for Women's Studies in

Education Occasional Papers No. 7, Toronto.

White, Michael V. (1982), 'Reading and rewriting: the production of an economic "Robinson Crusoe" ', *Southern Review*, **15** (2), 115--42.

White, Michael V. (1987), 'Robinson Crusoe', in John Eatwell, Murray Milgate and Peter Newman (eds), *The New Palgrave: A Dictionary of Economics*, vol. 4, New York: Stockton, pp. 217–18.

White, Michael V. (1994), 'Following strange gods: women in Jevons's political economy', in Peter Groenewegen (ed.), *Feminism and Political Economy in Victorian England*, Aldershot: Edward Elgar, pp. 46–78.

Whitford, Margaret (1989), 'Rereading Irigaray', in Teresa Brennan (ed.), *Between Feminism and Psychoanalysis*, London: Routledge, pp. 106–26.

Whitford, Margaret (1991a), *Luce Irigaray: Philosophy in the Feminine*, New York: Routledge.

Whitford, Margaret (1991b), 'Irigaray's body symbolic', *Hypatia*, **6** (3), 97–109.

Whyld, Janie (ed.) (1983), *Sexism in the Secondary Curriculum*, London: Harper & Row.

Wiegman, Robyn (1989), 'Economies of the body: gendered sites in *Robinson Crusoe* and *Roxana*', *Criticism*, **3** (1), 33–51.

Williams, Rhonda M. (1993), 'Race, deconstruction, and the emergent agenda of feminist economic theory', in Marianne A. Ferber and Julie A. Nelson (eds), *Beyond Economic Man: Feminist Theory and Economics*, Chicago: University of Chicago Press, pp. 144–52.

Woliver, Laura R. (1995), 'Reproductive technologies, surrogacy arrangements, and the politics of motherhood', in Martha Albertson Fineman and Isabel Karpin (eds), *Mothers in Law: Feminist Theory and the Legal Regulation of Motherhood*, New York: Columbia University Press, pp. 346–59.

Woolley, Frances R. (1993), 'The feminist challenge to neoclassical economics', *Cambridge Journal of Economics*, **17**, 485–500.

Worley, Sara (1995), 'Feminism, objectivity, and analytic philosophy', *Hypatia*, **10** (3), 138–56.

Wright, Elizabeth (ed.) (1992), *Feminism and Psychoanalysis: A Critical Dictionary*, Oxford: Blackwell.

Wright, Janet (1990), 'Wombs for rent', *Australian Left Review*, April, pp. 12–14.

Wylie, Alison, Kathleen Okruhlik, Leslie Thielen-Wilson and Sandra Morton (1989), 'Feminist critiques of science: the epistemological and methodological literature', *Women's Studies International Forum*, **12** (3), 379–88.

Yachetta, Lois (1995), Review of *Essays on the Economics of Discrimination*, edited by Emily P. Hoffman, *Feminist Economics*, **1** (2), 132–7.

Young, Alison (1993), 'Decapitation or feticide: the fetal laws of the universal subject', *Women: A Cultural Review*, **4** (3), 288–94.

Young, Iris Marion (1990), *Throwing Like a Girl and Other Essays in Feminist Philosophy and Social Theory*, Bloomington: Indiana University Press.

Young, Robert (1981), 'Post-structuralism: an introduction', in *Untying the Text: A Post-structuralist Reader*, Boston, Mass.: Routledge & Kegan Paul, pp. 1–28.

Zamagni, Stefano (ed.) (1995), *The Economics of Altruism*, Aldershot: Edward Elgar.

Zelizer, Viviana A. (1988), 'From baby farms to Baby M', *Society*, March/April, pp. 23–8.

Zellner, Harriet (1972), 'Discrimination against women, occupational segregation, and the relative wage', *American Economic Review*, **62** (2), 157–60.

Zellner, Harriet (1975), 'The determinants of occupational segregation', in Cynthia B. Lloyd (ed.), *Sex, Discrimination, and the Division of Labor*, New York: Columbia University Press, pp. 125–45.

Zerilli, Linda M.G. (1994), *Signifying Woman: Culture and Chaos in Rousseau, Burke, and Mill*, Ithaca, N.Y.: Cornell University Press.

Zipper, Juliet and Selma Sevenhuijsen (1987), 'Surrogacy: feminist notions of motherhood reconsidered', in Michelle Stanworth (ed.), *Reproductive Technologies: Gender, Motherhood and Medicine*, Cambridge: Polity Press, pp. 118–38.

Index